HISTORICAL TRACTS

OF

S. ATHANASIUS,

ARCHBISHOP OF ALEXANDRIA.

TRANSLATED,

WITH NOTES AND INDICES.

WIPF & STOCK · Eugene, Oregon

Wipf and Stock Publishers
199 W 8th Ave, Suite 3
Eugene, OR 97401

Historical Tracts
By S. aAthanasius, Archbishop of Alexandria and Atkinson, M.
Softcover ISBN-13: 978-1-6667-3429-4
Hardcover ISBN-13: 978-1-6667-2999-3
eBook ISBN-13: 978-1-6667-9000-9
Publication date 8/20/2021
Previously published by John Henry Parker, 1843

This edition is a scanned facsimile of the original edition published in 1843.

PREFACE.

THE Works of which this Volume is composed, being of an historical character, naturally require a Chronological Table of the principal events recorded in them, but the difficulties of forming any satisfactory statement, during the period to which they belong, are so great, that any arrangement can be but hypothetical, and must be accompanied with some notice of the difficulties themselves, and the various expedients which have been adopted with the view of overcoming them. Though such notice will be necessarily very imperfect, it shall here be attempted

1. *Interposition of Pope Julius in the affairs of the East.*

It is certain, that both the Eusebians and the Egyptian Bishops had recourse to Rome; that Athanasius went thither; that a synodal judgment was passed there; and that Legates went from S. Julius to Antioch; but the order and dates of these events are variously determined. For the sake of perspicuity, it will be necessary in the first place to take a view of the transactions to which dates are to be assigned; though it is impossible to do so, without prejudging some of the questions in dispute.

It appears then, that shortly after the return of S. Athanasius to Alexandria from his exile in Gaul, the Eusebian party brought charges against him before the three Emperors, (infr. pp. 18, 226,) and the Pope, (p. 37.) Their embassy or legation to the latter consisted of Macarius, Martyrius, and

Hesychius, (pp. 42, 47.) and they were met by a counter deputation from S. Athanasius, (pp. 44, 226,) supported, (p. 48,) or preceded, (p. 43,) by letters from many Catholic Bishops, (pp. 47, 70,) and by a letter to the Pope, (p. 38,) which an Alexandrian Council of from eighty, (p. 61,) to one hundred Bishops, (p. 14,) had written in his favour, (pp. 14, 17, and 48) The discussions which ensued at Rome perhaps were held before a Council of Bishops then present, (p. 46,) and ended in the defeat of the Eusebian legates, (p. 43,) one of whom abruptly left the city in consequence, (p. 44.) Julius, however, did not decide the matter at once, but at their suggestion, (pp. 39, 42, 226,) proposed a Council, (p. 11,) at which both Eusebians, (p. 54,) and Athanasius should attend, (p. 40,) and the Alexandrians have the choice of place, (p. 226.) Athanasius, who was otherwise disposed to betake himself to Rome, in consequence of the outrages of Gregory whom the Arian Council of the Dedication had sent to Alexandria in his place, (p. 227,) promptly obeyed the call (p. 49); and on his arrival at Rome, the Pope sent Elpidius and Philoxenus as legates to Antioch, (p. 39,) with a letter to the Eusebians, (p. 46,) repeating the invitation to a Council, (p. 41,) and fixing the day, (pp. 45, 227.) There they were detained over the time, ibid. and at length came back with a refusal on the part of the Orientals to attend (pp. 40, 46, 47); though the Eusebian legates had not only been the originators of the measure, but had gone so far as to offer to submit the question to the arbitration of the Pope, (p. 39.) Upon this Julius proceeded to hold a Council of fifty Bishops, (pp. 14, 39, 230,) at which Athanasius and others were pronounced innocent and admitted to communion, ibid. and in the name of which, (pp. 39, 46,) the Pope, eighteen months from the date of Athanasius's arrival, (p. 49,) proceeded to address a letter of remonstrance to the Orientals, who had written to him from Antioch.

This is a sketch of the history, and now to proceed to its chronology. The only date which is known for certain is that of the Eusebian Council of Antioch held A. D. 341.

PREFACE.

This we learn from Athanasius, de Syn. §. 25. " Ninety Bishops," he says, " met at the Dedication under the Consulate of Marcellinus and Probinus, in the 14th of the Indiction;" L. F. vol. 8, p. 109. As, in dating by the Indiction, the new year began in September, the Council must have assembled during the spring or summer of 341; nay, it would appear, in the first months of it, if Gregory, who was appointed in it to the See of Alexandria, began his persecution at Alexandria in that year. Gregory entered Alexandria during Lent, (infr. p. 7.) that is, either in Lent 341 while the Council was still sitting, or the Lent following. Upon Gregory's coming, Athanasius left Alexandria for Rome, that is, after Easter; thus Athanasius's visit to Rome commences in the spring of 341 or 342; unless indeed we suppose with Mansi, that Gregory's invasion and Athanasius's flight were prior to the Council of the Dedication, viz. in 340. He remained at Rome three years, (p. 158.) and in the fourth year was called by Constans to Milan. Now in the latter part of 345 the delegates of the Eusebians also came to Milan, Eudoxius, Martyrius, and Macedonius, (vid. L. F. vol. 8, p. 111.) with the Macrostich or Long Confession, which had been drawn up at Antioch in the beginning of the year. They presented themselves before a Council there, according to a letter of Liberius, of the date of 354; which rejected them; and that, according to the same letter, eight years before that date, which nearly agrees with Athanasius's account of the publication of the Macrostich. It is natural to connect this visit of the Eusebians to Milan with the summons of Athanasius by Constans to that city, and to conclude that the proceedings of the Council issued in the resolution which the Emperor adopted at this time to treat with his brother for the meeting of a General Council. If so, the date of Athanasius's journey to Rome is 342. And it certainly seems much more probable that Gregory should proceed to Alexandria the Lent after the Dedication, than that the ecclesiastical and military acts and movements [a] which attended his expedition should be despatched between January and Lent, which the date of 341 requires, i. e. did not Athanasius's words p. 226. on the other hand shew that the Eusebians were very much bent on the measure, and were likely to prosecute it promptly. And Baronius and others date the Councils of the Macrostich and of Milan at 344, not 345, which throws back the journey of Athanasius to 341. And moreover if the Anonymus Maffeianus, relied on by Mansi, be correct, the Council of Sardica was held at the end of 344, a date which may just allow time for a preliminary Council of Milan (in 344) between the Sardican Council and the end of three years from May 341. In this uncertainty about the year of Athanasius's journey to Rome, 341 may be more fitly taken than 342 or 340, as having the suffrages of more critics in its favour. But in this question does not consist the main difficulty of the chronology on the point before us, which is internal to the documents which are to follow, arising out of the relative not the absolute dates which they contain.

It appears that S. Athanasius was eighteen months at Rome before Pope Julius's letter, (p. 49;) that is, the Council of Rome, in or upon which he wrote it, was ending or just ended eighteen months after Athanasius's arrival, or in the month of October or rather November, since he set out for Rome after Easter. But the meeting of the Council was fixed for a day before the January preceding that November; because the Pope's legates who were sent into the East upon Athanasius's arrival at Rome are said, by being kept at Antioch till January, to be kept over the time

[a] Pagi after Schelstrate contends, that the Confession of faith and the Canons preceded the cause of Athanasius in the Council. Montfaucon and Tillemont, (with the exception of the Canon, which was expressly levelled at Athanasius, and which Montf does not notice as a Canon,) place it first of all. If there were at first orthodox Bishops at the Council, as is said, we cannot suppose, that Athanasius was condemned till after their departure. Schelstrate, who places matters of faith and discipline first, in his task of vindicating the Catholicity of the Council, is obliged to suppose its commencement in 340, in order to gain time for Gregory's expedition by Lent 341.

of meeting. Thus we have an interval of eleven months between the meeting and the termination. It follows then that the Council did not meet at the time proposed, *or* that it was continued for nearly a whole year, *or* that there were two Councils, one in December, the other in November. Now as to the last supposition, it is most improbable that the same Bishops of Italy should meet twice over at so short a period, and Julius and Athanasius speak distinctly of but one synodal *body*, (even supposing they are not clear about one meeting,) which both pronounced the innocence of Athanasius and commissioned Julius to write. Still less is it conceivable that the Council should be prolonged for ten or eleven months. Nor can we easily conjecture, what is at first sight plausible, a postponement of the day of meeting, for Julius seems positively to say that they met at the very time for which they had been convened. (p. 46.)

In this difficulty, which can on no hypothesis perhaps be satisfactorily removed, some critics have thrown the *fault*, as it may be called, upon one place in the history, others on another.

The form in which it has been above exhibited is that which arises out of the arrangement of facts and dates first suggested by Valesius, and adopted after him by Schelstrate, Pagi, Montfaucon, Coustant, Du Pin, S. Basnage, and others. It seems far more natural and less open to objections than any other; and perhaps the readiest explanation of the difficulty, which has been above described as attaching to it, is to consider the letter of Pope Julius to be later than the Italian Council by eleven months, and written in the ordinary Autumnal Synod (Baron. 342. 34.), to which, on occasion of the delay of the Eusebians, the Italian Council of December, might naturally delegate [b], as to a sort of Committee, the office of concluding negcciations with them and issuing the Council's sentence, whenever the legates of the

---

[b] Tillemont will be found to make a similar suggestion, vol. 7. pp. 706, 7. He supplies parallel instances.

Pope should return. What makes this the more probable is, that Julius speaks of Athanasius as being among the *Romans* eighteen months. "He continued here a year and six months,.... his presence overcame us all," p. 49, words which properly belong to Bishops residing in the neighbourhood, not to an Italian Council. It is observable, moreover, that Julius says, "the sentiments I am expressing are not those of myself alone, but of all the Bishops throughout Italy, *and in these parts*," ἐν τούτοις τοῖς μέρεσι, p. 46. (Baronius, however, adduces this passage in order to shew that S. Julius's first letter issued from a Council.) And he proceeds, "The Bishops *now too*, καὶ νῦν, assembled on the appointed day," as if there had been a former appointment, and that punctually kept; (though Valesius and Schelstrate understand the words, "I *again* write," which follow, to refer to Julius's former communication with the Eusebians before Athanasius's coming, as we may understand it still.) And that a delay of some kind was occasioned in the proceedings at Rome by the conduct of the Eusebians, is plain, as various critics observe, from Julius's words, p. 40, "I, when I had read your letter, after much consideration, *kept it to myself*, thinking that *after all* some of you would come.....but when no one arrived, and it became *necessary* that the letter should be produced, &c." This passage too accounts for the long interval between the departure of the legates from the Eusebians in January, and the Pope's Letter to them of the November following in answer.

Such is the disposition of the dates which is the most satisfactory on the whole; but it must not be concealed, that names of the greatest weight may be alleged in favour of other chronological arrangements. Such is Baronius, who has been followed by Labbe, Petavius, and others; such are Hermant, Papebroke, and Tillemont, who adopt a third hypothesis. Such again is Mansi, who follows an arrangement of his own, founded on a document which has come to light since the time of his predecessors.

PREFACE. ix

Baronius supposes two visits of Athanasius to Rome, and two Italian Councils held there. He refers to a statement of Socrates, as apparently the basis of the former of these suppositions; though Socrates is so inextricably perplexed in his account of the events and even of the names of persons which occur in the history, that it is difficult to determine what he does and what he does not say on this point. Baronius refers to Hist. ii. 11. where no such statement occurs. He may be taken, however, to say, (e. g. ii. 15.) that Athanasius after his acquittal at Rome returned to Alexandria before the violent entrance of Gregory, upon which he retired to Rome a second time. Accordingly, Baronius terminates the eighteen months some time before Lent, 342, which he considers the date of Gregory's entrance, or towards the close of 341, and places their commencement, that is, the first journey of Athanasius in the early part of 340, and the Council of Alexandria in 339. Further, since the termination of the eighteen months must coincide with the date of the Roman Council, which acquitted Athanasius, he supposes that Council to have been held in 341, before the outrages of Gregory, and before the return of the legates, whom he sends into the East in 340, previous to Athanasius' first journey, and brings back to Rome not till 342, when Julius holds a second Council, in which he writes his synodal letter.

Baronius urges in behalf of his two Councils that Pope Julius notices in his Letter written from the Council, the complaint of the Eusebians that Athanasius had been admitted to communion, which was undeniably the act of the Council of fifty Bishops. Valesius answers first by denying that Julius notices any such complaint, next by arguing that the act of the Council of fifty was not mere admission into communion, for Athanasius had never been out of communion, and of this the Eusebians might be complaining, but a formal recognition of his being, and deserving to be, in communion with the Church. And hence Athanasius says, that they gave him " the confirmation of their fellowship,"

p. 39. ἐκύρωσαν τὴν κοινωνίαν.[a] As to the question, which has been raised, whether the Pope suspended communion with Athanasius, it is treated of by Tillemont, vol. 8. p. 673.

Tillemont, though he agrees with Baronius in supposing two journeys of S. Athanasius to Rome, follows Papebroke in differing from him altogether in the dates at which he places them. He argues that the Council at Rome must be dated shortly after the Council of the Dedication at Antioch 341; after it, because Julius complains that the Eusebians had anticipated him [b], (p. 50.) and but shortly after, because they pleaded the suddenness of the summons to Rome as a reason for not going, whereas it had been sent them by the Pope's legates as far back as the foregoing year. And he considers that the legates set out in the year 340, because in Athanasius's Encyclical Letter, written in the spring of 341, mention is made (p. 11.) of an intention at Rome to hold a Council for settling the existing troubles, an intention moreover the news of which occasioned the Eusebians to assemble at Antioch in 341. Accordingly he places the Council of Rome in June of that year; and this, in spite of S. Julius's express statement that January, when the legates were dismissed from Antioch, was about (because just beyond) the time when the Council was held, meeting the difficulty by an arbitrary alteration of the text, of June for January. And he supposes the Council to continue by adjournment and representation till the return of the legates, when S. Julius wrote his letter to the Eusebians. Athanasius's eighteen months therefore terminated at this date, i. e. in the autumn of 341; but, as agreeing with Valesius in fixing Gregory's arrival at Alexandria in Lent of that year, Tillemont is obliged to suppose that the eighteen months were not consecutive, even if they were complete. He dates Athanasius's first coming as at the end of 339 [c]; considers that he

---

[b] Schelstrate of course, whom Pagi follows, will not allow any intentional anticipation on the part of the Council, which he maintains to be in its beginnings Catholic, and to have assembled at the end of 340 to dedicate the Aureum Dominicum

[c] The words μόνον ἀκούσας in Athanasius, infr. p 227 §. 11 init. are felt as a difficulty both by Tillemont and Montfaucon; by Montfaucon, as if shewing that his flight was before Gregory's coming; by Tillemont, as shewing that it was after Gregory's ordination

PREFACE. xi

returned to Alexandria in the course of 340 on the rumour of the Eusebian movements at Antioch, and retired a second time to Rome on the forcible entrance of Gregory during the Lent following.

Valesius argues against the double journey of Athanasius from the strong negative fact that Athanasius no where speaks of more than one, (vid. infr. pp. 39, &c. 158, 227, &c.) He considers too that he could not have returned to Alexandria without formal Letters from Constantius, which there is no appearance of his obtaining.

Mansi differs from other critics in this, that he rejects the testimony of Socrates, &c. upon which it rests that Gregory's appointment proceeded from the Council of the Dedication, and considers his violences at Alexandria to have taken place in Lent 340. He argues from the language of Athanasius in his Encyclical Letter and elsewhere that Gregory certainly was not elected by Bishops, and therefore not in a Council, (vid. infr. pp. 5, 64, 229, &c.) Yet surely, according to Socrates, &c. Athanasius was deposed by the Council "because he had violated a rule which they themselves then passed," viz. that he had exercised his episcopal office without the formal leave of a Council of Bishops; and it can hardly be supposed that, when the Eusebians took the pains to be thus formal, they had already despatched Gregory to take possession of the Alexandrian See. And Pope Julius's letter too, p. 50 fin. implies that the Council passed some act against Athanasius. Hence Schelstrate and Pagi maintain that he was not deposed till after the question of faith and at least some canons had been settled. Mansi, however, relies upon a document discovered by Maffei in the Veronese Library, presently to be mentioned, which anticipates the date of Athanasius's return after the Council of Sardica by some years, placing it on Oct. 21, 346. and assigning six years and six months for the length of his exile. In consequence he fixes Athanasius's flight from Gregory and journey to Rome at the beginning of 340, agreeing with Baronius and Papebroke in supposing that it was preceded, as Sozomen reports Hist. ii. 9. by a time of concealment. He places the Council of Rome at the end of the eighteen months after Athanasius's arrival, i. e. towards the end of 341. And he argues that the Council of the Dedication was held in the month of August, from the circumstance of St. Jerome's assigning the Council in his Chronicon to the fifth year of the Emperors, (as does Socrates Hist. ii. 8.) while the fourteenth of the Indiction, which is also its date, ended with the beginning of September. But the fifth year from Constantine's death began on May 22; and from the new Emperors' assumption of the title of Augustus, not in August as Mansi states, (vid. Suppl. Conc. p. 175) but on Sept. 9. vid. Tillem. Emp. t. 4. p. 312. l'Art de verifier les Dates, t. 1. p. 392.

The mention of the accession of the sons of Constantine leads to the notice of one date in which Schelstrate, Pagi, and Montfaucon, as well as Papebroke, and Tillemont, side with Baronius against Valesius, who wishes to make 337 instead of 338 the year of S. Athanasius's return from Gaul. Valesius argues in favour of 337, from the circumstance that Constantine the younger in his letter to the Church of Alexandria, (infr. p. 121.) which is dated June 17, designates himself as "Cæsar," not by the title of Augustus, which he assumed with his brothers the September after his accession, i. e. Sept. 9, 337. Valesius adds, that while the brothers were but Cæsars, Constantine would have the highest authority of the three, as being the eldest; as if thus accounting for Constantine's writing to the Alexandrians, not Constantius their sovereign. Tillemont, after Schelstrate and Pagi, urges in reply the testimony of Theodoret, who says that Athanasius was two years and four months at Treves; and as he arrived there not before the end of 335, (Tillem. Montf.) or in 336, (Baron. Schelstr) he did not leave till 338. Moreover, Constantine's letter was written too soon after his father's death, on the supposition of its belonging to 337, to allow even of his hearing of that event, much less of his speaking, as he does, of his father's wishes as regards Athanasius. It appears too that the three brothers met in Pannonia in 338, where Athanasius tells us, (infr. p. 159,) he had about this time an interview with Constantius, viz at Viminacium; it is natural then to suppose that the letter of Constantine was the consequence of the meetings then and there held. And while Athanasius, (infr. p. 225,) expressly says, that his return was the joint act of the three brothers, it is known that Constantius and Constans were at Viminacium in June 338, since one of their laws bears this date and place; not to say that, according to Epiphanius, Constantius's approbation of the return of Athanasius was given when that Emperor was at Antioch, which he is known to have been in October 338. (vid. Schelstrate, Pagi.) As to Valesius's difficulty about Constantine's title, Pagi solves it by observing that Constantine was writing to a Church under his brother's jurisdiction, and in such case he would naturally drop the title Augustus, though he was in possession of it. He refers to parallel instances. And as to Constantine's writing at all, it is sufficient to answer that Treves where Athanasius was staying was within his territory.

Valesius also maintains, that the Encyclical Letter was written on occasion of the second attack on the Alexandrian Church, by George in 356, not upon the first under Gregory. He is misled by the faults in the text noticed infr. p. 1, which Baronius had corrected from the necessity of the case, and which Montfaucon has been able to set right from one of his Mss. To meet the difficulty which the mention of Philagrius creates, of whose connection with Gregory we are informed by Athanasius himself, infr. p. 224, Pagi, who, as well as Schelstrate, follows Valesius in this point, supposes that there were two Prefects of the name of Philagrius, the second the son of the first. He supports this supposition by the mention which occurs, (ibid.) of a Philagrius, Vicar of Cappadocia, i. e. under the Prefect, and who cannot, he considers, be the man who had served the higher office of Prefect of Egypt. In this way would be explained the praise bestowed upon a Philagrius by Nazianzen, (vid. ibid. note b.) whom he supposes to be the second of the two.

2. *The Council of Sardica.*

If any period in the life of S. Athanasius might at first sight be considered free from chronological difficulties, it would be that which lies between his second and his third exiles. Baronius, Montfaucon, and Tillemont, whose dates we have found so discordant in the foregoing years, have hardly a subject of difference in those which follow. There is a general consent among them and the critics which come between them concerning the date of the Council of Sardica, the restoration of S. Athanasius, and the irruption of Syrianus and his flight. The great difficulties attaching to the Councils of Sirmium in these years scarcely fall into the narrative of his life. Thus stands the matter, if we confine ourselves to the discussions and researches of the seventeenth century. But in the course of the eighteenth a fresh source of information was discovered, which, while it added perplexity to the perplexed period which has already come under review, brought into serious difficulty the hitherto unquestioned dates of the Council of Sardica, and of S. Athanasius's return to Alexandria consequent upon it.

Maffei published from the Library of Verona a fragment of the Latin Version of Annals of the life of S. Athanasius, written apparently in Greek at Alexandria, and not very long after the times which it records. The high value which he sets upon this document, is confirmed by the judgment of Mansi and the Ballerini, the latter of whom call it an " aureum opusculum," Observ. in Noris. p. 834. and the former has made it the basis of a new chronological arrangement[d]. That it contains very great historical misstatements is evident at first sight; but it is a question whether these may not be attributed to the ignorance of the translator, errors in transcription, e. g. in numerals, and other causes; while on the other hand, were

[d] Vid. also Vallars. in Hieron. Chron. p. 793.

PREFACE. xv

the mistakes even so numerous and flagrant, an apparent internal consistency as well as plausible external support may be urged in behalf of those particular statements, on which are founded the corrections of the chronology of the historical period now under review.

In the very passage which is of main importance in the inquiry, and with which the fragment opens, we find a glaring error, at variance too with the account which follows. "Post Gregorii mortem Athanasius reversus est ex urbe Româ........et remansit quietus apud Alexandriam annis xvi. et mens. vi." whereas it is notorious, as the Annalist himself goes on to say, that he was driven into banishment again in little more than nine years.

In the paragraph that follows, the Author speaks of the Consuls of the year 349, as *Hypatius* and Catulinus, instead of Limenius; and of Eusebius of Nicomedia as then alive, who died in 341 or 342; and of the murder of Hermogenes at Constantinople, which took place at the same date. Mansi, however, has a very ingenious explanation of the mistake in the Consul's name.

Afterwards he speaks of Constans for Constantius, and Gregory for George.

The statement in which we are immediately concerned runs thus: "Et factus est, post Gregorii mortem Athanasius reversus est ex urbe Româ et partibus Italiæ et ingressus est Alexandriam, Phaophi xxiv. Consulibus Constantio iv. et Constante iii. hoc est post annos vi." The Consuls named belong to 346, and the Egyptian date, according to Mansi, corresponds to October 21; whereas the received date of Athanasius's return is 349, and is computed thus:—Sozomen Hist. iii. 12. places the Council of Sardica in the Consulate of Rufinus and Eusebius, that is, A.D. 347. From the Council an embassy or legation was sent by Constans to his brother, consisting of Euphrates and Vincentius. What happened to them at Antioch we read infr. p. 235, and it took place " at the season of the most holy Easter," which must be 348, Easter-Day being April 3; now Gregory died "about ten months after," p. 236; that is, in February 349, upon which Athanasius was restored to his see, ibid. But on the other hand, reckoning backwards, if his restoration took place, as the Annalist would have it, in 346, then Euphrates and Vincentius were at Antioch at Easter 345, and the Council took place in 344.

In another place the anonymous Annalist speaks of the irruption of Syrianus, infr. p. 206. as occurring, "Mechir xiii. die per noctem supervenientem xiv." or February 9, which answers to the received account infr. p. 294. and adds, " Hoc factum est post annos ix, et menses iii, ac dies xix, quam Italiâ reversus est Episcopus," a period, which, reckoning according to Alexandrian months of thirty days, consistently answers, as Maffei and Mansi observe, to the interval between Oct. 21, 346. and Feb. 9, 356. One cannot suppose then the date assigned, whatever be its value, to have been altered in transcription or translation. It is the date intended by the Author. Now in St. Jerome's Chronicon, the year assigned for Athanasius's return, is the tenth year of Constans, that is, this very year 346, though the date A.D. is there otherwise marked, viz. as 350 (349). Theodoret too reckons the length of Gregory's usurpation at six years, which, however treated, cannot be made to reach to 349. Moreover, if Euphrates was convicted of Arianism in 346, which is the date assigned to the Council of Cologne, he could not have been a legate from the Council of Sardica to Constantius in Easter 348; but this difficulty, so celebrated in controversy, vanishes, if for 348 we substitute 345, as the date of the visit of Euphrates to Antioch. It may be added, that in Surius's Edition of the Council of Sardica, the Consuls of 344 are named in the title; which is also the case in an ancient Ms. of the Collection of Mercator formerly contained in the Jesuit Library at Paris, though other chronological specifications are added inconsistent with this date.

What alterations in the chronology of the period seem to be

PREFACE.   xvii

required by this and other notices contained in the fragment under consideration, will be seen by inspecting Mansi's table, a specimen of which shall presently be given. Here the dates set down by the Annalist himself shall be set before the reader.

Entrance of S. Athanasius into Alexandria on his return from
  Italy.   Oct. 21, 346.
Legation of five Bishops from S. Athanasius to Constans
  [Constantius] at Milan.   May 19, 353.
Montanus the Palatine enters Alexandria, four days after,
  with Letters from the Emperor to S. Athanasius prohi-
  bitory of his legation.   May 23, 353.
Diogenes the Notary comes to Alexandria with a view
  of driving S. Athanasius from the city.   end of July, 355.
  he was there 4 months from the intercalation (after July)
  to Dec 22.
Syrianus enters Alexandria   Jan. 5, 356.
Breaks into the Church at night.   Feb. 9, 356.
George is driven from Alexandria   Oct. 2, 358.
Death of S. Athanasius.   May 3, 373.

It does not fall within the scope of this Preface to enter into the Chronology of the Councils of Milan, upon which so much has been written. On the critics who have treated the subject and their respective judgments, vid. Pagi, ann. 344. n. 4.

3. *Councils of Sirmium.*

Something was said on the subject of the Councils of Sirmium, in the eighth Volume of the Library of the Fathers, p. 160, in course of enumerating the Sirmian and other Confessions. Mansi, however, was scarcely referred to; and Zaccaria who has written after him not at all. A few words will be sufficient to supply the omission.

Socrates and Sozomen assign the condemnation of Photinus at Sirmium to a Council held there in 351. Baronius, Sirmond, and Gothofred, consider them mistaken, and fix it in the year 357, towards or at the end of which, Constantius came to that place, and remained there through the greater part or whole of 358, and part of 359, (Gothofred in Philost. p. 200. Mansi, Suppl. Conc. p. 182. ed. 1748.) Petavius, Tillemont, S. Basnage, &c. speak of three Councils or Conferences of Sirmium, placing them respectively in 351, 357, and 359. Gothofred three, in 357, 358, 359. Mansi three, in 358, 359, 359. Zaccaria makes in all five, viz. in 349, (in which indeed he follows Petavius,) 351, 357, (at which Hosius lapsed,) 357 (following Valesius and Pagi,) and 359. The main point of dispute is, whether there are *two* dates for Sirmian Councils, 351, and 357—9, or but *one*, and that, at the latter period, the former date, though assigned by Socrates, being in that case impossible; and the main argument in favour of Baronius and Mansi, who assert that there was but one, is the improbability, be it great or be it little, that there should have been two Councils or Conferences in that city, of an ecumenical not local character, within a few years of each other. There does not seem much more to be said than this, against Petavius and other advocates for 351 and 357.

This is evident from the mode in which Mansi draws out his argument. He urges that Socrates and Sozomen, the two writers who date the Council at 351, nevertheless state, that "George, Bishop of Alexandria," was present at it, that is, George of Cappadocia, who was not consecrated till 356, and was not driven from Alexandria till the end of August, (or Oct. 2, according to the Anonymus,) 358. The Council then was held towards the end of that year, a date at which we happen to know that Constantius was making a long stay at Sirmium. Such seems the utmost of Mansi's argument. Tillemont had already urged the mention of George to shew that there was a Sirmian Council at a later date, but it does follow from thence, as Tillemont well understands, that still Photinus was not condemned at an earlier Council held in 351. Now the reasons for the latter opinion, with the replies made to them, are as follows: 1. Socrates dates in this place by naming the Consuls (of the foregoing year,—there were no Consuls in 351,) and is never wrong, according to Petavius, when he dates by the Consuls. Mansi, however, denies this, and Zaccaria concedes it, vid. also infr. p. xxi. 2. The Council of Sirmium, says Tillemont, was composed of Bishops of the East, yet held in Illyricum, all which agrees with the date 351, when the West was under the power of usurpers; Mansi accounts for the fact by alleging that the West had already declared its judgment in two Councils held against Photinus at Rome and Milan. 3. Basil of Ancyra, who was the life of the Council against Photinus, opposed himself at Ancyra to the Council of 357 or 358; which obliges us to distinguish between the two Councils. Mansi explains by stating, what was the fact, that there were two parties, Arians and Semi-Arians, at the Council, and that when the latter, of which Basil was the leader, left it, the former stayed and passed the Confession which Hosius subscribed, and Basil, &c. at Ancyra repudiated. 4. Germinius, who succeeded Photinus in the see of Sirmium, sat as Bishop as early as the Council of Milan, 355; it is answered, that at least he was Bishop of Cyzicus before the deposition of Photinus. 5. Theodore, who subscribed the formulary against Photinus, was dead in 355; that is, if the Theodore who subscribed was the Bishop of Heraclea, and this formulary the confession which Liberius signed. vid. Hilar. Fragm. vi. 7. 6. Cecropius of Nicomedia, says Zaccaria against Mansi, though not against Baronius, was present at the Council, but he was killed in the earthquake in that city, August 28, 358. 7. Pagi too observes, that the disputation between Basil and Photinus was taken down, according to Epiphanius, Hær. 71. p. 829. by "Callicrates, registrar of Rufinus the Prefect;" now if Prætorian Prefect be meant, Rufinus was Prefect of Illyricum 349—352. Exceptores or registrars were attached to all judges, Gothofr. Cod. Theod. t. 2. p. 459. but they are especially connected with Prætorian Prefects by Gothofred, ibid. Pancirollus Not. Dign. p. 36. and Lami Erud. Apost. p. 262.

4 *The year of S. Athanasius's death.*

Though there is nothing in the following Treatises which leads specially to a discussion of the year of S Athanasius's death, yet since it is one of the principal points of controversy in a history which, as we have seen, abounds in chronological difficulties, and is closely connected with passages which occur below, it will not be out of place here to set down the opinions of various critics on the subject. Many of them are collected together in Fontanini's Dissertation appended to his Historia Literaria Aquileiensis.

Socrates places his death in the Consulate of Gratian ii. and Probus, that is, in 371; in which he is followed by Petavius; Hermant in his Life of S. Athanasius; P. F. Chifflet, (upon Ep. Paulin. 29) Paulin. Illustr. part. 2. c. 11. p. 150; Papebroke in vit. Ath. p. 248; and Sollerius (who answers Pagi and Montfaucon in a very disagreeable tone) de Patriarchis Alexandrinis, Act. SS. in t. 5. Jun.

Baronius; Valesius (Theod. Hist. iv. 22.); Renaudot, Hist. Patriarch. Alex. p. 95; and Fontanini *supr.* adopt the date of 372, from the duration of his Episcopate being 46 years, (on which there is a general agreement,) and its commencement in 326. Sollerius too confesses, that of the two he should prefer 372 to 373, de Patr. Alex. n. 213. and it can hardly be doubted, that this date would have, what may be called, the second votes of the advocates both of 371 and of 373.

Cardinal Noris in his Censur. in Not. Garner. (Opp. t. 3. p. 1178.) in correction of a former statement in his Hist. Pelag. in which he agreed with Baronius; his Editors the Ballerini in their Obss p. 834; Bucherius (in Victor. Can. Pasch.); Pagi; Quesnel (Leon. Opp. t. 2. p. 1545. ed. Baller.); Du Pin, making S. Athanasius's Episcopate "more than 48 years;" Oudinus (in supplem. Script. Eccles.); Tillemont; Montfaucon; Ceillier (Hist. des Aut. Eccles.); S. Basnage (Annal.); Le Quien (Or. Christ t 2. p. 400.); Scip. Maffei (Osserv. Lett.

t. 3.); and Mansi in the Dissertation quoted above, (though he speaks respectfully of Sollerius's objections, in Pag. Ann. 372. 9.) argue in favour of 373. This last opinion, which Montfaucon is considered to have established, in his Vit. Ath. and a " Dissertatio de tempore mortis Alex. Ep. Alex. ac de anno ob. Athan. M." (which has not fallen in the way of the present writer,) is founded principally upon S. Proterius's Paschal Epistle.

Little seems to be adduced in favour of 371, beyond the circumstance of Socrates mentioning the Consuls of that year, a mode of dating which, according to Baronius, may ordinarily be trusted, (in Ann. 69. n. 36.) that is, in the case of public acts or contemporary events, as Montfaucon observes, Fontan. Diss. p. 444. Petavius, however, says, Socrates nunquam temere, aut falso notas Consulares adhibet, de Phot. Hær. c. 2. p. 379; on this point, however, something has occurred above, p. xix. After alleging the evidence of Socrates, Sollerius, who is the latest of the above advocates of the year 371, does little more than attempt to adjust that date with other existing chronological data, and to refute objections.

The most obvious difficulty in his hypothesis is, that Socrates himself, in the very passage in which he mentions the Consuls of 371, states that S. Athanasius was Bishop for 46 years, which, since he did not succeed Alexander till 326, will bring the date of his death to 372 or 373. A controversy follows, whether his consecration was at the end of 326, or at the beginning. S Alexander died, according to the Coptite History, as late as April 17 (326); but according to Athanasius himself, infr. p. 88. and Theodoret, within five months after the reception of the Meletians, (which followed upon the termination of the Nicene Council, i. e. upon Aug. 25, 325,) and therefore in the beginning of 326, or the end of 325. Epiphanius too reports, that S. Alexander died the year of the Nicene Council, Hær. 69. 11. (though he adds what invalidates his testimony, or rather turns it the other way,) and his Festival is fixed in the Roman Martyrology on

Feb. 26. Next comes the question of the interval between Alexander's death and Athanasius's ordination, which Sollerius of course wishes to curtail as much as possible. With this view he refers to the words of the Alexandrian Council, infr. p. 22, which he interprets to imply, that the vacancy in the see was immediately filled, and he maintains, after Papebroke, that the Greek Feast-Day of S. Athanasius, Jan. 18, was really the day of his consecration, i. e. in 326. However, though this be granted for argument's sake, even then the 46 years of S. Athanasius's Episcopate extend to January 372, i. e. beyond May 2, (his day of death,) 371. Nor can we suppose, that Socrates merely uses round numbers, when he speaks of 46 years, for S. Cyril expressly tells us, that Athanasius's Episcopate was "46 *whole* years;" and Theodoret, Sozomen, the Arabian writers, (Renaudot Hist. Patr. Alex. p. 96.) and others say the same thing. Yet Rufinus, who was in Egypt about the time of Athanasius's death, certainly says only, that he died in his 46th year.

And here at first sight is an argument in favour of 372, rather than 373; Papebroke and Fontanini observe, that S. Athanasius would have been Bishop 47 not 46 years on supposition of the latter date. But this depends on the time of year at which his Episcopate commenced. Sollerius maintains above, that it dates from January 18; but Montfaucon (in his Monitum in correction of his Vit. Athan.) and Tillemont place the death of S. Alexander on the 17th or 18th of April, following the Jacobite Chronicon of Abraham Eckellensis, as above cited, and other Coptite, as well as Abyssinian Calendars. To the five months spoken of above by Athanasius and Theodoret, must in this case be added, as indeed is reasonable, the time consumed in the return of S. Alexander from Nicæa to Alexandria, and the proceedings in reconciliation of the Meletians, which will make up the whole interval between August 25, and the April following. Again, S Athanasius's consecration does not seem to have followed immediately upon the death of his predecessor, infr

p. 22. which will carry down the beginning of his Episcopate far into the year 326; and if we date it from the middle or the end, and much more if, as the Ballerini propose, we fix it on Jan. 18, 327, then 46 years and some months, or as it is natural that S. Cyril should express it, 46 whole years, will bring us to May 2, (the received day of his death,) 373. The known duration then of S. Athanasius's Episcopate does not decide between 372 and 373, being consistent with the latter date as well as with the former. Other arguments, decisive against 371, but available for both 372 and 373, are deducible from the date of the coming of Valens to Antioch, where, as Socrates tells us, he was staying at the time of S. Athanasius's death; and of Melania's visit to Alexandria, when Athanasius gave her Macarius's sheep-skin,—a proof, says Montfaucon, that Athanasius was not dead then, a proof, says Fontanini, that he was dying.

The direct evidence in favour of 373 has been mentioned above. It consists in the Paschal Epistle of S. Proterius, a contemporary of S. Leo, which is contained in Petavius's Doctr. Temp. t. 2. who, however, p. 889. ed. 1627. as Sollerius and Fontanini after him, thinks the text corrupt and untrustworthy, as it evidently is in part. Sollerius also argues against it as irrelevant in its context, and unmeaning. It is confirmed by S. Jerome's Chronicon, which places Athanasius's death in the 10th year of Valens; and by the Coptite History, which, by dating it on a Thursday, fixes it in 373; and especially by Maffei's fragment, of which so much has been said above. Collateral evidence is gained from the date of the consecration of S. Basil 370, who, when he was Bishop, corresponded with S. Athanasius, which, under the circumstances, could hardly have been the case, had Athanasius died in 372. Sollerius, however, suggests, that the Athanasius addressed by S. Basil was Athanasius of Ancyra, at one time an Arianizer, though afterwards zealous for orthodoxy, n. 250.

It only remains to exhibit the historical events which have

come under review according to the respective chronologies which different critics have adopted.

Dates according to Valesius, Schelstrate, Pagi, Montfaucon, Sam. Basnage.

	A.D.
S. Athanasius returns from Gaul	337. *V.*
	338. *S. P. M. B.*
leaving Treves end of June, *M.*	
Three Eusebian Legates sent to Rome.	339. *V. S. P. M. B.*
Council of Alexandria.	340. *S. P. M. B.*
Council of the Dedication.	341. *V S. P. M. B.*
in beginning of Year, *V.* end of 340, till January 341, *S.* before Sept *P.* to anticipate Roman, *Bar.* not to anticipate Roman, *S. P.*	
Entrance of Gregory into Alexandria. Lent.	341. *V. P. M. B*
Athanasius writes his Encyclical Letter.	341. *M.*
in concealment, *M.*	
[in 356 according to *V. S. P.*]	
S. Athanasius escapes to Rome.	341. *V. S. P. M. B.*
March or April, *S. P.* after Easter, (April 19,) *V.* May *M.* after Council of Dedication, *P.*	
Legates set out from Rome to the Eusebians.	341. *V. S. P. B.*
before Athanasius arrives there, and in beginning of Year, *V.*	
after Athanasius's arrival, in March or April, *S. P.* May, *M.*	
Legates arrive at Antioch.	341. *S. P.*
in April or May or June, *S.* in June, *P.*	
Legates set out from Antioch.	342. *V. S. M. B.*
January, *S. B. M*	
they return in March or April, *S.*	
Council of Rome, in which Athanasius is acquitted.	342. *V. S. P. M. B.*
October, *S. B.* or November, *M.*	
The Pope's Letter to the Eusebians.	342. *V. M. B. M.*

Baronius and Petavius.

Athanasius returns from Gaul.	338. *B. P.*
The three Eusebian Legates, Macarius, &c. sent to Rome.	339. *B. P.*
Council of Alexandria.	339. *B.*
The Legates sent from the Pope to the Eusebians.	340. *B.*

PREFACE.

Athanasius comes to Rome (first time) beginning of	340.	*B. P.*
Council of the Dedication at Antioch,	341.	*B. P.*
to anticipate Roman Council, *B.*		
First Council of Rome, in which Athanasius is acquitted.	341.	*B. P.*
Athanasius returns immediately to Alexandria,	341.	*B. P.*
end of year, or beginning of next, *B.*		
Eusebians send back the Legates.	341.	*B. P.*
after the Council of Rome, *B.* before it, *P.*		
Entrance of Gregory into Alexandria, Lent	342.	*B. P.*
Athanasius retreats from Alexandria into a place of concealment.	342.	*B. P.*
He writes his Encyclical Letter.	342.	*B.*
The Pope's Legates return to Rome.	342.	*B.*
Second Council of Rome.	342.	*B.*
The Pope's Letter to the Eusebians.	342.	*B.*
Athanasius comes to Rome (second time).	342.	*B. P.*

Papebroke, Tillemont.

S. Athanasius returns from Gaul.	338.	*P. T.*
The three Eusebian Legates sent to Rome.	339.	*T.*
Council of Alexandria.	339.	*P. T.*
S. Athanasius goes to Rome.	339.	*P. T.*
and his 18 months begin, *T.* September, *P.*		
The Legates sent from the Pope to the Eusebians,	340.	*T.*
immediately after Sept. 339. *P.*		
S. Athanasius returns to Alexandria,	end of 340.	*P. T.*
Council of the Dedication.	341.	*P. T.*
beginning of Year, *T.*		
before September, *T.*		
Entrance of Gregory into Alexandria, Lent.	341.	*P. T.*
S. Athanasius writes his Encyclical Letter.	341.	*P. T.*
He leaves Alexandria and retreats to Rome.	341.	*P. T.*
after Easter, *T.*		
The Pope's Legates leave Antioch.	341.	*P. T.*
in June not January, *P. T.*		
Council of Rome,	June 341.	*P. T.*
opened before return of Legates, *P.*		
sitting till August or September, *T.*		
The Pope's Letter to the Eusebians.	341.	*T.*
August or September, *T.*		

xxvi   PREFACE.

Mansi.

Entrance of Gregory into Alexandria.	Lent, 340.
S. Athanasius leaves Alexandria for a place of concealment.	May, 340.
He goes to Rome.	June, 340.
Council of the Dedication.	August, 341.
Council of Rome.	End of 341.

	Baron.	Pag.	Mont.	Tillem.	Mans.
Macrostich is drawn up by Arian Council of Antioch.	344.	345.	344.	345.	end of 343.
It is rejected by the Westerns in the Council of Milan.	344.	346.	345.	345.	344.
when the Arian Legates leave the Assembly in anger.	344.	346.	345.	345.	346.
Council of Sardica.	347.	347.	347.	347.	end of 344.
Sardican Legates at Antioch. Easter,	348.	348.	348.	348.	345.
Death of the usurper Gregory, Jan. or Feb.	349.	349.	349.	349.	346.
Council of Cologne deposes Euphrates.	346.	346.		346.	346.
Council of Milan against Photinus, at which Valens and Ursacius appear.	350.	347.	347.	347.	346.
Council of Jerusalem.	350.	349.	349.	349.	346.
S. Athanasius returns to Alexandria.	350.	349.	349.	349.	346. Oct. 21
First Sirmian Council against Photinus.	357.	351	351.	351.	358.
Montanus comes to Alexandria.	351.	353.	353 or 354.		353. end of May
Diogenes the Notary attempts to drive S. Athanasius from Alexandria	354.	355.	355.	355.	355. end of July.
Irruption of Syrianus into the Church, Feb 9.	356.	356.	356.	356.	356.
George is driven from Alexandria.	357.			358.	358. Oct. 2.
Second Sirmian Council or Conference, in which was passed the "blasphemia," vol. 8. p 161.	Beg of 357.	End of 357.	357.	357	359.
Council of Ancyra just before Easter.	357.	358.		358.	359.
Third Sirmian Council or Conference	357.	358.	359.	359. May 22.	359.
Council of Ariminum, July 21.	359.	359.	359.	359.	359.
Death of S. Athanasius, May 2.	372	373.	373.	373 probably	373.

PREFACE.

Before concluding, it is necessary to observe, that in the references in the notes or margin, S. Athanasius's Works are designated by their Latin titles for the sake of clearness; and " Hist. Arian." is the same work as " ad Mon." There is some unavoidable irregularity in the mode of reference to former Volumes of this series, e. g. " Libr. F." with the Volume specified, is equivalent to " Oxf. Tr.'" or " O. T." or to the name of the Treatise with " Tr." added. Also the reference is sometimes made according to pages, sometimes according to sections &c. Consistency has not been thought of much consequence in a matter of this kind, where clearness and conciseness of reference were rather to be consulted in each particular case.

Also it may be right to refer the reader to a Letter addressed to Montfaucon on the words θάλλων, or " boughs," infr. p. 270. in the Collectio Nova (t. ii. in Cosm. p. 18); and to a note of Quesnel's on S. Leo, (t. 3. p. xlvii. ed. Baller.) who observes, that Siscia, infr. p. 60. is not a province, but the city of that name in Pannonia.

And it should be added to page 13, that Tillemont dates the Apologia contra Arian. not earlier than A.D. 356. arguing from the mention of the banishment of Liberius and Hosius. Also in note g, p. 49, justice is not done to Baronius's view of Athanasius's double journey to Rome, as the foregoing pages will shew. And in p. 76, note m, Thomassin is quoted not to corroborate Febronius's interpretation, but principle.

Also in p. 46, Valesius Obss. Eccles. i. 2. p. 174. understands Eusebius himself by οἱ περὶ Εὐσέβιον §. 26. Montfaucon observes, that Eusebius alone is spoken of in §. 1. He adds, " res hic in dubio versatur." Baronius adduces the phrase as used in the Encyclical Letter in proof that it was written while Eusebius was still alive, but Valesius denies the argument on grammatical grounds, Obss. Eccl. i. 7 fin. Montfaucon, however, observes, in his Monitum prefixed to that Letter, that in matter of fact the phrase is never used by S. Athanasius of Eusebius's party after E.'s death, but always κοινωνοὶ τῶν περὶ E. or κληρόνομοι τῆς ἀσεβείας τοῦ E.

Also with reference to the subject of note n, p. 77. it should be observed, that the majority of critics side with Du Cange against Gothofred on the meaning of the word Canalis. "Those Bishops," says Baronius, were " in Canalio, qui sedes haberent in cursu publico, viâ scilicet quâ equi publici per stationes singulas dispositi essent ad iter agendum." An. 347. 55. " Qui præerant sacris urbium, quæ regiæ viæ insidebant," says Noris, professing his agreement with Baronius, Opp. t. 4. p. 623. Pitiscus also, " qui sedes habent in cursu publico," *in voc.* So also Kiesling, adding, " intelliguntur hoc nomine urbes, seu potius civitates, in quibus Episcopi sedem habuerunt fixam." de Discipl. Cleric. p. 13. Beveridge reports Zonaras and Balsamon as furnishing the same interpretation; " cities which are in the public ways, or canal, through which travellers pass without trouble, as water flows in an aqueduct." Pandect. t. 1. p. 507.

For the Translation, the Editors have to express their acknowledgments to the Rev. MILES ATKINSON, M.A. late Fellow of Lincoln College.

J. H. N.

Dec. 4, 1843.

CONTENTS.

	Page
1. Encyclical Epistle, addressed to all Bishops every where, A.D. 341. (*Ep. Encycl.*)	1
2. Apology against the Arians, written about A.D. 350. (*Apol. contr. Arian.*)	13
3. Encyclical Epistle, addressed to the Bishops of Egypt and Libya, A.D. 356. (*ad Ep. Æg.*)	125
4. Apology addressed to the Emperor Constantius, A.D. 356. (*ad Constant.* or *Ap. ad Const.*)	154
5. Apology for his flight, A.D. 357 or 358. (*de Fug.*)	189
6. Epistle to Serapion concerning the death of Arius, A.D. 358—360. (*ad Serap. de Mort. Ar.*)	210
7. Epistle to the Monks, A.D. 358, or later. (*Ep. ad Mon.*)	215
8. History of the Arians, written A.D. 358—360. (*ad Mon.* or *Hist. Arian.*)	219
Appendix. S. Alexander's Deposition of Arius, and Encyclical Epistle, A.D. 321. (*Alex. Encycl. Ep.*)	297

HISTORICAL TRACTS.

I.

ENCYCLICAL EPISTLE

OF THE

BLESSED ATHANASIUS,

BISHOP OF ALEXANDRIA.

[S. Athanasius wrote the following Epistle in the year 341. In that year the Eusebians held the famous Council of the Dedication at Antioch, vid. Athan. de Syn. §. 25. (Libr. F. vol 8 p 109, &c.) Here they appointed Gregory to the see of Alexandria in the place of Athanasius, whom they had already condemned and denounced at the Synod of Tyre, A.D. 335. Gregory was by birth a Cappadocian, and, (if Nazianzen speaks of the same Gregory, which some critics doubt,) studied at Alexandria, where S. Athanasius had treated him with great kindness and familiarity, though Gregory afterwards took part in propagating the calumny against him of having murdered Arsenius. Gregory was on his appointment dispatched to Alexandria with Philagrius Prefect of Egypt, and their proceedings on their arrival are related in the following Encyclical Epistle, which S Athanasius forwarded immediately upon his retreat from the city to all the Bishops of the Catholic Church. It is less correct in style, as Tillemont observes, than other of his works, as if composed in haste. In the Editions previous to the Benedictine, it was called an "Epistle to the Orthodox every where," but Montfaucon has been able to restore the true title. He has been also able from his MSS. to make a far more important correction, which has cleared up some very perplexing difficulties in the history All the Editions previous to the Benedictine read "George" throughout for "Gregory," and "Gregory" in the place where "Pistus" occurs. Baronius, Tillemont, &c had already made the alterations from the necessity of the case.]

To his fellow-Ministers[1] in every place, beloved Lords, Athanasius sends health in the Lord.

[1] συλλειτουργοῖς.

1. OUR sufferings have been dreadful beyond endurance, and it is impossible to describe them in suitable terms; but

§. 1.

ENCYC. LETT.

Judg. 19, 19.

in order that the dreadful nature of the events which have taken place may be more readily apprehended, I have thought it good to bring to your notice a history out of the Scriptures. It happened that a certain Levite was injured in the person of his wife; and, when he considered the exceeding greatness of the pollution, (for the woman was a Hebrew, and of the tribe of Judah,) being astounded at the outrage which had been committed against him, he divided his wife's body, as the Holy Scripture relates in the Book of Judges, and sent a part of it to every tribe in Israel, in order that it might be understood that an injury like this pertained not to himself only, but extended to all alike; and that, if the people sympathised with him in his sufferings, they might avenge him; or if they neglected to do so, might bear the disgrace of being considered thenceforth as themselves guilty of the wrong. The messengers whom he sent related what had happened; and they that heard and saw it, declared that such things had never been done from the day that the children of Israel came up out of Egypt. So every tribe of Israel was moved, and all came together against the offenders, as though they had themselves been the sufferers; and at last the perpetrators of this iniquity were destroyed in war, [1] ἀνάθεμα and became a curse[1] in the mouths of all: for the assembled people considered not their kindred blood, but regarded only the crime they had committed. You know the history, brethren, and the particular account of the circumstances given in Scripture. I will not therefore describe them more in detail, since I write to persons acquainted with them, and as I am anxious to represent to your piety our present circumstances, which are even worse than those to which I have referred. For my object in reminding you of this history is this, that you may compare those ancient transactions with what has happened to us now, and perceiving how much these last exceed the other in cruelty, may be filled with greater indignation on account of them, than were the people of old against those offenders.

2. For the treatment we have undergone, surpasses the bitterness of any persecution, and the calamity of the Levite was but small, when compared with the enormities which have now been committed against the Church; or rather such

deeds as these were never before heard of in the whole world, or the like experienced by any one. In that case it was but a single woman that was injured, and one Levite who suffered wrong; now the whole Church is injured, the priesthood insulted, and worst of all, piety[1] is persecuted by impiety. On that occasion the tribes were astounded, each at the sight of part of the body of one woman; but now the members of the whole Church are seen divided from one another, and are sent abroad some to you, and some to others, bringing word of the insults and injustice which they have suffered. Be ye therefore also moved, I beseech you, considering that these wrongs are done unto you no less than unto us; and let every one lend his aid, as feeling that he is himself a sufferer, lest shortly the Ecclesiastical Canons, and the faith of the Church be corrupted. For both are in danger, unless God shall speedily by your hands amend what has been done amiss, and the Church be avenged on her enemies. For our Canons[a] and our forms were not given to the Churches at the present day, but were wisely and safely transmitted to us from our forefathers. Neither had our faith its beginning at this time, but it came down to us from the Lord through His disciples[b]. That therefore the ordinances which have been preserved in the Churches from old time until now, may not be lost in our days, and the trust which has been committed to us required at our hands; rouse yourselves, brethren, as being stewards of the mysteries of God, and seeing them now seized upon by aliens. Further particulars of our condition you will learn from the bearers of our letters, but I was anxious myself to write you a brief account thereof, that you may know for certain, that such things have never before been committed against the Church, from the day that our Saviour, when He was taken up, gave command to His disciples, saying, *Go ye, and make disciples of all nations, baptizing them in the name of the Father, and of the Son, and of the Holy Ghost.*

[1] εὐσέβεια, orthodoxy, vid. vol. viii p 1, note a.

Mat. 28, 19.

---

[a] vid. Beveridg. Cod. Can Illustr. 1. 3. §. 2. who comments on this passage at length. Allusion is also made to the Canons in Apol cont. Arian. §. 69.

[b] vid. Athan. de Syn. §. 4. (Oxf. Tr. p. 78, and note o.) Orat. 1. § 8. (ib.d. p. 191) Tertull. Præscr. Hær. §. 29. (O. T. p. 462, and note c.)

3. Now the outrages which have been committed against us, and against the Church are these. While we were holding our assemblies in peace, as usual, and while the people were rejoicing in them, and advancing in godly conversation, and while our fellow-ministers in Egypt, and the Thebais, and Libya, were in love and peace both with one another and with us; on a sudden the Prefect of Egypt puts forth a public letter, bearing the form of an edict, and declaring that one Gregory from Cappadocia was coming to be my successor, supported by his own body-guard. This announcement confounded every one, for such a proceeding was entirely novel, and now heard of for the first time. The people however assembled still more constantly in the Churches[c], for they very well knew that neither they themselves, nor any Bishop or Presbyter, nor in short any one had ever complained against me, and they saw that Arians only were on his side, and were aware also that he was himself an Arian, and was sent by the Eusebians to the Arian party. For you know, brethren, that the Eusebians have always been the supporters and associates of the impious heresy of the Arian fanatics[1], by whose means they have ever carried on their designs against me, and were the authors of my banishment into Gaul.

[1 ἀρειομανιτῶν. vid. Ath. Oxf. Tr. viii. p. 91, note q.]

4. The people, therefore, were justly indignant and exclaimed against the proceeding, calling the rest of the magistrates and the whole city to witness, that this novel and iniquitous attempt was now made against the Church, not on the ground of any charge brought against me by Ecclesiastical persons, but through the wanton assault of the Arian heretics. For even if there had been any complaint generally prevailing against me, it was not an Arian, or one professing Arian doctrines, that ought to have been chosen to supersede me; but according to the Ecclesiastical Canons, and the direction of Paul, when the people were *gathered together, and the*

---

[c] Assembling in the Churches seems to have been a sort of protest or demonstration, sometimes peaceably, but sometimes in a less exceptionable manner,—peaceably, during Justina's persecution at Milan. Ambros Ep. i 20. August. Confess. ix. 15. but at Ephesus after the third Ecumenical Council the Metropolitan shut up the Churches, took possession of the Cathedral, and succeeded in repelling the imperial troops Churches were asylums, vid. Cod. Theodos. ix. 45. §. 4. &c. at the same time arms were prohibited.

spirit of them that ordain, *with the power of our Lord Jesus Christ,* all things ought to have been enquired into and transacted canonically, in the presence of those among the laity and clergy who demanded the change, and not that a person brought from a distance by Arians, as if making a traffic of the title of Bishop, should with the support and strong arm of heathen magistrates, thrust himself upon those who neither demanded nor desired his presence, nor indeed knew any thing of what had been done. Such proceedings tend to the dissolution of all Ecclesiastical rules, and compel the heathen to blaspheme, and to suspect that our appointments are not made according to a divine rule, but as a matter of traffic and patronage [1].

5. Thus was this notable appointment of Gregory brought about by the Arians, and such was the beginning of it. And what outrages he committed on his entry into Alexandria, and of what great evils that event was the cause, you may learn both from our letters, and by enquiry of those who travel among you. While the people were offended at such an unusual proceeding, and in consequence assembled in the Churches, in order to prevent the impiety of the Arians from mingling itself with the faith of the Church, Philagrius who has long been a persecutor of the Church and her virgins, and is now Prefect[d] of Egypt, an apostate already, and a fellow-countryman of Gregory, a man too of no respectable character, and moreover supported by the Eusebians, and therefore full of zeal against the Church; this person, by means of promises which he afterwards fulfilled, succeeded in gaining over the heathen multitude, with the Jews and disorderly persons, and having excited their passions, sent them in a body with swords and clubs into the Churches to attack the people.

6. What followed upon this it is by no means easy to describe: indeed it is not possible to set before you a just representation of the circumstances, nor even could one recount a small part of them without tears and lamentations. Have such deeds as these ever been made the subjects of tragedy

[1] O. T. viii. p. 190, note c. §. 3.

---

[d] The Prefect of Egypt was called Augustalis as having been first appointed by Augustus, after his victories over Antony. He was of the Equestrian, not, as other Prefects, of the Senatorian order. He was the imperial officer, as answering to Propraetors in the Imperial Provinces. vid. Hofman, in voc.

among the ancients? or has the like ever happened before in time of persecution or of war? The Church and the holy Baptistery were set on fire, and straightway groans, shrieks, and lamentations, were heard through the city; while the citizens in their indignation at these enormities, cried shame upon the governor, and protested against the violence used to them. For the holy and undefiled virgins[e] were stripped naked, and suffered treatment which is not to be named, and if they resisted, they were in danger of their lives. Monks were trampled under foot and perished; some were hurled headlong; others were destroyed with swords and clubs, others were wounded and beaten. And oh! what deeds of impiety and iniquity were committed upon the Holy Table! They offered birds and pine cones[f] in sacrifice, singing the praises of their idols, and blaspheming even in the very Churches our Lord and Saviour Jesus Christ, the Son of the living God. They burned the books of Holy Scripture which they found in the Church; and the Jews, the murderers of our Lord, and the godless heathen entering irreverently (O strange boldness!) the holy Baptistery, stripped themselves naked, and acted such a disgraceful part, both by word and deed, as one is ashamed even to relate. Certain impious men also, following the examples set them in the bitterest persecutions, seized upon the virgins, and widows, and having tied their hands together, dragged them along, and endeavoured to make them blaspheme and deny the Lord, and when they refused to do so, they beat them violently and trampled them under foot.

§. 4. 7. In addition to all this, after such a notable and illustrious entry into the city, the Arian Gregory, taking pleasure in these calamities, and as if desirous to secure to the heathens and Jews, and those who had wrought these evils upon us, a prize and price of their iniquitous success, gave up the Church to be plundered by them. Upon this licence of iniquity and disorder, their deeds were worse than in time of war, and more cruel than those of robbers. Some of them

---

[e] The sister of S. Antony was one of the earliest known inmates of a nunnery, vit. Ant. § 2 3. They were called by the Catholic Church by the title, "Spouse of Christ." Apol. ad Const. §. 33.

[f] The θύος or suffitus of Grecian sacrifices generally consisted of portions of odoriferous trees. vid. Potter. Antiqu. ii. 4. Some translate the word here used, (στροβίλους,) "shell-fish."

plundered whatever fell in their way; others divided among themselves the sums which individuals had laid up there[g]; the wine, of which there was a large quantity, they either drank or emptied out or carried away; they plundered the store of oil, and every one took as his spoil the doors and chancel rails; the candlesticks they forthwith laid aside in the wall [1], and lighted the candles of the Church before their idols: in a word, rapine and death pervaded the Church.

TR.I.4.

[1] ἐν τῷ τοι-
(ᵖ) χίῳ
τοιχάρ-
χοι for
deacons.
Apost.
Const.ii.
57. Cle-
ment.
p. 615.
from
idea of
navis or
nave.
2 δύσσι-
βεῖς·
3 ἀπομα-
φοριζόμι-
ναι.

8. And the impious[2] Arians, so far from feeling shame that such things should be done, added yet further outrages and cruelty. Presbyters and laymen had their flesh torn, virgins were stripped of their veils[3], and led away to the tribunal of the governor, and then cast into prison, others had their goods confiscated, and were scourged; the bread of the ministers and virgins was intercepted. And these things were done even during the holy season of Lent[h], about the time of Easter; a time when the brethren were keeping fast, while this notable person Gregory exhibited the disposition of a Caiaphas, and, together with that Pilate the Governor, furiously raged against the pious worshippers of Christ. Going into one of the Churches on the Preparation[i], in company with the Governor and the heathen multitude, when he saw that the people regarded with abhorrence his forcible entry among them, he caused that most cruel person, the Governor, publicly to scourge in one hour, four and thirty virgins and married women, and men of rank, and to cast them into prison. Among whom there was one virgin, who, being fond of reading, had the Psalter in her hands, at the time when he caused her to be publicly scourged: the book was seized by the officers, and the virgin herself shut up in prison.

9. When all this was done, they did not stop even here; but consulted how they might act the same part in the other

§. 5.

---

[g] Churches, as heathen temples before them, were used for deposits. At the sack of Rome, Alaric spared the Churches and their possessions; nay, he himself transported the costly vessels of St. Peter into his Church.

[h] Lent and Passion Week was the season during which Justina's persecution of St. Ambrose took place, and the proceedings against St. Chrysostom at Constantinople. On the Paschal Vigils, vid. Tertull. ad Uxor. ii. 4. p. 426, note n Oxf. Tr.

[i] παρασκευή, i. e. Good Friday. The word was used for Friday generally as early as S Clem Alex. Strom. vii. p 877. ed. Pott. vid. Constit. Apostol. v 13. Pseudo-Ign. ad Philipp. 13

8 *In consequence Athanasius withdraws from the city.*

ENCYC. LETT.
[1] μανίαν

Church, where I principally abode during those days; and they were eager to extend their fury[1] to this Church also, in order that they might hunt out and dispatch me. And this would have been my fate, had not the grace of Christ assisted me, if it were only that I might escape to relate these few particulars concerning their conduct. For seeing that they were exceedingly mad against me, and being anxious that the Church should not be injured, nor the virgins that were in it suffer, nor additional murders be committed, nor the people again outraged, I withdrew myself from among them, remembering the words of our Saviour, *If they persecute you in this city, flee ye into another.* I judged from the mischief they had done to one Church, that there was no outrage they would forbear to perpetrate against the other, especially since they had not reverenced even the Lord's day[2] on this holy Festival, but on that day when our Lord delivered all men from the bonds of death, they had shut up in prison the people of His Church; and Gregory and his associates, as if fighting against our Saviour, and depending upon the support of the Governor, had turned into mourning this day of liberty to the servants of Christ. The heathens were rejoiced to do this, for they abhor that day; and Gregory perhaps did but fulfil the commands of the Eusebians, when he forced the Christians to mourn under the infliction of bonds.

Mat. 10, 23.

[2] Easter Day.

10. With these acts of violence has the Governor seized upon the Churches, and has given them up to Gregory and the Arian fanatics. Thus, those persons who were excommunicated by us for their impiety, now glory in the plunder of our Churches; while the people of God, and the Clergy of the Catholic Church are compelled either to have communion with the impiety of the Arian heretics, or else to forbear entering into them. Moreover, by means of the Governor, Gregory has exercised no small violence towards the captains of ships and others who pass over sea, torturing and scourging some, putting others in bonds, and casting them into prison, in order to oblige them not to resist his iniquities, and to convey letters[3] from him. And not satisfied with all this, that he may glut himself with my blood, he has caused his savage associate the Governor, to prefer an indictment

[3] i.e. letters of communion

against me, as in the name of the people, before the most religious Emperor Constantius, which contains such odious charges, that if they were true, I ought not only to be banished, but should deserve to suffer a thousand deaths. The person who drew it up is an apostate from Christianity, and a shameless worshipper of idols, and they who subscribed it are heathens, and keepers of idol temples, and others of them Arians. In short, not to make my letter tedious to you, a persecution rages here, and such a persecution as was never before raised against the Church. For in former instances a man at least might pray while he fled from his persecutors, and be baptized while he lay in concealment. But now their extreme cruelty has imitated the godless conduct of the Babylonians For as they falsely accused Daniel, so does the notable Gregory now accuse before the Governor those who pray in their houses, and watches every opportunity to insult their ministers, so that through his violent conduct, the souls of many are endangered from missing baptism, and many who are in sickness and sorrow have no one to visit them, a calamity which they bitterly lament, accounting it worse than their sickness. For while the ministers of the Church are under persecution, the people who condemn the impiety of the Arian heretics choose rather thus to be sick and to run the risk, than that a hand of the Arians should come upon their heads.

11. Gregory then is an Arian, and has been sent to the Arian party, for none demanded him, but they only; and accordingly as a hireling and a stranger, he makes use of the Governor to inflict these dreadful and cruel deeds upon the people of the Catholic Churches, as not being his own. For since Pistus, whom the Eusebians formerly appointed over the Arians, was justly anathematized and excommunicated for his impiety by you the Bishops of the Catholic Church, as you all know, on our writing to you concerning him, they have now, therefore, in like manner sent this Gregory to them; and lest they should a second time be put to shame, by our again writing against them, they have employed foreign force against me, in order that, having obtained possession of the Churches, they may seem to have escaped all suspicion of being Arians. But in this too they have

been mistaken, for none of the people of the Church are with them, except the heretics only, and those who have been excommunicated for their crimes, and such as have been compelled by the Governor to dissemble.

12. This then is the plot of the Eusebians, which they have long been devising and bringing to bear; and now have succeeded in accomplishing through the false charges which they have made against me before the Emperor. Notwithstanding, they are not yet content to be quiet, but even now seek to kill me, and they make themselves so formidable to my friends, that they are all driven into banishment, and expect death at their hands. But you must not for this stand in awe of their iniquity, but on the contrary avenge: and shew your indignation at this their unprecedented conduct against me For if when one member suffers all the members suffer with it, and, according to the blessed Apostle, we ought to weep with them that weep, let every one, now that so great a Church as this is suffering, avenge its wrongs, as though he were himself the sufferer. For we have a common Saviour, who is blasphemed by them, and Canons belonging to us all, which they are transgressing. If while any of you had been sitting in your Church, and while the people were assembled with you, without any blame, some one had suddenly come under plea of an edict to be your successor, and had acted the same part towards you, would you not have been indignant? would you not have demanded to be righted? If so, then it is right that you should be indignant now, lest if these things be passed over unnoticed, the same mischief shall by degrees extend itself to every Church, and so our schools of religion be turned into a market-house and an exchange.

§. 7. 13. You are acquainted with the history of the Arian fanatics, beloved, for you have often, both individually and in a body, condemned their impiety; and you know also that the Eusebians, as I said before, are engaged in the same heresy; for the sake of which they have long been carrying on a conspiracy against me. And I have represented to you, what has now been done, both for them and by them, with greater cruelty than is usual even in time of war, in order that after the example set before you in the history which I related at the beginning, you may entertain a zealous hatred of their wickedness, and reject those who have committed such enormities against the Church. If the brethren at Rome last year, before these things had happened, and on account of their former misdeeds, wrote letters to call a Council, that these evils might be set right, (fearing which, the Eusebians took care previously to throw the Church into confusion, and desired to destroy me, in order that they might thenceforth be able to act as they pleased without fear, and might have no one to call them to account,) how much more ought you now to be indignant at these outrages, and to condemn them, seeing they have added this to their former misconduct.

14. I beseech you, overlook not such proceedings, nor suffer the famous Church of the Alexandrians to be trodden down by heretics. In consequence of these things the people and their ministers are separated from one another, as one might expect, silenced by the violence of the Prefect, yet abhorring the impiety of the Arian fanatics. If therefore Gregory shall write unto you, or any other in his behalf, receive not his letters, brethren, but tear them in pieces and put the bearers of them to shame, as the ministers of impiety and wickedness. And even if he presume to write to you after a friendly fashion, nevertheless receive them not. Those who bring his letters convey them only from fear of the Governor, and on account of his frequent acts of violence. And since it is probable that the Eusebians will write to you concerning him, I was anxious to admonish you beforehand, so that you may herein imitate God, who is no respecter of persons, and may drive out from before you those that come from them; because for the sake of the Arian fanatics they caused persecutions, rape of virgins, murders, plunder of the Church's property, burnings and blasphemies in the Churches, to be committed by the heathens and Jews at such a season. The impious and mad Gregory cannot deny that he is an Arian, being proved to be so by the person who writes his letters. This is his secretary Ammon, who was cast out of the Church long ago by my predecessor the blessed Alexander for his many crimes and for his impiety.

15. For all these reasons, therefore, vouchsafe to send me a

reply, and condemn these impious men; so that even now the ministers and people of this place, seeing your orthodoxy and hatred of wickedness, may rejoice in your concord in the Christian faith, and that those who have been guilty of these lawless deeds against the Church may be reformed by your letters, and brought at last, though late, to repentance. Salute the brotherhood that is among you. All the brethren that are with me salute you. Fare ye well, and remember me, and the Lord preserve you continually, most truly beloved Lords.

II.

AN APOLOGY

OF OUR

HOLY FATHER ATHANASIUS,

ARCHBISHOP OF ALEXANDRIA,

AGAINST THE ARIANS.

[The following Apology, or Defence of his conduct, was written by S. Athanasius between A.D. 349—352, after his return from his second exile upon the Council of Sardica. It is scarcely more than a collection of exculpatory documents, which might serve as a record of his innocence. These documents extend from A.D. 300, to A.D. 350, of which those between 340 and 350, are placed first. "This Apology," says Montfaucon, "is the most authentic source of the history of the Church in the first half of the fourth century. Athanasius is far superior to any other historians of the period, both from his bearing for the most part a personal testimony to the facts he relates, and from his great accuracy and use of actual documents. On the other hand, Ruffinus, Socrates, Sozomen, Theodoret, must not be used without extreme caution, unless they adduce documents, which is seldom the case." He proceeds to give instances; for this reason it will not be worth while in this work, nor was it in the foregoing, to compare Athanasius's statements with those of other historians, or to use the latter except in connecting the line of the narrative. The charges which he notices are as follow: —that he had been clandestinely consecrated, that he had imposed a duty on Egyptian linen, that he had assisted Philumenus with money, when in rebellion against the Emperor; that he had sanctioned the overthrow of a Communion Table and breaking of one of the Communion Vessels; that he had killed a Meletian Bishop named Arsenius; that he had been the cause of many executions or murders after his return from Gaul; that he had sold for his own benefit the corn bestowed by Constantine on the widows of the Church, and that he had stopped the supplies of corn intended for Constantinople.]

INTRODUCTION.

1. I supposed that, after so many proofs of my innocence had been given, my enemies would have shrunk from further

enquiry, and would now have condemned themselves for their false accusations of others. But as they are not yet abashed, though they have been so clearly convicted, but, as insensible to shame, persist in their slanderous reports against me, professing to think that the whole matter ought to be tried over again, (not that they may have judgment passed on them, for that they avoid, but in order to harass me, and to disturb the minds of the simple,) I therefore thought it necessary to make my defence unto you, that you may listen to their murmurings no longer, but may denounce their wickedness and base calumnies. And it is only to you, who are men of sincere minds, that I offer a defence: as for the contentious, I appeal confidently to the decisive proofs which I have against them. For my cause needs not a second judgment; which has already been given, and not once or twice only, but many times. First of all, it was tried in my own country in an assembly of nearly one hundred of its Bishops[a]; a second time at Rome, when, in consequence of Letters from Eusebius, both they and we were summoned, and more than fifty Bishops met[b]; and a third time in the great Council assembled at Sardica[c] by order of the most religious Emperors Constantius and Constans, when my enemies were degraded as false accusers, and the sentence that was passed in my favour received the suffrages of more than three hundred Bishops, out of the provinces of Egypt, Libya, and Pentapolis, Palestine, Arabia, Isauria, Cyprus, Pamphylia, Lycia, Galatia, Dacia, Mysia, Thrace, Dardania, Macedonia, Epirus, Thessaly, Achaia, Crete, Dalmatia, Siscia, Pannonia, Noricum, Italy, Picenum, Tuscany, Campania, Calabria, Apulia, Bruttia, Sicily, the whole of Africa, Sardinia, Spain, Gaul, and Britain.

2. Added to these was the testimony[d] of Ursacius and Valens, who had formerly calumniated me, but afterwards changed their minds, and not only gave their assent to the sentence

---

[a] The Council of Sardica says eighty, which is a usual number in Egyptian Councils. (vid Tillemont, vol 8 p 74.) There were about ninety Bishops in Egypt, the Thebais, and Libya The present Council was held in 339, or 340. Its Synodal Epistle is contained below, §. 3. and is particularly addressed to Pope Julius, § 20.

[b] This was held in 341. Julius's Letter is found below, § 21.

[c] In A D. 347, though Marsi, contrary to other writers, maintains its date to be 344. vid. §. 44. infr.

[d] vid. infr. § 58. This was A.D. 349.

that was passed in my favour, but also confessed that they themselves and the rest of my enemies were false accusers; for men who make such a change and such a recantation of course reflect upon the Eusebians, for with them they had contrived the plot against me. Now after a matter has been examined and decided on such clear evidence by so many eminent Bishops, every one will confess that further discussion is unnecessary; else, if an investigation be instituted at this time, it may be again discussed and again investigated, and there will be no end of this trifling.

3. Now the decision of so many Bishops was sufficient to confound those who would still fain pretend some charge against me. But when my enemies also bear testimony in my favour and against themselves, declaring that the proceedings against me were a conspiracy, who is there that would not be ashamed to doubt any longer? The law requires that in the mouth of two or three witnesses judgments shall be settled, and we have here this great multitude of witnesses in my favour, with the addition of the proofs afforded by my enemies, so much so that those who still continue opposed to me no longer attach any importance to their own arbitrary[e] judgment, but now have recourse to violence, and in the place of fair reasoning seek to injure[f] those by whom they were exposed. For this is the chief cause of vexation to them, that the measures they carried on in secret, contrived by themselves in a corner, have been brought to light and disclosed by Valens and Ursacius; for they are well aware that their recantation not only clears those whom they have injured, but condemns them.

4. Indeed this led to their degradation in the Council of Sardica, as mentioned before, and with good reason; for, as the Pharisees of old, when they undertook the defence of Paul, gave clear judgment against the conspiracy which they and the Jews had formed against him; and as the blessed David was proved to be persecuted unjustly when the

T<small>R</small>. II. 1, 2.

§. 2.

[e] ὡς ἠθέλησαν vid. infr. §. 14. de Decr. §. 3 de Syn §. 13. ad Ep. Ag §. 5.
[f] This implies that Valens and Ursacius were subjected to some kind of persecution, which is natural. They relapsed in 351, when Constantius on the death of Constans came into possession of his brother's dominions; and professed to have been forced to their former recantation by the latter Emperor.

persecutor confessed, *I have sinned, my son David;* so it was with these men; being overcome by the truth they became suppliants, and addressed a letter to that effect to Julius Bishop of Rome. They wrote also to me desiring to be on terms of peace with me, though they have spread such reports concerning me; and probably even now they are covered with shame, on seeing that those whom they sought to destroy by the grace of the Lord are still alive. Consistently also with this conduct they anathematized Arius and his heresy; for knowing that the Eusebians had conspired against me in behalf of their own misbelief, and of nothing else, as soon as they had determined to confess their calumnies against me, they immediately renounced also that antichristian heresy for the sake of which they had falsely asserted them.

CHAP. I.

ENCYCLICAL LETTER OF THE COUNCIL OF EGYPT.

1. THE following are the letters written in my favour by the Bishops in the several Councils; and first the letter of the Egyptian Bishops.

The holy Council assembled at Alexandria, out of Egypt, the Thebais, Libya, and Pentapolis, to the Bishops of the Catholic Church every where, brethren beloved and greatly longed for, sendeth health in the Lord.

Dearly beloved brethren, we might have put forth a defence of our brother Athanasius[1], as respects the conspiracy of the Eusebians against him, and complained of his sufferings at their hands, and have exposed all their false charges, either at the beginning of their conspiracy or upon his arrival at Alexandria. But circumstances did not permit it then, as you also know; and lately, after the return of the Bishop Athanasius, we thought that they would be confounded and covered with shame at their manifest injustice: in consequence we prevailed with ourselves to remain silent. Since, however, after all his severe sufferings, after his retirement into Gaul, after his sojourn in a foreign and far distant country in the place of his own, after his narrow escape from death through their calumnies, but for the clemency of the Emperor,—distress which would have satisfied even the most cruel enemy,—still they are insensible to shame, and are again raging against the Church and Athanasius; and from indignation at his deliverance venture on still more atrocious schemes against him, and are ready with any accusation, fearless of the words in holy Scripture, *A false witness shall not be unpunished;* and, *The mouth that*

§. 3.
[1] συλλειτουργόν.

Prov. 19, 5.
Wisd. 1, 11.

belieth slayeth the soul; we therefore are unable longer to hold our peace, being amazed at their wickedness and at the insatiable love of contention displayed in their treacherous proceedings.

2. For see, they cease not to disturb the ear of royalty with fresh reports against us; they cease not to write letters of deadly import, for the destruction of the Bishop who is the enemy of their impiety. For again have they written to the Emperors against him; again are they conspiring against him, charging him with a butchery which has never taken place; again they wish to shed his blood, accusing him of a murder that never was committed, (for at that former time would they have murdered him by their calumnies, had we not found favour with the Emperor;) again they are urgent, to say the least, that he should be sent into banishment, while they pretend to lament the miseries of the exiles, as though they had been exiled by him. They lament before us things that have never been done, and, not satisfied with what has been done to him, desire to add thereto other and more cruel treatment.

3. So mild are they and merciful, and of so just a disposition; or rather (for the truth shall be spoken) so wicked are they and malicious; obtaining respect through fear and by threats, rather than by their piety and justice, as becomes Bishops. They have dared in their letters to the Emperors to pour forth language such as no contentious person would employ even among those that are without; they have charged him with a number of murders and butcheries, and that not before a Governor, or any other superior officer, but before the three Augusti; nor shrink they from any journey however long, provided only all the greater courts may be filled with their accusations. For indeed, dearly beloved, their business consists in accusations, and that of the most solemn character, forasmuch as the tribunals to which they make their appeal are the most solemn of any upon earth. And what other end do they propose by these investigations, except to move the Emperor to capital punishment?

§. 4   4. Their own conduct therefore, and not that of Athanasius, is the fittest subject for lamentation and mourning, and one would more properly lament them, for such actions ought to be bewailed, since it is written, *Weep ye not for the dead, neither bemoan him but weep sore for him that goeth away, for he shall return no more.* For their whole letter speaks of nothing but his death; and their endeavour is to kill, whenever they may be permitted, or if not, to drive into exile. And this they were permitted to do by the most religious father of the Emperors, who gratified their fury by the banishment of Athanasius, though not by his death. Now that this is not the conduct even of ordinary Christians, (nay, even of heathens,) much less of Bishops, who profess to teach others righteousness, we suppose that your Christian consciences must at once perceive. How can they forbid others to accuse their brethren, who themselves become their accusers, and that to the Emperors? How can they teach compassion for the misfortunes of others, who cannot rest satisfied even with our banishment? For there was confessedly a general sentence of banishment against us Bishops, and we all looked upon ourselves as banished men: and now again we consider ourselves as restored with Athanasius to our native country, and in the place of our former lamentations and mourning over him, as having the greatest encouragement and grace,—which may the Lord continue to us, nor suffer the Eusebians to destroy!

Tr. II.
4, 5.
Jer. 22, 10.

5. Even if their charges against him were true, here is a certain charge against them, that against the precept of Christianity, and after his banishment and trials, they have assaulted him again, and accuse him of murder, and butchery, and other crimes, which they sound in the royal ears against the Bishops. But how exceeding manifold is their wickedness, and what manner of men think you them, when every word they speak is false, every charge they bring a calumny, and there is no truth whatever either in their speeches or their writings! However, let us now enter upon these matters, and meet their last charges. This will prove, that in their former representations in the Council and at the trial their conduct was dishonourable, or rather their words untrue, besides exposing them for what they have now advanced.

6. We are indeed ashamed to make any defence against such charges. But since our reckless accusers lay hold of any charge, and allege that murders and butcheries were

§. 5.

committed after the return of Athanasius, we beseech you to bear with our answer though it be somewhat long; for circumstances constrain us. No murder was committed either by Athanasius or on his account, since our accusers, as we said before, compel us to enter upon this strange apology. Slaughter and imprisonment are foreign to our Church. No one did Athanasius commit into the hands of the executioner; and the prison, so far as he was concerned, was never disturbed. Our sanctuaries are now, as they have always been, pure, and honoured only with the Blood of Christ and His pious worship. Neither Presbyter nor Deacon was destroyed by Athanasius; he perpetrated no murder, he caused the banishment of no one. Would that they had never caused the like to him, nor given him actual experience of it! No one here was banished on his account; no one at all except Athanasius himself the Bishop of Alexandria, whom they banished, and whom, now that he is restored, they again seek to entangle in the same or even a more cruel plot than before, setting their tongues to speak all manner of false and deadly words against him.

7. For, behold, they now attribute to him the acts of the magistrates; and although they plainly confess in their letter that the Prefect of Egypt passed sentence upon certain persons, they now are not ashamed to impute this sentence to Athanasius; and that, though he had not at the time entered Alexandria, but was yet on his return from his place of exile. Indeed he was then in Syria; since we must needs adduce in his defence his length of way from home, that a man may not be responsible for the actions of a Governor or Prefect of Egypt But supposing Athanasius had been in Alexandria, what were the proceedings of the Prefect to Athanasius? However, he was not even in the country; and what the Prefect of Egypt did was not done on ecclesiastical grounds, but for reasons which you will learn from the records, which, after we understood what they had written, we made diligent enquiry for, and have transmitted to you. Since then they now raise a cry against certain things which were never done either by him or for him, as though they had certainly taken place, and testify against such evils as though they were assured of their existence; let them inform us from what

Council they obtained their knowledge of them, from what proofs, and in the course of what investigation? But if they have no such evidence to bring forward, and nothing but their own mere assertion, we leave it to you to consider as regards their former charges also, how the things took place, and why they so speak of them. In truth, it is nothing but calumny, and a plot of our enemies, and anger full of atrocious projects, and an impiety in behalf of the Arian fanatics[1], which is frantic against true godliness, and desires to root out the orthodox, so that henceforth the advocates of impiety may preach without fear whatever doctrines they please. The history of the matter is as follows:—

8. When Arius, from whom the heresy of the Arian fanatics has its name, was cast out of the Church for his impiety by Bishop Alexander, of blessed memory, the Eusebians, who are the disciples and partners of his impiety, considering themselves also to have been ejected, wrote frequently to the Bishop Alexander, beseeching him not to keep the heretic Arius out of the Church. But when Alexander in his piety towards Christ refused to admit that impious man, they directed their resentment against Athanasius, who was then a Deacon, because in their busy enquiries they had heard that he was much in the familiarity of Alexander the Bishop, and much honoured by him. And their hatred of him was greatly increased after they had experience of his piety[2] towards Christ, in the Council assembled at Nicæa, wherein he spoke boldly against the impiety of the Arian fanatics. But when God raised him to the Episcopate, their long-cherished malice burst forth into a flame, and fearing his orthodoxy and resistance of their impiety, they (and especially Eusebius, who was smitten with a consciousness of his own evil doings,) engaged in all manner of treacherous designs against him. They prejudiced the Emperor against him; they frequently threatened him with Councils; and at last assembled at Tyre; and to this day they cease not to write against him, and are so implacable that they even find fault with his appointment to the Episcopate[a], taking every means

Tr. II. 5, 6.

[1] or Ariomaniacs, *passim.*

[2] i.e. orthodoxy, *passim.*

---

[a] The Eusebians alleged that, fifty-four Bishops of the two parties of S. Alexander and Meletius being assembled for the election, and having sworn to elect by the common voice, six or seven of these broke their oaths in

of shewing their enmity and hatred towards him, and spreading false reports for the sole purpose of thereby destroying his character.

9. However, the very misrepresentations which they now are making, do but convict their former statements of being falsehoods, and a mere conspiracy against him. For they say, that " after the death of the Bishop Alexander, a certain few having mentioned the name of Athanasius, six or seven Bishops elected him clandestinely in a secret place:" and this is what they wrote to the Emperors, having no scruple about asserting the greatest falsehoods. Now that the whole multitude and all the people of the Catholic Church assembled together as with one mind and body, and cried, shouted, that Athanasius should be Bishop of their Church, made this the subject of their public prayers to Christ, and conjured us to grant it for many days and nights, neither departing themselves from the Church, nor suffering us to do so; of all this we are witnesses, and so is the whole city, and the province too. Not a word did they speak against him, as these persons represented, but gave him the most excellent titles they could devise, calling him the good, the pious, Christian, an ascetic[b], a genuine Bishop. And that he was elected by a majority of our body in the sight and with the acclamations of all the people, we who elected him also testify, who are surely more credible witnesses than those who were not present, and now spread these false accounts.

10. But yet Eusebius[1] finds fault with the appointment of Athanasius,—he who perhaps never received any appointment

[1] Of Nicomedia.

favour of S Athanasius, whom no one had thought of, and consecrated him in secret to the great surprise and scandal of both ecclesiastical and lay persons. vid Socr 11. 17 Philostorgius (A.D. 425) adds particulars, explanatory or corrective of this statement, of which the Bishops in the text do not seem to have heard, viz. that Athanasius with his party one night seized on the Church of St Dionysius, and compelled two Bishops whom he found there to consecrate him against their will, that he was in consequence anathematized by all the other Bishops, but that, fortifying himself in his position, he sent in his election to the Emperor, and by this means obtained its confirmation. Hist. 11. 16. It appears, in matter of fact, that S. Athan was absent at the time of his election; as Socrates says, in order to avoid it, or as Epiphanius, on business at the Court, these reasons are compatible.

[b] It is contested whether S. Athan. was ever one of S. Antony's monks, the reading of a passage in the commencement of his Vit. Ant., which would decide the question, varying in different MSS. The word " ascetic" is used of those who lived a life, as afterwards followed in Monasteries, in the Ante-Nicene times.

to his office at all; or if he did, has himself rendered it invalid[c]. For he had first the See of Berytus, but leaving that he came to Nicomedia. He left the one contrary to the law, and contrary to the law invaded the other; he deserted his own See for he failed in affection, and took possession of another's though he failed in a plea; he lost his love for the first in his lust for another, nor retained that love for the second which his lust had occasioned. For, behold, withdrawing himself from the second, again he takes possession of another's, casting an evil eye all around him upon the cities of other men, and thinking that godliness[1] consists in wealth and in the greatness of cities, and making light of the heritage of God to which he had been appointed; not knowing that *where even two or three are gathered in the name of the Lord, there is the Lord in the midst of them;* not considering the words of the Apostle, *I will not boast in another man's labours;* not perceiving the charge which he has given, *Art thou bound unto a wife? seek not to be loosed.* For if this expression applies to a wife, how much more does it apply to a Church, and to the same Episcopate; to which whosoever is bound ought not to seek another, lest he prove an adulterer according to holy Scripture.

TR. II. 6, 7.

[1] *εὐσέ-βειαν*, ortho-doxy, (vid. 1 Tim. 6, 5.) Mat. 18, 20. 2 Cor. 10, 15. 1 Cor. 7, 27.

11. But though conscious of these his own misdoings, he has boldly undertaken to arraign the appointment of Athanasius, to which honourable testimony has been borne by all; and he ventures to reproach him with his deposition, though he has been deposed himself, and has a standing proof of his deposition in the appointment of another. How could either he or Theognius[d] degrade another, after they had been degraded themselves, which is sufficiently proved by the appointment of others in their room? For you know very well that

§. 7.

---

[c] The Canons of Nicæa and Sardica were absolute against translation, but, as Bingham observes, Antiqu. vi. 4. §. 6. only as a general rule. The so-called Apostolical Canons except "a reasonable cause" and the sanction of a Council, one of the Councils of Carthage prohibit them when subserving ambitious views, and except for the advantage of the Church. Vid. list of translations in Socr. Hist. vii. 36. Cassiodor. Hist. xii. 8. Niceph. Hist. xiv. 39. Cotelier adds others ad Can. Apost. 14.

[d] Or Theogris; he was, as well as Eusebius, a pupil of Lucian's, and was deposed together with him after the Nicene Council for communicating with Arians. Constantine banished them to Gaul, they were recalled in the course of two or three years. He was dead by the date of the Council of Sardica.

APOL. AG. AR. there were appointed instead of them Amphion to Nicomedia and Chrestus to Nicæa, in consequence of their own impiety and connection with the Arian fanatics, who were rejected by the Ecumenic Council. But while they desire to set aside that true Council, they endeavour to give that name to their own unlawful combination[1]; while they are unwilling that the decrees of the Council should be enforced, they desire to enforce their own decisions; and they use the name of a Council, while they refuse to submit themselves to one so great as this. Thus they care not for Councils, but only pretend to do so in order that they may root out the orthodox, and annul the decrees of the true and great Council against the Arians, in support of whom, both now and heretofore, they have ventured to assert these falsehoods against the Bishop Athanasius. For their former statements resembled those they have now made, viz. that disorderly meetings were held at his entrance[2], with lamentation and mourning, the people indignantly refusing to receive him. Now such was not the case, but, on the other hand, joy and cheerfulness prevailed, and the people ran together, hastening to obtain the desired sight of him. The Churches were full of rejoicings, and thanksgivings were offered up to the Lord every where; and all the Ministers and Clergy beheld him with such feelings, that their souls were possessed with delight, and they esteemed that the happiest day of their lives. Why need we mention the inexpressible joy that prevailed among us Bishops, for we have already said that we counted ourselves to have been partakers in his sufferings?

§. 8. 12. Now this being confessedly the truth of the matter, although it is very differently represented by them, what weight can be attached to that Council or trial of which they make their boast? Since they presume thus to controvert the circumstances of a case which they did not witness, which they have not examined, and for which they did not meet, and to write as though they were assured of the truth of their statements, how can they claim credit respecting those matters for the consideration of which they say that they did meet together? Will it not rather be believed that they have acted both in the one case and in the other

[1] Eusebian Council of Tyre, A.D. 335.

[2] On his return from Gaul, A.D. 338.

out of enmity to us? For what kind of a Council of Bishops was then held? Was it an assembly which aimed at the truth? Was not almost every one among them our enemy? Did not the attack of the Eusebians upon us proceed from their zeal for the Arian fanaticism? Did they not urge on the others of their party? Have we not always written against them as professing the doctrines of Arius? Was not Eusebius of Cæsarea in Palestine accused by our confessors of sacrificing to idols[e]? Was not George proved to have been degraded by the blessed Alexander[f]? Were not they charged with various offences, some with this, some with that?

13. How then could such men entertain the purpose of holding a meeting against us? How can they have the boldness to call that a Council, at which a single Count presided, which an executioner attended, and where a chief jailor instead of the Deacons of the Church introduced us into Court, and where the Count only spoke, and all present held their peace, or rather obeyed his directions? The removal of those Bishops who seemed to deserve it, was prevented at his desire; and when he gave the order we were dragged about by soldiers;—or rather the Eusebians gave the order, and he was subservient to their will. In short, dearly beloved, what kind of Council was that, the object of which was banishment and murder at the pleasure of the Emperor? And of what nature were their charges?—for here is matter of still greater astonishment. There was one Arsenius whom they declared to have been murdered; and they also complained that a chalice belonging to the sacred mysteries had been broken.

14. Now Arsenius is alive, and prays to be admitted to our communion. He waits for no other testimony to prove that he is still living, but himself confesses it, writing in his own person to our brother Athanasius, whom they

---

[e] At the Council of Tyre, Potamo an Egyptian Bishop and Confessor asked Eusebius what had happened to *him* in prison during the persecution, Epiph. Hær. 68, 7. as if hinting at his cowardice. It appears that Eusebius was prisoner at Cæsarea with S. Pamphilus; yet he never mentions the fact himself, which is unlike him, if it was producible.

[f] George, Bishop of Laodicea, had been degraded when a Priest by S. Alexander, for his profligate habits as well as his Arianism. Athan. speaks of him elsewhere as reprobated even by his party. de Fug. 26.

positively asserted to be his murderer. The impious wretches were not ashamed to accuse him of having murdered a man who was at a great distance from him, being separated by an immense tract both of land and water, and whose abode at that time no one knew. Nay, they even had the boldness to remove him out of sight, and place him in concealment, though he had suffered no injury; and, if it had been possible, they would have transported him to another world, nay, or have taken him from life in earnest, so that either by a true or false statement of his murder they might in as good earnest destroy Athanasius. But thanks to divine Providence for this also, which permitted them not to succeed in their injustice, but presented Arsenius alive to the eyes of all men, who has clearly proved their conspiracy and calumnies. He does not withdraw from us as murderers, nor hate us as having injured him, (for indeed he has suffered no evil at all;) but he desires to hold communion with us; he wishes to be admitted among us, and has written to this effect.

§. 9. 15. Nevertheless they laid their plot against Athanasius, accusing him of having murdered a person who was still alive; and those same men are the authors of his banishment[1]. For it was not the father of the Emperors, but their calumnies, that sent him into exile. Consider whether this is not the truth. When nothing was discovered to the prejudice of our brother Athanasius, but still the Count threatened him with violence, and was very zealous against him, the Bishop[g], in order to avoid this violence, went up[2] to the most religious Emperor, where he protested against the Count and their conspiracy against him, and requested either that a lawful Council of Bishops might be assembled,

[1] by Constantine into Gaul, A.D. 335.

[2] i. e to Constantinople.

---

[g] The circumstances of this appeal, which are related by Athan below, §. 86. are thus summed up by Gibbon; "Before the final sentence could be pronounced at Tyre, the intrepid primate threw himself into a bark which was ready to hoist sail for the imperial city. The request of a formal audience might have been opposed or eluded, but Athanasius concealed his arrival, watched the moment of Constantine's return from an adjacent villa, and boldly encountered his angry sovereign as he passed on horseback through the principal street of Constantinople. So strange an apparition excited his surprise and indignation; and the guards were ordered to remove the importunate suitor, but his resentment was subdued by involuntary respect; and the haughty spirit of the Emperor was awed by the courage and eloquence of a Bishop, who implored his justice and awakened his conscience." Hist. xxi. Athan. was a small man in person.

or that the Emperor would himself receive his defence concerning the charges they brought against him. Upon this the Emperor wrote in anger, summoning them before him, and declaring that he would hear the cause himself, and for that purpose he also ordered a Council to be held. Whereupon the Eusebians went up and charged Athanasius, not with the same offences which they had published against him at Tyre, but with an intention of detaining the vessels laden with corn, as though Athanasius had been the man to pretend that he could stop the exports of corn from Alexandria to Constantinople.

16. Certain of our friends were present at the palace with Athanasius, and heard the threats of the Emperor upon receiving this report. And when Athanasius exclaimed against the calumny, and positively declared that it was not true; (for how, he argued, should he a poor man, and in a private station, be able to do such a thing?) Eusebius did not hesitate publicly to repeat the charge, and swore that Athanasius was a rich man, and powerful, and able to do any thing, from which it might be supposed that he had used this language. Such was the accusation these venerable Bishops proffered against him. But the grace of God proved superior to their wickedness, for it moved the pious Emperor to mercy, who instead of death passed upon him the sentence of banishment. Thus their calumnies, and nothing else, were the cause of this. For the Emperor, in the letter which he previously wrote, complained of their conspiracy, censured their machinations, and condemned the Meletians as unrighteous and deserving of execration; in short, expressed himself in the severest terms concerning them. For he was greatly moved when he heard the story of the dead alive; he was moved at hearing of this murder of one who lived after it without loss of life. We have sent you the letter.

17. But these marvellous Eusebians, to make a show of refuting the truth of the case, and the statements contained in this letter, put forward the name of a Council, and ground its proceedings upon the authority of the Emperor. Hence the attendance of a Count at their meeting, and the soldiers as guards of the Bishops, and royal letters com-

pelling the attendance of any persons whom they required. But observe here the strange character of their machinations, and the inconsistency of their bold measures, so that by some means or other they may take Athanasius away from us. For if as Bishops they claimed for themselves alone the judgment of the case, what need was there for the attendance of a Count and soldiers? or how was it that they assembled under the sanction of royal letters? Or if they required the Emperor's countenance and wished to derive their authority from him, why did they then entrench upon his judgment? and when he declared in the letter which he wrote, that the Meletians were profligate calumniators, and that Athanasius was most innocent, and enlarged upon the pretended murder of the living, how was it that they determined that the Meletians had spoken the truth, and that Athanasius was guilty of the offence; and were not ashamed to make the living dead, living both after the Emperor's judgment, and at the time when they met together, and who even until this day is amongst us? So much concerning the case of Arsenius.

§. 11. 18. And as for the chalice belonging to the mysteries, what was it, or where was it broken by Macarius? for this is the report which they spread up and down. But for Athanasius, even his accusers would not have ventured to blame him, had they not been suborned by them. However, they attribute the origin of the offence to him; although it ought not to be imputed even to Macarius who is clear of it. And they are not ashamed to parade the sacred mysteries before Catechumens, and worse than that, even before heathens [h]: whereas, they ought to attend to what is written, *It is good to keep close the secret of a king;* and as the Lord has charged us, *Give not that which is holy unto the dogs, neither cast ye your pearls before swine.* We ought not then to parade the holy mysteries before the uninitiated, lest the heathen in their ignorance deride them, and the Cate-

---

[h] This period, when Christianity was acknowledged by the state but not embraced by the population, is just the time when we hear most of this Reserve as a principle. While Christians were but a sect, persecution enforced a discipline, and when they were commensurate with the nation, faith made it unnecessary. We are now returned to the state of the fourth century.

chumens being over-curious be offended. However, what was the chalice, and where and before whom was it broken? It is the Meletians who make the accusation, who are not worthy of the least credit, for they have been schismatics and enemies of the Church, not of a recent date, but from the times of the blessed Peter, Bishop and Martyr[i]. They formed a conspiracy against Peter himself; they calumniated his successor Achillas; they accused Alexander even before the Emperor, and being thus well versed in these arts, they have now transferred their enmity to Athanasius, acting altogether in accordance with their former wickedness. For as they slandered those that have been before him, so now they have slandered him. But their calumnies and false accusations have never prevailed against him until now, that they have got the Eusebians for their assistants and patrons, on account of the impiety[1] which these have adopted from the Arian fanatics, which has led them to conspire against many Bishops, and among the rest Athanasius.

[Tr II. 11.]

[1 i. e. heresy, passim.]

19. Now the place where they say the chalice was broken, was not a Church; there was no Presbyter in occupation of the place; and the day on which they say that Macarius did the deed, was not the Lord's day. Since then there was no Church there; since there was no one to perform the priest's office; and since the day did not require the use of it[k]; what was this sacred chalice, and when, or where was it broken? There are many cups, it is plain, both in private houses, and in the public market; and if a person breaks one of them, he is not guilty of impiety. But the chalice which belongs to the mysteries, and which if it be broken intentionally, makes the perpetrator of the deed an impious person, is found only among those who are lawfully appointed to preside over the Church. This is the only description that can be given of this kind of chalice; there is none other; of this you drink prior to the people; this you have received according to the canon of the Church[2]; this belongs only to those who preside

[2 vid. Can. Ap. 65.]

---

[i] Meletius, Bishop of Lycopolis in the Thebaid, being deposed for lapsing in the Dioclesian Persecution, separated from the Catholic Church and commenced a succession of his own in Egypt. In the same persecution S. Peter suffered.

[k] This seems to imply that the Holy Communion was only celebrated on Sundays in the Egyptian Churches.

APOL.
AG. AR.
[1] προσί-
νυν

over the Catholic Church, for to you only it appertains to have the first taste[1] of the Blood of Christ, and to none besides. But as he who breaks a sacred cup is an impious person, much more impious is he who treats the Blood of Christ with contumely: and he does so who performs this mystical rite contrary to the rule of the Church;—(we say this, not as if a chalice even of the schismatics was broken by Macarius, for there was no chalice there at all; how should there be? where there was neither Lord's house nor any one belonging to the Church, nay, it was not the time of the celebration of the mysteries;)—now such a person is the notorious Ischyras, who was never appointed to his office by the Church, and when Alexander admitted the Presbyters that had been ordained by Meletius, he was not even numbered amongst them; and therefore did not receive ordination even from that quarter.

§. 12. 20. By what means then did Ischyras become a Presbyter[1]? who was it that ordained him? was it Colluthus? for this is the only supposition that remains. But it is well known, and no one has any doubt about the matter, that Colluthus died a Presbyter, and that every ordination of his was invalid, and that all that were ordained by him during the schism were reduced to the condition of laymen, and in that rank appear in the congregation. How then can it be believed that a private person, occupying a private house, had in his possession a sacred chalice? But the truth is, they gave the name of Presbyter at the time to a private person, and gratified him with this title to support him in his iniquitous conduct towards us; and now as the reward of his accusations they procure for him the erection of a Church. So that this man had then no Church; but as the reward of his malice and subserviency to them in accusing us, he receives now what he had not before; nay, perhaps they have even remunerated his services with the Episcopate, for so he goes about reporting, and accordingly behaves towards us with great insolence. Thus are such rewards as these now bestowed by Bishops upon accusers and calumniators; though indeed it is reasonable, in the case of an accomplice,

[1] Vid. Bp. Taylor, Episcop. Assert § 32. Potter on Church Gov. ch v

that as they have made him a partner in their proceedings, so they should also make him their associate in their own Episcopate. But this is not all; give ear yet further to their proceedings at that time.

21. Being unable to prevail against the truth, though they had thus set themselves in array against it, and Ischyras having proved nothing at Tyre, except that he was a calumniator, and the calumny ruining their plot, they defer proceedings until they obtain fresh evidence, and propose to send to the Mareotis certain of their party to enquire diligently into the matter. Accordingly they dispatched secretly, with the assistance of the civil power, persons to whom we openly objected on many accounts, as being of the party of Arius, and therefore our enemies; namely, Diognius, Maris, Theodorus, Macedonius, and two others, young both in years and mind[m], Ursacius and Valens from Pannonia, who, after they had undertaken this long journey for the purpose of obtaining justice against their enemy, set out again from Tyre for Alexandria. They did not shrink from becoming witnesses themselves, although they were the judges, but openly adopted every means of furthering their design, and undertook any labour or journey whatsoever in order to bring to a successful issue the conspiracy which was in progress. They left the Bishop Athanasius detained in a foreign country while they themselves entered their enemy's city, as if to have their revel both against his Church and against his people. And what was more outrageous still, they took with them the accuser Ischyras, but would not permit Macarius, the accused person, to accompany them, but left him in custody at Tyre. For " Macarius the Presbyter of Alexandria" was made answerable for the charge far and near.

22. They therefore entered Alexandria alone with the accuser, their partner in lodging, board, and wine-cup, and taking with them Philagrius the Prefect of Egypt they proceeded to the Mareotis, and there carried on the investigation by themselves, all their own way, with the forementioned person. Although the Presbyters frequently begged that they might

TR. II. 12—14.

§. 13.

§. 14.

[m] Vid also Athan ad Ep. Æg. 7 Euseb. Vit. c. iv. 43. Hilar ad Const. 5. Fragm. i. 12.

be present, they would not permit them. The Presbyters both of the city and of the whole country desired to attend, that they might detect who and whence the persons were who were suborned by Ischyras. But they forbade the Ministers to be present, while they carried on the examination concerning the Church, the chalice, the table, and the holy things, before the heathen; nay, worse than that, they summoned heathen witnesses during the enquiry concerning the sacred chalice; and those persons who they affirmed were taken out of the way by Athanasius by means of the summons of the Receiver-general, and they knew not where in the world they were, these same individuals they brought forward before themselves and the Prefect only, and avowedly used their testimony, whom they affirmed without shame to have been secreted by the Bishop Athanasius.

23. But here too their only object is to effect his death, and so they again pretend that persons are dead who are still alive, following the same method they adopted in the case of Arsenius. For the men are living, and are to be seen in their own country; but to you who are at a great distance from the spot they give a tragical representation of the matter as though they had disappeared, in order that, as the evidence is so far removed from you, they may falsely accuse our brother-minister, as though he used violence and the civil power; whereas they themselves have in all respects acted by means of that power and the countenance of others. For their proceedings in the Mareotis were parallel to those at Tyre; and as there a Count attended with military assistance, and would permit nothing either to be said or done contrary to their pleasure, so here also the Prefect of Egypt was present with a band of men, frightening all the members of the Church, and permitting no one to give true testimony. And what was the strangest thing of all, the persons who came, whether as judges or witnesses, or, what was more likely, in order to serve their own purposes and those of Eusebius, lived in the same place with the accuser, even in his house, and there seemed to carry on the investigation as they pleased.

§. 15. 24. We suppose you are not ignorant what outrages they committed at Alexandria; for they are reported every where.

Outrages of the Arian party at Alexandria.

They attacked the holy virgins and brethren with naked swords; they beat with scourges their persons, esteemed honourable in the sight of God, so that their feet were lamed by the stripes, whose souls are whole and sound in purity and all good works[1]. The trades[2] were excited against them; and the heathen multitude was set to strip them naked, to beat them, wantonly to insult them, and to threaten them with their altars and sacrifices. And one coarse fellow, as though license had now been given them by the Prefect in order to gratify the Bishops, took hold of a virgin by the hand, and dragged her towards an altar that happened to be near, imitating the practice of compelling to offer sacrifice in time of persecution. When this was done, the virgins took to flight, and a shout of laughter was raised by the heathen against the Church; the Bishops being in the place, and occupying the very house where this was going on; and from which, in order to obtain favour with them, the virgins were assaulted with naked swords, and were exposed to all kinds of danger, and insult, and wanton violence. And this treatment they received during a season of fasting[3], and at the hands of persons who themselves were feasting with the Bishops in that house.

TR. II. 15, 16.

[1] Hist. Arian. 12.

[2] ἐργασίαι (?)

[3] supr. p. 7.

25. Foreseeing these things, and reflecting that the entrance of enemies into a place is no ordinary calamity, we protested against this commission And Alexander[n], Bishop of Thessalonica, considering the same, wrote to the people residing there, discovering the conspiracy, and testifying of the plot. They indeed reckon him to be one of themselves, and account him a partner in their designs; but they only prove thereby the violence they have exercised towards him. For even the profligate Ischyras himself was only induced by fear and violence to proceed in the matter, and was obliged by force to undertake the accusation. As a proof of this, he wrote himself to our brother Athanasius[4], confessing that nothing of the kind that was alleged had taken place there,

§. 16.

[4] infr. §. 64.

---

[n] This Alexander had been one of the Nicene Fathers, in 325, and had the office of publishing their decrees in Macedonia, Greece, &c. He was at the Council of Jerusalem ten years after, at which the Church of the Holy Sepulchre was consecrated, and afterwards Arius admitted to communion. His influence with the Court party seems to have been great, judging from Count Dionysius's tone in speaking of him, infr §. 81

but that he was suborned to make a false statement. This declaration he made, though he was never admitted by Athanasius as a Presbyter, nor received that title from him as a boon, nor was entrusted by way of recompense with the erection of a Church, nor expected the bribe of a Bishopric; all of which he obtained from them in return for undertaking the accusation. Moreover, his whole family held communion with us[1], which they would not have done had they been injured in the slightest degree.

26. Now to prove that these things are facts and not mere assertions, we have the testimony[2] of all the Presbyters of the Mareotis°, who always accompany the Bishop in his visitations, and who also wrote at the time against Ischyras. But neither those of them who came to Tyre were allowed to declare the truth[3], nor could those who remained in the Mareotis obtain permission to refute the calumnies of Ischyras[4]. Copies also of the letters of Alexander, and of the Presbyters, and of Ischyras, will prove the same thing. We have sent also the letter of the father of the Emperors, in which he expresses his indignation that the murder of Arsenius was charged upon any one while the man was still alive, as also his astonishment at the variable and inconsistent character of their accusations with respect to the chalice, since at one time they accused the Presbyter Macarius, at another the Bishop Athanasius, of having broken it with his hands. He declares also on the one hand that the Meletians are calumniators, and on the other that Athanasius is perfectly innocent.

27. And are not the Meletians calumniators, and above all John[5], who after coming into the Church, and communicating with us, after condemning himself, and no longer taking any part in the proceedings respecting the chalice, when he saw the Eusebians zealously supporting the Arian fanatics, though they had not the daring to cooperate with them openly, but were attempting to employ others as their masks, undertook a character, as an actor in the heathen theatres[6]? The subject of the drama was the contest of the

Marginal notes:
APOL. AG. AR.
[1] vid. infr. §. 63 fin. §. 85 fin.
§. 17.
[2] infr. §. 74.
[3] infr. § 79.
[4] §. 72 fin.
[5] Arcaph. infr. 65 fin. head of the Meletians.
[6] vid. infr. §. 37. 46. vol. 8. p. 127. note g.

° The district, called Mareotis from a neighbouring lake, lay in the territory and diocese of Alexandria, to the west. It consisted of various large villages, with handsome Churches, and resident Priests, and of hamlets which had none, of the latter was "the Peace of Secontaruri," (infr. §. 85) where Ischyras lived.

Arians; the real design of the piece being their success, but John and his partizans being appended and playing the parts, in order that under colour of these, the supporters of the Arians, in the garb of judges, might drive away the enemies of their impiety, firmly establish their impious doctrines, and bring the Arians into the Church. And those who wish to drive out true godliness[1] strive all they can to prevail by ungodliness[1]; they who have chosen the part of that impiety[1] which wars against Christ, endeavour to destroy the enemies thereof, as though they were impious[1] persons; and they impute to us the breaking of the chalice, for the purpose of making it appear that Athanasius, equally with themselves, is guilty of impiety[1] towards Christ.

28. For what means this mention of the sacred chalice by them? Whence comes this religious[1] regard for the chalice among those who support impiety[1] towards Christ? Whence comes it that Christ's chalice is known to them who know not Christ? How can they who profess to honour that chalice, dishonour the God of the chalice? or how can they who lament over the chalice, seek to murder the Bishop who celebrates the mysteries therewith? for they would have murdered him, had it been in their power. And how can they who lament the loss of the throne that was Episcopally covered[2], seek to destroy the Bishop that sat upon it, to the end that both the throne may be without its Bishop, and that the people may be deprived of godly[1] doctrine? It was not then the chalice, nor the murder, nor any of those portentous deeds they talk about, that induced them to act thus; but the forementioned heresy of the Arians, for the sake of which they conspired against Athanasius and other Bishops, and still continue to wage war against the Church.

29. Who are they that have really been the cause of murders and banishments? Are not these? Who are they that, availing themselves of external support, conspire against the Bishops? Are not the Eusebians they, and not Athanasius, as in their letters they pretend? Both he and others have suffered at their hands. Even at the time of which we speak, four Presbyters[3] of Alexandria, though they had not even proceeded to Tyre, were banished by their means. Who then are they whose conduct calls for tears and lamentations?

Tr. II. 17.

[1] εὐσέ-βεια, &c. vid.

supr. p. 3. ref. 1.

[2] cathedræ velatæ, Aust. ap. Bingh. viii. 6. §. 10.

[3] vid. their names infr. §. 40.

APOL.
AG. AR. Does not theirs, who after they have been guilty of one course of persecution, do not scruple to add to it a second, but have recourse to all manner of falsehood, in order that they may destroy a Bishop who will not give way to their impious heresy? Hence arises the enmity of the Eusebians; hence their proceedings at Tyre, hence their pretended trials; hence also now the letters which they have written even without any trial, expressing the utmost confidence in their statements; hence their calumnies before the father of the Emperors, and before the most religious Emperors themselves.

§. 18. 30. For it is necessary that you should know what is now reported to the prejudice of our brother Athanasius, in order that you may thereby be led to condemn their wickedness, and may perceive that they desire nothing else but to murder him. A quantity of corn was given by the father of the Emperors for the support of certain widows, some to be of Libya, and some out of Egypt. They have all received it up to this time, Athanasius getting nothing therefrom, but the trouble of assisting them. But now, although the recipients themselves make no complaint, but acknowledge that they have received it, Athanasius has been accused of selling all the corn, and appropriating the profits to his own use: and the Emperor wrote to this effect about it, charging him with the offence in consequence of the calumnies which had been raised against him. Now who are they that have raised these calumnies? Is it not those who after they have been guilty of one course of persecution, scruple not to set on foot another? Who are the authors of those letters which are said to have come from the Emperor? Are not the Arians who are so zealous against Athanasius, and scruple not to speak and write any thing? No one would pass over persons who have acted as they have done, in order to entertain suspicion of others. Nay, the proof of their calumny appears to be most evident, for they are anxious under cover of it, to take away the corn from the Church, and to give it to the Arians. And this circumstance more than any other, brings the matter home to the authors of this design and their principals, who scrupled neither to set on foot a charge of murder against Athanasius, and as a base means of prejudicing the Emperor against him, nor yet to take away from the Clergy[1] of the Church the subsistence of the poor, in order that in fact they might make gain for the heretics.

31. We have sent also the testimony of our brother ministers in Libya, Pentapolis, and Egypt, from which likewise you may learn the false accusations which have been brought against Athanasius. And these things they do, in order that, the professors of true godliness being henceforth induced by fear to remain quiet, the heresy of the impious Arians may be introduced in place of the truth. But thanks be to your piety, dearly beloved, that you have frequently anathematized the Arians in your letters, and have never given them admittance into the Church. The exposure of the Eusebians is also easy, and ready at hand. For behold, after their former letters concerning the Arians, of which also we have sent you copies, they now openly stir up the Arian fanatics against the Church, though the whole Catholic Church has anathematized them; they have appointed a Bishop[2] over them; they distract the Churches with threats and alarms, that they may gain assistants in their impiety in every part. Moreover, they send Deacons to the Arians, who openly join their assemblies; they write letters to them, and receive answers from them, thus making schisms in the Church, and holding communion with them; and they send to every part, commending their heresy, and repudiating the Church, as you will perceive from the letters they have addressed to the Bishop of Rome[3], and perhaps to yourselves also. You perceive therefore, dearly beloved, that these things are not undeserving of vengeance: they are indeed dreadful and alien from the doctrine of Christ.

32. Wherefore we have assembled together, and have written to you, to request of your Christian wisdom to receive this our declaration and sympathize with our brother Athanasius, and to shew your indignation against the Eusebians who have essayed such things, in order that such malice and wickedness may no longer prevail against the Church. We call upon you to be the avengers of such injustice, reminding you of the injunction of the Apostle, *Put away from among yourselves that wicked person.* Wicked indeed is their conduct, and unworthy

TR. II. 18, 19.
1 τῶν κλήρων, f. χηρῶν, Montf.
§. 19.

[2] Pistus.

[3] vid. infr. §. 21.

1 Cor. 5, 13.

of your communion. Wherefore give no further heed to them, though they should again write to you against the Bishop Athanasius; (for all that proceeds from them is false;) not even though they subscribe their letter with names[p] of Egyptian Bishops. For it is evident that it will not be we who write, but the Meletians[1], who have ever been schismatics, and who even unto this day make disturbances and raise factions in the Churches. For they ordain improper persons, and all but heathens; and they are guilty of such actions as we are ashamed to set down in writing, but which you may learn from those whom we have sent unto you, and who will deliver to you our letter.

§. 20. 33. Thus wrote the Bishops of Egypt to all Bishops, and to Julius Bishop of Rome.

[1] infr. §. 73.

[p] The Eusebians availed themse'ves of the subscriptions of the Meletians, as at Philippopolis, Hilar. Fragm. 3.

CHAP. II.

LETTER OF POPE JULIUS TO THE EUSEBIANS AT ANTIOCH.

1. THE Eusebians also wrote to Julius, and thinking to frighten me, requested him to call a Council, and to be himself the judge, if he so pleased[1]. When therefore I went up to Rome, Julius wrote to the Eusebians, as was suitable, and sent moreover two of his own Presbyters[a], Elpidius and Philoxenus[2]. But they, when they heard of me, were thrown into confusion, as not expecting my going up thither, and they declined the proposed Council, alleging unsatisfactory reasons for so doing, but in truth they were afraid lest the things should be proved against them which Valens and Ursacius afterwards confessed[3]. However, more than fifty Bishops assembled, in the place where the Presbyter Vito held his congregation[4], and they acknowledged my defence, and gave me the confirmation[5] both of their fellowship and their loving hospitality. On the other hand, they expressed great indignation against the Eusebians, and requested that Julius would write to the following effect to those of their number who had written to him. Which accordingly he did, and sent it by the hand of Count Gabianus.

[1] A.D. 340. vid. Hist.
Arian. § 11.
? May,
A.D. 341.

[3] infr. §. 58.
[4] συνῆγεν
[5] vid. infr. p. 60, ref. 2.

2. The Letter of Julius[6].

Julius to his dearly beloved brethren[b], Danius, Flacillus, Narcissus, Eusebius, Maris, Macedonius, Theodorus, and &c.

[6] A.D. 342, but 341.
Tillem. &c.

---

[a] Vito and Vincentius, Presbyters, had represented Silvester at Nicæa. Liberius sent Vincentius, Bishop, and Marcellus, Bishop, to Constantius, and again Lucifer, Bishop, and Eusebius, Bishop. St. Basil suggests that Damasus should send Legates into the East, Ep. 69. The Council of Sardica, Can. 5. recognised the Pope's power of sending Legates into foreign Provinces to hear certain appeals; "ut de *Latere suo* Presbyterum mittat" vid. Thomassin. de Eccl. Disc. Part 1 II 117.

[b] By Danius, which had been considered the same name as Dianæus, Bishop of Cæsarea in Cappadocia, Montfaucon in loc. understands the notorious Arian, Bishop of Nicæa, called variously Diognius, (supr. § 13.) Theognius, (infr. §. 28.) Theognis, (Philostorg Hist. II 7.) Theogonius, (Theod Hist. 1. 19.) and assigns some ingenious and probable reasons for his supposition. vid. supr. p. 23, note d. Flacillus, Arian Bishop of Antioch, as Athan. names him, is called Placillus,(in St. Jerome's Chronicon, p 785) Placitus, (Soz. III. 5.) Flacitus, (Theod Hist. 1. 21.) Theodorus was Arian Bishop of Heraclea, whose Comments on the Psalms are supposed to be those which bear his name in Corderius's Catena.

APOL. AG. AR. their friends, who have written to me from Antioch, sends health in the Lord.

§. 21. I have read your letter[c] which was brought to me by my Presbyters Elpidius and Philoxenus, and I am surprised to find that, whereas I wrote to you in charity and with conscious sincerity, you have replied to me in an unbecoming and quarrelsome temper; for the pride and arrogance of the writers is plainly exhibited in that letter. Yet such feelings are inconsistent with the Christian faith; for what was written in a charitable spirit ought likewise to be answered in a spirit of charity and not of contention. And was it not a token of charity to send Presbyters to sympathize with them that are in suffering, and to desire those who had written to me to come hither, that the questions at issue might obtain a speedy settlement, and all things be duly ordered, so that our brethren might no longer be exposed to suffering, and that you might escape further imputation? But something seems to shew that your temper is such, as to force us to conclude that the terms in which you appear to pay honour[1] to us, are with some dissimulation modified in their meaning. The Presbyters also whom we sent to you, and who ought to have returned rejoicing, did on the contrary return sorrowful on account of the proceedings they had witnessed among you. And I, when I had read your letter, after much consideration, kept it to myself, thinking that after all some of you would come, and there would be no need to bring it forward, lest if it should be openly exhibited, it should grieve many of our brethren here. But when no one arrived, and it became necessary that the letter should be produced, I declare to you, they were all astonished, and were hardly able to believe that such a letter had been written by you at all; for it is expressed in terms of strife rather than of charity.

3 Now if the author of it wrote with an ambition of exhibiting his power of language, such a practice surely is more

[1] τιμᾷν

---

[c] Some of the topics contained in the Eusebian Letter are specified in Julius's answer. It acknowledged, besides, the high dignity of the See of Rome, as being "The School (φροντιστήριον) of the Apostles and the Metropolis of orthodoxy from the beginning," but added that "doctors came to it from the east, and that they ought not themselves to hold the second place, for they were superior in virtue, though not in their Church." And they said that they would hold communion with Julius if he would agree to their depositions and substitutions in the Eastern Sees. Soz. iii. 8.

suitable for other subjects: in ecclesiastical matters, it is not a display of eloquence that is needed, but the observance of Apostolic Canons, and an earnest care not to offend one of the little ones of the Church. For it were better for a man, according to that ecclesiastical sentence, that a millstone were hanged about his neck, and that he were drowned in the sea, than that he should offend even one of the little ones. But if such a letter was written, because certain persons through a narrow feeling[1] took offence among themselves, (for I will not impute it to all); it were better not to entertain any such feeling of offence at all, at least not to let the sun go down upon their vexation; and certainly not to give it room to exhibit itself in writing.

4. Yet what has been done that is a just cause of offence? or in what respect was my letter to you such? Was it, that I invited[2] you to be present at a Council? You ought rather to have received the proposal with joy. Those who have confidence in their proceedings, or as they choose to term them, in their decisions, are not wont to be angry, if such decision is enquired into by others; they rather shew all boldness, seeing that if they have given a just decision, it can never prove to be the reverse. The Bishops who assembled in the great Council of Nicæa agreed, not without the will of God, that the decisions of one Council should be examined in another[d], to the end that the judges, having before their eyes that other trial which was to follow, might be led to investigate matters with the utmost caution, and that the parties concerned in their sentence might have assurance that the judgment they received was just, and not dictated by the enmity of their former judges. Now if you are unwilling that such a practice should be adopted in your own case, though it is of ancient standing, and has been noticed and recommended by the great Council, your refusal is not becoming; for it is unreasonable that a custom which

---

[d] As this determination does not find a place among the now received Canons of the Council, the passage in the text becomes of great moment in the argument in favour of the twenty Canons extant in Greek being but a portion of those passed at Nicæa vid Alber. Dissert. in Hist. Eccles. vii. Abraham Ecchellensis has argued on the same side, (apud Colet. Concil. t. ii. p. 399. Ed. Ven. 1728) also Baronius, though not so strongly Ann. 325. nn. 157, &c. and Montfaucon in loc. Natalis Alexander, Sæc. 4. Dissert. 28. argues against the larger number, and Tillemont, Mem. t. 6. p. 674

APOL. AG. AR.

has once obtained in the Church, and been established by Councils, should be set aside by a few individuals.

5. For a further reason they cannot justly take offence in this point. When the persons whom you the Eusebians dispatched with your letters, I mean Macarius the Presbyter, and Martyrius and Hesychius the Deacons, arrived here, and found that they were unable to withstand the arguments of the Presbyters who came from Athanasius, but were confuted and exposed on all sides, they then requested me to call a Council together[1], and to write to Alexandria to the Bishop Athanasius, and also to the Eusebians, in order that a just judgment might be given in the presence of all parties. And they undertook in that case to prove all the charges which had been brought against Athanasius. For Martyrius and Hesychius had been publicly detected by us, and the Presbyters of the Bishop Athanasius had withstood them with great confidence: indeed, if one must tell the truth, the party of Martyrius had been utterly overthrown; and this it was that led them to desire that a Council might be held. Now supposing that they had not desired a Council, but that I had been the person to propose it, in discouragement of[2] those who had written to me, and for the sake of our brethren who complain that they have suffered injustice; even in that case the proposal would have been reasonable and just, for it is agreeable to ecclesiastical practice, and well pleasing to God. But when those persons, whom you the Eusebians considered to be trustworthy, when even they wished me to call the brethren together, it was inconsistent in the parties invited to take offence, when they ought rather to have shewn all readiness to be present. These considerations shew that the display of anger in the offended persons is unreasonable, and their refusal to meet the Council is unbecoming, and has a suspicious appearance. Does any one find fault, if he sees that done by another, which he would allow if done by himself? If, as you write, the decrees of any Council have an irreversible force, and he who has given judgment on a matter is dishonoured, if his sentence is examined by another; consider, dearly beloved, who are they that dishonour Councils? who are setting aside the decisions of former judges?

6. Not to inquire at present into every individual case, lest

[1] A. D. 340.

[2] σκύλαι

I should appear to press too heavily on certain parties, the last instance that has occurred, and which every one who hears it must shudder at, will be sufficient in proof of the others which I omit. The Arians who were excommunicated for their impiety by Alexander, the late Bishop of Alexandria, of blessed memory, were not only proscribed by the brethren in the several cities, but were also anathematized by the whole body assembled together in the great Council of Nicæa. For theirs was no ordinary offence, neither had they sinned against man, but against our Lord Jesus Christ Himself, the Son of the living God. And yet these persons who were proscribed by the whole world, and branded in every Church, are said now to have been admitted to communion again; which I think you ought to hear with indignation. Who then are the parties who dishonour Councils? Are not they who have set at nought the voices of the Three hundred[e], and have preferred impiety to godliness?

7. The heresy of the Arian fanatics[1] was condemned and proscribed by the whole body of Bishops every where; but the Bishops Athanasius and Marcellus have many supporters who speak and write in their behalf. We have received testimony in favour of Marcellus, that he resisted the advocates of the Arian doctrines in the Council of Nicæa; and in favour of Athanasius, that at Tyre nothing was brought home to him, and that in the Mareotis, where the Reports against him are said to have been drawn up, he was not present. Now you know, dearly beloved, that *ex parte* proceedings are of no weight, but bear a suspicious appearance. Nevertheless, these things being so, we, in order to be accurate, and neither shewing any prepossession in favour of yourselves, nor of those who wrote in behalf of the other party, invited those who had written to me to come hither, that, since there were many who wrote in their behalf, all things might be enquired into in a Council, and neither the guiltless might be condemned, nor the guilty be accounted innocent. We then are not the parties who dishonour Councils, but they who at once and recklessly have received the Arians whom

TR. II.
23.

§. 23.

[1] ἀρειο-
μανιτῶν,
supr. p.
4. ref. 1.

---

[e] The number of the Fathers at the Nicene Council is generally considered to have been 318, the number of Abraham's servants, Gen. 14, 14. Anastasius (Hodeg. 3. fin.) referring to the first three Ecumenical Councils, speaks of the faith of the 318, the 150, and the 200.

all had condemned, and contrary to the decision of the judges. The greater part of those judges have now departed, and are with Christ; but some of them are still in this life of trial, and are indignant at learning that certain persons have set aside their judgment.

§. 24.   8. We have also been informed of the following circumstance by those who were at Alexandria. A certain Carpones, who had been excommunicated by Alexander for Arianism, was sent hither[1] by one Gregory with certain others, also excommunicated for the same heresy. However, I had learnt the matter also from the Presbyter Macarius, and the Deacons Martyrius and Hesychius[2]. For before the Presbyters of Athanasius arrived, they urged me to send letters to one Pistus at Alexandria, though at the same time the Bishop Athanasius was there. And when the Presbyters of the Bishop Athanasius came, they informed me that this Pistus was an Arian, and that he had been excommunicated[3] by the Bishop Alexander and the Council of Nicæa, and then ordained by one Secundus, whom also the great Council excommunicated as an Arian. This statement the party of Martyrius did not gainsay, nor did they deny that Pistus had received his ordination from Secundus. Now consider, after this who are most justly liable to blame? I, who could not be prevailed upon to write to the Arian Pistus; or those, who advised me to do dishonour to the great Council, and to address the impious as if they were godly persons? Moreover, when the Presbyter Macarius, who had been sent hither by Eusebius with Martyrius and the rest, heard of the opposition which had been made by the Presbyters of Athanasius, while we were expecting his appearance with Martyrius and Hesychius, he decamped in the night, in spite of a bodily ailment; which leads us to conjecture that his departure arose from shame on account of the exposure which had been made concerning Pistus. For it is impossible that the ordination of the Arian Secundus should be considered valid[4] in the Catholic Church. This would indeed be dishonour to the Council, and to the Bishops who composed it, if the decrees they framed, as in the presence of God, with such extreme earnestness and care, should be set aside as nugatory.

§. 25.   9. If, as you write[5], the decrees of all Councils ought to be of force, according to the precedent in the case of Novatus[f] and Paul of Samosata, certainly the sentence of the Three hundred ought not to be reversed, certainly a Catholic Council ought not to be set at nought by a few individuals. For the Arians are heretics as they, and the like sentence has been passed both against the one and the other. And, after such bold proceedings as these, who are they that have lighted up the flame of discord? for in your letter you blame us for having done this. Have we, who have sympathized with the sufferings of the brethren, and have acted in all respects according to the Canon; or they who contentiously and contrary to the Canon have set aside the sentence of the Three hundred, and dishonoured the Council in every way? For not only have the Arians been received into communion, but Bishops also have adopted the practice of removing from one place to another[2]. Now if you really believe that all Bishops have the same and equal authority[3], and you do not, as you assert, account of them according to the magnitude of their cities, he that is entrusted with a small city ought to abide in the place committed to him, and not from disdain of his trust to remove to one that has never been put under him; despising that which God has given him, and making much of the vain applause of men. You ought then, dearly beloved, to have come and not declined, that the matter may be brought to a conclusion; for this is what reason demands.

[1] Tr. II. 25. 1. e. Novatian.
[2] vid. supr. p. 23.
[3] Cyprian. de Unit. Eccl. 4. O. T.

10. But perhaps you were prevented by the time fixed upon for the Council, for you complain in your letter that the interval before the day we appointed[4] was too short. But[4] this, dearly beloved, is a mere excuse. Had certain of you set out to come, and the day arrived before them, the interval allowed would then have been proved to be too short. But when persons do not wish to come, and detain even my Presbyters up to the month of January[5], it is the mere excuse of those who have no confidence in their cause; otherwise, as I said before, they would have come, not regarding the length of the journey, not considering the shortness of the

[4] προθεσμία, vid. Cyr. Cat. O. T. pp. 3, 246.
[5] A. D. 342. Tillem. reads June.

---

[f] The instance of Novatian makes against the Eusebians, because for some time after Novatian was condemned in the West, his cause was not abandoned in the East. Tillemont, Mem. t. 7. p. 277.

time, but trusting to the justice and reasonableness of their cause. But perhaps they did not come on account of the aspect of the times[1], for again you declare in your letter, that we ought to have considered the present circumstances of the East, and not to have desired you to come. Now if as you say you did not come because the times were such, you ought to have considered such times beforehand, and not to have become the authors of schism, and of mourning and lamentation in the Churches. But as the matter stands, men, who have been the cause of these things, shew that it is not the times that are to blame, but the determination of those who will not meet a Council.

§. 26. 11. But I wonder also how you could ever have written that part of your letter, in which you say, that I alone wrote, and not to all of you, but to the Eusebians only. In this complaint one may discover more of readiness to find fault than of regard for truth. I received the letters against Athanasius from none other than those connected with Martyrius and Hesychius, and I necessarily wrote to them who had written against him. Either then the Eusebians ought not alone to have written, apart from you all, or else you, to whom I did not write, ought not to be offended that I wrote to them who had written to me. If it was right that I should address my letter to you all, you also ought to have written with them; but now, considering what was reasonable, I wrote to them who had addressed themselves to me, and had given me information. But if you were displeased because I alone wrote to them, it is but consistent that you should also be angry, because they wrote to me alone. But for this also, dearly beloved, there was a fair and reasonable cause. Nevertheless it is necessary that I should acquaint you that, although I only wrote, yet the sentiments I expressed were not those of myself alone, but of all the Bishops throughout Italy and in these parts I indeed was unwilling to cause them all to write, lest the others should be overpowered by their number. The Bishops however assembled on the appointed day, and agreed in these opinions, which I again write to signify to you; so that, dearly beloved, although I alone address you, yet you may be assured that these are the sentiments of all. Thus much for the excuses, not reason-

[1] the Persian war. Hist. Arian. § 11.

able, but unjust and suspicious, which some of you have alleged for your conduct.

12. Now although what has already been said were sufficient to shew that we have not admitted to our communion our brothers Athanasius and Marcellus either too readily, or unjustly, yet it is but fair briefly to set the matter before you. Eusebius's friends wrote formerly against the friends of Athanasius, as you also have written now; but a great number of Bishops out of Egypt and other provinces wrote in his favour. Now in the first place, your letters against him are inconsistent with one another, and the latter have no sort of agreement with the former, but in many instances the former are answered by the latter, and the latter are impeached by the former. Now where there is this contradiction in letters, no credit whatever is due to the statements they contain. In the next place, if you require us to believe what you have written, it is but consistent that we should not refuse credit to those who have written in his favour[1]; especially, considering that you write from a distance, while they are on the spot, are acquainted with the man, and the events which are occurring there, and testify in writing to his manner of life, and positively affirm that he has been the victim of a conspiracy throughout

13. Again, a certain Bishop Arsenius was said at one time to have been destroyed by Athanasius, but we have learned that he is alive, nay, that he is on terms of friendship with him. He has positively asserted that the Reports drawn up in the Mareotis were *ex parte* ones, for that neither the Presbyter Macarius, the accused party, was present, nor yet his Bishop, Athanasius himself. This we have learnt, not only from his own mouth, but also from the Reports which Martyrius and Hesychius brought to us[2]; for we found on reading them, that the accuser Ischyras was present there, but neither Macarius, nor the Bishop Athanasius; and that the Presbyters of Athanasius desired to attend, but were not permitted. Now, dearly beloved, if the trial was to be conducted honestly, not only the accuser, but the accused also ought to have been present. As the accused party Macarius attended at Tyre, as well as the accuser Ischyras, when nothing was proved against him, so not only ought the

accuser to have gone to the Mareotis, but also the accused, so that he might be present when he was convicted, or if he was acquitted, might have opportunity to expose the calumny. But now, as this was not the case, but the accuser only went out thither, with those to whom Athanasius objected, the proceedings wear a suspicious appearance.

§. 28. 14. And he complained also that the persons who went to the Mareotis went against his wish, for that Theognius, Maris, Theodorus, Ursacius, Valens, and Macedonius, who were the persons they sent out, were of suspected character. This he shewed not by his own assertion merely, but from a letter of Alexander who was Bishop of Thessalonica; for he produced a letter written by him to Dionysius[1], the Count who presided in the Council, in which he shews most clearly that there was a conspiracy on foot against Athanasius. He has also brought forward a genuine document, all in the handwriting of the accuser Ischyras himself[2], in which he calls God Almighty to witness that no chalice was broken, nor table overthrown, but that he had been suborned by certain persons to invent these accusations. Moreover, when the Presbyters of the Mareotis arrived[3], they positively affirmed that Ischyras was not a Presbyter of the Catholic Church, and that Macarius had not committed any such offence as the other had laid to his charge. The Presbyters and Deacons also who came to us testified in the fullest manner in favour of the Bishop Athanasius, strenuously asserting that none of those things which were alleged against him were true, but that he was the victim of a conspiracy.

15. And all the Bishops of Egypt and Libya wrote and protested[4] that his ordination was lawful and strictly ecclesiastical, and that all that you had advanced against him was false, for that no murder had been committed, nor any persons despatched on his account, nor any chalice broken, but that all was false. Nay, the Bishop Athanasius also shewed from the *ex parte* Reports drawn up in the Mareotis, that a Catechumen was examined and said[5], that he was within with Ischyras, at the time when they say Macarius the Presbyter of Athanasius burst into the place; and that others who were examined said,—one, that Ischyras was in a small cell[6],—and another, that he lay behind the door, being sick at that very

[1] infr. §. 80
[2] §. 64.
[3] §. 74.
[4] supr. §. 6. p. 22.
[5] infr. §. 83.
[6] ἐν κελλίῳ

time, when they say Macarius came thither. Now from these representations of his, we are naturally led to ask the question, How was it possible that a man who was lying behind the door sick could get up, conduct the service, and offer the Oblations? and how could it be that Oblations were offered in the presence of Catechumens[1]? for if there were Catechumens present, it was not yet the time for presenting the Oblations. These representations, as I said, were made by the Bishop Athanasius, and he shewed from the Reports, what was also positively affirmed by those who were with him, that Ischyras has never been a Presbyter at all in the Catholic Church, nor has ever appeared as a Presbyter in the assemblies of the Church; for not even when Alexander admitted those of the Meletian schism, by the indulgence of the great Council, was he named by Meletius among his Presbyters, as they deposed[2]; which is the strongest argument possible that he was not even a Presbyter of Meletius; for otherwise, he would certainly have been numbered with the rest. Besides, it was shewn also by Athanasius from the Reports, that Ischyras had spoken falsely in other instances: for he set up a charge respecting the burning of certain books, when, as they pretend, Macarius burst in upon them, but was convicted of falsehood by the witnesses he himself brought to prove it.

16. Now when these things were thus represented to us, and so many witnesses appeared in his favour, and so much was advanced by him in his own justification, what did it become us to do? what did the Canon[3] of the Church require of us, but that we should not condemn him, but rather receive him and treat him as a Bishop, as we have done? Moreover, besides all this he continued here a year and six months[g], expecting the arrival of yourselves and of whoever chose to come. His presence overcame us all, for he would not have been here, had he not felt confident in his cause; and he came not of his own accord, but on a summons[4] by

TR. II. 28, 29.

[1] Bingh. Ant. x. 5. § 8.

[2] infr. §. 71.

[3] pp. 3. 45. 55.

[4] κληθείς

---

g Valesius, Montfaucon, and Coustant, consider these eighteen months to run from about May 341, upon Gregory's usurpation, to October or November 342, when the Council of Rome terminated, as Schelstrate also thinks. Baronius and Tillemont follow Socrates in supposing two journeys of Athan to Rome, and that the eighteen months began in 339 or 340, and had a break in them, during which he returned to Alexandria

letter from us, in the manner in which we wrote to you. But still you complain after all of our transgressing the Canons. Now consider, who are they that have so acted? we who received this man after such ample proof of his innocence, or they who being at Antioch at the distance of six and thirty posts[h]; appointed a stranger to be Bishop, and sent him to Alexandria with a military force; a thing which was not done even when Athanasius was banished into Gaul, though it would have been done then, had he been really proved guilty of the offence. But when he returned, of course he found his Church unoccupied and waiting for him.

§. 30. 17. But now I am ignorant under what colour these proceedings have been conducted. In the first place, if the truth must be spoken, it was not right, when we had written to summon a Council, that any persons should anticipate its decisions[1]: and in the next place, it was not fitting that such novel proceedings should be adopted against the Church. For what Canon of the Church[1], or what Apostolical tradition warrants this, that when the Church was at peace, and so many Bishops were in unanimity with Athanasius the Bishop of Alexandria, Gregory should be sent thither, a stranger to the city, not having been baptized there, nor known to the general body, and desired neither by Presbyters, nor Bishops, nor Laity—that he should be ordained at Antioch, and sent to Alexandria, accompanied not by Presbyters, nor by Deacons of the city, nor by Bishops of Egypt, but by soldiers? for they who came hither complained that this was the case.

[1] p. 41, note d, p. 55.

18. Even supposing that Athanasius was in the position of a criminal after the Council, this appointment ought not to have been made thus illegally and contrary to the Canon of the Church, but the Bishops of the province ought to have

---

[h] or rather, halts, μοναί. They are enumerated in the Itinerary of Antoninus, and are set down on Montfaucon's plate The route passes over the Delta to Pelusium, and then coasts all the way to Antioch These μοναί were day's journeys, Coustant in Hilar. Psalm 118, Lit 5 2. or half a day's journey, Herman. ibid, and were at unequal intervals, Ambros in Psalm 118, Serm. 5 § 5. Gibbon says that by the government conveyances, " it was easy to travel an 100 miles in a day along the Roman roads." ch. 11. Μονή or mansio properly means the building, where soldiers or other public officers rested at night, (hence its application to monastic houses.) Such buildings included granaries, stabling, &c vid. Cod. Theod. ed. Gothofr. 1665. t. 1. p. 47. t. 2. p. 507. Ducange Gloss. t. 4. p. 426 Col. 2.

[1] The Eusebians kept the Pope's legates, and hastened their own Council of the Dedication by way of anticipating him in their decision.

ordained one in that very Church, of that very Priesthood, of that very Clergy¹; and the Canons² received from the Apostles ought not thus to be set aside. Had this offence been committed against any one of you, would you not have exclaimed against it, and demanded justice as for the transgression of the Canons? Dearly beloved, we speak honestly, as in the presence of God, and declare, that this proceeding was neither pious, nor lawful, nor ecclesiastical. Moreover, the account which is given of the conduct of Gregory on his entry into the city, plainly shews the character of his appointment. In such peaceful times, as those who came from Alexandria declared them to have been, and as the Bishops also represented in their letters, the Church was set on fire³; Virgins were stripped; Monks were trodden under foot; Presbyters and many of the people were scourged and suffered violence, Bishops were cast into prison, multitudes were dragged about from place to place; the holy Mysteries^k, about which they accused the Presbyter Macarius, were seized upon by heathens and cast upon the ground; and all to constrain certain persons to admit the appointment of Gregory. Such conduct plainly shews who they are that transgress the Canons. Had the appointment been lawful, he would not have had recourse to illegal proceedings to compel the obedience of those who in a legal way resisted him. And notwithstanding all this, you write that perfect peace prevailed in Alexandria and Egypt. Surely not, unless the works of peace are entirely changed, and you call such doings as these peace.

[Tr. II. 30, 31. ¹ vid. Bingh. Ant. II. 11. § 7. ² pp. 3, 50 ³ supr. p. 6.]

19. I have also thought it necessary to point out to you this circumstance, viz. that Athanasius positively asserted that Macarius was kept at Tyre under a guard of soldiers, while only his accuser accompanied those who went to the Mareotis⁴; and that the Presbyters who desired to attend the inquiry were not permitted, while the said inquiry respecting the chalice and the Table was carried on before the Prefect and his band, and in the presence of Heathens and Jews.

[§. 31. ⁴ p. 31.]

---

^k Athan. only suggests this, supr. p. 6. S. Hilary says the same of the conduct of the Arians at Toulouse, " Clerks were beaten with clubs; Deacons bruised with lead; nay, even *on Christ Himself* (the Saints understand my meaning) hands were laid." Contr. Constant. 11.

APOL. AG. AR. This at first seemed incredible, but it was proved to have been so from the Reports; which caused great astonishment to us, as I suppose, dearly beloved, it does to you also. Presbyters, who are the ministers of the Mysteries, are not permitted to attend, but an enquiry concerning Christ's Blood and Christ's Body is carried on before an external[1] judge, in the presence of Catechumens, nay, worse than that, before Heathens and Jews, who have so bad a name in regard to Christianity. Even supposing that an offence had been committed, it should have been investigated legally in the Church and by the Clergy, not by heathens who abhor the Word and know not the Truth. I am persuaded that both you and all men must perceive the nature and magnitude of this sin. Thus much concerning Athanasius.

[1] ἐξωτικοῦ

§. 32. 20. With respect to Marcellus[1], forasmuch as you have charged him also of impiety towards Christ, I am anxious to inform you, that when he was here, he positively declared that what you had written concerning him was not true; but being nevertheless requested by us to give an account of his faith, he answered in his own person with the utmost boldness, so that we were obliged to acknowledge that he maintains nothing except the truth. He made a confession[2] of the same godly doctrines concerning our Lord and Saviour Jesus Christ as the Catholic Church confesses, and he affirmed that he had held these opinions for a very long time, and had not recently adopted them: as indeed our Presbyters[3], who were at a former date present at the Council of Nicæa, testified to his orthodoxy, for he maintained then, as he has done now, his opposition to Arianism, (on which point it is right to admonish you, lest any of you admit such heresy, instead of abominating it as alien from *sound doc-*

[2] vid. Epiph. Hær. 72. 2, 3. and p. 73. infr.

[3] Vincentius and Vito.

1 Tim. 1. 10.

[1] Julius here acquits Marcellus, but it would seem that he did not eventually preserve himself from heretical notions, even if he deserved a favourable judgment at this time. Athan. sides with him, de Fug. 3. Hist. Arian. 6 but Epiphanius records, that on his asking Athanasius what he (Athan) thought of Marcellus, a smile came on his face, and he implied that there was some unsoundness in Marcellus's views which perhaps he did not like to expose Hær 72. n 4. And S. Hilary says that Athan separated him from his communion, as agreeing with Photinus his disciple, Fragm. ii. 23. Sulpicius says the same. He is considered heretical by S. Epiphanius, *loc. cit* S. Basil, Epp 69, 125, 263, 265 S. Chrysostom in Hebr. Hom. ii. 2. Theodoret, Hær. ii. 10. vid. Petav. de Trin. i. 13. who condemns him, and Bull far more strongly Def. F N. ii. 1. §. 9. Montfaucon defends him, (in a special Dissertation, Collect Nov. tom. 2.) and Tillemont, Mem. tom. 7. p. 513. and Natalis Alex. Sæc iv. Dissert. 30.

trine.) Seeing then that he professed orthodox opinions, and had testimony to his orthodoxy, what, I ask again in his case, ought we to have done, except to receive him as a Bishop, as we did, and not reject him from our communion?

21. These things I have written, not so much for the purpose of defending their cause, as in order to convince you, that we acted justly and canonically[1] in receiving these persons, and that you are contentious without a cause. But it is your duty to use your anxious endeavours and to labour by every means to correct the irregularities which have been committed contrary to the Canon, and to secure the peace of the Churches; so that the peace of our Lord which has been given to us may remain, and the Churches may not be divided, nor you incur the charge of being authors of schism. For I confess, your past conduct is an occasion of schism rather than of peace.

22. For not only the Bishops Athanasius and Marcellus came hither and complained of the injustice that had been done them, but many other Bishops also[m], from Thrace, from Cœle-Syria, from Phœnicia and Palestine, and Presbyters not a few, and others from Alexandria and from other parts, were present at the Council here, and in addition to their other statements, lamented before all the assembled Bishops the violence and injustice which the Churches had suffered, and affirmed that similar outrages to those which had been committed in Alexandria had occurred in their own Churches, and in others also. Again, there lately came Presbyters with letters from Egypt and Alexandria, who complained that many Bishops and Presbyters who wished to come to the Council were prevented, for they said that, since the departure of Athanasius[n] even up to this time, Bishops who are confessors[o] have been beaten with stripes, that others have been cast into prison, and that but lately aged men, who have been an exceedingly long period in the Episcopate, have been

---

[m] The names of few are known; perhaps Marcellus, Asclepas, Paul of Constantinople, Lucius of Adrianople. vid. Montf. in loc. Tillem. Mem. tom. 7. p. 272.

[n] These outrages took place immediately on the dismission of Elpidius and Philoxenus, the Pope's legates, from Antioch. Athan. Hist. Ar. 12.

[o] e.g Saparammon and Potamo, both Confessors, who were of the number of the Nicene Fathers, and had defended Athan. at Tyre, were, the former banished, the latter beaten to death. vid. infr. Hist. Ar. 12.

given up to be employed in the public works, and nearly all the Clergy of the Catholic Church with the people are the objects of plots and persecutions. Moreover they said that certain Bishops and other brethren had been banished for no other reason than to compel them against their will to communicate with Gregory and his Arian associates. We have heard also from others, what is confirmed by the testimony of the Bishop Marcellus, that a number of outrages, similar to those which were committed at Alexandria, have occurred also at Ancyra in Galatia[p]. And in addition to all this, those who came to the Council reported against some of you (for I will not mention names) certain charges of so dreadful a nature that I have declined setting them down in writing: perhaps you also have heard them from others. It was for this cause especially that I wrote to desire[1] you to come, that you might be present to hear them, and that all irregularities might be corrected and differences healed. And those who were called for these purposes ought not to have refused, but to have come the more readily, lest by failing to do so they should be suspected of what was alleged against them, and be thought unable to prove what they had written.

§. 34. 23. Now according to these representations, since the Churches are thus afflicted and treacherously assaulted, as our informants positively affirmed, who are they that have lighted up the flame of discord[2]? We, who grieve for such a state of things and sympathize with the sufferings of the brethren, or those who have brought these things about? While then such extreme confusion existed in every Church, which was the cause why those who visited us came hither, I wonder how you could write that unanimity prevailed in the Churches. These things tend not to the edification of the Church, but to her destruction; and those who rejoice in them are not sons of peace, but of confusion: but our *God is not* a God *of confusion, but of peace.* Wherefore, as the God and Father of our Lord Jesus Christ knows, it was from a regard for your good name,

---

[1] προτρεπόμενος

[2] vid. supr. p. 45.

1 Cor. 14, 33.

[p] The Pseudo-Sardican Council, i. e. the Eusebians at Philippopolis, retort this accusation on the party of Marcellus, Hilar. Fragm. iii 9. but the character of the outrages fixes them on the Arians. vid. infr. p. 71, note h.

and with prayers that the Churches might not fall into confusion, but might continue as they were regulated[1] by the Apostles, that I thought it necessary to write thus unto you, to the end that you might at length discountenance those who through the effects of their mutual enmity have brought the Churches to this condition. For I have heard, that it is only a certain few[2] who are the authors of all these things.

TR. II. 34, 35.
[1] ἐκανο-νίσθη, vid. p. 51, infr. §. 69.
[2] ad Ep. Æg. 5. de Syn. 5.

24. Now, as having bowels of mercy, take ye care to correct, as I said before, those irregularities which have been committed contrary to the Canon, so that if any mischief has already befallen, it may be healed through your zeal. And write not that I have preferred the communion of Marcellus and Athanasius to yours, for such like complaints are no indications of peace, but of contentiousness and hatred of the brethren. For this cause I have written the foregoing, that you may understand that we acted not unjustly in admitting them to our communion, and so may cease this strife. If you had come hither, and they had been condemned, and had appeared unable to produce reasonable evidence in support of their cause, you would have done well in writing thus. But seeing that, as I said before, we acted agreeably to the Canon, and not unjustly, in holding communion with them, I beseech you for the sake of Christ, suffer not the members of Christ to be torn asunder, neither trust to prejudices, but seek rather the peace of the Lord. It is neither holy nor just, in order to gratify the narrow-spirit[1] of a few persons, to reject those who have never been condemned, and thereby to grieve the Spirit. But if you think that you are able to prove any thing against them, and to confute them face to face, let those of you who please come hither: for they also promised that they would be ready to establish completely the truth of those things which they have reported to us.

[1] μικρο-ψυχίαν supr. p. 41.

25. Give us notice therefore of this, dearly beloved, that we may write both to them, and to the Bishops who will have again to assemble, so that the guilty may be condemned in the presence of all, and confusion no longer prevail in the Churches. What has already taken place is enough: it is enough surely that Bishops have been sentenced to banish-

§. 35.

ment in the presence of Bishops; of which it behoves me not to speak at length, lest I appear to press too heavily on those who were present on those occasions. But if one must speak the truth, matters ought not to have proceeded so far; their private feelings[1] ought not to have been suffered to reach their present pitch. Let us grant the "removal," as you write, of Athanasius and Marcellus, from their own places, yet what must one say of the case of the other Bishops and Presbyters who, as I said before, came hither from various parts, and who complained that they also had been forced away, and had suffered the like injuries? O dearly beloved, the decisions of the Church are no longer according to the Gospel, but tend only to banishment and death[2]. Supposing, as you assert, that some offence rested upon those persons, the case ought to have been conducted against them, not after this manner, but according to the Canon of the Church[3]. Word should have been written of it to us all[q], that so a just sentence might proceed from all. For the sufferers were Bishops, and Churches of no ordinary note, but those which the Apostles themselves had governed in their own persons[r].

26. And why was nothing said to us concerning the Church of the Alexandrians in particular? Are you ignorant that the custom has been for word to be written first to us, and then for a just sentence to be past from this place[s]? If then any such suspicion rested upon the Bishop there, notice thereof ought to have been sent to the Church of this place; whereas, after neglecting to inform us, and proceeding on their own authority as they pleased, now they desire to

---

APOL. AG. AR.

[1] μικροψυχίας p. 55.

[2] Hist. Arian. §. 67.

[3] p. 53.

---

[q] Coustant in loc. fairly insists on the word "all," as shewing that S. Julius does not here claim the prerogative of judging *by himself* all Bishops whatever, and that what follows relates merely to the Church of Alexandria.

[r] St. Peter (Greg. M. Epist. vii. Ind. 15. 40) or St. Mark (Leo, Ep 9) at Alexandria. St Paul at Ancyra in Galatia, (Tertull contr Marcion. iv 5.) vid Coustant. in loc

[s] Socrates says somewhat differently, "Julius wrote back....that they acted against the Canons, because they had not called him to a Council, the Ecclesiastical Canon commanding that the Churches ought not to make Canons beside the will of the Bishop of Rome." Hist. ii. 17. Sozomen in like manner, "for it was a sacerdotal law, to declare invalid whatever was transacted beside the will of the Bishop of the Romans." Hist iii 10. vid. Pope Damasus ap. Theod Hist. v. 10. Leon. Epist. 14. &c. In the passage in the text the prerogative of the Roman see is limited, as Coustant observes, to the instance of Alexandria; and we actually find in the third century a complaint lodged against its Bishop Dionysius with the Pope

obtain our concurrence in their decisions, though we never condemned him. Not so have the Constitutions[t] of Paul, not so have the traditions of the Fathers directed; this is another form of procedure, a novel practice. I beseech you, readily bear with me: what I write is for the common good. For what we have received from the blessed Apostle Peter[u], that I signify to you; and I should not have written this, as deeming that these things were manifest unto all men, had not these proceedings so disturbed us. Bishops are forced away from their sees and driven into banishment, while others from different quarters are appointed in their place; others are treacherously assailed, so that the people have to grieve for those who are forcibly taken from them, while, as to those who are sent in their room, they are obliged to give over seeking the man whom they desire, and to receive those they do not.

27. I ask[1] of you, that such things may no longer be, but that you will denounce in writing those persons who attempt them; so that the Churches may no longer be afflicted thus, nor any Bishop or Presbyter be treated with insult, nor any one be compelled to act contrary to his judgment, as they have represented to us, lest we become a laughing-stock among the heathen, and above all, lest we excite the wrath of God against us. For every one of us shall give account in the Day of judgment of the things which he has done in this life. May we all be possessed with the mind of God! so that the Churches may recover their own Bishops, and rejoice evermore in Jesus Christ our Lord; through Whom to the Father be glory, for ever and ever. Amen.

---

[t] διατάξεις. St. Paul says οὕτως ἐν ταῖς ἐκκλησίαις διατάσσομαι. 1 Cor. vii. 17. τὰ δὲ λοιπὰ διατάξομαι Ibid xi. 34 vid. Pearson, Vind. Ignat p 298 Hence Coustant in loc. Athan. would suppose Julius to refer to 1 Cor. v. 4. which Athan. actually quotes, Ep. Encycl. §. 2. supr. pp 4 5. Pearson *loc. cit.* considers the διατάξεις of the Apostles, as a collection of regulations and usages, which more or less represented, or claimed to represent, what may be called St. Paul's *rule*, or St. Peter's *rule*, &c.

Coteller considers the διατάξεις as the same as the διδαχαί, the "doctrine" or "teaching" of the Apostles. Præfat in Const Apost. So does Beveridge, Cod. Can. Illustr 1. 9 §. 5.

[u] [Petri] in Sede suâ vivit potestas et excellit auctoritas. Leon. Serm. iii 3. vid. contra Barrow on the Supremacy, p 116. ed. 1836. "not one Bishop, but all Bishops together through the whole Church, do succeed St. Peter, or any other Apostle."

APOL. AG. AR. I pray for your health in the Lord, brethren dearly beloved and greatly longed for.

§. 36.   28. Thus wrote the Council of Rome by Julius Bishop of Rome.

CHAP. III.

LETTERS OF THE COUNCIL OF SARDICA TO THE CHURCHES OF EGYPT AND OF ALEXANDRIA, AND TO ALL CHURCHES.

1. But when, notwithstanding, the Eusebians proceeded without shame, disturbing the Churches, and plotting the ruin of many, the most religious Emperors Constantius and Constans being informed of this, commanded[1] the Bishops from both the West and East to meet together in the city of Sardica. In the mean time Eusebius[2] died: but a great number assembled from all parts, and we challenged the associates of Eusebius to submit to a trial. But they, having before their eyes the things that they had done, and perceiving that their accusers had come up to the Council, were afraid to do this; but, while all beside met with honest intentions, they again brought with them the Counts[3] Musonianus[a] and Hesychius the Castrensian[b], that, as their custom was, they might effect their own aims by their authority. But when the Council met without the Counts, and no soldiers were permitted to be present, they were confounded, and conscience-stricken, because they could no longer obtain what judgment they wished, but such only as reason and truth[4] required. We, however, frequently repeated our challenge, and the Council of Bishops called upon them to come forward, saying, "You have come for the purpose of undergoing a trial, why then do you now withdraw yourselves? Either you ought not to have come, or having come, not to conceal yourselves. Such conduct will prove

[1] ἐκέλευ-σαν
[2] of Nicomedia
[3] Hist. Ar. 15.
[4] ὁ τῆς ἀληθείας λόγος, vid. p. 72.

---

[a] Musonian was originally of Antioch, and his name Strategius, he had been promoted and honoured with a new name by Constantine, for whom he had collected information about the Manichees. Amm. Marc. xv. 13. §. 1. In 354, he was Prætorian Prefect of the East. (vid. Libr of F O. T. vol viii. p. 73, note a.) Libanius praises him.

[b] The Castrensians were the officers of the palace; castra, as στρατόπεδον, infr. §. 86 being at this time used for the Imperial Court. vid. Gothofred in Cod. Theod. vi. 30. p. 218. Ducange in voc.

APOL. AG. AR. your greatest condemnation. Behold, Athanasius and his friends are here, whom you accused while absent; if therefore you think that you have any thing against them, you may convict them face to face. But if you pretend to be unwilling to do so, while in truth you are unable, you plainly shew yourselves to be calumniators, and the Council will give sentence against you accordingly." When they heard this they were self-condemned, (for they were conscious of their machinations and fabrications against us,) and were ashamed to appear, thereby proving themselves to have been guilty of many base calumnies.

2. The holy Council therefore denounced their indecent and suspicious flight[1], and admitted us to make our defence; and when we had related their conduct towards us, and proved the truth of our statements by witnesses and other evidence, they were filled with astonishment, and all acknowledged that our opponents had good reason to be afraid to meet the Council, lest their guilt should be proved before their faces. They said also, that probably they had come from the East, supposing that Athanasius and his friends would not appear, but that, when they saw them confident in their cause, and challenging a trial, they fled. They accordingly received us as injured persons who had been falsely accused, and confirmed[2] yet more towards us their fellowship and loving hospitality[3] But they deposed Eusebius's associates in wickedness, who had become even more shameless than himself, viz Theodorus[4] of Heraclea, Narcissus of Neronias, Acacius[5] of Cæsarea, Stephanus[6] of Antioch, Ursacius and Valens of Pannonia, Menophantus of Ephesus, and George[7] of Laodicæa; and they wrote to the Bishops in all parts of the world, and to the diocese[8] of each of the injured persons, in the following terms

[1] to Philippopolis.
[2] ἐκύρω-σαν κ. τ. λ.
p 38, ref. 5.
[3] ἀγάπης.
[4] p. 39, note b.
[5] vol. 8, p. 7. p.
[6] Hist. Arian. §. 20.
[7] p. 25. f.
[8] παροι-κία

3. *Letter of the Council of Sardica to the Church of Alexandria.*

The Holy Council, by the grace of God assembled at Sardica, from[9] Rome, Spain, Gaul, Italy, Campania, Calabria, Apulia, Africa, Sardinia, Pannonia, Mysia, Dacia, Noricum, Siscia, Dardania, the other Dacia, Macedonia, Thessaly, Achaia, Epirus, Thrace, Rhodope, Palestine, Arabia, Crete,

[9] vid. supr. p. 14. where Isauria, Thessaly, Sicily, Bri-

and Egypt, to their dearly beloved brethren, the Presbyters and Deacons, and to all the Holy Church of God abiding at Alexandria, sends health in the Lord.

We were not ignorant, but the fact was well known to us, even before we received the letters of your piety, that the supporters of the abominated heresy of the Arians were practising many dangerous machinations, rather to the destruction of their own souls, than to the injury of the Church. For this has ever been the object of their unprincipled craft; this is the deadly design in which they have been continually engaged; viz. how they may best expel from their places and persecute all who are to be found any where of orthodox sentiments, and maintaining the doctrine of the Catholic Church, which was delivered to them from the Fathers. Against some they have laid false accusations; others they have driven into banishment; others they have destroyed by the punishments inflicted on them. Thus also they endeavoured by violence and tyranny to surprise the innocence of our brother and fellow Bishop Athanasius, and therefore conducted their enquiry into his case without any scrupulous care, without any faith, without any sort of justice Accordingly having no confidence in the part they had played on that occasion, nor yet in the reports they had circulated against him, but perceiving that they were unable to produce any certain evidence respecting them, when they came to the city of Sardica, they were unwilling to meet the Council of all the holy Bishops. From this it became evident that the decision of our brother and fellow-Bishop Julius was a just one[1]; for after cautious deliberation and care he had determined, that we ought not to hesitate at all about holding communion with our brother Athanasius. For he had the credible testimony of eighty Bishops, and was also able to advance this fair argument in his support, that by the mere means of our dearly beloved brethren his own Presbyters, and by correspondence, he had defeated the designs of the Eusebians, who relied more upon violence than upon a judicial enquiry.

4. Wherefore all the Bishops from all parts determined upon holding communion with Athanasius on the ground that he was innocent. And let your charity also observe, that when

Side notes: Tr. II. 36, 37. tain, &c. added. Also Theod. Hist. ii. 6. vid. p 78.r.1. §. 37.

[1] vid. infr p. 80, note p.

he came to the holy Council assembled at Sardica, the Bishops of the East were informed of the circumstance, as we said before, both by letter, and by injunctions conveyed by word of mouth, and were summoned[1] by us to be present. But, being condemned by their own conscience, they had recourse to unbecoming excuses, and set themselves to avoid the enquiry. They demanded that an innocent man should be rejected from our communion, just as if he had been guilty, not considering how unbecoming, or rather how impossible, such a proceeding was. And as for the Reports which were framed in the Mareotis by certain most wicked and most profligate youths[2], to whose hands one would not commit the very lowest office of the ministry, it is certain that they were *ex parte* statements. For neither was our brother the Bishop Athanasius present on the occasion, nor the Presbyter Macarius who was accused by them. And besides, their enquiry, or rather their falsification of facts, was attended by the most disgraceful circumstances. Sometimes heathens, sometimes Catechumens, were examined, not that they might declare what they knew, but that they might assert those falsehoods which they had been taught by others. And when you Presbyters, who were anxious in the absence of your Bishop, desired to be present at the enquiry, in order that you might shew the truth, and disprove falsehood, no regard was paid to you; they would not permit you to be present, but drove you away with insult.

5. Now although their calumnies have been most plainly exposed before all men by these circumstances; yet we found also, on reading the Reports, that that most iniquitous person, Ischyras, who has obtained from them the empty title of Bishop as his reward for the false accusation, had convicted himself of calumny. He declares in the Reports that at the very time when, according to his positive assertions, Macarius entered his cell, he lay there sick, whereas the Eusebians have had the boldness to write that Ischyras was standing up and offering the oblations, when Macarius came in[3].

6. The base and slanderous charge which they next alleged against him, has become well-known to all men. They raised a great outcry, affirming that Athanasius had committed murder, and had destroyed one Arsenius a Meletian

Bishop, whose loss they pretended to deplore with feigned lamentations and untrue tears, and demanded that the body of a living man, as if a dead one, should be given up to them. But their fraud was easily detected: one and all knew that the person was alive, and was numbered among the living[1].

Tr. II. 38, 39.

[1] pp. 26, 47.

7. And when these men, who are ready upon any opportunity, perceived their falsehoods detected, (for Arsenius shewed himself alive, and so proved that he had not been destroyed, and was not dead,) yet they would not rest, but proceeded to other calumnies[2], and to slander Athanasius by a fresh expedient. Well; our brother, dearly beloved, was not confounded, but again in the present case also with great boldness challenged them to the proof, and we too prayed and exhorted them to come to the trial, and if they were able, to establish their charge against him. O great arrogance! O dreadful pride! or rather, if one must say the truth, O evil and guilt-stricken conscience! for this is the view which all men take of it.

[2] vid. supr. 36. infr. §. 87.

8. Wherefore, dearly beloved brethren, we admonish and exhort you, above all things to maintain the right faith of the Catholic Church. You have undergone many severe and grievous trials; many are the insults and injuries which the Catholic Church has suffered, but *he that endureth to the end the same shall be saved.* Wherefore even though they shall still recklessly assail you, let your tribulation be unto you for joy. For such afflictions have a share in martyrdom, and such confessions and tortures as yours will not be without their reward, but ye shall receive the prize from God. Therefore strive above all things in support of the sound faith, and of the innocence of your Bishop and our brother Athanasius. We also have not held our peace, nor been negligent of what concerns your comfort, but have deliberated and done whatsoever the claims of charity demand. We sympathize with our suffering brethren, and their afflictions we consider as our own.

Matt. 10, 22.

9. Accordingly we have written to beseech our most religious and godly Emperors, that their Graces would give orders for the release of those who are still suffering from affliction and oppression, and would command that none of

§. 39.

the magistrates, whose duty it is to attend only to civil causes, give judgment upon Clergy^c, nor henceforward in any way, on pretence of providing for the Churches, attempt any thing against the brethren; but that every one may live, as he prays and desires to do, free from persecution, from violence and fraud, and in quietness and peace may follow the Catholic and Apostolic Faith. As for Gregory, who has the reputation of being illegally ordained by the heretics, and has been sent by them to your city, we wish your unanimity to understand, that he has been degraded by a judgment of the whole sacred Council, although indeed he has never at any time been considered to be Bishop at all. Wherefore receive gladly your Bishop Athanasius, for to this end we have dismissed him in peace. And we exhort all those who either through fear, or through the intrigues of certain persons, have held communion with Gregory, that now being admonished, exhorted, and persuaded by us, they withdraw from that his accursed communion, and straight-way unite themselves to the Catholic Church.

§. 40.

10. Forasmuch as we have learnt that Aphthonius, Athanasius the son of Capito, Paul, and Plutio, our fellow Presbyters[1], have also suffered from the machinations of the Eusebians, so that some of them have had trial of exile, and others have fled on peril of their lives, we have in consequence thought it necessary to make this known unto you, that you may understand that we have received and acquitted them also, being aware that whatever has been done by the Eusebians against the Orthodox has tended to the glory and commendation of those who have been attacked by them. It were fitting that your Bishop and our brother Athanasius should make this known to you respecting them, to his own respecting his own; but as for more abundant testimony he wished the holy Council also to write to you, we deferred not to do so, but hastened to signify this unto you, that you may receive them as we have done, for they also are deserving of praise, because through their piety towards Christ they have been thought worthy to endure violence at the hands of the heretics.

---

^c vid. Bingham Antiqu. v 2. §. 5. &c. Gieseler Eccl. Hist. vol 1 p 242 Bassi. Biblioth. Jur. t. 1. p. 276. Bellarm. de Cleric 28.

11. What decrees have been past by the holy Council against those who are at the head of the Arian heresy, and have offended against you, and the rest of the Churches, you will learn from the subjoined documents[1]. We have sent them to you, that you may understand from them that the Catholic Church will not overlook those who offend against her.

Tr. II. 40, 41.

[1] vid. Encycl. Letter, infr. p. 69.

12. *Letter of the Council of Sardica to the Bishops of Egypt and Libya.*

The holy Council, by the grace of God assembled at Sardica, to the Bishops of Egypt and Libya, their fellow ministers and dearly beloved brethren, sends health in the Lord.

We were not ignorant[d], but the fact was well known to us, even before we received the letters of your piety, that the supporters of the abominated heresy of the Arians were practising many dangerous machinations, rather to the destruction of their own souls, than to the injury of the Church. For this has ever been the object of their craft and villainy: this is the deadly design in which they have been continually engaged, viz. how they may best expel from their places and persecute all who are to be found any where of orthodox sentiments, and maintaining the doctrine of the Catholic Church, which was delivered to them from the Fathers. Against some they have laid false accusations; others they have driven into banishment; others they have destroyed by the punishments inflicted on them. Thus also they endeavoured by violence and tyranny to surprise the innocence of our brother and fellow Bishop Athanasius, and therefore conducted their enquiry into his case without any scrupulous care, without any faith, without any sort of justice. Accordingly, having no confidence in the part they had played on that occasion, nor yet in the reports they had circulated against him, but perceiving that they were unable to produce any certain evidence respecting them, when they came to the city of Sardica, they were unwilling to meet the Council of all the holy Bishops. From this it became evident that the decision of our brother and fellow Bishop

§. 41.

---

d It will be observed that this Letter is nearly a transcript of the foregoing It was first printed in the Benedictine Edition.

Julius was a just one; for after cautious deliberation and care he had decided, that we ought not to hesitate at all about holding communion with our brother Athanasius. For he had the credible testimony of eighty Bishops, and was also able to advance this fair argument in his support, that by the mere means of our dearly beloved brethren his own Presbyters, and by correspondence, he had defeated the designs of the Eusebians, who relied more upon violence, than upon a judicial enquiry.

13. Wherefore all the Bishops from all parts determined upon holding communion with Athanasius on the ground that he was innocent And let your charity also observe, that when he came to the holy Council assembled at Sardica, the Bishops of the East were informed of the circumstance, as we said before, both by letter, and by injunctions conveyed by word of mouth, and were invited by us to be present. But, being condemned by their own conscience, they had recourse to unbecoming excuses, and began to avoid the enquiry. They demanded that an innocent man should be rejected from our communion, just as if he had been guilty, not considering how unbecoming, or rather how impossible, such a proceeding was. And as for the reports which were framed in the Mareotis by certain most wicked and abandoned youths, to whose hands one would not commit the very lowest office of the ministry, it is certain that they were *ex parte* statements. For neither was our brother the Bishop Athanasius present on the occasion, nor the Presbyter Macarius, who was accused by them. And besides, their enquiry, or rather their falsification of facts, was attended by the most disgraceful circumstances. Sometimes Heathens, sometimes Catechumens, were examined, not that they might declare what they knew, but that they might assert those falsehoods which they had been taught by others. And when you Presbyters, who were anxious in the absence of your Bishop, desired to be present at the enquiry, in order that you might shew the truth, and disprove falsehood, no regard was paid to you; they would not permit you to be present, but drove you away with insult.

14. Now although their calumnies have been most plainly exposed before all men by these circumstances; yet we

found also, on reading the Reports, that that most iniquitous person Ischyras, who has obtained from them the empty title of Bishop as his reward for the false accusation, had convicted himself of calumny. He declares in the Reports, that at the very time when, according to his positive assertions, Macarius entered his cell, he lay there sick; whereas the Eusebians have had the boldness to write that Ischyras was standing up and offering the oblations, when Macarius came in.

15. The base and slanderous charge which they next alleged against him has become well known unto all men. They raised a great outcry, affirming that Athanasius had committed murder, and destroyed one Arsenius a Meletian Bishop, whose loss they pretended to deplore with feigned lamentations, and untrue tears, and demanded that the body of a living man, as if a dead one, should be given up to them. But their fraud was easily detected; one and all knew that the person was alive, and was numbered among the living

16. And when these men, who are ready upon any opportunity, perceived their falsehood detected, (for Arsenius shewed himself alive, and so proved that he had not been destroyed, and was not dead,) yet they would not rest, but proceeded to add other to their former calumnies, and to slander Athanasius by a fresh expedient. Well: our brother, dearly beloved, was not confounded, but again in the present case also with great boldness challenged them to the proof, and we too prayed and exhorted them to come to the trial, and if they were able, to establish their charge against him. O great arrogance! O dreadful pride! or rather, if one must say the truth, O evil and guilt-stricken conscience! for this is the view which all men take of it.

17. Wherefore, dearly beloved brethren, we admonish and exhort you, above all things, to maintain the right faith of the Catholic Church. You have undergone many severe and grievous trials; many are the insults and injuries which the Catholic Church has suffered, but *he that endureth to the end, the same shall be saved.* Wherefore, even though they shall still recklessly assail you, let your tribulation be unto you for joy. For such afflictions have a share in martyrdom, and such confessions and tortures as yours will not be with-

Tr. II. 41, 42

§. 42.

Mat. 10, 22.

out their reward, but ye shall receive the prize from God. Therefore, strive above all things in support of the sound Faith, and of the innocence of your Bishop and our brother Athanasius. We also have not held our peace, nor been negligent of what concerns your comfort, but have deliberated and done whatever the claims of charity demand. We sympathize with our suffering brethren, and their afflictions we consider as our own, and have mingled our tears with yours. And you, brethren, are not the only persons who have suffered: many others also of our brethren in ministry have come hither, bitterly lamenting these things.

18. Accordingly, we have written to beseech our most religious and godly Emperors, that their Graces would give orders for the release of those who are still suffering from affliction and oppression, and would command that none of the magistrates, whose duty it is to attend only to civil causes, give judgment upon Clergy, nor henceforward in any way, on pretence of providing for the Churches, attempt any thing against the brethren, but that every one may live, as he prays and desires to do, free from persecution, from violence and fraud, and in quietness and peace may follow the Catholic and Apostolic Faith. As for Gregory who has the reputation of being illegally ordained by the heretics, and who has been sent by them to your city, we wish your unanimity to understand, that he has been degraded by the judgment of the whole sacred Council, although indeed he has never at any time been considered to be a Bishop at all. Wherefore receive gladly your Bishop Athanasius; for to this end we have dismissed him in peace. And we exhort all those, who either through fear, or through the intrigues of certain persons, have held communion with Gregory, that being now admonished, exhorted, and persuaded by us, they withdraw from his accursed communion, and straightway unite themselves to the Catholic Church.

19. What decrees have been passed by the holy Council against Theodorus, Narcissus, Stephanus, Acacius, Menophantus, Ursacius, Valens, and George[¹], who are the heads of the Arian heresy, and have offended against you and the rest of the Churches, you will learn from the subjoined documents. We have sent them to you, that your piety may

assent to our decisions, and that you may understand from them, that the Catholic Church will not overlook those who offend against her.

Tr. II. 43, 44.

20. *Encyclical Letter of the Council of Sardica.*

The holy Council[1], by the grace of God, assembled at Sardica, to their dearly beloved brethren, the Bishops and fellow-Ministers of the Catholic Church every where, sends health in the Lord.

[1] vid. Theod. Hist. ii. 6. Hil. Fragm. ii.

The Arian fanatics have dared repeatedly to attack the servants of God, who maintain the right faith; they attempted to substitute a spurious doctrine, and to drive out the orthodox; and at last they made so violent an assault against the Faith, that it became known to the piety of our most religious Emperors. Accordingly, the grace of God assisting them, our most religious Emperors have themselves assembled us together out of different provinces and cities, and have permitted this holy Council to be held in the city of Sardica; to the end that all dissension may be done away, and all false doctrine being driven from us, Christian godliness may alone be maintained by all men. The Bishops of the East also attended, being exhorted to do so by the most religious Emperors, chiefly on account of the reports they have so often circulated concerning our dearly beloved brethren and fellow-ministers Athanasius Bishop of Alexandria, and Marcellus Bishop of Ancyro-Galatia. Their calumnies have probably already reached you, and perhaps they have attempted to disturb your ears, that you may be induced to believe their charges against those innocent men, and that they may obliterate from your minds any suspicions respecting their own wicked heresy. But they have not been permitted to effect this to any great extent; for the Lord is the Defender of His Churches, who endured death for their sakes and for us all, and provided access to heaven for us all through Himself. When therefore the Eusebians wrote long ago to Julius our brother and Bishop of the Church of the Romans, against our fore-mentioned brethren, that is to say, Athanasius, Marcellus, and Asclepas[e], the Bishops from the

§. 44.

[e] Asclepas, or Asclepius of Gaza, Epiph. Hær. 69. 4. was one of the Nicene Fathers, and according to Theod. Hist. i. 27. was at the Council of Tyre, which

other parts wrote also, testifying to the innocence of our fellow-minister Athanasius, and declaring that the representations of the Eusebians were nothing else but mere falsehood and calumny.

21. And indeed their calumnies were clearly proved by the fact that, when they were called[1] to a Council by our dearly beloved fellow-minister Julius, they would not come, and also by what was written to them by Julius himself For had they had confidence in the measures and the acts in which they were engaged against our brethren, they would have come. And besides, they gave a still more evident proof of their conspiracy by their conduct in this great and holy Council. For when they arrived at the city of Sardica, and saw our brethren Athanasius, Marcellus, Asclepas, and the rest, they were afraid to come to a trial, and though they were repeatedly invited to attend, they would not obey the summons. Although all we Bishops met together, and above all that man of an happy old age, Hosius, one who on account of his age, his confession, and the many labours he has undergone, is worthy of all reverence; and although we waited and besought them to come to the trial, that in the presence of our fellow-ministers they might establish the truth of those charges which they had circulated and written against them in their absence; yet they would not come, when they were thus called, as we said before, thus giving proof of their calumnies, and almost proclaiming to the world by this their refusal, the plot and conspiracy in which they have been engaged. They who are confident of the truth of their assertions are able to make them good against their opponents face to face. But as they would not meet us, we think that no one can now doubt, however they may again have recourse to their bad practices, that they possess no proof against our brethren, but calumniate them in their absence, while they avoid their presence.

[1] κληθίν-τας

Athan also attended, but only by compulsion. According to the Eusebians at Philippopolis, they had deposed him about 330, if the Council of Sardica was held 347. They state, however, at the same time, that he had been condemned by Athanasius and Marcellus. vid. Hilar. Fragm. iii. 13. Sozomen, Hist iii 8. says that they deposed him on the charge of having overturned an altar; and, after Athan. infr. §. 47. that he was acquitted at Sardica on the ground that Eusebius of Cæsarea and others had reinstated him in his see, (before 339.) There is mention of a Church built by him in Gaza, ap. Bolland. Febr. 26. Vit. S. Porphyr. n 20. p. 648.

22. They fled, dearly beloved brethren, not only on account of the calumnies they had uttered, but because they saw that those had come who had various charges to advance against them. For chains and iron were brought forward which they had used; persons appeared who had returned from banishment, there came also our brethren, kinsmen of those who were still detained in exile, and friends of such as had perished through their means. And what was the most weighty ground of accusation, Bishops were present, one [f] of whom brought forward the iron and the chains which they had caused him to wear, and others testified to the deaths which had been brought about by their calumnies. For they had proceeded to such a pitch of madness, as even to attempt to destroy Bishops; and would have destroyed them, had they not escaped their hands. Our fellow-minister, Theodulus of blessed memory [g], died during his flight from their false accusations, orders having been given in consequence of these to put him to death. Others also exhibited sword-wounds; and others complained that they had been exposed to the pains of hunger through their means. Nor were they ordinary persons who testified to these things, but whole Churches, in whose behalf legates appeared [h], and told us of soldiers sword in hand, of multitudes armed with clubs, of the threats of judges, of the use of forged letters For there were read certain forged letters of Theognius against our fellow-ministers Athanasius, Marcellus, and Asclepas, written with the design of exasperating the Emperors against them; and those who had then been Deacons of Theognius proved the fact In addition to these things, we heard of virgins stripped naked, Churches

---

[f] Perhaps Lucius of Hadrianople, says Montfaucon, referring to Apol. de Fug §. 3. vid. also Hist Arian 19

[g] Theodulus, Bishop of Trajanopolis in Thrace, who is here spoken of as deceased, seems to have suffered this persecution from the Eusebians upon their retreat from Sardica, vid. Athan. Hist Arian § 19. We must suppose then with Montfaucon, that the Council, from whom this letter proceeds, sat some considerable time after that retreat, and that the proceedings spoken of took place in the interval. Socrates, however, makes Theodulus survive Constans, who died 350. Hist ii. 26.

[h] The usual proceeding of the Arians was to retort upon the Catholics the charges which they brought against them, supr. p. 54, note p. Accordingly, in their Encyclical from Philippopolis, they say that " a vast multitude had congregated at Sardica, of wicked and abandoned persons, from Constantinople and Alexandria, who lay under charges of murder, blood, slaughter, robbery, plunder, spoiling, and all nameless sacrileges and crimes, who had broken altars, burnt Churches, ransacked private houses, &c. &c. Hil. Fragm iii 19.

APOL. AG. AR.

burnt, ministers in custody, and all for no other end, but only for the sake of the accursed heresy of the Arian fanatics, whose communion whoso refused was forced to suffer these things.

23. When they perceived then how matters lay, they were in a strait what course to choose. They were ashamed to confess all that they had done, but were unable to conceal it any longer. They therefore came to the city of Sardica, that by their appearance there they might seem to remove suspicion from themselves of the guilt of such things. But when they saw those whom they had calumniated, and those who had suffered at their hands; when they had before their eyes their accusers and the proofs of their guilt, they were unwilling to come forward, though invited by our fellow-ministers Athanasius, Marcellus, and Asclepas, who with great freedom complained of their conduct, and urged and challenged them to the trial, promising not only to refute their calumnies, but also to bring proof of the offences which they had committed against their Churches. But they were seized with such terrors of conscience, that they fled; and in doing so they exposed their own calumnies, and confessed by running away the crimes of which they had been guilty.

§. 46.

24. But although their malice and their calumnies have been plainly manifested on this as well as on former occasions, yet that they may not devise means of practising a further mischief in consequence of their flight, we have considered it advisable to examine the part they have played according to the principles of truth[1]; this has been our purpose, and we have found them calumniators by their acts, and authors of nothing else than a plot against our brethren in ministry. For Arsenius, who they said had been murdered by Athanasius, is still alive, and is numbered among the living; from which we may infer that the reports they have circulated on other subjects are fabrications also. And whereas they spread abroad a rumour concerning a chalice, which they said had been broken by Macarius the Presbyter of Athanasius, those who came from Alexandria, the Mareotis, and the other parts, testified that nothing of the kind had taken place. And the Egyptian Bishops[2] who wrote to Julius our brother in ministry, positively affirmed that there

[1] supr p. 59. ref. 2. Orat 1. O. T. p. 227 init.

[2] p. 30.

did not exist among them even any suspicion whatever of such a thing. Tʀ. II. 46, 47.

25. Moreover, the Reports, which they say they have to produce against him, are, as is notorious, *ex parte* statements; and even in the formation of these very Reports, Heathens and Catechumens were examined; one of whom, a Catechumen, said[1] in his examination that he was present in the room, when Macarius broke in upon them; and another declared, that Ischyras of whom they speak so much, lay sick in his cell at the time; from which it appears that the Mysteries were never celebrated at all, because Catechumens were present, and also that Ischyras was not there, but was lying sick on his bed. Besides, this wicked wretch Ischyras, who has falsely asserted, as he was convicted of doing, that Athanasius had burnt some of the sacred books, has himself confessed that he was sick, and was lying in his bed when Macarius came; from which it is plain that he is a slanderer. Nevertheless, as a reward for these his calumnies, they have given to this very Ischyras the title of Bishop, although he has never been even a Presbyter. For two Presbyters, who were once associated with Meletius, but were afterwards received by Alexander, Bishop of Alexandria, of blessed memory, and are now with Athanasius, appeared before the Council, and testified that he was not even a Presbyter of Meletius, and that Meletius never had either Church or Minister in the Mareotis. And yet this man, who has never been even a Presbyter, they have now brought forward as a Bishop, that by this name they may have a means of overpowering those who are within hearing his calumnies. [1] pp. 48, 49.

26 The book of our brother Marcellus was also read, by which the fraud of the Eusebians were plainly discovered. For what Marcellus had advanced by way of enquiry[2], they falsely represented as his professed opinion; but when the subsequent parts of the book were read, and the parts preceding these queries, his faith was found to be correct. He had never pretended, as they positively affirmed[3], that the word of God had His beginning from holy Mary, nor that His kingdom had an end; on the contrary he had written that His kingdom was both without beginning and without end. §. 47. [2] vid. de Decr. O. T. vol.8. p. 44, e. [3] de Syn. O. T. p. 110, note r.

APOL. Our brother Asclepas also produced Reports which had been
AG. AR. drawn up at Antioch in the presence of his accusers and
Eusebius of Cæsarea, and proved that he was innocent by
¹p.70.e. the sentence of the Bishops who judged his cause¹. They
had good reason therefore, dearly beloved brethren, for
disobeying our frequent summons, and for deserting the
Council. They were driven to this by their own consciences;
but their flight only confirmed the proof of their calumnies,
and caused those things to be believed against them, which
their accusers, who were present, were asserting and arguing.
But besides all these things, they had not only received
those who were formerly degraded and ejected on account of
the Arian heresy, but had even promoted them to a higher
station, advancing Deacons to the Presbytery, and of Presbyters making Bishops, for no other end, but that they might
disseminate and spread abroad impiety, and corrupt the
orthodox faith.

§. 48. 27. Their present leaders are, after Eusebius, Theodorus of
Heraclea, Narcissus of Neronias in Cilicia, Stephanus of
Antioch, George of Laodicea, Acacius of Cæsarea in Palestine, Menophantus of Ephesus in Asia, Ursacius of Singi-
donum in Mysia, and Valens of Mursia in Pannonia¹. These
men would not permit those who came with them from the
East to meet the holy Council, nor even to approach the Church
of God; but as they were coming to Sardica, they held Councils
in various places by themselves, and made an engagement under
threats, that when they came to Sardica, they would not at
all appear at the trial, nor attend the assembling of the holy
Council, but simply coming, and making known their arrival
as a matter of form, would speedily take to flight. This we have
been able to ascertain from our brethren in ministry, Macarius
of Palestine and Asterius of Arabiaᵏ, who after coming in their
company, separated themselves from their unbelief. These
came to the holy Council, and complained of the violence they
had suffered, and said that no orthodox act proceeded from
them; adding that there were many among them who adhered

---

¹ Vid. supr. p. 31, note m. p. 60. ref. 4. &c. vol 8 p. 74, note d. About Stephanus, vid infr. Hist. Arian §. 20.
ᵏ These two Bishops were soon after the Council banished by Eusebian influence into upper Libya, where they suffered extreme ill usage. vid. infr. Hist. Arian. §. 18.

to the true doctrine, but were prevented by those men from coming hither, by means of the threats and promises which they held out to those who wished to separate from them. On this account it was that they were so anxious that all should abide in one dwelling, and would not suffer them to be by themselves even for the shortest space of time.

TR. II. 48, 49.

28. Since then it became us not to hold our peace, nor to pass over unnoticed their calumnies, imprisonments, murders, scourgings, conspiracies by means of forged letters, outrages, stripping of the virgins, banishments, destruction of the Churches, burnings, translations from small cities to larger dioceses, and above all, the rising of the accursed Arian heresy by their means against the orthodox faith; we have therefore pronounced our dearly beloved brethren and fellow-ministers Athanasius, Marcellus, and Asclepas, and those who minister to the Lord with them, to be innocent and clear of offence, and have written to the diocese of each, that the people of each Church may know the innocence of their own Bishop, and may esteem him as their Bishop and expect his coming.

§. 49.

29. And as for those who like wolves[1] have invaded their Churches, Gregory at Alexandria, Basil at Ancyra, and Quintianus at Gaza, let them neither give them the title of Bishop, nor hold any communion at all with them, nor receive letters[2] from them, nor write to them. And for Theodorus, Narcissus, Acacius, Stephanus, Ursacius, Valens, Menophantus, and George, although the last from fear did not come from the East, yet because he was degraded by the blessed Alexander, and because both he and the others were connected with the Arian fanaticism, as well as on account of the charges which he against them, the holy Council has unanimously deposed them from the Episcopate, and we have decided that they not only are not Bishops, but that they are unworthy of holding communion with the faithful.

[1] vid. Acts 20, 29.

[2] p 8. ref. 3.

30. For they who separate the Son and alienate the Word from the Father, ought themselves to be separated from the Catholic Church and to be alien from the Christian name. Let them therefore be anathema to you, because they have adulterated the word of truth. It is an Apostolic injunction, *If any man preach any other Gospel unto you than that ye have* Gal.1,9.

APOL. AG. AR. *received, let him be accursed.* Charge your people that no one hold communion with them, for there is no *communion of light with darkness;* put away from you all these, for 2 Cor. 6, 14. 15. there is no *concord of Christ with Belial.* And take heed, dearly beloved, that ye neither write to them, nor receive letters from them; but desire rather, brethren and fellow-ministers, as being present in spirit with our Council, to assent to our judgments by your subscriptions[1], to the end that concord may be preserved by all our fellow-ministers every where. May Divine Providence protect and keep you, dearly beloved brethren, in sanctification and joy.

I, Hosius, Bishop, have subscribed this, and all the rest likewise.

31. This is the letter which the Council of Sardica sent to those who were unable to attend, and they on the other hand gave their judgment in accordance; and the following are the names both of those Bishops who subscribed in the Council, and of the others also

§. 50. Hosius of Spain[m], Julius of Rome by his Presbyters Archidamus and Philoxenus, Protogenes of Sardica, Gaudentius, Macedonius, Severus[1], Prætextatus[2], Ursicius[3], Lucillus[4], Eugenius, Vitalius, Calepodius, Florentius[5], Bassus, Vincentius[6], Stercorius, Palladius, Domitianus, Chalbis, Gerontius, Protasius[7], Eulogus, Porphyrius[8], Dioscorus, Zozimus, Januarius, Zozimus, Alexander, Eutychius, Socrates, Diodorus, Martyrius, Eutherius, Eucarpus, Athenodorus, Irenæus, Julianus, Alypius, Jonas, Aetius[9], Restitutus, Marcellinus, Aprianus, Vitalius, Valens, Hermogenes, Castus, Domitianus, Fortunatius[10], Marcus, Annianus, Heliodorus, Musæus, Asterius, Paregorius,

[1] of Ravenna.
[2] of Barcelona.
[3] of Brescia.
[4] of Verona.
[5] of Merida.
[6] of Capua.
[7] of Milan.
[8] of Philippi.
[9] of Thessalonica.
[10] of Aquilea.

[1] In like manner the Council of Chalcedon was confirmed by as many as 470 subscriptions, according to Ephrem, (Phot. Bibl. p. 801) by 1600 according to Eulogius, (ibid. p. 877.) i. e. of Bishops, Archimandrites, &c.

[m] Hosius is called by Athan. the father and the president of the Council. Hist. Arian. 15. 16. Roman controversialists here explain why Hosius does not sign himself as the Pope's legate, De Marc. Concord v. 4. Alber. Dissert ix and Protestants why his legates rank before all the other Bishops, even before Protogenes, Bishop of the place. Basnage, Ann. 347. 5 Febronius considers that Hosius signed here and at Nicæa, as a sort of representative of the civil, and the Legates of the ecclesiastical supremacy. de Stat. Eccl. vi. 4. And so Thomassin, " Imperator velut exterior Episcopus: præfuit autem summus Pontifex, ut Episcopus interior." Dissert. in Conc x 14. The Pope never attended in person the Eastern Councils St. Leo excuses himself on the plea of its being against usage. Epp. 37. and 93.

of the Council of Sardica. 77

Plutarchus, Hymeræus, Athanasius, Lucius, Amantius, Arius, Tr. II. Asclepius, Dionysius, Maximus[1], Tryphon, Alexander, Antigonus, Ælianus, Petrus, Symphorus, Muscnius, Eutychus, Philologius, Spudasius, Zozimus, Patricius, Adolius, Sapricius. [50 of Lucca.]

From Gaul the following; Maximianus[2], Verissimus[3], Victurus, Valentinus[4], Desiderius, Eulogius, Sarbatius, Dyscolius, Severinus[5], Satyrus, Martinus, Paulus, Optatianus, Nicasius, Victor[6], Sempronius, Valerinus, Pacatus, Jesses, Ariston, Simplicius, Metianus, Amantus[7], Amilhanus, Justinianus, Victorinus[8], Saturnilus, Abundantius, Donatianus, Maximus. [2 of Treves. 3 of Lyons. 4 of Arles. 5 of Sens. 6 of Worms. 7 of Strasbourgh.]

From Africa; Nessus, Gratus[9], Megasius, Coldæus, Rogatianus, Consortius, Rufinus, Manninus, Cessilianus, Herennianus, Marianus, Valerius, Dynamius, Myzonius, Justus, Celestinus, Cyprianus, Victor, Honoratus, Marinus, Pantagathus, Felix, Bandius, Liber, Capito, Minervalis, Cosmus, Victor, Hesperio, Felix, Severianus, Optantius, Hesperus, Fidentius, Salustius, Paschasius. [8 of Paris. 9 of Carthage.]

From Egypt, Liburnius, Amantius, Felix, Ischyrammon, Romulus, Tiberinus, Consortius, Heraclides, Fortunatius, Dioscorus, Fortunatianus, Bastamon, Datyllus, Andreas, Serenus, Arius, Theodorus, Evagoras, Helias, Timotheus, Orion, Andronicus, Paphnutius, Hermias, Arabion, Psenosiris, Apollonius, Muis, Sarapampon[10], Philo, Philippus, Apollonius, Paphnutius, Paulus, Dioscorus, Nilammon, Serenus, Aquila, Aotas, Harpociation, Isac, Theodorus, Apollos, Ammonianus, Nilus, Heraclius, Arion, Athas, Arsenius, Agathammon, Theon, Apollonius, Helias, Paninuthius, Andragathius, Nemesion, Sarapion, Ammonius, Ammonius, Xenon, Gerontius, Quintus, Leonides, Sempronianus, Philo, Heraclides, Hieracys, Rufus, Pasophius, Macedonius, Apollodorus, Flavianus, Psaes, Syrus, Apphus, Sarapion, Esaias, Paphnutius, Timotheus, Elurion, Gaius, Musæus, Pistus, Heraclammon, Hero, Helias, Anagamphus, Apollonius, Gaius, Philotas, Paulus, Tithoes, Eudæmon, Julius. [10 p. 53, note o. and §. 78.]

Those in the cross roads[n] of Italy are, Probatius, Viator,

[n] οἱ ἐν τῷ κανακλίῳ τῆς Ἰταλίας "Canalis est, non via regia aut militaris, verum via transversa, quæ in regiam seu basilicam influit, quasi æquæ cana-

APOL.
AG. AR.
Facundinus, Joseph, Numedius, Sperantius, Severus, Heraclianus, Faustinus, Antoninus, Heraclius, Vitalius, Felix, Crispinus, Paulianus.

From Cyprus; Auxibius, Photius, Gerasius, Aphrodisius, Irenicus, Nunechius, Athanasius, Macedonius, Triphyllius, Spyridon, Norbanus, Sosicrates.

From Palestine; Maximus, Aetius, Arius, Theodosius, Germanus, Silvanus, Paulus, Claudius, Patricius, Elpidius, Germanus, Eusebius, Zenobius, Paulus, Petrus.

These are the names of those who subscribed to the acts of the Council; but there are very many beside, out of Asia, Phrygia, and Isauria[1], who wrote in my behalf before this Council was held, and whose names, nearly sixty-three in number, may be found in their own letters. They amount altogether to three hundred and forty-four°.

[1] p. 60. r. 9.

lis in alveum." Gothofred. in Cod. Theod. vi. de Curiosis, p. 196. who illustrates the word at length. Du Cange on the contrary, *in voc* explains it of "the high road." Tillemont professes himself unable to give a satisfactory sense to it. vol. viii. p. 685.

° There is great uncertainty what was the actual number of Bishops present at the Council. Athan. Hist. Arian. §. 15. says 170, while Theodoret names 250. Hist. ii. 6. If the Western Bishops, whose signatures are given by Athan. in the text to the number of 163, were all present, it might have been conjectured that he was speaking of the Western only; but he expressly includes the Eastern. In that case, subtracting the 73 or 80 Eusebians, so small a majority of orthodox remains, that it is incredible, considering the notorious dexterity and unscrupulousness of the Eusebians in Synodal meetings, that they should have been obliged to secede. Athan. says, supr §. 1. that the Letter of the Council was signed in all by more than 300. It will be observed, that Athan.'s numbers in the text do not accurately agree with each other. The subscriptions enumerated are 284, to which 63 being added, make a total of 347, not 344.

CHAP. IV.

IMPERIAL AND ECCLESIASTICAL ACTS IN CONSEQUENCE OF THE DECISION OF THE COUNCIL OF SARDICA.

1. WHEN the most religious Emperor Constantius heard of these things, he sent for me, having written privately to his brother Constans of blessed memory, and to me three several times in the following terms.

2. Constantius Victor Augustus to Athanasius.

Our benignant clemency will not suffer you to be any longer tempest-tossed by the wild waves of the sea; for our unwearied piety has not lost sight of you, while you have been bereft of your native home, deprived of your goods, and have been wandering in savage wildernesses. And although I have for a long time deferred expressing by letter the purpose of my mind concerning you, principally because I expected that you would appear before us of your own accord, and would seek a relief of your sufferings; yet forasmuch as fear, it may be, has prevented you from fulfilling your intentions, we have therefore addressed to your fortitude letters full of our bounty, to the end that you may use all speed and without fear present yourself in our presence, thereby to obtain the enjoyment of your wishes, and that, having experience of our grace, you may be restored again to your friends. For this purpose I have besought my Lord and brother Constans Victor Augustus in your behalf, that he would give you permission to come, in order that you may be restored to your country with the consent of us both, receiving this as a pledge of our favour.

3. *The Second Letter.*

Although we made it very plain to you in a former letter that you may without hesitation come to our Court, because

APOL. AG. AR.
¹ Gothof. in Cod Theod. viii 5. p. 507.

we greatly wished to send you home, yet, we have further sent this present letter to your fortitude, to exhort you without any distrust or apprehension, to place yourself in the public conveyances¹, and to hasten to us, that you may enjoy the fulfilment of your wishes.

4. *The Third Letter.*

Our pleasure was, while we abode at Edessa, and your Presbyters were there, that, on one of them being sent to you, you should make haste to come to our Court, in order that you might see our face, and straightway proceed to Alexandria. But as a long period has elapsed since you received letters from us, and you have not yet come, we are therefore desirous to remind you again, that you may endeavour to present yourself before us with all speed, and so may be restored to your country, and obtain the accomplishment of your prayers. And for your fuller information we have sent Achitas the Deacon, from whom you will be able to learn our earnest desires concerning you, and that you may now secure the objects of your prayers.

5. Such was the tenour of the Emperor's letter; on receiving which I went up to Rome to bid farewell to the Church and the Bishop: for I was at Aquileia when it was written. The Church was filled with all joy, and the Bishop Julius rejoiced with me in my return and wrote to the Church ᵖ; and as I passed along, the Bishops of every place sent me on my way in peace. The letter of Julius was as follows.

ᵖ " They acquainted Julius the Bishop of Rome with their case; and he, according to the prerogative (προνόμια) of the Church in Rome, fortified them with letters in which he spoke his mind, and sent them back to the East, restoring each to his own place, and remarking on those who had violently deposed them. They then set out from Rome, and on the strength (θαρροῦντι) of the letters of Bishop Julius, take possession of their Churches." Socr. ii. 15. It must be observed, that in the foregoing sentence Socrates has spoken of "*imperial* Rome." Sozomen says, "Whereas the care of all (κηδεμονίας) pertained to him on account of the dignity of his see, he restored each to his own Church, iii. 8. " I answer," says Barrow, " the Pope did not restore them *judicially*, but *declaratively*, that is, declaring his approbation of their right and innocence, did admit them to communion....Besides, the Pope's proceeding was taxed, and protested against, as irregular;....and, lastly, the restitution of Athanasius and the other Bishops had no complete effect, till it was confirmed by the synod of Sardica, backed by the imperial authority." Suprem. p. 360. ed. 1836.

Letter of Pope Julius to the Alexandrians.

6. Julius to the Presbyters, Deacons, and people abiding at Alexandria.

<small>Tr. II. 52, 53. §. 52.</small>

I congratulate you, beloved brethren, that you now behold the fruit of your faith before your eyes; for any one may see that such indeed is the case with respect to my brother and fellow-Bishop Athanasius, whom for the innocency of his life, and by reason of your prayers, God hath restored to you again. Wherefore it is easy to perceive, that you have continually offered up to God pure prayers and full of love. Being mindful of the heavenly promises, and of the conversation that leads to them, which you have learnt from the teaching of this my brother, you knew certainly and were persuaded by the right faith that is in you, that he, whom you always had as present in your most pious minds, would not be separated from you for ever. Wherefore there is no need that I should use many words in writing to you; for your faith has already anticipated whatever I could say to you, and has by the grace of God procured the accomplishment of the common prayers of you all. Therefore, I repeat again, I congratulate you, because you have preserved your souls unconquered in the faith; and I also congratulate no less my brother Athanasius, in that, though he has endured many afflictions, he has at no time been forgetful of your love and earnest desires towards him. For although for a season he seemed to be withdrawn from you in body, yet has he continued to live as always present with you in spirit[1].

<small>[1] Athan. here omits a paragraph in his own praise. vid. Socr. ii. 23.</small>

7. Wherefore he returns to you now more illustrious than when he went away from you. Fire tries and purifies the precious metals, gold and silver: but how can one describe the worth of such a man, who, having passed victorious through the perils of so many tribulations, is now restored to you, being pronounced innocent not by my voice only, but by the voice of the whole Council[2]? Receive therefore, dearly beloved brethren, with all godly honour and rejoicing, your Bishop Athanasius, together with those who have been partners with him in so many labours. And rejoice that you have now obtained the fulfilment of your prayers, after that in your salutary writings, you have given meat and drink to your Pastor, who, so to speak, longed and thirsted after your

<small>[2] p. 56, note s. p. 80, note p.</small>

godliness. For while he sojourned in a foreign land, you were his consolation; and you refreshed him during his persecutions by your most faithful minds and spirits. And it delights me now to conceive and figure to my mind the joy of every one of you at his return, and the pious greetings of the multitude, and the glorious festivity of those that run to meet him. What a day will that be to you, when my brother comes back again, and your former sufferings terminate, and his much-prized and desired return inspires you all with an exhilaration of perfect joy! The like joy it is mine to feel in a very great degree, since it has been granted me by God, to be able to make the acquaintance of so eminent a man.

8. It is fitting therefore that I should conclude my letter with a prayer[1]. May Almighty God, and His Son our Lord and Saviour Jesus Christ, afford you continual grace, giving you a reward for the admirable faith which you displayed in your noble confession in behalf of your Bishop, that He may impart unto you and unto them that are with you, both here and hereafter, those better things, which *eye hath not seen, nor ear heard, neither hath entered into the heart of man, the things which God hath prepared for them that love Him*; through our Lord Jesus Christ, through whom to Almighty God be glory for ever and ever Amen. I pray, dearly beloved brethren, for your health and strength in the Lord

§. 54. 9. The Emperor, when I came to him with these letters, received me kindly, and sent me forward to my country and Church, addressing the following to the Bishops, Presbyters, and People.

10 Victor Constantius, Maximus, Augustus, to the Bishops and Presbyters of the Catholic Church.

The most reverend Athanasius has not been deserted by the grace of God, but although for a brief season he was subjected to trials to which human nature is liable, he has obtained from the superintending Providence such an answer to his prayers as was meet, and is restored by the will of the Most High, and by our sentence, at once to his country and to the Church, over which by divine permission he presided.

Wherefore, in accordance with this, it is fitting that it should be provided by our clemency, that all the decrees which have heretofore been passed against those who held communion with him, be now consigned to oblivion, and that all suspicions respecting them be henceforward set at rest, and that an immunity, such as the Clergy who are associated with him formerly enjoyed, be duly confirmed to them. Moreover to our other acts of favour towards him we have thought good to add the following, that all persons of the sacred catalogue[1] should understand, that an assurance of safety is given to all who adhere to him, whether Bishops, or other Clergy. And union with him will be a sufficient guarantee, in the case of any person, of an upright intention. For whoever, acting according to a better judgment and part, shall choose to hold communion with him, we order, in imitation of that Providence which has already gone before, that all such should have the advantage of the grace which by the will of the Most High is now offered to them from us. May God preserve you.

Tr. 11. 54, 55.

[1] vid. Bingh. Antiqu. 1.5.§.10.

11. *The Second Letter.*

Victor Constantius, Maximus, Augustus, to the people of the Catholic Church at Alexandria.

Desiring as we do your welfare in all respects, and knowing that you have for a long time been deprived of episcopal superintendence, we have thought good to send back to you your Bishop Athanasius, a man known to all men for the uprightness that is in him, and for his personal deportment. Receive him, as you are wont to receive every one, in a suitable manner, and, putting him forth as your succour in your prayers to God, endeavour to preserve continually that unanimity and peace according to the order of the Church, which is at the same time becoming in you, and most advantageous for us. For it is not becoming that any dissension or faction should be raised among you, so subversive of the prosperity of our times. We desire that this offence may be altogether removed from you, and we exhort you to continue stedfastly in your accustomed prayers, and to make him, as we said before, your advocate and helper towards God. So that, when this your determination, dearly

§. 55.

beloved, has influenced the prayers of all men, even the heathen who are still addicted to the false worship of idols may eagerly desire to come to the knowledge of our sacred worship.

12. Again therefore we exhort you to continue in these things, and gladly to receive your Bishop, who is sent back to you by the decree of the Most High, and by our desire, and determine to greet him cordially with all your soul and with all your mind. For this is what is both becoming in you, and agreeable to our clemency. In order that all occasion of excitement and sedition may be taken away from those who are maliciously disposed, we have by letter commanded the magistrates who are among you to subject to the vengeance of the law all whom they find to be factious. Wherefore taking into consideration both these things, our desire in accordance with the will of the Most High, and our regard for you and for concord among you, and the punishment that awaits the disorderly, observe such things as are proper and suitable to the order of our sacred religion, and receiving the fore-mentioned Bishop with all reverence and honour, take care to offer up with him your prayers to God, the Father of all, in behalf of yourselves, and for the wellbeing of your whole lives.

§. 56. 13. Having written these letters, he also commanded that the decrees, which he had formerly sent out against me in consequence of the calumnies of the Eusebians, should be abolished, and removed from out the Orders of the Duke and the Prefect of Egypt, and Eusebius the Decurion[1] was sent to withdraw them from the Order-books. His letter on this occasion was as follows.

[1] member of the Curia or Council.

14. Victor, Constantius, Augustus, to Nestorius[2].

(*And in the same terms, to the Governors of Augustamnica, the Thebais, and Libya.*)

[2] Prefect of Egypt, vid p. 5, note d.

Whatever Orders are found to have been passed heretofore, tending to the injury and dishonour of those who hold communion with the Bishop Athanasius, we wish them to be now erased. For we desire that whatever immunities his Clergy possessed before, they should again possess the same. And we wish this our Order to be observed, that when the Bishop Athanasius is restored to his Church, those who hold communion with him may enjoy the immunities which they have always enjoyed, and which the rest of the Clergy enjoy; so that they may have the satisfaction of being on an equal footing with others.

^{Tr. II. 56, 57.}

15. Being thus set forward on my journey, as I passed through Syria, I met with the Bishops of Palestine, who when they had called a Council[1] at Jerusalem, received me courteously, and themselves also sent me on my way in peace, and addressed the following letter to the Church and the Bishops.

§. 57.

[1] Hist. Arian. 25.

16. The Holy Council, assembled at Jerusalem, to the brethren in ministry in Egypt and Libya, and to the Presbyters, Deacons, and People at Alexandria, dearly beloved brethren, and greatly longed for, sends health in the Lord.

We cannot give worthy thanks to the God of all, dearly beloved, for the wonderful things which He has done at all times, and especially at this time with respect to your Church, in restoring to you your pastor and lord[2], and our fellow-minister Athanasius. For who ever hoped that his eyes would see what you are now actually enjoying? Of a truth, your prayers have been heard by the God of all, who cares for His Church, and has looked upon your tears and groans, and has therefore heard your petitions. For ye were as sheep scattered and fainting, not having a shepherd. Wherefore the true Shepherd, who careth for His own sheep, has visited you from heaven, and has restored to you him whom you desire. Behold, we also, being ready to do all things for the peace of the Church, and being prompted by the same affection as yourselves, have saluted him before you; and communicating with you through him, we send you these greetings, and our offering of thanksgiving, that you may know that you are united in one bond of love with him and with us. You are bound to pray also for the piety of our most religious Emperors, who, when they knew your earnest longings after him, and his innocency, determined to restore him to you with all honour. Wherefore receive him with uplifted hands, and take good heed that you offer up due thanksgivings on his behalf to God who has bestowed these blessings upon you; so that you may continually rejoice

[2] κύριον, infr. p. 86.

with God and glorify our Lord, in Christ Jesus our Lord, through whom to the Father be glory for ever. Amen.

17. I have set down here the names of those who subscribed this letter, although I have mentioned them before[1]. They are these; Maximus, Aetius, Arius, Theodorus[2], Germanus, Silvanus, Paulus, Patricius, Elpidius, Germanus, Eusebius, Zenobius, Paulus, Macrinus[3], Petrus, Claudius.

18. When Ursacius and Valens witnessed these proceedings, they forthwith condemned themselves for what they had done, and going up to Rome, confessed their crime, declared themselves penitent, and sought forgiveness[4], addressing the following letters to Julius Bishop of ancient Rome, and to myself. Copies of them were sent to me from Paulinus, Bishop of Tibur[5].

19. *A Translation from the Latin of a Letter[6] to Julius, concerning the recantation of Ursacius and Valens[q].*

Ursacius and Valens to the most blessed Lord[7], Pope Julius.

Whereas it is well known that we have heretofore in letters laid many grievous charges against the Bishop Athanasius, and whereas, when we were corrected by the letters of your Goodness[8], we were unable to render an account of our conduct, by reason of the circumstance which we notified unto you; we do now confess before your Goodness, and in the presence of all the Presbyters our brethren, that all the reports which have heretofore come to your hearing respecting the case of the aforesaid Athanasius, are falsehoods and fabrications, and are utterly inconsistent with his character. Wherefore we earnestly desire communion with the aforesaid Athanasius, especially since your Piety, with your characteristic generosity, has vouchsafed to pardon our

---

q "I have always entertained some doubts," says Gibbon, " concerning the retractation of Ursacius and Valens Their Epistles to Julius Bishop of Rome, and to Athanasius himself, are of so different a cast from each other, that they cannot both be genuine. The one speaks the language of criminals, who confess their guilt and infamy, the other of enemies, who solicit on equal terms an honourable reconciliation." ch xxi. note 118. Surely this is just the difference of tone in which an apology is made to a superior, and to an equal (ἀδελφῷ), except by very generous, or by deeply repentant, persons. Athan.'s account of it, infr. p. 239, r 2. is quite in accordance. It will be observed too that they appear to have made their peace with Rome with the view of being defended by the Pope against Athanasius.

error. But we also declare, that if at any time the Eastern
Bishops, or Athanasius himself, with an evil intent, should
wish to bring us to judgment for this offence, we will not
attend contrary to your judgment and desire. And as for
the heretic Arius and his supporters, who say that once the
Son was not, and that the Son is made of that which was
not, and who deny that Christ is God[1] and the Son of God
before the worlds, we anathematize them both now and for
evermore, as also we set forth in our former declaration at
Milan[2]. We have written this with our own hands, and we
profess again, that we have renounced for ever, as we said
before, the Arian heresy and its authors.

I Ursacius subscribed this my confession in person, and
likewise I Valens.

TR. II.
58.

[1] not in Latin.

[2] A.D. 346, 7, or 8.

20. Ursacius and Valens, Bishops, to their Lord[3] and Brother,
the Bishop Athanasius.

[3] κυρίῳ, vid. infr. p. 95.

Having an opportunity of sending by our brother and
fellow Presbyter Musæus, who is coming to your Charity, we
salute you affectionately, dearly beloved brother, through
him, from Aquileia, and pray you, being as we trust in
health, to read our letter. You will also give us confidence,
if you will return to us an answer in writing. For know that
we are at peace with you, and in communion with the
Church, of which the salutation prefixed to this letter is a
proof. May Divine Providence preserve you, my Lord[4], our
dearly beloved brother!

[4] κυρίε

21. Such were their letters, and such the sentence and the
judgment of the Bishops in my behalf. But in order to
prove that they did not act thus to ingratiate themselves, or
under compulsion[5], in any quarter, I desire, with your permission, to recount the whole matter from the beginning, so that
you may perceive that the Bishops wrote as they did with
upright and just intentions, and that Ursacius and Valens,
though they were slow to do so, at last confessed the truth

[5] p. 15, note f.

CHAP. V.[1]

[1] Second part of Apology.

DOCUMENTS CONNECTED WITH THE CHARGES OF THE MELETIANS AGAINST ST. ATHANASIUS.

§. 59. 1. PETER was Bishop among us before the persecution, and during the course of it he suffered martyrdom. When Meletius, who held the title of Bishop in Egypt, was convicted of many crimes, and among the rest of offering sacrifice to idols, Peter deposed him in a general Council of the Bishops. Whereupon Meletius did not appeal to another Council, or attempt to justify himself before those who should come after, but made a schism, so that they who espoused his cause are even yet called Meletians instead of Christians[2]. He began immediately to revile the Bishops, and made false accusations, first against Peter himself, and after him against Achillas, and after Achillas against Alexander[3] And he thus practised craftily, following the example of Absalom, to the end that, as he was disgraced by his deposition, he might by his calumnies mislead the minds of the simple. While Meletius was thus employed, the Arian heresy arose, and in the Council of Nicæa, when that heresy was anathematized, and the Arians were excommunicated, the Meletians on whatever grounds[r] (for it is not necessary now to mention the reasons of this proceeding) were received into the Church Five months however had not elapsed when the blessed Alexander died, and the Meletians, who ought to have remained quiet, and to have been grateful that they were received on any terms, like dogs unable to forget their vomit, began again to trouble the Churches.

[2] vol viii. p. 180, note f.
[3] ad Ep. Æg. §. 22. supr. p. 29.
vid. 2 Pet 2, 22.

[r] Meletius had the name of Bishop secured to him, but was interdicted from all Episcopal functions Those who had been ordained by him were received to communion and allowed to continue in ministerial duties, on condition that they gave precedence in their own Church or Diocese to those whom Alexander had ordained, and performed no ecclesiastical act without leave of the Catholic Bishop; but when the Catholic Bishop in each place died, they were to be considered capable of succeeding. Athan. speaks more openly against this arrangement infr. § 71. vid. vol. viii. p. 181, note g.

2. Upon learning this, Eusebius, who had the lead in the Arian heresy, sends and bribes the Meletians with large promises, becomes their secret friend, and arranges with them for their assistance on any occasion when he might wish for it. At first he sent to me, urging me to admit the Arians to communion[1], and threatening me in his verbal communications, which he requested me in his letters. And when I refused, declaring that it was not right that those who had invented heresy contrary to the truth, and had been anathematized by the Ecumenical[2] Council, should be admitted to communion, he caused the Emperor also, Constantine, of blessed memory, to write to me, threatening me, in case I should not receive the Arians, with those afflictions, which I have before undergone, and which I am still suffering. The following is a part of his letter. Syncletius and Gaudentius, officers of the palace[3], were the bearers of it.

Tr. II. 59, 60.

[1] *ad Ep. Æg. 19.*

[2] *supr. §. 7. and vol 8. p. 49, note o.*

[3] παλατῖνοι, vid. Apol. ad Const. §. 19.

3. *Part of a Letter from the Emperor Constantine.*

Having therefore knowledge of my will, grant free admission to all who wish to enter into the Church. For if I learn that you have hindered or excluded any who claim to be admitted into communion with the Church, I will immediately send some one who shall depose you by my command, and shall remove you from your place.

4. When upon this I wrote and endeavoured to convince the Emperor, that that anti-Christian[4] heresy had no communion with the Catholic Church, Eusebius forthwith, availing himself of the occasion which he had agreed upon with the Meletians, writes and persuades them to invent some pretext, so that, as they had practised against Peter and Achillas and Alexander, they might also lay a plot for me, and might spread abroad reports to my prejudice. Accordingly, after seeking for a long time, and finding nothing, they at last agree together, with the advice of the Eusebians, and fabricate their first accusation by means of Ision, Eudæmon, and Callinicus[5], respecting the linen vestments[6], to the effect that I had imposed a law upon the Egyptians, and had required its observance of them first. But when certain Presbyters of mine were found to be present, and the Emperor took cognizance of the matter,

§. 60.

[4] χριστομάχῳ, vol. 8. p. 6, note n.

[5] infr. § 71 fin.

[6] στιχάριον, ecclesiastical, vid. Du Cange.

they were condemned, (the Presbyters were Apis and Macarion,) and the Emperor wrote, condemning Ision, and ordering me to appear before him. His letters were as follows[1]. * * *

APOL. AG. AR

[1] they are lost.

5. Eusebius, having intelligence of this, persuades them to wait; and when I arrive, they next accuse Macarius of breaking the chalice, and bring against me the most heinous accusation possible, viz. that, being an enemy of the Emperor, I had sent a purse of gold to one Philamenus. The Emperor therefore heard us on this charge also in suburb Psammathia[2], when they, as usual, were condemned, and driven from the presence; and, as I returned, he wrote the following letter to the people.

[2] suburb of Nicomedia, infr. §. 65.

6. Constantine Maximus, Augustus, to the people of the Catholic Church at Alexandria

§. 61. Dearly beloved brethren, I greet you well, calling upon God, who is the chief witness of my good-will towards you, and on the Only-begotten, the Author of our Law, who is Sovereign over the lives of all men, and who hates dissensions. But what shall I say to you? That I am in good health? Nay, but I should be able to enjoy better health and strength, if you were possessed with mutual love one towards another, and had rid yourselves of your enmities, through which, in consequence of the storms excited by contentious men, we have left the haven of brotherly love. Alas! what perverseness is this! What evil consequences are produced every day by the tumult of envy which has been stirred up among you! Hence it is that an evil character attaches to the people of God. Whither has the faith of righteousness departed? For we are so involved in the mists of darkness, not only through manifold errors, but through the faults of ungrateful men, that we bear with those who favour folly, and though we are aware of them, take no heed of those who beat down goodness and truth. What strange inconsistency is this! We do not convict our enemies, but we follow the example of robbery which they set us, whereby the most pernicious errors, finding no one to oppose them, easily, if I may so speak, make a way for themselves. Is there no understanding among us, for the credit of our common nature, since we are thus neglectful of T<small>R</small>. II. the injunctions of the Law? 61, 62.

7. But some one will say, that that mutual love which nature prompts is exercised among us. But, I ask, how is it that we who have the law of God for our guide, in addition to the light of nature, thus tolerate the disturbances and disorders raised by our enemies, who set every thing in a flame, as it were, with firebrands? How is it, that having eyes, we see not, neither understand, though we are surrounded by the intelligence of the law? What a stupor has seized upon our senses, that we are thus neglectful of ourselves, although God admonishes us of these things! Is it not an intolerable calamity? and ought we not to esteem such men as our enemies, and not the household and people of God? For they are infuriated against us, desperate as they are: they lay grievous crimes to our charge, and persecute us as enemies.

8. And I would have you yourselves to consider with what §. 62 exceeding madness they do this. The foolish men carry their maliciousness at their tongues' end. They carry about with them a sort of sullen anger, so that, by way of retaliation, they smite one another, and give us a share in the punishment which they inflict upon themselves. The good teacher is accounted an enemy, while he who clothes himself with the vice of envy, contrary to all justice makes his gain of the gentle temper of the people; he ravages, and consumes, he decks himself out, and recommends himself with false praises; he subverts the truth, and corrupts the faith, until he finds out a hole and hiding place for his conscience. Thus their very perverseness makes them wretched, while they impudently prefer themselves to places of honour, however unworthy they may be Ah! what a mischief is this! they say, " Such an one is too old, such an one is a mere boy; the office belongs to me, it is due to me, since it is taken away from him. I will gain over all men to my side, and then I will endeavour with my power to ruin him." Plain indeed is this proclamation of their madness to all the world, the sight of companies, and gatherings, and rowers under command[1] in their offensive cabals. Alas! [1] ἀρχαιρεσίαν what preposterous conduct is ours, if I may say it! Do they make an exhibition of their folly in the Church of God?

APOL. AG. AR.

And are they not yet ashamed of themselves? Do they not yet blame themselves? Are they not smitten in their consciences, so that they now at length shew that they entertain a proper sense of their deceit and contentiousness? Theirs is the mere force of envy, supported by those baneful influences which naturally belong to it. But those wretches have no power against your Bishop. Believe me, brethren, their endeavours will have no other effect than this, after they have worn down our days, to leave to themselves no place of repentance in this life

9. Wherefore I beseech you, lend help to yourselves; receive kindly our love, and with all your strength drive away those who desire to obliterate from among us the grace of unanimity; and looking unto God, love one another. I received graciously your Bishop Athanasius, and addressed him in such a manner, as being persuaded that he was a man of God. It is for you to understand these things, not for me to judge of them. I thought it becoming that the most Reverend Athanasius himself should convey my salutation to you, knowing his kind care of you, which, in a manner worthy of that peaceable faith which I myself profess, is continually engaged in the good work of declaring saving knowledge, and will be furnished with a word of exhortation for you. May God preserve you, dearly beloved brethren

Such was the letter of Constantine.

§. 63. 10. After these occurrences the Meletians remained quiet for some time, but afterwards shewed their hostility again, and contrived the following plot, with the aim of pleasing those who had hired their services. The Mareotis is a region of Alexandria, in which Meletius was not able to make a schism. Now while the Churches still existed within their appointed limits, and all the Presbyters had congregations in them, and while the people were living in peace, a certain person named Ischyras[1], who was not a Clergyman, but depraved in his habits, endeavoured to lead astray the people of his own village, declaring himself to be a Clergyman. Upon learning this, the Presbyter of the place, informed me of it when I was going through my visitation of the Churches, and I sent Macarius the Presbyter with him to summon Ischyras. They found him sick and lying in his cell, and

[1] supr. pp. 30. 48. 62.

charged his father to admonish his son not to continue any such practices as had been reported against him. But when he recovered from his sickness, being prevented by his friends and his father from pursuing the same course, he fled over to the Meletians, and they communicate with the Eusebians, and at last that calumny is invented by them, that Macarius had broken a chalice, and that a certain Bishop named Arsenius had been murdered by me. Arsenius they placed in concealment, in order that he might seem taken off, when he did not make his appearance; and they carried about a hand pretending that he had been cut to pieces. As for Ischyras, whom they did not even know, they began to spread a report that he was a Presbyter, in order that what he said about the chalice might mislead the people. Ischyras, however, being censured by his friends, came to me weeping, and said that no such thing as they had reported had been done by Macarius, and that himself had been suborned by the Meletians to invent this calumny. And he wrote the following letter

11. To the Blessed Pope[1] Athanasius, Ischyras sends health in the Lord.

As when I came to you, my Lord[2] Bishop, desiring to be received into the Church, you reproved me for what I formerly said, as though I had proceeded to such lengths of my own free choice, I therefore submit to you this my apology in writing, in order that you may understand, that violence was used towards me, and blows inflicted on me by Isaac and Heraclides, and Isaac of Letopolis, and those of their party. And I declare, and take God as my witness in this matter, that of none of the things which they have stated, do I know you to be guilty. For no breaking of a chalice or overturning of the holy Table ever took place, but they compelled me by their violent usage to assert all this. And this defence I make and submit to you in writing, desiring and claiming for myself to be admitted among the members of your congregation. I pray that you may have health in the Lord.

12. I submit this my handwriting to you the Bishop Athanasius in the presence of the Presbyters, Ammonias of Dicella,

Heraclius of Phascus, Boccon of Chenebris, Achillas of Myrsine, Didymus of Taphosiris, and Justus from Bomotheus; and of the Deacons, Paul, Peter, and Olympius, of Alexandria, and Ammonius, Pistus, Demetrius, and Gaius, of the Mareotis.

§. 65.   13. Notwithstanding this statement of Ischyras, they again spread abroad the same charges against me every where, and also reported them to the Emperor Constantine. He had heard before of the affair of the chalice in Psammathia[1], when I was there, and had detected the falsehood of my enemies. But now he wrote to Antioch to Dalmatius[s] the Censor, requiring him to institute a judicial enquiry respecting the murder. Accordingly the Censor sent me notice to prepare for my defence against the charge. Upon receiving his letters, although at first I paid no regard to the thing, because I knew that nothing of what they said was true, yet seeing that the Emperor was moved, I wrote to my brethren in Egypt, and sent a deacon, desiring to learn something of Arsenius, for I had not seen the man for five or six years. Well, not to relate the matter at length, Arsenius was found in concealment, in the first instance in Egypt, and at last my friends discovered him still in concealment at Tyre. And what was most remarkable, even when he was discovered he would not confess that he was Arsenius, until he was convicted in court before Paul, who was then Bishop of Tyre, and at last out of very shame he could not deny it.

14. This he did in order to fulfil his contract with the Eusebians, lest, if he were discovered, the game they were playing should at length be broken up; which in fact came to pass. For when I wrote the Emperor word, that Arsenius was discovered, and reminded him of what he had heard in Psammathia concerning Macarius the Presbyter, he stopped the proceedings of the Censor's court, and wrote condemning the proceedings against me as calumnious, and commanded

[1] vid. §. 60.

[s] Dalmatius was the name of father and son, the brother and nephew of Constantine. Socrates, Hist. i 27. gives the title of Censor to the son; but the Alexandrian Chronicon (according to Tillemont, Empereurs, vol. 4. p. 657.) gives it to the father. Valesius, and apparently Tillemont, think Socrates mistaken. The younger Dalmatian was created Cæsar by Constantine a few years before his death, and, as well as his brother Hannibalian, and a number of other relatives, was put to death by Constantius, or his ministers and the soldiery, on the death of his father. vid Athan. Hist. Mon. 69.

the Eusebians to return, who were coming into the East to appear against me. Now in order to shew that they accused me of having murdered Arsenius, (not to bring forward the letters of many persons on the subject,) it shall be sufficient only to produce one from Alexander the Bishop of Thessalonica, from which the tenor of the rest may be inferred. He then being acquainted with the reports which Archaph, who is also called John, circulated against me on the subject of the murder, and having heard that Arsenius was alive, wrote as follows.

15 Letter of Alexander.

To his dearly beloved son and brother like-minded, the Lord[1] Athanasius, Alexander the Bishop sends health in the Lord.

I congratulate the most excellent Serapion, that he is striving so earnestly to adorn himself with holy habits, and is thus advancing to higher praise the memory of his father. For, as the Holy Scripture somewhere says, *though his father die, yet he is as though he were not dead* for he has left behind him a memorial of his life. What my feelings are towards the ever-memorable Sozon, you yourself, my lord[2], are not ignorant, for you know the sacredness of his memory, as well as the excellent disposition of the young man. I have received only one letter from your reverence, which I had by the hands of this youth. I mention this to you, my lord, that you may know that I have received it. Our dearly beloved brother and deacon Macarius, afforded me great pleasure by writing to me from Constantinople, that the false accuser Archaph had met with disgrace, for having given out before all men that a live man had been murdered. That he will receive from the righteous Judge, together with all the tribe of his associates, that punishment which his crimes deserve, the infallible Scriptures assure us. May the Lord of all preserve you for very many years, my most excellent lord[3].

16. And they who lived with Arsenius bear witness, that he was kept in concealment for this purpose, that they might pretend his death; for in searching after him we found the following person, and he in consequence wrote the following

APOL. AG AR.

letter to John, who supported this false accusation against me.

17. To his dearly beloved brother John, Pinnes, Presbyter of the Monastery of Ptemencyrcis, in the district of Anteopolis, sends greeting.

I wish you to know, that Athanasius sent his deacon into the Thebais, to search every where for Arsenius; and Pecysius the Presbyter, and Sylvanus the brother of Helias, and Tapenacerameus, and Paul monk of Hypsele, whom he first fell in with, confessed that Arsenius was with us. Upon learning this we caused him to be put on board a vessel, and to sail to the lower countries with Helias the monk. Afterwards the deacon returned again suddenly with certain others, and entered our monastery, in search of the same Arsenius, and him they found not, because, as I said before, we had sent him away to the lower countries; but they conveyed me together with Helias the monk, who took him out of the way, to Alexandria, and brought us before the Duke[t], when I was unable to deny, but confessed that he was alive, and had not been murdered: the monk also who took him out of the way confessed the same. Wherefore I acquaint you with these things, Father, lest you should determine to accuse Athanasius; for I said that he was alive, and had been concealed with us, and all this is become known in Egypt, and it cannot any longer be kept secret.

[1] μονῆς

I, Paphnutius, monk of the same monastery[1], who wrote this letter, heartily salute you. I trust that you are in health.

18. The following also is the letter which the Emperor wrote when he learnt that Arsenius was found to be alive.

[2] vid. supr. p. 93.

19. Victor, Constantine, Maximus, Augustus, to the Pope[2] Athanasius.

§. 68. Having read the letters of your wisdom, I felt the inclination to write in return to your gravity, and to exhort you that you would endeavour to restore the people of God to

---

[t] According to the system of government introduced by Dioclesian and Constantine, there were thirty-five military commanders of the troops, under the Magistri militum, and all of these bore the name of duces or dukes; the comites, or counts, were ten out of the number, who were distinguished as companions of the Emperor. vid. Gibbon, ch. 17. Three of these dukes were stationed in Egypt.

tranquillity, and to merciful feelings. For in my own mind
I hold these things to be of the greatest importance, that we
should cultivate truth, and ever keep righteousness in our
thoughts, and have pleasure especially in those who walk in
the right way of life But as concerning those who are
deserving of all execration, I mean the most perverse and
ungodly Meletians, who have at last stultified themselves by
their folly, and are now raising unreasonable commotions by
envy, uproar, and tumult, thus making manifest their own
ungodly dispositions, I will say thus much. You see that
those who they pretended had been slain with the sword, are
still amongst us, and in the enjoyment of life. Now what
could be a stronger presumption against them, and one so
manifestly and clearly tending to their condemnation, as that
those whom they declared to have been murdered, are yet in
the enjoyment of life, and accordingly will be able to speak
for themselves?

20. But this further accusation was advanced by these same
Meletians. They positively affirmed that you, rushing in
with lawless violence, had seized upon and broken a chalice,
which was deposited in the most Holy Place; than which
there certainly could not be a more serious charge, nor a
more grievous offence, had such a crime actually been
perpetrated. But what manner of accusation is this? What
is the meaning of this change and variation and difference in
the circumstances of it, insomuch that they now transfer this
same accusation to another person[1], a fact which makes it
clearer, so to speak, than the light itself, that they designed
to lay a plot for your wisdom? After this who can be willing
to follow them, men that have fabricated such charges to the
injury of another, seeing too that they are hurrying themselves on to ruin, and are conscious that they are accusing
you of false and feigned crimes? Who then, as I said, will
follow after them, and thus go headlong in the way of
destruction; in that way in which it seems they alone
suppose that they have hope of safety and of help? But if
they were willing to walk according to a pure conscience,
and to be directed by the best wisdom, and to go in the way
of a sound mind, they would easily perceive that no help can
come to them from Divine Providence, while they are given

[1] pp. 48, 49.

up to such doings, and tempt their own destruction. I should not call this a harsh judgment of them, but the simple truth.

21. And finally, I will add, that I wish this letter to be read frequently by your wisdom in public, that it may thereby come to the knowledge of all men, and especially reach the ears of those who thus act, and thus raise disturbances; for the judgment which is expressed by me according to the dictates of equity is confirmed also by real facts. Wherefore, seeing that in such conduct there is so great criminality, let them understand that I so judge of them; and that I have come to this determination, that if they excite any further commotion of this kind, I will myself in person take cognizance of the matter, and that not according to the ecclesiastical, but according to the civil laws, and so I will find them out, because they seem to be offenders not only against human kind, but against the divine doctrine itself. May God ever preserve you, dearly beloved brother!

§. 69. 22. But that the wickedness of the calumniators might be more fully displayed, behold Arsenius also wrote to me after he was discovered in his place of concealment; and as the letter which Ischyras had written confessed the falsehood of their accusation, so that of Arsenius proved their maliciousness still more completely.

> 23 To the blessed Pope Athanasius, Arsenius, Bishop of those who were heretofore under Meletius in the city of the Hypselites, together with the Presbyters and Deacons, wishes much health in the Lord.
>
> Being earnestly desirous of peace and union with the Catholic Church, over which by the grace of God you are appointed to preside, and wishing to submit ourselves to the Canon of the Church, according to the ancient rule [u], we write unto you, dearly beloved Pope, and declare in the name of the Lord, that we will not for the future hold communion with those who continue in schism, and are not at peace with the Catholic Church, its Bishops, Presbyters, and Deacons. Neither will we take part with them if they wish

---

[u] vid. supr. p. 3, note a, the (so called) Apostolical Canon apparently referred to here, is Can. 27. according to Beveridge.

to establish any thing in a Council; neither will we send letters of peace¹ unto them nor receive such from them; neither yet without the consent of you our Metropolitan will we publish any decree concerning Bishops, or on any other general Ecclesiastical question; but we will yield obedience to all the Canons that have heretofore been ordained, after the example of the Bishops˟ Ammonian, Tyrannus, Plusian, and the rest. Wherefore we beseech your goodness to write to us speedily in answer, and likewise to our fellow-ministers concerning us, informing them that we will henceforth abide by the fore-mentioned resolution and will be at peace with the Catholic Church, and at unity with our fellow-ministers in every part. And we are persuaded that your prayers, being acceptable unto God, will so prevail with Him, that this peace shall be firm and indissoluble unto the end, according to the will of God the Lord of all, through Jesus Christ our Lord.

24. The sacred Ministry that is under you, we and those that are with us salute. Very shortly, if God permit, we will come unto your goodness. I, Arsenius, pray that you may be strong in the Lord for many years, most blessed Pope.

But a stronger and clearer proof of the calumny is the recantation of John, of which the most godly Emperor Constantine of blessed memory is a witness, for knowing how John had accused himself, and having received letters from him expressing his repentance, he wrote to him as follows.

25. Constantine Maximus Augustus to John.

The letters which I have received from your prudence were extremely pleasing to me, because I learned from them what I very much longed to hear, that you had laid aside every narrow feeling², had joined the communion of the Church as became you, and were now in perfect concord with the most reverend Bishop Athanasius. Be assured therefore that so far I entirely approve of your conduct; because, dismissing all occasions of quarrel, you have done

---

˟ 1. e. Meletian Bishops who had conformed; or, since they are not in the list, §. 71. Catholic Bishops with whom the conforming party were familiar; or Meletians after the return of Meletius. vid. Tillemont, Mem. vol. 8. p. 658.

that which is pleasing to God, and have embraced the unity of His Church. In order therefore that you obtain the accomplishment of your wishes, I have thought it right to grant you permission to enter the public conveyance[y], and to come to the court' of my clemency. Let it then be your care to make no delay; but as this letter gives you authority to use the public conveyance, come to me immediately, that you may have your desires fulfilled, and by appearing in my presence may enjoy that pleasure which it is fit for you to receive. May God preserve you continually, dearly beloved brother.

---

[y] On the "cursus publicus," vid. Gothofred. in Cod. Theod. viii. tit. 5. It was provided for the journeys of the Emperor, for persons whom he summoned, for magistrates, ambassadors, and for such private persons as the Emperor indulged in the use of it, which was gratis. The use was granted by Constantine to the Bishops who were summoned to Nicæa, as far as it went, in addition though aliter Valesius in loc to other means of travelling Euseb. v. Const. iii. 6 The cursus publicus brought the Bishops to the Council of Tyre. ibid. iv. 43. In the conference between Liberius and Constantius, Theod. Hist. ii. 13. it is objected that the cursus publicus is not sufficient to convey Bishops to the Council which Liberius proposes, he answers that the Churches are rich enough to convey their Bishops as far as the sea. Thus S. Hilary was compelled, (datâ evectionis copiâ, Sulp Sev Hist ii 57) to attend at Seleucia, as Athan. at Tyre. Julian complains of the abuse of the cursus publicus, perhaps with an allusion to these Councils of Constantius. vid. Cod Theod viii. tit. 5 l. 12 where Gothofred quotes Liban.Epitaph in Julian. (vol. i. p 569. ed Reiske.) Vid. the well-known passage of Ammianus, who speaks of the Councils being the ruin of the res vehicularia Hist xxi. 16. The Eusebians at Philippopolis say the same thing. Hilar. Fragm iii 25. The Emperor provided board and perhaps lodging for the Bishops at Ariminum; which the Bishops of Aquitaine, Gaul, and Britain, declined, except three British from poverty. Sulp. Hist. ii. 56. Hunneric in Africa, after assembling 466 Bishops at Carthage, dismissed them without modes of conveyance, provision, or baggage Victor. Utic. Hist. iii. init. In the Emperor's letter previous to the assembling of the sixth Ecumenical Council, A.D. 678, (Harduin. Conc. t. 3. p. 1048 fin) he says he has given orders for the conveyance and maintenance of its members. Pope John VIII. reminds Ursus, Duke of Venice, (A.D. 876.) of the same duty of providing for the members of a Council, " secundum pios principes, qui in talibus munificè semper erant intenti " Colet. Concil. (Ven. 1730) t. xi. p. 14.

[z] στρατόπεδον. vid. Chrys. on the Statues, p. 118, note d. Gothofr. in Cod. Theod vl. 32. l. 1. Castra sunt ubi Princeps est ibid. 35 l. 15. also Kiesling. de Discipl. Cler. i. 5. p. 16 Beveridge in Can Apost 83. interprets στρατία of any civil engagement as opposed to clerical.

CHAP. VI.

DOCUMENTS CONNECTED WITH THE COUNCIL OF TYRE.

1. Thus ended the conspiracy The Meletians were repulsed §. 71. and covered with shame; but notwithstanding this the Eusebians still did not remain quiet, for it was not for the Meletians but for the Arians that they cared, and they were afraid lest, if the proceedings of the former should be stopped, they should no longer find persons to play the parts[1], by whose assistance they might bring in that heresy. They therefore again stirred up the Meletians, and persuaded the Emperor to give orders that a Council should be held afresh at Tyre, and Count Dionysius was despatched thither, and a military guard was given to the Eusebians. Macarius also was sent as a prisoner to Tyre under a guard of soldiers, and the Emperor wrote to me, and laid a peremptory command upon me, so that, however unwilling, I was obliged to go. The whole conspiracy may be understood from the letters which the Bishops of Egypt wrote; but it will be necessary to relate how it was contrived by them in the outset, that so may be perceived the malice and wickedness that was exercised against me.

 p. 34, r. 6.

2. There are in Egypt, Libya, and Pentapolis, nearly one hundred Bishops, none of whom laid any thing to my charge; none of the Presbyters found any fault with me; none of the people spoke aught against me; but it was the Meletians who were ejected by Peter, and the Arians, that divided the plot between them, while the one party claimed to themselves the right of accusing me, the other of sitting in judgment on the case. I objected to the Eusebians as being my enemies on account of the heresy; next, I shewed in the following manner that the person who was called my accuser was not a Presbyter at all. When Meletius was admitted into communion, (would that he had never been so admitted[2]) the blessed[3] Alexander who knew his craftiness required of him a catalogue of the Bishops whom he said he had in

[2] p. 88, note r. [3] μακα-ρίτης, infr. pp. 161, 162.

Egypt, and of the Presbyters and Deacons that were in Alexandria itself, and if he had any in the country adjoining. This the Pope Alexander did, lest Meletius, assuming full liberty of action in the Church, should sell ordination to many, and thus continually, by a fraudulent procedure, put in whatever ministers he pleased. Accordingly he made out the following catalogue of those in Egypt.

3. *A catalogue presented by Meletius to the Bishop Alexander.*

I, Meletius of Lycus, Lucius of Antinopolis, Phasileus of Hermopolis, Achilles of Cusæ, Ammonius of Diospolis.

In Ptolemais, Pachymes of Tentyræ.

In Maximianopolis, Theodorus of Coptus.

In Thebais, Cales of Hermethes, Colluthus of Upper Cynus, Pelagius of Oxyrynchus, Peter of Heracleopolis, Theon of Nilopolis, Isaac of Letopolis, Heraclides of Niciopolis, Isaac of Cleopatris, Melas of Arsenoitis.

In Heliopolis, Amos of Leontopolis, Ision of Athribis.

In Pharbethus, Harpocration of Bubastus, Moses of Phacusæ, Callinicus of Pelusium, Eudæmon of Tanis, Ephraim of Thmuis.

In Sais, Hermæon of Cynus and Busiris, Soterichus of Sebennytus, Pininuthes of Phthenegys, Chronius of Metelis, Agathammon of the district of Alexandria.

In Memphis, John who was ordered by the Emperor to be with the Archbishop[1]. These are those of Egypt.

And the Clergy that he had in Alexandria were Apollonius Presbyter, Irenæus Presbyter, Dioscorus Presbyter, Tyrannus Presbyter. And Deacons; Timotheus Deacon, Antinous Deacon, Hephæstion Deacon. And Macarius Presbyter of Parembole[2].

4. These Meletius presented in person to the Bishop Alexander, but he made no mention of the person called Ischyras, nor ever professed at all that he had any Clergy in the Mareotis. Notwithstanding our enemies did not desist from their attempts, but still he that was no Presbyter was feigned to be one, for there was the Count ready to use compulsion towards us, and soldiers hurried us about[3]. But

even then the grace of God prevailed: for they could not convict Macarius in the matter of the chalice; and Arsenius, whom they reported to have been murdered by me, stood before them alive and shewed the falseness of their accusation. When therefore they were unable to convict Macarius, the Eusebians, who became enraged that they had lost the prey of which they had been in pursuit, persuaded the Count Dionysius who is one of them to send to the Mareotis, in order to see whether they could not find out something there against the Presbyter, or rather that they might at a distance patch up their plot as they pleased in my absence: for this was their aim. However, when I represented that the journey to the Mareotis was a superfluous undertaking, (for that they ought not to pretend that statements were defective which they had been employed upon so long, and ought not now to defer the matter; for they had said whatever they thought they could say, and now being at a loss what to do, they were making pretences,) or if they must needs go to the Mareotis, that at least the suspected parties should not be sent,—the Count was convinced by my reasoning, with respect to the suspected persons; but they did any thing rather than what I proposed, for the very persons whom I objected against on account of the Arian heresy, these were they who specially went, viz Diognius, Maris, Theodorus, Macedonius, Ursacius, and Valens. Again, letters were written to the Prefect of Egypt, and a military guard was provided; and, what was remarkable and altogether most suspicious, they caused Macarius the accused party to remain behind under a guard of soldiers, while they took with them the accuser [1].

5. Now who after this does not see through this conspiracy? Who does not clearly perceive the wickedness of these Eusebians? For if a judicial enquiry must needs take place in the Mareotis, the accused ought also to have been sent thither. But if they did not go for the purpose of such an enquiry, why did they take the accuser? It was enough that he had not been able to prove the fact. But this they did in order that they might carry on their designs against the absent Presbyter, whom they could not convict when present, and might concoct a plan as they pleased. For when

TR. II.
72.

[1] supr. p 31

the Presbyters of Alexandria and of the whole district found fault with them because they were there by themselves, and required that they too might be present at their proceedings, (for they said that they knew both the circumstances of the case, and the history of the person named Ischyras,) they would not allow them; and although they had with them Philagrius the Prefect of Egypt, who was an apostate, and heathen soldiers, during an enquiry which it was not becoming even for Catechumens to witness, they would not admit the Clergy, lest there as well as at Tyre there might be those who would expose them.

§. 73. 6. But in spite of these precautions they were not able to escape detection: for the Presbyters of the City and of the Mareotis, perceiving their evil designs, addressed to them the following protest.

7. To Theognius, Maris, Macedonius, Theodorus, Ursacius, and Valens, the Bishops who have come from Tyre, these from the Presbyters and Deacons of the Catholic Church of Alexandria under the most reverend Bishop Athanasius.

It was incumbent upon you when you came hither and brought with you the accuser, to bring also the Presbyter Macarius; for trials are appointed by holy Scripture to be so constituted, that the accuser and accused may stand up together. But since neither you brought Macarius, nor our most reverend Bishop Athanasius came with you, we claimed for ourselves the right of being present at the investigation, that we might see that the enquiry was conducted impartially, and might ourselves be convinced of the truth. But when you refused to allow this, and wished, in company only with the Prefect of Egypt and the accuser, to do whatever you pleased, we confess that we entertained an evil suspicion of the affair, and perceived that your coming was only the act of a cabal and a conspiracy. Wherefore we address to you this letter, to be a testimony before a genuine Council, that it may be known to all men, that you have carried on an *ex parte* proceeding and for your private ends, and have desired nothing else but to form a conspiracy against us. A copy of this, lest it should be kept secret by you, we have transmitted also to Palladius the Controller[a] of Augustus. For what you have already done causes us to suspect you, and to reckon on the like conduct from you hereafter.

Tr II. 73, 74.

I Dionysius Presbyter have delivered this letter, Alexander Presbyter, Nilaras Presbyter, Longus Presbyter, Aphthonius Presbyter, Athanasius Presbyter, Amyntius Presbyter, Pistus Presbyter, Plution Presbyter, Dioscorus Presbyter, Apollonius Presbyter, Serapion Presbyter, Ammonius Presbyter, Gaius Presbyter, Rhinus Presbyter, Œthales Presbyter.

Deacons; Marcellinus Deacon, Appianus Deacon, Theon Deacon, Timotheus Deacon, a second Timotheus Deacon.

8. This is the letter, and these the names of the Clergy of the city; and the following was written by the Clergy of the Mareotis, who know the character of the accuser, and who were with me in my visitation.

§. 74.

9. To the holy Council of blessed Bishops of the Catholic Church, all the Presbyters and Deacons of the Mareotis send health in the Lord.

Knowing that which is written, *Speak that thine eyes have seen*, and, *A false witness shall not be unpunished;* we testify what we have seen, especially since the conspiracy which has been formed against our Bishop Athanasius has made our testimony necessary. We wonder how Ischyras ever came to be reckoned among the number of the Ministers of the Church, which is the first point we think it necessary to mention. Ischyras never was a Minister of the Church; but when formerly he represented himself to be a Presbyter of Colluthus, he found no one to believe him, except only his own relations. For he never had a Church, nor was ever considered a Clergyman, by those who lived but a short distance from his village, except only, as we said before, by his own relations. But, notwithstanding he assumed this designation, he was deposed in the presence of our Father Hosius at the Council which assembled at

Prov 25, 7. Sept. 19, 5.

---

[a] Curiosus; the Curiosi (in curis agendis) were properly the overseers of the public roads, Ducange in voc. but they became in consequence a sort of imperial spy, and were called the Emperor's eyes. Gothofr. in Cod.Theod. t 2. p. 194. ed. 1665. Constantius confined them to the school of the Agentes in rebus, (infr Apol. ad Const. §. 10.) under the Master of the Offices. Gothofr. ibid. p. 192

Alexandria, and was reduced to the condition of a layman, and so he continued subsequently, being deprived of his pretended claim to the priesthood. Of his character we think it unnecessary to speak, as all men have it in their power to become acquainted therewith But since he has falsely accused our Bishop Athanasius of breaking a chalice and overturning a table, we are necessarily obliged to address you on this point.

10. We have said already that he never had a Church in the Mareotis, and we declare before God as our witness, that no chalice was broken, nor table overturned by our Bishop, nor by any one of those who accompanied him; but all that is alleged respecting this affair is mere calumny. And this we say, not as having been absent from the Bishop, for we are all with him when he makes his visitation of the Mareotis, and he never goes about alone, but is accompanied by all the Presbyters and Deacons, and by a considerable number of the people. Wherefore we make these assertions, as having been present with him during the whole of the visitation which he made amongst us, and testify that neither was a chalice ever broken, nor table overturned, but the whole story is false, as the accuser himself also witnesses under his own hand[1]. For when, after he had withdrawn with the Meletians, and had reported these things against our Bishop Athanasius, he wished to be admitted to communion, he was not received, although he wrote and confessed under his own hand that none of these things were true, but that he had been suborned by certain persons to say so.

§. 75. 11. Wherefore also Theognius, Theodorus, Maris, Macedonius, Ursacius, and Valens, came into the Mareotis, and when they found that none of these things were true, but it was likely to be discovered that they had framed a false accusation against our Bishop Athanasius, the party of Theognius being themselves his enemies, caused the relations of Ischyras and certain Arian fanatics[2] to say whatever they wished. For none of the people spoke against the Bishop but these persons, through a dread of Philagrius the Prefect of Egypt, and by threats and with the support of the Arian fanatics[2], accomplished whatever they desired. For when we came to disprove the calumny, they would not permit us, but cast us out, while they admitted whom they pleased to a participation in their schemes, and concerted matters with them, influencing them by fear of the Prefect Philagrius. Through his means they prevented us from being present, that we might discover whether those who were suborned by them were members of the Church or Arian fanatics. And you also, dearly beloved Fathers, know, as you teach us, that the testimony of enemies avails nothing. That what we say is the truth the handwriting[1] of Ischyras testifies, as do also the facts themselves, because when we were conscious that no such thing as was pretended had taken place, they took with them Philagrius, that through fear of the sword and by threats they might frame whatever plots they wished. These things we testify as in the presence of God; we make these assertions as knowing that there will be a judgment held by God; desiring indeed all of us to come to you, but being content with these letters which we send to you, that they may be instead of the presence of those who cannot come.

TR. II. 75, 76.

[1] χείρ, infr. Apol. ad Const. §. 11.

I, Ingenius Presbyter, pray that you may be strong in the Lord, dearly beloved Fathers Theon P. Ammonas P. Heraclius P. Boccon P. Tryphon P. Peter P Hierax P. Serapion P. Marcus P. Ptollarion P. Gaius P. Dioscorus P. Demetrius P. Thyrsus P.

Deacons; Pistus D. Apollos D. Serras D. Pistus D. Polynicus D. Ammonius D. Maurus D. Hephæstus D. Apollos D. Metopas D. Apollos D Serapas D. Meliphthongus D. Lucius D. Gregoras D

12. *The same to the Controller, and to Philagrius, at that time Prefect of Egypt*

§. 76.

To Flavius Philagrius, and to Flavius Palladius, Ducenary[b], Officer of the Palace[c], and Controller, and to Flavius Antoninus, Commissary of Provisions[3], and Centenary of my Lords, the most illustrious Prefects of the sacred Prætorium, these from the Presbyters and Deacons of the Mareotis, a district of the

[2] vid. p. 89, r. 3.
[3] βιαρχῷ

---

[b] On the different kinds of Ducenaries, vid. Gothofr. in Cod Theod xi. 7. leg. 1. Here, as in Euseb Hist vii. 30. the word stands for a Procurator, whose annual pay amounted to 200 sestertia vid Salmas in Hist. Aug. t. 1. p 533. In like manner a Centenary is one who receives 100.

108 *The Clergy of the Mareotis to the Prefect and Controller*

APOL. AG. AR. Catholic Church which is under the most Reverend Bishop Athanasius, we address this testimony by those whose names are under-written:—

Whereas Theognius, Maris, Macedonius, Theodorus, Ursacius, and Valens, as if sent by all the Bishops who assembled at Tyre, came into our Diocese alleging that they had received orders to investigate certain ecclesiastical affairs, among which they spoke of the breaking of a chalice belonging to the Lord, of which information was given them by Ischyras, whom they brought with them, and who says that he is a Presbyter, although he is not,—for he was ordained by the Presbyter Colluthus who pretended to the Episcopate, and was afterwards ordered by a whole Council, by Hosius and the Bishops that were with him, to take the place of a Presbyter, as he was before; and accordingly all that were ordained by Colluthus, resumed the same rank which they held before, and so Ischyras himself proved to be a layman,—and the Church, which he says he has, never was a Church at all, but a small dwelling house belonging to an orphan boy of the name of Ision;—for this reason we have offered this testimony, adjuring you by Almighty God, and by our Lords Constantine Augustus, and the most illustrious Cæsars his sons, to bring these things to the knowledge of their piety. For neither is he a Presbyter of the Catholic Church, nor does he possess a Church, nor has a chalice ever been broken, but the whole story is false and an invention.

[1] A.D. 335. Dated in the Consulship[1] of Julius Constantius the most illustrious Patrician[c], brother of the most religious Emperor Constantine Augustus, and of Rufinus Albinus, most illus-
[2] August. trious men, on the tenth day of the month Thoth[2].

These were the letters of the Presbyters.

§. 77.   13. The following also are the letters and protests of the Bishops who came with us to Tyre, when they discovered the conspiracy and plot.

---

[c] The title Patrician was revived by Constantine as a personal distinction It was for life, and gave precedence over all the great officers of state except the Consul. It was usually bestowed on favourites, or on ministers as a reward of services. Gibbon, Hist. ch. 17 This

Julius Constantius, who was the father of Julian, was the first who bore the title, with L Optatus, who had been consul the foregoing year. Illustrissimus was the highest of the three ranks of honour. ibid.

14. To the Bishops assembled at Tyre, most honoured Lords, those of the Catholic Church who have come from Egypt with Athanasius send health in the Lord.

We suppose that the conspiracy which has been formed against us by Eusebius, Theognius, Marus, Narcissus, Theodorus, and Patrophilus, is no longer uncertain. From the very beginning we all demurred, through our fellow-minister Athanasius, to the holding of the inquiry in their presence, knowing that the presence of even one enemy only, much more of many, is able to disturb and injure the hearing of a cause. And you also yourselves know the enmity which they entertain, not only towards us, but towards all the orthodox, how that for the sake of the fanaticism of Arius, and his impious doctrine, they direct their assaults, they form conspiracies against all. And when, being confident in the truth, we desired to shew the falsehood, which the Meletians had employed against the Church, the Eusebians endeavoured by some means or other to interrupt our representations, and strove eagerly to set aside our testimony, threatening those who gave an honest judgment, and insulting others, for the sole purpose of carrying out the design they had against us. Your divinely inspired[1] piety, most honoured Lords, was probably ignorant of their conspiracy, but we suppose that it has now been made manifest.

[1] ἔνθεος

15. For indeed they have themselves plainly disclosed it; for they desired to send to the Mareotis those of their party who are suspected by us, so that, while we were absent and remained here, they might disturb the people and accomplish what they wished. They knew that the Arian fanatics, and Colluthians[d] and Meletians, were enemies of the Catholic Church, and therefore they were anxious to send them, that in the presence of our enemies they might devise against us whatever schemes they pleased. And those of the Meletians who are here, even four days previously, (as they knew that this inquiry was about to take place,) despatched at evening certain of their party, as a post, for the purpose of collecting Meletians out of Egypt into the Mareotis, because there were

---

[d] Colluthus formed a schism on the doctrine that God was not the cause of any sort of evil, e. g did not inflict pain and suffering. Though a Priest, he took on himself to ordain, even to the Priesthood. vid supr. p. 30, note l. St. Alexander even seems to imply that he did so for money. Theod. Hist. 1 3.

none at all there, and Colluthians and Arian fanatics, from other parts, and to prepare them to speak against us. For you also know that Ischyras himself confessed before you, that he had not more than seven persons in his congregation. When therefore we heard that, after they had made what preparations they pleased against us, and had sent these suspected persons, they were going about to each of you, and requiring your subscriptions, in order that it might appear as if this had been done with the consent of you all; for this reason we hastened to write to you, and to present this our testimony, declaring that we are the objects of a conspiracy under which we are suffering by and through them, and demanding that having the fear of God in your minds, and condemning their conduct in sending whom they pleased without our consent, you would refuse your subscriptions, lest they pretend that those things are done by you, which they are contriving only among themselves.

16. Surely it becomes those who are in Christ, not to regard men, but to prefer the truth before all things. And be not afraid of their threatenings, which they employ against all, nor of their plots, but rather fear God. If it was at all necessary that persons should be sent to the Mareotis, we also ought to have been there with them, in order that we might convict the enemies of the Church, and point out those who were aliens, and that the investigation of the matter might be impartial. For you know that the Eusebians contrived that a letter should be presented, as coming from the Colluthians, the Meletians, and Arians, and directed against us: but it is evident that these enemies of the Catholic Church speak nothing that is true concerning us, but say every thing against us. And the law of God forbids an enemy to be either a witness or a judge. Wherefore as you will have to give an account in the day of judgment, receive this testimony, and recognising the conspiracy which has been framed against us, beware, if you are requested by them, of doing any thing against us, and of taking part in the designs of the Eusebians. For you know, as we said before, that they are our enemies, and are aware why Eusebius of Cæsarea became such last year. We pray that you may be in health, greatly beloved Lords [1].

[1] κύριοι

17. To the most illustrious Count Flavius Dionysius, from the Bishops of the Catholic Church in Egypt who have come to Tyre[1].

Tr. II. 78. §. 78.

[1] nearly verbatim as the foregoing.

We suppose that the conspiracy which has been formed against us by Eusebius, Theognius, Maris, Narcissus, Theodorus, and Patrophilus, is no longer uncertain. From the very beginning we all demurred, through our fellow-minister Athanasius, to the holding of the inquiry in their presence, knowing that the presence of even one enemy only, much more of many, is able to disturb and injure the hearing of a cause. For their enmity is manifest which they entertain, not only towards us, but also towards all the orthodox, because they direct their assaults, they form conspiracies against all. And when, being confident in the truth, we desired to shew the falsehood which the Meletians had employed against the Church, the Eusebians endeavoured by some means or other to interrupt our representations, and strove eagerly to set aside our testimony, threatening those who gave a honest judgment and insulting others, for the sole purpose of carrying out the design they had against us. Your goodness was probably ignorant of the conspiracy which they have formed against us, but we suppose that it has now been made manifest.

18. For indeed they have themselves plainly disclosed it; for they desired to send to the Mareotis those of their party who are suspected by us, so that, while we were absent, and remained here, they might disturb the people and accomplish what they wished. They knew that Arian fanatics, Colluthians, and Meletians were enemies of the Church, and therefore they were anxious to send them, that in the presence of our enemies, they might devise against us whatever schemes they pleased. And those of the Meletians who are here, even four days before, (as they knew that this inquiry was about to take place,) despatched at evening two individuals of their own party, as a post, for the purpose of collecting Meletians out of Egypt into the Mareotis, because there were none at all there, and Colluthians, and Arian fanatics, from other parts, and to prepare them to speak against us. And your goodness knows that he himself

confessed before you, that he had not more than seven persons in his congregation. When therefore we heard that, after they had made what preparations they pleased against us, and had sent these suspected persons, they were going about to each of the Bishops and requiring their subscriptions, in order that it might appear that this was done with the consent of them all; for this reason we hastened to refer the matter to your honour, and to present this our testimony, declaring that we are the objects of a conspiracy, under which we are suffering by and through them, and demanding of you that having in your mind the fear of God, and the pious commands of our most religious Emperor, you would no longer tolerate these persons, but condemn their conduct in sending whom they pleased without our consent.

I Adamantius Bishop have subscribed this letter, Ischyras, Ammon, Peter, Ammonianus, Tyrannus, Taurinus, Sarapammon, Œlurion, Harpocration, Moses, Optatus, Anubion, Saprion, Apollonius, Ischyrion, Arbæthion, Potamon, Paphnutius, Heraclides, Theodorus, Agathammon, Gaius, Pistus, Athas, Nicon, Pelagius, Theon, Paninuthius, Nonnus, Ariston, Theodorus, Irenæus, Blastammon, Philippus, Apollos, Dioscorus, Timotheus of Diospolis, Macarius, Heraclammon, Cronius, Muis, James, Ariston, Artemidorus, Phinees, Psais, Heraclides.

19. *Another from the same.*

The Bishops of the Catholic Church who have come from Egypt to Tyre, to the most illustrious Count Flavius Dionysius.

Perceiving that many conspiracies and plots are being formed against us through the machinations of Eusebius, Narcissus, Flacillus, Theognius, Maris, Theodorus, and Patrophilus, (against whom we wished at first to enter an objection, but were not permitted,) we are constrained to have recourse to the present appeal. We observe also that great zeal is exerted in behalf of the Meletians, and that a plot is laid against the Catholic Church in Egypt in our persons. Wherefore we address this letter to you, beseeching you to bear in mind the Almighty Power of God, who defends the kingdom of our most religious and godly Emperor Constantine, and to reserve the hearing of the affairs which concern us for the most religious Emperor himself. For it is but reasonable, since you were commissioned by his Majesty, that you should reserve the matter for him upon our appealing to his piety. We can no longer endure to be the objects of the treacherous designs of the fore-mentioned Eusebians, and therefore we demand that the case be reserved for the most religious and godly Emperor, before whom we shall be able to set forth our own and the Church's just claims. And we are convinced that when his piety shall have heard our cause, he will not condemn us. Wherefore we again adjure you by Almighty God, and by our most religious Emperor, who, together with the children of his piety, has thus ever been victorious[1] and prosperous these many years, that you proceed no further, nor suffer yourself to move at all in the Council in relation to our affairs, but reserve the hearing of them for his piety. We have likewise made the same representations to my Lords[2] the orthodox Bishops.

20. Alexander[3], Bishop of Thessalonica, on receiving these letters, wrote to the Count Dionysius as follows.

21. The Bishop Alexander to my Lord[4] Dionysius.

I see that a conspiracy has evidently been formed against Athanasius; for they have determined, I know not on what grounds, to send all those to whom he has objected, without giving any information to us, although it was agreed that we should consider together who ought to be sent. Take care therefore that nothing be done rashly, (for they have come to me in great alarm, saying that the wild beasts have already roused themselves, and are going to rush upon them; for they had heard it reported, that John had sent certain,) lest they be beforehand with us, and concoct what schemes they please. For you know that the Colluthians[5] who are enemies of the Church, and the Arians, and Meletians, are all of them leagued together, and are able to work much evil. Consider therefore what is best to be done, lest some mischief befal, and we be subject to censure, as not having judged the matter fairly. Great suspicions are also entertained of these persons, lest, as being devoted to the Meletians,

TR. II.
79, 80.

[1] pp 79 and 96, p. 119, r. 2.

[2] κυρίοις μου.

§. 80.
[3] p. 33, note n.

[4] δεσπότῃ μου.

[5] p. 109, note d.

114   Letter of Count Dionysius to the Eusebians.

APOL. AG. AR. ¹atTyre. they should go through those Churches whose Bishops are here¹, and raise an alarm amongst them, and so disorder the whole of Egypt. For they see that this is already taking place to a great extent.

22. In consequence of this, the Count Dionysius wrote to the Eusebians as follows

§. 81.   23 This is what I have already mentioned to my lords
²perhaps associated with Flacillus², that Athanasius has come forward
president of and complained that those very persons have been sent
Council, whom he objected to; and crying out that he has been
vid.p.39, wronged and deceived. Alexander the lord of my soul has
note b. also written to me on the subject; and that you may
perceive that what his Excellence has said is reasonable, I
have subjoined his letter to be read by you. Remember
also what I wrote to you before: I impressed upon your
Excellences, my lords, that the persons who were sent
ought to be commissioned by the general vote and decision
of all. Take care therefore lest our proceedings fall under
censure, and we give just grounds of blame to those who are
disposed to find fault with us. For as the accuser's side
ought not to suffer any oppression, so neither ought the
defendant's. And I think that there is no slight ground of
blame against us, when my lord Alexander appears to
disapprove of what we have done.

§. 82.   24. While matters were proceeding thus we withdrew from
Jer.9,2. them, as from *an assembly of treacherous men*, for whatsoever they pleased they did, whereas there is no man in
the world but knows that *ex parte* proceedings cannot
stand good. This the divine law determines; for when the
blessed Apostle was suffering under a similar conspiracy and
Acts 24, was brought to trial, he demanded, saying, *The Jews from*
18. 19.   *Asia ought to have been here before thee, and object, if they
had ought against me.* On which occasion Festus also,
when the Jews wished to lay such a plot against him, as
Acts 25, these men have now laid against me, said, *It is not the*
16.   *manner of the Romans to deliver any man to die, before
that he which is accused have the accuser face to face,*

and have licence to answer for himself concerning the crime laid against him. But the Eusebians have both had the boldness to pervert the law, and have acted more unjustly even than those unjust persons. For they did not proceed privately at the first, but when in consequence of our being present they found themselves weak, then they straightway went out, like the Jews, and took counsel together alone, how they might destroy us and bring in their heresy, as they demanded Barabbas. For this purpose it was, as they have themselves confessed, that they did all these things.

Tr II. 82, 83.

25. Although these circumstances were amply sufficient for our vindication, yet in order that the wickedness of these men and the freeness of the truth might be more fully exhibited, I have not felt averse to repeat them again, in order to shew that they have acted in a manner inconsistently with themselves, and as men scheming in the dark have fallen foul upon one another, and while they desired to destroy us have like insane persons wounded themselves. For in their investigation of the subject of the Mysteries, they questioned Jews, they examined Catechumens[1], "Where were you," they said, "when Macarius came and overturned the Table?" They answered, "We were present within doors," whereas there could be no oblation if Catechumens were present. Again, although they had written word every where, that Macarius came and overthrew every thing, while the Presbyter was standing and celebrating the Mysteries, yet when they questioned whomsoever they pleased, and asked them, "Where was Ischyras when Macarius rushed in?" those persons answered that he was lying sick in a cell. Now he that was lying could not be standing, nor could one that lay sick in his cell offer the oblation. Besides whereas Ischyras said that certain books had been burnt by Macarius, the witnesses who were suborned to give evidence, declared that nothing of the kind had been done, but that Ischyras spoke falsely. And what is most remarkable, although they had again written word every where, that those who were able to give evidence had been concealed by us, yet these persons made their appearance, and they questioned them, and were not ashamed to find it proved on all sides that they were

§. 83.

[1] vid. p. 73.

slanderers, and had acted in this matter clandestinely, and according to their pleasure. For they prompted the witnesses by signs, while the Prefect threatened them, and the soldiers pricked them with their swords; but the Lord revealed the truth, and shewed them to be slanderers. Therefore also they concealed the Records of their proceedings, which they retained themselves, and charged those who wrote them to keep out of sight, and to communicate to no one whomsoever. But in this too also they were disappointed; for the person who wrote them was Rufus, who is now public executioner in the Augustalian[1] prefecture, and is able to testify to the truth of this; and the Eusebians sent them to Rome by the hands of their own friends, and Julius the Bishop transmitted them to me. And now they are mad with rage, because we have obtained and read what they wished to conceal.

§. 84. 26. As such was the character of their machinations, so they very soon shewed plainly the reasons of their conduct. For when they went away, they took the Arians with them to Jerusalem, and there admitted them to communion, having sent out a letter concerning them, part[2] of which, and the beginning, is as follows.

27. The holy Council by the grace of God assembled at Jerusalem, to the Church of God which is in Alexandria, and to the Bishops, Presbyters, and Deacons, in all Egypt, the Thebais, Libya, Pentapolis, and throughout the world, sends health in the Lord.

Having come together out of different Provinces to a great meeting which we have held for the consecration of the Martyry of the Saviour, which has been appointed to the service of God the King of all and of His Christ, by the zeal of our most religious Emperor Constantine, the grace of God hath afforded us more abundant rejoicing of heart; which our most religious Emperor himself hath occasioned us by his letters, wherein he hath stirred us up to do that which is right, putting away all envy from the Church of God, and driving far from us all malice, by which the members of God have been heretofore torn asunder, and that we should with single and peaceable minds receive the Arians, whom envy, that enemy of all goodness, has caused for a season to be excluded from the Church. Our most religious Emperor has also in his letter testified to the correctness of their faith, which he has ascertained from themselves, himself receiving the profession of it from them by word of mouth, and has now made manifest to us by subjoining a written declaration of their orthodox belief.

28. Every one that hears of these things must see through their treachery. For they made no concealment of what they were doing; unless perhaps they confessed the truth without wishing it. For if I was the hindrance to the admittance of the Arians into the Church, and if they were received while I was suffering from their plots, what other conclusion can be arrived at, than that these things were done on their account, and that all their proceedings against me, and the story which they fabricated about the breaking of the chalice and the murder of Arsenius, were for the sole purpose of introducing impiety into the Church, and of preventing their being condemned as heretics? For this was what the Emperor threatened long ago in his letters to me. And they were not ashamed to write in the manner they did, and to affirm that those persons whom the whole Ecumenical Council anathematized held orthodox sentiments. And as they undertook to say and do any thing without scruple, so they were not afraid to meet together in a corner, in order to overthrow, as far as was in their power, the authority of so great a Council.

29. Moreover, the price which they paid for false testimony yet more fully manifests their wickedness and impious intentions. The Mareotis, as I have already said, is a district of Alexandria, in which there has never been either a Bishop or a Chorepiscopus[e]; but the Churches of the whole district are subject to the Bishop of Alexandria, and each Presbyter has under his charge one of the largest villages, which are about ten or more in number[f]. Now the village in which Ischyras lives, is a very small one, and possesses so few inhabitants, that there has never been a Church built there,

---

[e] That Chorepiscopi were real Bishops, vid. Bevereg. in Conc. Ancyr. Can. 13. Routh in Conc. Neocæs. Can. 13. referring to Rhabanus Maurus. Thomassin on the other hand denies that they were Bishops, Discipl. Eccl. 1. 2. c. 1.

[f] Ten under each Presbyter. Vales. ad Socr. Hist. 1 27. Ten altogether, Montfaucon in loc. with more probability; and so Tillemont, vol. 8. p. 20.

but only in the adjoining village. Nevertheless, they determined, contrary to ancient usage [g], to nominate a Bishop for this place, and not only so, but even to appoint one, who was not so much as a Presbyter. Knowing as they did the unusual nature of such a proceeding, yet being constrained by the promises they had given in return for his false impeachment of me, they submitted even to this, lest that abandoned person, if he were ill-treated by them, should disclose the truth, and thereby shew the wickedness of the Eusebians. Notwithstanding this, he has no Church, nor a people to obey him, but is scouted by them all, like a dog [h], although they have even caused the Emperor to write to the Receiver-General [1], (for every thing is in their power,) commanding that a Church should be built for him, that being possessed of that, his statement may appear credible about the chalice and the table. They caused him immediately to be nominated a Bishop, because if he were without a Church, and not even a Presbyter, he would appear to be a false accuser, and a fabricator of the whole matter. Nevertheless he possesses but an empty title, as he has no people [2], and even his own relations are not obedient to him, and the letter also has failed to accomplish its purpose, remaining only as a convincing proof of the utter wickedness of himself and the Eusebians. It runs as follows.

[1] Catholicus, p. 32. Apol. ad Const. §. 10.

[2] pp. 108, 110.

30. *The Letter of the Receiver-General.*

Flavius Hemerius sends health to the Tax-collector [3] of the Mareotis.

[3] Exactor.

Ischyras the Presbyter having petitioned the piety of our Lords, Cæsars Augusti, that a Church might be built in the district of the Peace of Secontarurus [4], their divinity has commanded that this should be done as soon as possible. Take care therefore, as soon as you receive the copy of the sacred Edict, which with all due veneration is placed above, and the Reports which have been formed before my sanctity, that you

[4] p. 34, note o.

---

[g] It was against the Canon of Sardica, and doubtless against ancient usage, to ordain a Bishop for so small a village, vid. Bingham, Antiqu II. 12. who, however, maintains by instances, that at least small towns might be sees Also it was against usage that a layman, as Ischyras, should be made a Bishop ibid. 10. § 4, &c. St. Hilary, however, makes him a Deacon. Fragm. II. 16

[h] Dogs without owners, and almost in a wild state, abound, as is well known, in Eastern cities; vid. Psalm lix. 6, 14, 15. 2 Kings ix. 35, 36 and for the view taken in Scripture of dogs, vid. Bochart, Hieroz. II. 56.

quickly make an abstract of them, and transfer them to the Order book, so that the sacred command may be put in execution.

^{Tr. II.
85, 86.}

31. While they were thus plotting and scheming, I went up[1] and represented to the Emperor the unjust conduct of the Eusebians, for he it was who had commanded the Council to be held, and his Count presided at it. When he heard my report, he was greatly moved, and wrote to them as follows.

^{1 §. 86.
I p. 26,
r. 2.}

32. Victor[2], Constantine, Maximus, Augustus, to the Bishops assembled at Tyre.

^{2 Euseb.
v. Const.
u. 48.}

I know not what the decisions are which you have arrived at in your Council amidst noise and tumult; but somehow the truth seems to have been perverted in consequence of certain confusions and disorders, in that you, through your mutual contentiousness, which you are resolved should prevail, have failed to perceive what is pleasing to God. However, it will rest with Divine Providence to disperse the mischiefs which manifestly are found to arise from this contentious spirit, and to shew plainly to us, whether you, while assembled in that place, have had any regard for the truth, and whether you have made your decisions uninfluenced by either favour or enmity. Wherefore I wish you all to assemble with all speed before my piety, in order that you may render in person a true account of your proceedings.

33. The reason why I have thought good to write thus to you, and why I summon you before me by letter, you will learn from what I am going to say. As I was entering on a late occasion our all-happy home of Constantinople, which bears our name, (I chanced at the time to be on horseback,) on a sudden the Bishop Athanasius, with certain others whom he had with him, approached me in the middle of the road, so unexpectedly, as to occasion me much amazement. God, who knoweth all things, is my witness, that I should have been unable at first sight even to recognise him, had not some of my attendants, on my naturally enquiring of them, informed me both who it was, and under what injustice he was suffering. I did not however enter into any conversation with him at that time, nor grant him an interview, but

APOL. AG. AR.

¹ στρατό-
πεδον,
p. 100,
note z.
² πρά-
ττοντα
³ λα-
τρείας

when he requested to be heard I refused, and all but gave orders for his removal: when with increasing boldness he claimed only this favour, that you should be summoned to appear, that he might have an opportunity of complaining before me in your presence, of the ill-treatment which he has met with. As this appeared to me to be a reasonable request, and suitable to the times, I willingly ordered this letter to be written to you, in order that all of you, who constituted the Council which was held at Tyre, might hasten without delay to the Court¹ of my clemency, so as to prove by facts that you had passed an impartial and uncorrupt judgment. This, I say, you must do before me, whom not even you will deny to be a true servant of God².

34. For indeed through my devotion³ to God, peace is preserved every where, and the Name of God is truly worshipped even by the barbarians, who have hitherto been ignorant of the truth. And it is manifest, that he who is ignorant of the truth, does not know God. Nevertheless, as I said before, even the barbarians have now come to the knowledge of God, by means of me, His true servant¹, and have learned to fear Him whom they perceive from actual facts to be my shield and protector every where. And from this chiefly they have come to know God, whom they fear through the dread which they have of me. But we, who profess to set forth (for I will not say to guard) the holy mysteries of His Goodness, we, I say, engage in nothing but what tends to dissension and hatred, and, in short, whatever contributes to the destruction of mankind. But hasten, as I said before, and all of you with all speed come to us, being persuaded that I shall endeavour with all my might to amend what is amiss, so that those things specially may be preserved and firmly established in the law of God, to which no blame nor dishonour may attach; while the enemies of the law, who under pretence of His holy Name bring in manifold and divers blasphemies, shall be scattered abroad, and entirely crushed, and utterly destroyed.

¹ " Once in an entertainment, at which he (Constantine) received Bishops, he made the remark that he too was a Bishop, using pretty much these words in my hearing, ' You are Bishops of matters within the Church, I am appointed by God to be Bishop of matters external to it.' " Euseb. Vit. Const. iv. 24. vid. supr. p. 76, note m.

35. When the Eusebians read this letter, being conscious of what they had done, they prevented the rest of the Bishops from going up, and only themselves went, viz. Eusebius, Theognius, Patrophilus, the other Eusebius, Ursacius, and Valens. And they no longer said any thing about the chalice and Arsenius, (for they had not the boldness to do so,) but inventing another accusation which concerned the Emperor himself, they declared before him, that Athanasius had threatened that he would cause the corn to be withheld which was sent from Alexandria to his own home[1]. The Bishops Adamantius, Anubion, Agathammon, Arbethion, and Peter, were present and heard this. It was proved also by the anger of the Emperor; for although he had written the preceding letter, and had condemned their injustice, as soon as he heard such a charge as this, he was immediately incensed, and instead of granting me a hearing, he sent me away into Gaul. And this again shews their wickedness further: for when the younger Constantine, of blessed memory, sent me back home, remembering what his father had written, he also wrote as follows.

[1] Constantinople.

36. Constantine Cæsar, to the people of the Catholic Church of the city of Alexandria.

I suppose that it has not escaped the knowledge of your pious minds, that Athanasius, the interpreter of the adorable Law, was sent away into Gaul for a time, with the intent that, as the savageness of his bloodthirsty and inveterate enemies persecuted him to the hazard of his sacred life[2], he[2 κιφαλῆς] might thus escape suffering some irremediable calamity, through the perverse dealing of those evil men. In order therefore to escape this, he was snatched out of the jaws of his assailants, and was ordered to pass some time under my government, and so was supplied abundantly with all necessaries in this city, where he lived, although indeed his celebrated virtue, relying entirely on divine assistance, set at nought the sufferings of adverse fortune. Now seeing that it was the fixed intention of our Lord[3] Constantine Augustus, my[3 διωσί- της] Father, to restore the said Bishop to his own place, and to your most beloved piety, but he was taken away by that fate which is common to all men, and went to his rest before he could accomplish his wish; I have thought proper to fulfil that intention of the Emperor of sacred memory which I have inherited from him. When he comes to present himself before you, you will learn with what reverence he has been treated. Indeed it is not wonderful, whatever I have done on his behalf; for the thoughts of your longing desire for him, and the appearance of so great a man, moved my mind, and urged me thereto. May Divine Providence continually preserve you, dearly beloved brethren.

Dated from Treves the 15th before the Calends of July[1].

[1] June 17. A.D. 338.

§. 88. 37. This being the reason why I was sent away into Gaul, who, I ask again, does not plainly perceive the intention of the Emperor, and the murderous spirit of the Eusebians, and that the Emperor did this in order to prevent their forming some more desperate scheme? for he listened to them with a sincere purpose[k]. Such were the practices of the Eusebians, and such their machinations against me. Who that has witnessed them will deny that nothing has been done in my favour out of partiality, but that that great number of Bishops both individually and collectively wrote as they did in my behalf and condemned the falsehood of my enemies justly, and in accordance with the truth? Who that has observed such proceedings as these will deny that Valens and Ursacius had good reason to condemn themselves, and to write as they did, to accuse themselves on their repentance, choosing rather to suffer shame for a short time, than to undergo the punishment of false accusers for ever and ever[1]?

§. 89. 38. Wherefore also my blessed brothers in ministry, acting justly and according to the laws of the Church, while certain

[k] ἱστήκουσι γὰρ ἀπλῶς. Montfaucon in Onomast. (Athan. t. 2. ad calc.) points out some passages in his author, where ἱστακούειν like ὑπακούειν, means "to answer." vid Apol ad Const. §. 16. init. Orat. iii. 27 fin.

[1] Here ends the second part of the Apology, as is evident by turning back to §. 58. (supra, p 87 fin) to which this paragraph is an allusion. The express object of the second part was to prove, what has now been proved by documents, that Valens and Ursacius did but succumb to plain facts which they could not resist. It is observable too from this passage that the Apology was written before their relapse, i. e. before A.D 351, or 352. The remaining two sections are written after 357, as they mention the fall of Liberius and Hosius, and speak of Constantius in different language from any which has been found above. vid. Libr. F. vol. 8. p. 90, note p.

affirmed that my case was doubtful, and endeavoured to compel them to annul the sentence which was passed in my favour, have now endured all manner of sufferings, and have chosen rather to be banished than to see the judgment of so many Bishops reversed. Now if those genuine Bishops had withstood by words only those who plotted against me, and wished to undo all that had been done in my behalf; or if they had been ordinary men, and not the Bishops of illustrious cities, and the heads of great Churches, there would have been room to suspect that in this instance they too had acted contentiously and in order to gratify me. But when they not only endeavoured to convince by argument, but also endured banishment, and one of them is Liberius Bishop of Rome, (for although he did not endure to the end the sufferings of banishment, yet he remained in his exile for two years, being aware of conspiracy formed against me,) and since there is also the great Hosius, together with the Bishops of Italy, and of Gaul, and others from Spain, and from Egypt, and Libya, and all those from Pentapolis, (for although for a little while, through fear of the threats of Constantius, he seemed not to resist them, yet the great violence and tyrannical power exercised by Constantius, and the many insults and stripes inflicted on him, prove that it was not because he gave up my cause, but through the weakness of old age, being unable to bear the stripes, that he yielded to them for a season,) therefore I say, it is altogether right that all, as being fully convinced, should hate and abominate the injustice and the violence which they have used towards me; especially as it is well known that I have suffered these things on account of nothing else but the Arian impiety.

39. Now if any one wishes to become acquainted with my case, and the falsehood of the Eusebians, let him read what has been written in my behalf, and let him hear the witnesses, not one, or two, or three, but that great number of Bishops; and again let him attend to the witnesses of these proceedings, Liberius and Hosius, and their associates, who when they saw the attempts made against me, chose rather to endure all manner of sufferings than to give up the truth, and the judgment which had been pronounced in my favour.

APOL. AG. AR. And this they did with an honourable and righteous intention, for what they suffered proves to what straits the other Bishops were reduced. And they are memorials and records against the Arian heresy, and the wickedness of the false accusers, and afford a pattern and model for those who come after, to contend for the truth unto death, and to abominate the Arian heresy which fights against Christ[1], and is a forerunner of Antichrist[2]; and not to believe those who attempt to speak against me. For the defence put forth, and the sentence given, by so many Bishops of high character, are a trustworthy and sufficient testimony in my behalf.

[1] χριστο-μάχον, vol. 8. p. 6, note n.
[2] ibid. p. 79, note q.

III.

ENCYCLICAL EPISTLE

OF OUR HOLY

FATHER ATHANASIUS,

ARCHBISHOP OF ALEXANDRIA,

TO THE BISHOPS OF EGYPT AND LIBYA,

AGAINST THE ARIANS.

[The Circular Epistle which follows was addressed by S Athanasius to the Bishops of his Patriarchate in the beginning of 356, immediately after his flight from Egypt on the outrages committed against the Church by Syrianus. Some indeed have referred it to the year 361, with some plausibility, on the ground of a passage in § 22, where he speaks of the Arians being "declared heretics 36 years ago and cast out of the Church by decree of the whole Ecumenical Council," i. e. 325. However, if a stop is placed after "ago," the former clause may be made to refer to S. Alexander's condemnation of them, as Montfaucon observes. On the other hand it is plainly proved from §. 7, that it was written just as the Arians were sending George of Cappadocia to Alexandria, i. e. before Easter 356, and after Feb. 9, the date of Athanasius's leaving Alexandria. The stress too which is laid upon maintaining the Nicene Creed, and the notice of the Arian appeal to Scripture, and the respectful language he uses of Constantius, all agree with the date 356, if corroboration is necessary. There is very little in this Epistle which is not contained in his other Treatises, and a considerable portion is of a doctrinal character. It was written on occasion of an attempt made by the Arians to seduce the Bishops addressed into subscribing one of the specious Creeds of which so much is read in the history of the times; but nothing can be gathered of the circumstances from collateral sources The Treatise was formerly put at the head of the Orations against the Arians, and numbered as the first of them]

CHAP. I.

1. ALL things whatsoever our Lord and Saviour Jesus Christ, as Luke hath written, *both did and taught,* He did for our salvation, for which He appeared in the world; for He came, §. 1. vid. Acts1,1.

as John saith, *not to condemn the world, but that the world through Him might be saved.* And among the rest we have especially to admire this instance of His goodness, that He was not silent concerning those who should fight against us, but plainly told us beforehand, that, when those things should come to pass, we might straightway be found with minds established by His teaching. For He said, *There shall arise false prophets and false Christs, and shall shew great signs and wonders; insomuch that, if it were possible, the very elect shall be deceived. Behold, I have told you before.* Manifold indeed and beyond human conception are the instructions and gifts of grace which He has laid up in us; as the pattern of heavenly conversation, power against devils, the adoption of sons, and that exceeding great and singular grace, the knowledge of the Father and of the Word Himself, and the gift of the Holy Ghost. But the mind of man is prone to evil exceedingly; moreover, our adversary the devil, envying us the possession of such great blessings, goeth about seeking to snatch away the seed of the word which is sown within us. Wherefore as if by His prophetic warnings He would seal up His instructions in our hearts as His own peculiar treasure, the Lord said, *Take heed that no man deceive you. for many shall come in My name, saying, I am he; and the time draweth near; and they shall deceive many· go ye not therefore after them.*

2. This is a great gift which the Word has bestowed upon us, that we should not be deceived by appearances, but that, howsoever these things are concealed, we should distinguish them by the grace of the Spirit. For whereas the inventor of wickedness and great spirit of evil, the devil, is utterly hateful, and as soon as he shews himself is rejected[1] of all men,—as a serpent, as a dragon, as a lion seeking whom he may seize upon and devour,—therefore he conceals and covers what he really is, and craftily personates that Name which all men desire, so that deceiving by a false appearance, he may bind fast in his chains those whom he has led astray. And as if one that desired to kidnap the children of others during the absence of their parents, should personate their appearance, and so putting a cheat on the affections of the offspring, should carry them far away and destroy them;

in like manner this evil and wily spirit the devil, having no confidence in himself, and knowing the love which men bear to the truth, puts on the resemblance thereof, and so spreads his poison among those that follow after him. [Tr. III. 1—3.]

3. Thus he deceived Eve, not speaking his own, but artfully adopting the words of God, and perverting their meaning. Thus he suggested evil to the wife of Job, persuading her to feign affection for her husband, while he taught her to blaspheme God. Thus does the crafty spirit mock men by false appearances, deluding and drawing each into his own pit of wickedness. When of old he deceived the first man Adam, thinking that through him he should have all men subject unto him, he exulted with great boldness and said, *My hand hath found as a nest the riches of the people; and as one gathereth eggs that are left, have I gathered all the earth; and there was none that moved the wing, or opened the mouth, or peeped.* But when the Lord came upon earth, and the enemy made trial of His human economy, being unable to deceive the flesh which He had taken upon Him, from that time forth He, who promised Himself the occupation of the whole world, is for His sake mocked even by children: that proud one is mocked as a sparrow[1]. For now the infant child lays his hand upon the hole of the asp, and laughs at him that deceived Eve; and all that rightly believe in the Lord tread under foot him that said, *I will ascend above the heights of the clouds: I will be like the Most High.* [§. 2.] [Is. 10, 14.] [1 vid. Job 40, 24. Sept.] [Is. 14, 14.]

4. Thus he suffers and is dishonoured; and although he still ventures with shameless confidence to disguise himself, yet now, wretched spirit, he is detected the rather by them that bear the Sign on their foreheads; yea, more, he is rejected of them, and is humbled, and put to shame. For even if, now that he is a creeping serpent, he shall transform himself into an angel of light, yet his deception will not profit him; for we have been taught that *though an angel from heaven preach unto us any other gospel than that we have received, he shall be accursed.* And although, again, he conceal his natural falsehood, and pretend to speak truth with his lips; yet are we *not ignorant of his devices*, but are able to answer him in the words spoken by the Spirit against him; *But* [vid. Gal. 1, 8. 9.] [§. 3.] [2 Cor. 2, 11.]

Satan being hateful in himself pretends to be holy.

unto the ungodly, said God, why dost thou preach *My laws?* and, *Praise is not seemly in the mouth of a sinner.* For even though he speak the truth, the deceiver is not worthy of credit.

5. And whereas Scripture has shewn this, when relating his wicked artifices against Eve in Paradise, so the Lord also reproved him,—first in the mount, when He laid open *the folds of his breast-plate*¹, and shewed who the crafty spirit was, and proved that it was not one of the saints², but Satan that was tempting Him. For He said, *Get thee behind me, Satan; for it is written, Thou shalt worship the Lord thy God, and Him only shalt thou serve.* And again, when He put a curb in the mouths of the devils that cried after Him from the tombs. For although what they said was true, and they lied not then, saying, *Thou art the Son of God,* and *the Holy One of God;* yet He would not that the truth should proceed from an unclean mouth, and especially from such as them, lest under pretence thereof they should mingle with it their own malicious devices, and sow³ them while men slept. Therefore He suffered them not to speak these words, neither would He have us to suffer such, but hath charged us by His own mouth, saying, *Beware of false prophets, which come to you in sheeps' clothing, but inwardly they are ravening wolves;* and by the mouth of His Holy Apostles, *Believe not every spirit.*

6. Such is the method of our adversary's operations; and of the like nature are all these inventions of heresies, each of which has for the father of its own device the devil, who changed and became a murderer and a liar from the beginning. But being ashamed to profess his hateful name, they usurp the glorious Name of our Saviour *which is above every name*, and deck themselves out in the language of Scripture, speaking indeed the words, but stealing away the true meaning thereof; and so disguising by some artifice their false inventions, they also become the murderers of those whom they have led astray. For to what benefit do Marcion and Manichæus receive the Gospel while they reject the Law⁴? For the New Testament arose out of the Old, and bears witness to the Old; if then they reject this, how can they receive that which proceeds from it? Thus Paul was an Apostle of the Gospel, *which God promised*

afore by His prophets in the holy Scriptures; and our Lord Himself said, *Search the Scriptures, for they are they which testify of Me.* How then shall they confess the Lord, unless they first search the Scriptures which are written concerning Him? And the disciples say that they have found Him, *of whom Moses and the Prophets did write.*

^{TR.III. 3, 4. Rom. 1, 2. John 5, 39. John 1, 45.}

7. And to what end do the Sadducees retain the Law, if they receive not the Prophets[1]? For God who gave the Law, Himself promised in the Law that He would raise up Prophets also, so that the same is Lord both of the Law and of the Prophets, and he that denies the one must of necessity deny the other also. And again, how can the Jews receive the Old Testament, unless they acknowledge the Lord whose coming was expected according to it? For had they believed the writings of Moses, they would have believed the words of the Lord; for He said, *He wrote of Me.* Moreover, what are the Scriptures to Paul[2] of Samosata, who denies the Word of God and His incarnate Presence[3], which is signified and declared both in the Old and New Testament? And of what use are the Scriptures to the Arians also, and why do they bring them forward, men who say that the Word of God is a creature, and like the Gentiles, *serve the creature more than* God *the Creator?* Thus each of these heresies, in respect of the peculiar impiety of its invention[4], has nothing in common with the Scriptures. And their advocates are aware of this, that the Scriptures are very much, or rather altogether, opposed to the doctrines of every one of them; but for the sake of deceiving the more simple sort, (such as are those of whom it is written in the Proverbs, *The simple believeth every word,*) they pretend like their *father the devil*[5] to study and to quote the language of Scripture, in order that they may appear by their words to have a right belief, and so may persuade their wretched followers to believe contrary to the Scriptures[6].

^{1 vid Prideaux, Conn ii. 5 (vol.3. p. 474. ed. 1725.) John 5, 46. 2 vol. 8. p. 16, note 1. 3 ibid. p 252, note g. Rom. 1, 25. 4 ἱδινοίας Prov. 14, 15. John 8, 5. 5 Orat. ii.73,74. vol. 8. p. 9, note 3 6 ibid p. 189.}

8. Assuredly in every one of these heresies the devil has thus disguised himself, and has suggested to them words full of craftiness. The Lord spake concerning them, that *there shall arise false Christs and false prophets, so that they shall deceive many.* Accordingly the Devil has come,

^{Mat.24, 24.}

K

speaking by each and saying, " I am Christ, and the truth is with me;" and he has made them, one and all, to be liars like himself. And strange it is, that while all heresies are at variance with one another concerning the mischievous inventions which each has framed, they are united together only by the common purpose of lying[1]. For they have one and the same father that has sown in them all the seeds of falsehood Wherefore the faithful Christian and true disciple of the Gospel, having grace to discern spiritual things, and having built the house of his faith upon a rock, stands continually firm and secure from their deceits. But the simple person, as I said before, that is not thoroughly grounded in knowledge, such an one, considering only the words that are spoken and not perceiving their meaning[2], is immediately drawn away by their wiles. Wherefore it is good and needful for us to pray that we may receive the gift of discerning spirits, so that every one may know, according to the precept of John, whom he ought to reject and whom to receive as friends and of the same faith. Now one might write at great length concerning these things, if one desired to go into details respecting them; for the impiety and perverseness of heresies will appear to be manifold and various, and the craft of the deceivers to be very terrible But since holy Scripture is of all things most sufficient[3] for us, therefore recommending to those who desire to know more of these matters, to read the Divine word, I now hasten to set before you that which most claims attention, and for the sake of which principally I have written these things.

§. 5.   9. I have heard during my sojourn in these parts[4], (and they were true and orthodox brethren that informed me,) that certain professors of Arian opinions have met together, and have drawn up a confession of faith to their own liking, and that they intend to send word to you, that you must either subscribe to what pleases them, or rather to what the Devil has inspired them with, or in case of refusal must suffer banishment. They have indeed already begun to molest the Bishops of these parts; and thereby have plainly manifested their disposition. For inasmuch as they have framed this document only for the purpose of inflicting

Attempt of Arians to substitute a Creed for the Nicene.

banishment or other punishments, what does such conduct prove them to be, but enemies of the Christians, and friends of the Devil and his angels? and especially, since they spread abroad what they like contrary to the mind of that gracious Prince, our most religious Emperor Constantius[1]. And this they do with great craftiness, and, as appears to me, chiefly with two ends in view; first, that by obtaining your subscriptions, they may seem to remove the evil repute that rests upon the name of Arius, and may escape notice themselves as if not professing his opinions; and again, that by putting forth these statements they may cast a shade over the Council of Nicæa[2], and the confession of faith which was then put forth against the Arian heresy.

10. But this proceeding does but prove the more plainly their own maliciousness and heterodoxy. For had they believed aright, they would have been satisfied with the confession put forth at Nicæa by the whole Ecumenic Council; and had they considered themselves calumniated and falsely called Arians, they ought not to have been so eager to innovate upon what was written against Arius, lest what was directed against him might seem to be aimed at them also. This however is not the course they pursue, but they conduct the struggle in their own behalf, just as if they were Arius. Observe how entirely they disregard the truth, and how every thing they say and do is for the sake of the Arian heresy. For in that they dare to question those sound definitions of the faith, and take upon themselves to produce others contrary to them, what else do they but accuse the Fathers, and stand up in defence of that heresy which they opposed and protested against? And what they now write proceeds not from any regard for the truth, as I said before, rather they do it as in mockery and by an artifice, for the purpose of deceiving men, that by sending about their letters they may engage the ears of the people to listen to these notions, and so put off the time when they will be brought to trial, and that by concealing their impiety from observation, they may have room to extend their heresy, which *like a gangrene* eats its way every where.

11. Accordingly they disturb and disorder every thing, and yet are never satisfied with their own proceedings. For

---

TR. III.
[5, 6]

[1] vol 8, p 90, note p.

[2] ibid. p 84, note b.

[3] ibid. p 49, note o, de Syn. passim.

[4] p. 35, r. 1.

2 Tim. 2, 17.
§. 6.

every year, as if they were going to draw up a contract, they meet together and pretend to write about the faith, whereby they expose themselves the more to ridicule and disgrace, because their expositions are rejected, not by others, but by themselves[1]. For had they had any confidence in their previous statements, they would not have desired to draw up others; nor again, rejecting these last, would they now have set down the one in question, which no doubt true to their custom, they will again alter, after a very short interval, and as soon as they shall find a pretence for their customary plotting against certain persons. For when they have a design against any, then it is that they make a great shew of writing about the faith, that, as Pilate washed his hands, so they by a like proceeding may destroy those who rightly believe in Christ, hoping that, as making definitions about the faith, they will appear, as I have repeatedly said, to be free from the charge of false doctrine.

12. But they will not be able to hide themselves, nor to escape; for they continually become their own accusers[2] even while they defend themselves. Justly so, since instead of answering those who bring proof against them, they do but persuade themselves to believe whatever they wish. And when is an acquittal obtained, upon the criminal becoming his own judge? Hence it is that they are always writing, and always altering their own previous statements, and thus they shew an uncertain faith[3], or rather a manifest unbelief and perverseness. And this, it appears to me, must needs be the case with them; for since, having fallen away from the truth, and desiring to overthrow that sound confession of faith which was drawn up at Nicæa, they have, in the language of Scripture, *loved to wander, and have not refrained their feet;* therefore, like Jerusalem of old, they labour and toil in these their changes, sometimes writing one thing, and sometimes another, but only for the sake of gaining time, and that they may continue enemies of Christ[4], and deceivers of mankind.

§. 7. 13. Who then, that has any real regard for truth, will be willing to suffer these men any longer? who will not justly reject their expositions? who will not denounce their audacity, that being but few[5] in number, they would have their decisions to prevail over every thing, and as desiring the supremacy of their own meetings, held in corners and suspicious in their circumstances, would forcibly cancel the decrees of an uncorrupt, pure, and Ecumenic Council? Men who have been promoted by the Eusebians for advocating this Antichristian heresy, venture to define articles of faith, and while they ought to be brought to judgment as criminals, like Caiaphas, they take upon themselves to judge. They compose a Thalia[1], and would have it received as a standard of faith, while they are not yet themselves determined what they believe.

14. Who does not know that Secundus[2] of Pentapolis, who was several times degraded long ago, was received by them for the sake of the Arian fanaticism; and that George[3] now of Laodicea, and Leontius the Eunuch, and before him Stephanus, and Theodorus of Heraclea[4], were promoted by them? Ursacius and Valens also, who from the first were instructed by Arius as young men[5], though they had been formerly degraded from the Priesthood, afterwards got the title of Bishops on account of their impiety; as did also Acacius, Patrophilus[6], and Narcissus, who have been most forward in all manner of impiety. These were degraded in the great Council of Sardica; Eustathius also now of Sebastea, Demophilus and Germinius[7], Eudoxius and Basil, who are supporters of that impiety, were advanced in the same manner. Of Cecropius[8], and him they call Auxentius, and of Epictetus[9] the stage-player, it were superfluous for me to speak, since it is manifest to all men, in what manner, on what pretexts, and by what enemies of ours these were promoted, that they might play their false charges against the orthodox Bishops who were the objects of their designs. For although they resided at the distance of eighty posts[10], and were unknown to the people, yet on the ground of their impiety they were able to procure for themselves the title of Bishop. For the same reason also they have now[11] hired one George of Cappadocia, whom they wish to impose upon you. But no respect is due to him any more than to the rest, for there is a report in these parts that he is not even a Christian, but is devoted to the worship of idols, and he has a hangman's temper[12]. And this person, such as he is described to be, they have taken

Tr. III.
7.

[1] vol 8. p. 94, &c.

[2] ibid pp. 88, 89 supr. p. 44.
[3] supr p. 25, note f.
[4] supr. p 60
[5] supr. p. 31, note m.
[6] omitted and rightly
(P) supr. p. 68.
[7] vol 8 pp. 85, 86.
[8] of Nicomedia.
[9] vid Hist Mon § 74 fin.

[10] supr. p 50, note h.

[11] p 125.

[12] vol. 8. p. 134, note f.

134 *Words bad, though Scriptural, which proceed from bad men,*

LETT. TO EG. LIB.
into their ranks, that they may be able to injure, to plunder, and to slay; for in these things he is a great proficient, but is ignorant of the very principles of the Christian faith.

§. 8.   15. Such are the machinations of these men against the truth: but their designs are manifest to all the world, though they attempt in ten thousand ways, like eels, to elude the grasp, and to escape detection as enemies of Christ. Wherefore I beseech you, let no one among you be deceived, no one seduced by them; rather, considering that a sort of judaical impiety is invading the Christian faith, be ye all zealous for the Lord; hold fast, every one, the faith we have received from the Fathers, which they who assembled at Nicæa recorded in writing[1], and endure not those who endeavour to innovate thereon. And however they may quote phrases out of the Scripture, endure not their compositions; however they may speak the language of the orthodox, yet attend not to what they say, for they speak not with an upright mind, but putting on such language like sheeps' clothing, in their hearts they think with Arius, after the manner of the devil[2] who is the author of all heresies. For he too made use of the words of Scripture, but was put to silence by our Saviour. For if he had indeed meant them as he used them, he would not have fallen from heaven; but now having fallen through his pride[3], he artfully dissembles in his speech, and oftentimes maliciously endeavours to lead men astray by the subtleties and sophistries of the Gentiles.

16. Had these expositions of theirs proceeded from the orthodox[4], from such as the great Confessor Hosius, and Maximinus[5] of Gaul, or his successor, or from such as Philogonius and Eustathius[6], Bishops of the East[7], or Julius and Liberius of Rome, or Cyriacus of Mysia[8], or Pistus and Aristæus of Greece, or Silvester and Protogenes of Dacia, or Leontius and Eupsychius of Cappadocia, or Cecilian of Africa, or Eustorgius of Italy, or Capito of Sicily, or Macarius of Jerusalem, or Alexander of Constantinople, or Pederos of Heraclea, or those great Bishops Meletius, Basil, and Longianus, and the rest from Armenia and Pontus, or Lupus and Amphion from Cilicia, or James and the rest from Mesopotamia, or our own blessed Alexander, with others of the

[1] vol. 8, p 49, note p.
[2] supr. p. 129.
[3] Cypr. Treat. tr. p 24, note a.
[4] vol. 8, p. 17, note m.
[5] supr. p. 77, r. 2.
[6] at Nicæa as most of the others.
[7] i. e. of Antioch
[8] of Paphos p Leont in Nest. 1. p 550. [ed. Can.]

for they do but serve as their cloak.

same sentiments as these;—there would then have been nothing to suspect in their statements, for the minds of apostolical men are sincere and incapable of fraud. But when they proceed from those who are hired to advocate the cause of heresy, and since, according to the divine proverb, *The words of the wicked are to lie in wait,* and *The mouth of the wicked poureth out evil things,* and *The counsels of the wicked are deceit:* it becomes us to watch and be sober, brethren, as the Lord has said, lest any deception arise from subtlety of speech and craftiness; lest any one come and pretend to say, 'I preach Christ,' and after a little while he be found to be Antichrist. These indeed are Antichrists, whosoever come to you in the cause of the Arian fanaticism.

Tr.III. 8, 9.
§. 9.

Prov. 12, 6 15, 28. 12, 5.

17. For what defect is there among you, that any one need to come to you from without? Or, of what do the Churches of Egypt and Libya and Alexandria stand so much in need, that these men should make a purchase[1] of the Episcopate as of wood and goods, and intrude into Churches which do not belong to them? Who is not aware, who does not perceive clearly, that they do all this in order to support their impiety? Wherefore although they should make themselves mute, or although they should bind on their garments larger borders than the Pharisees, and pour themselves forth in long speeches, and practise the tones of their voice[2], they ought not to be believed; for it is not the mode of speaking, but the intentions of the heart and a godly conversation that recommend the faithful Christian. And thus the Sadducees and Herodians, although they had the law in their mouths, were put to rebuke by our Saviour, who said unto them, *Ye do err, not knowing the Scriptures, nor the power of God* and all men witnessed the exposure of those who pretended to quote the words of the Law, as being in their minds heretics and enemies of God[3]. Others indeed they deceived by these professions, but when our Lord became man they were not able to deceive Him; for *the Word was made flesh,* who *knoweth the thoughts of men that they are vain.* Thus He exposed the evasions of the Jews, saying, *If God were your Father, ye would love Me, for I proceeded forth from the Father, and am come to you*[4]. In like manner these men seem now to act; for they disguise their real sentiments, and

[1] Ap. ad Const. §. 28.
Hist. Arian. §. 73, supr.

[2] vid. Basil Ep 223.

[3] θεομάχοι John 1, 14.
Ps. 94, 11.
John 8, 42. 16, 28.

[4] ἥκω, vid. Hipp. contr. Noet. 16. and vol. 8, p 98, l 1.

make use of the language of Scripture in their writings, which they hold forth as a bait for the ignorant, that they may inveigle them into their own wickedness.

§. 10.   18. Consider, whether this be not so. If, when there is no reason for their doing so, they write confessions of faith, it is a superfluous, and perhaps also a mischievous proceeding, because, when no question is proposed for consideration, they give occasion for controversy of words, and unsettle the simple hearts of the brethren, disseminating among them such notions as have never entered into their minds. And if they profess to clear themselves in regard to the Arian heresy, they ought first to remove the seeds of those evils which have sprung up, and to proscribe those who produced them, and then in the room of former statements to set forth others which are sound; or else let them openly vindicate the opinions of Arius, that they may no longer covertly but openly shew themselves enemies of Christ[1], and that all men may fly from them as from the sight of a serpent. But now they keep back those opinions, and for a pretence write on other matters; just as if a surgeon, when summoned to attend a person wounded and suffering, should upon coming in to him say not a word concerning his wounds, but proceed to discourse about his sound limbs. Such an one would be chargeable with utter stupidity, for saying nothing on the matter for which he came, but discoursing on those other points in which he was not needed. Yet just in the same manner these men omit those matters which concern their heresy, and take upon themselves to write on other subjects, whereas, if they had any regard for the Faith, or any love for Christ, they ought first to remove out of the way those blasphemous expressions uttered against Him, and then in the room of them to speak and to write sound words. But this they neither do themselves, nor permit those that desire to do so, whether it be from ignorance, or through craft and artifice.

§ 11.   19. If they do this from ignorance they must be charged with rashness, because they affirm positively concerning things that they know not; but if they dissemble knowingly, their condemnation is the greater, because while they overlook nothing in consulting for their own interests, in writing about

[1] p. 132, r. 4.

faith in our Lord they make a mockery, and do any thing rather than speak the truth; they keep back those particulars respecting which their heresy is accused, and merely bring forward passages out of the Scriptures. Now this is a manifest robbery of the truth, and a practice full of all iniquity; and so I am sure your piety will readily perceive it to be from the following illustrations. No person being accused of adultery defends himself as innocent of theft; nor would any one in prosecuting a charge of murder suffer the accused parties to defend themselves by saying, 'We have not committed perjury, but have preserved the deposit which was entrusted to us.' This would be mere child's play, instead of a refutation of the charge and a demonstration of the truth. For what has murder to do with a deposit, or adultery with theft? The crimes are indeed related to each other as proceeding from the same evil heart; yet in respect to the refutation of an alleged offence, they have no connection with each other.

20. Accordingly as it is written in the Book of Jesus the son of Nave, when Achan was charged with theft, he did not excuse himself with the plea of his zeal in the wars, but being convicted of the offence was stoned by all the people. And when Saul was charged with negligence and a breach of the law, he did not benefit his cause by alleging his conduct on other matters. For a defence in one sort will not operate to obtain an acquittal in another sort; but if all things should be done according to law and justice, a man must defend himself in those particulars wherein he is accused, and must either disprove the past, or else confess it with the promise that he will do so no more. But if he is guilty of the crime, and will not confess, but in order to conceal the truth speaks on other points instead of the one in question, he shews plainly that he has acted amiss; nay, and is conscious of his delinquency. But what need of many words, seeing that these persons are themselves the accusers of the Arian heresy? For since they have not the boldness to speak out, but conceal their blasphemous expressions, it is plain that they know that this heresy is separate and alien from the truth. But since they conceal this and are afraid to speak, it is necessary for me to strip off the veil from their

138 *Athanasius's apology for uttering Arian statements.*

LETT. TO EG. LIB.

¹ vol. 8, p. 216, note c.

impiety, and to expose the heresy to public view, knowing as I do the statements which the Arians formerly made, and how they were cast out of the Church, and degraded from the Clergy. But here first I ask for pardon¹ of the foul words to which I am about to give utterance, since I use them, not because I thus think, but in order to convict the heretics.

CHAP. II.

1. Now the Bishop Alexander of blessed memory cast Arius §. 12. out of the Church for holding and maintaining the following sentiments[1]: "God was not always a Father: The Son was [1 vol 8. pp. 10, 94, 185.] not always: But whereas all things were made out of nothing, the Son of God also was made out of nothing: And since all things are creatures, He also is a creature and a production[2]: And since all things once were not, but were [2 ποίημα] afterwards made, there was a time when the Word of God Himself was not; and He was not before He was begotten[3], [3 γεννη-θῆναι, vol 8, p. 272.] but He had a beginning[4] of existence: For He was then begotten when God determined to produce[5] Him: For He [4 ἀρχήν] also is one among the rest of His works. And since He is [5 δημι-ουργῆσαι] by nature changeable[6], and only continues good because He [6 τρεπ-τός, vid. chooses by His own free will, He is capable of being changed, vol. 8. as are all other things, whenever he wishes. And therefore p. 230, God, as foreknowing that He would be good, gave Him by note a.] anticipation that glory which He would have obtained afterwards by His virtue; and He is now become good by His works which God foreknew." Accordingly they say, that Christ is not truly God, but that He is called God on account of His participation in God's nature, as are all other creatures. And they add, that He is not that Word which is by nature in the Father, and is proper to His Substance, nor is He His proper wisdom by which He made this world; but that there is another Word[7] which is [7 ibid. properly[8] in the Father, and another Wisdom which is p. 101. properly in the Father, by which Wisdom also He made [8 ἴδιος] this Word, and that the Lord Himself is called the Word by a fiction[9] in regard of things endued with reason[10], and is [9 κατ' called the Wisdom fictitiously in regard of things endued ἐπίνοιαν with wisdom. Nay, they say that as all things are in sub- [11. 38.]

stance separate and alien from the Father, so He also is in all respects separate and alien from the substance of the Father, and properly belongs to things made and created, and is one of them; for He is a creature, and a production, and a work.

2. Again, they say that God did not create us for His sake, but Him for our sakes. For they say, " God was alone, and the Word was not with Him, but afterwards when He would create us[1], then He made Him; and from the time He was made, He called Him the Word, and the Son, and the Wisdom, in order that He might create us by Him. And as all things subsisted by the will of God, and did not exist before; so He also was made by the will of God, and did not exist before. For the Word is not the proper and natural Offspring of the Father, but was Himself made by grace: for God who existed before made by His will the Son who did not exist, by which will also He made all things, and produced, and created, and willed them to be[2]."

Moreover they say also, that Christ is not the natural and true power of God; but as *the locust* and *the cankerworm* are called a power[3], so also He is called the power of the Father. Furthermore he said, that the Father cannot be described by the Son, and that the Son can neither see nor know the Father perfectly and exactly[4]. For having a beginning of existence, He cannot know Him that is without beginning; but what He knows and sees, He knows and sees in a measure proportionate to His capacity[5], as we also know and see in proportion to our powers. And he added also, that the Son not only does not know His own Father exactly, but that He does not even know His own nature[6].

§. 13.   3. For maintaining these and the like opinions Arius was declared a heretic; for myself, while I have merely been writing them down, I have been cleansing myself[7] by thinking of the contrary doctrines, and by possessing my mind with the idea of the true faith. For the Bishops who all assembled from all parts at the Council of Nicæa, stopped their ears when they heard these statements, and all with one voice condemned this heresy on account of them, and anathematized it, declaring it to be alien and estranged from the faith of the Church It was no necessity which led the judges to this decision, but they all by free choice vindicated the truth[a]: and they did so justly and rightly. For infidelity is coming in through these men, or rather a Judaism beside the Scriptures, which has close upon it Gentile superstition, so that he who holds these opinions can no longer be called a Christian, for they are all contrary to the Scriptures.

4. John, for instance, saith, *In the beginning was the Word;* but these men say, " He was not, before He was begotten."[1] And again he has written, *And we are in Him that is true, even in His Son Jesus Christ; this is the true God, and eternal life;* but these men, as if in contradiction to this, allege that Christ is not the true God, but that He is only called God, as are other creatures, in regard of His participation in the divine nature. And the Apostle blames the Gentiles, because they worship creatures, saying, *They served the creature more than God the Creator*[1] But if these men say that the Lord is a creature, and worship Him as a creature, how do they differ from the Gentiles? If they hold this opinion, is not this passage also against them; and does not the blessed Paul write as blaming them? The Lord also says, *I and My Father are One.* and *He that hath seen Me, hath seen the Father*[2]; and the Apostle who was sent by Him to preach, writes, *Who being the Brightness of His glory, and the express Image of His Person.* But these men dare to separate them, and to say that He is alien from the substance and eternity of the Father; and impiously to represent Him as changeable, not perceiving, that by speaking thus, they make Him to be, not one with the Father, but one with created things. Who does not see, that the brightness cannot be separated from the light[3], but that it is by nature proper to it, and co-existent with it, and is not

Tr.III. 13.

John 1, 1.

1 John 5, 20.

Rom. 1, 25.
1 supr.
p. 129, vol 8.
p. 191, note d.

John 10, 30; 14, 9.
2 ibid.
p. 229, note g.
Heb. 1, 3.

3 ibid.
p. 48.

---

[a] " Know," says St Athan. to Jovian, " that these things have been preached from the beginning, and this Creed the Fathers who assembled at Nicæa confessed, and to these have been awarded the suffrages of all the Churches every where in their respective places..... And thou knowest that, should there be some few who are in opposition to this faith, they cannot create any prejudice against it, the whole world maintaining the Apostolical Creed." Athan. Ep. ad Jov. §.2 " Whether it be persecutions or afflictions or threats from our sovereign, or cruelties from persons in office, ...we endured it on behalf of the Apostolical faith, &c." Theod. Hist. v. 9. vid Keble on Primitive Trad. p 122. 10. " Let each boldly set down his faith in writing, having the fear of God before his eyes." Conc. Chalced. Sess.1. Hard. t.2. p. 273. "Give diligence without fear, favour, or dislike, to set out the faith in its purity." ibid. p. 285.

produced after it? Again, when the Father says, *This is My beloved Son*, and when the Scriptures say that *He is the Word* of the Father, by whom *the heavens were established*, and in short, *All things were made by Him;* these inventors of new doctrines and fables represent that there is another Word, and another Wisdom of the Father, and that He is only called the Word and the Wisdom by a fiction in regard of things endued with reason, while they perceive not the absurdity of this[1].

§. 14. 5. But if He be styled the Word and the Wisdom by a fiction on our account, what He really is they cannot tell[2]. For if the Scriptures affirm that the Lord is both these, and yet these men will not allow Him to be so, it is plain that in their impious opposition to the Scriptures they would deny His existence altogether. The faithful are able to conclude this truth both from the voice of the Father Himself, and from the Angels that worshipped Him, and from the Saints that have written concerning Him; but these men, as they have not a pure mind, and cannot bear to hear the words of holy men who teach of God, may be able to learn something even from the devils who resemble them, for they spoke of Him, not as if there were many beside, but, as knowing Him alone, they said, *Thou art the Holy One of God*, and the *Son of God*. He also who suggested to them this heresy[3], while tempting Him in the mount, said not, 'If thou also be a Son of God,' as though there were others beside Him, but, *If Thou be the Son of God*, as being the only one. But as the Gentiles, having renounced the notion of one God, have sunk into polytheism, so these wonderful men, not believing that the Word of the Father is one, have come to adopt the idea of many words, and they deny Him that is really God and the true Word, and have dared to conceive of Him as a creature, not perceiving how full of impiety is such an opinion. For if He be a creature, how is He at the same time the Creator of creatures? or how the Son and the Wisdom and the Word? For the Word is not created, but begotten; and a creature is not a Son, but a production. And if all creatures were made by Him, and He is also a creature, then by whom was He made? Productions must of necessity proceed from some one; as in fact they proceeded from the Word; because He was not Himself a production, but the Word of the Father. And again, if the Wisdom in the Father be beside the Lord, then there is a Wisdom in a Wisdom: and if the Word of God be the Wisdom of God, then there is a Word in a Word: and if the Word of God be the Son of God, then there is a Son produced in the Son.

6. How is it that the Lord has said, *I am in the Father, and the Father in Me,* if there be another in the Father, by whom the Lord Himself also was made? And how is it that John, passing over that other, relates of this One, saying, *All things were made by Him; and without Him was not any thing made*[1]? If all things that were made by the will of God were made by Him, how can He be Himself one of the things that were made? And when the Apostle says, *For whom are all things, and by whom are all things,* how can these men say, that we were not made for Him, but He for us? If it be so, He ought to have said, "For whom the Word was made;" but He saith not so, but, *For whom are all things, and by whom are all things,* thus proving these men to be heretical and false.

7. But further, as they have had the boldness to say that there is another Word in God, and since they cannot bring any clear proof of this from the Scriptures, let them but shew one work of His, or one work of the Father that was made without this Word; so that they may seem to have some ground at least for this their imagination[2]. The works of the true Word are manifest to all, and according to the evidence they afford is He known by them. For as, when we see the creation, we conceive of God as the Creator of it; so when we see that nothing is without order therein, but that all things move and continue with order and design, we have an idea of a Word of God who is over all and governs all. This too the holy Scriptures testify, declaring that He is the Word of God, and that *all things were made by Him, and without Him was not any thing made.* But of that other Word, of whom they speak, there is neither word nor work that they have to shew. Nay, even the Father Himself, when He says, *This is My beloved Son,* signifies that besides Him there is none other.

Tr.III. 14, 15.

§. 15. John 14, 10. John 1, 3. [1] vol. 8. p. 208, note a. Heb. 2, 10.

[2] ἐπίνοιας John 1, 3. Mat. 17, 5.

8. It appears then that so far as these doctrines are concerned, these wonderful men have now joined themselves to the Manichees. For these also confess the existence of a good God, so far as the mere name goes, but they are unable to point out any of His works either visible or invisible. But inasmuch as they deny Him who is truly and indeed God, the Maker of heaven and earth, and of all things invisible, they are mere inventors of fables. And this appears to me to be the case with these evil-minded men. They see the works of the true Word who alone is in the Father, and yet they deny Him, and make to themselves another Word[1], whose existence they are unable to prove either by His works or by the testimony of others. Unless it be that they have adopted a fabulous notion of God, that He is a compound being like man, speaking and then changing His words, and as a man exercising understanding and wisdom; not perceiving to what absurdities[2] they are reduced by such an opinion. For if God has a succession of words[3], they certainly must consider Him as a man. And if those words proceed from Him and then vanish away, they are guilty of a greater impiety, because they resolve into nothing what proceeds from the self-existent God. If they conceive that God doth at all beget, it were surely better and more religious to say that He is the Father of One Word, who is the fulness of His Godhead, in whom are hidden the treasures of all knowledge, and that He is co-existent with His Father, and that all things were made by Him; rather than to suppose God to be the Father of many words which are no where to be found, or to represent Him who is simple in His nature as compounded of many[4], and as being subject to human passions[5] and variable.

9. Next, whereas the Apostle says, *Christ the power of God and the wisdom of God,* these men reckon Him but as one among many powers; nay, worse than this, they compare Him, transgressors as they are, with the cankerworm and other irrational creatures which are sent by Him for the punishment of men. Next, whereas the Lord says, *No one knoweth the Father, save the Son;* and again, *Not that any man hath seen the Father, save He which is of the Father;* are not these indeed enemies of God[6] which say that the Father

is neither seen nor known of the Son perfectly? If the Lord says, *As the Father knoweth Me, even so know I the Father,* and if the Father knoweth not the Son partially, are they not mad to pretend that the Son knoweth the Father only partially, and not fully? Next, if the Son has a beginning of existence, and all things likewise have a beginning, let them say, which is prior to the other. But indeed they have nothing to say, neither can they with all their craft prove such a beginning of the Word. For He is the true and proper Offspring of the Father, and *in the beginning was the Word, and the Word was with God, and the Word was God.* With regard to their assertion, that the Son knows not His own nature[1], it is superfluous to reply to it, except only so far as to condemn their madness, for how does not the Son know Himself, when He imparts to all men the knowledge of His Father and of Himself, and blames those who know Them not?

^{Tr III 16, 17 John 10, 15}

^{John 1, 1.}

^{1 οὐσίαν}

10. But it is written[2], say they, *The Lord created Me in the beginning of His ways for His works.* O untaught and insensate that ye are! He is called also in the Scriptures, *servant*, and *son of a handmaid*, and *lamb*, and *sheep*, and it is said that He suffered toil, and thirst, and was beaten, and endured pain. But there is plainly a reasonable ground and cause[3], why such representations as these are given of Him in the Scriptures; and it is because He became man and the Son of man, and took upon Him the form of a servant, which is the human flesh: for *the Word*, says John, *was made flesh.* And since He became man, no one ought to be offended at such expressions; for it is proper to man to be created, and born, and formed, to suffer toil and pain, to die and to rise again from the dead. And as, being the Word and Wisdom of the Father, He has all the attributes of the Father, His eternity, and His unchangeableness, and is like Him in all respects and in all things[4], and is neither before nor after, but co-existent with the Father, and is the very form[5] of the Godhead, and is the Creator, and is not created: (for since He is in substance like[6] the Father, He cannot be a creature, but must be the Creator, as Himself hath said, *My Father worketh hitherto, and I work.*) so being made man, and bearing our flesh,

^{§. 17 2 Orat 11. 18—72 Prov. 8, 22 Ps. 116, 16 &c.}

^{3 vol. 8. p. 22.}

^{John 1, 14.}

^{4 vol. 8. p 115, note e.}
^{5 εἶδος, ibid.}
^{p. 154, note e.}
^{6 ibid.}
^{p. 210, note e.}
^{John 5, 17.}

He is necessarily said to be created and made, and to have all the attributes of the flesh; howsoever these men, like Jewish vintners, who mix their wine with water[1], debase the Word, and subject His Godhead to their notions of created things.

11. Wherefore the Fathers were with reason and justice indignant, and anathematized this most impious heresy; which these persons are now cautious of and keep back, as being easy to be disproved and unsound[2] in every part of it. These that I have set down are but a few of the arguments which go to condemn their doctrines; but if any one desires to enter more at large into the proof against them, he will find that this heresy is not far removed from the Gentile superstitions, and that it is the lowest and the very dregs of all the other heresies. These last are in error either concerning the body or the incarnation of the Lord, falsifying the truth, some in one way and some in another, or else they deny that the Lord has come at all, as the Jews erroneously suppose. But this alone more madly than the rest has dared to assail the very Godhead, and to assert that the Word is not at all[3], and that the Father was not always a father; so that one might reasonably say that that Psalm was written against them; *The fool hath said in his heart, There is no God*[4] *Corrupt are they, and become abominable in their doings.*

§. 18. 12. "But," say they, "we are strong, and are able to defend our heresy by our many devices." They would have a better answer to give, if they were able to defend it, not by artifice nor by Gentile sophisms, but by the simplicity of the faith. If however they have confidence in it, and know it to be in accordance with the doctrines of the Church, let them openly express their sentiments; for no man when he hath lighted a candle putteth it under a bushel[5], but on a candlestick, and so it gives light to all that come in. If therefore they are able to defend it, let them record in writing the opinions above imputed to them, and expose their heresy bare to the view of all men, as they would a candle, and let them openly accuse the Bishop Alexander, of blessed memory, as having unjustly ejected[6] Arius for professing these opinions; and let them blame the

Council of Nicæa for putting forth a written confession of Tr.III. the true faith in opposition to their impiety. But they will 18, 19. not do this, I am sure, for they are not so ignorant of the evil nature of these notions which they have invented and are ambitious of spreading abroad; but they know well enough, that although they may at first lead astray the simple by vain deceit, yet their imaginations will soon be extinguished, *as the light of the ungodly*, and themselves Job 18, branded every where as enemies of the Truth. 5. ¹vol. 8.

13. Therefore although they do all things foolishly, and p. 193. speak as fools, yet in this at least they have acted wisely, as *children of this world*, hiding their candle under a bushel, Luke 16, that it may be supposed to give light, and lest, if it appear, it 8. be condemned and extinguished. Thus when Arius himself, the author of the heresy, and the associate of Eusebius, was summoned through the interest of the Eusebians to appear before Constantine Augustus of blessed memory², and was ² vid. required to present a written declaration of his faith, the Ep. ad Serap. wily man wrote one, but kept out of sight the peculiar infr. expressions of his impiety, and pretended, as the Devil did, to quote the simple words of Scripture, just as they are written. And when the blessed Constantine said to him, " If thou holdest no other opinions in thy mind besides these, take the Truth to witness for thee; the Lord will repay thee if thou swear falsely:" the wretched man swore that he held no other, and that he had never either spoken or thought otherwise than as he had now written. But as soon as he went out he dropped down, as if paying the penalty of his crime, and *falling headlong burst asunder in* Acts 1, *the midst.* 18.

14. Death, it is true, is the common end of all men, and we §. 19. ought not to insult the dead, though he be an enemy, for it is uncertain whether the same event may not happen to ourselves before evening. But the end of Arius was not after an ordinary manner, and therefore it deserves to be related. The Eusebians threatening to bring him into the Church, Alexander the Bishop of Constantinople resisted them, but Arius trusted to the violence and menaces of Eusebius. It was the Sabbath, and he expected to join communion³ on the following day. There was therefore a ³ συνά- γισθαι

148 *The death of Arius has not been a warning to them.*

LETT. TO EG. LIB.

great struggle between them, the Eusebians threatening, Alexander praying. But the Lord, being judge of the case, decided against the unjust party, for the sun had not set, when the necessities of nature compelled him to that place, where he fell down, and was forthwith deprived of communion with the Church and of his life together. The blessed[1] Constantine hearing of this soon after, was struck with wonder to find him thus convicted of perjury. And indeed it was then evident to all that the threats of the Eusebians had proved of no avail, and the hope of Arius had become vain. It was shewn too that the Arian fanaticism was rejected from communion[2] by our Saviour both here and in the Church of the first-born in heaven.

[1] μακαρίτης
[2] ἀκοινώνητος

15. Now who will not wonder to see the unrighteous ambition of these men, whom the Lord has condemned;—to see them vindicating the heresy which the Lord has pronounced excommunicate, (since He did not suffer its author to enter into the Church,) and not fearing that which is written, but attempting impossible things? *For the Lord of hosts hath purposed, and who shall disannul it?* and whom the Lord hath condemned, who shall justify? Let them however in defence of their own imaginations write what they please; but do you, brethren, as *bearing the vessels of the Lord,* and vindicating the doctrines of the Church, examine this matter, I beseech you; and if they write in other terms than those above recorded as the language of Arius, then condemn them as hypocrites, who hide the poison of their opinions, and like the serpent flatter with the words of their lips. For, though they thus write, they have associated with them those who were formerly rejected[3] with Arius. Such as Secundus[4] of Pentapolis, and the Clergy who were convicted at Alexandria, and they write to them in Alexandria. But, what is most astonishing, they have caused us and our friends to be persecuted, although the most religious Emperor Constantine sent us back in peace to our country and Church, and shewed his concern for the harmony of the people. But now they have caused the Churches to be given up to these men, thus proving to all that for the sake of the Arians the whole conspiracy against us and the rest has been carried on from the beginning.

Is. 14, 27.

Is. 52, 11.

[3] p 151, note a.
[4] supr. p. 14. vol 8. p. 88.

16. Now while such is their conduct, how can they claim credit for what they write? Had the opinions they have put in writing been orthodox, they would have expunged from their list of books the Thalia of Arius, and have rejected the scions of the heresy, viz. those disciples of Arius, and the partners of his impiety and his punishment. But since they have not renounced these[1], it is manifest to all that their sentiments are not orthodox, though they write them over ten thousand times[2]. Wherefore it becomes us to watch, lest some deception be conveyed under the clothing of their phrases, and they lead away certain from the true faith. And if they venture to advance the opinions of Arius, when they see themselves proceeding in a prosperous course, nothing remains for us but to use great boldness of speech, remembering the predictions of the Apostle, which he wrote to forewarn us of such like heresies, and which it becomes us to repeat

17. For we know that, as it is written, *in the latter times some shall depart from the sound faith*[3], *giving heed to seducing spirits, and doctrines of devils, that turn from the truth;* and, *as many as will live godly in Christ shall suffer persecution. But evil men and seducers shall wax worse and worse, deceiving and being deceived.* But none of these things shall prevail over us, nor *separate us from the love of Christ*, though the heretics threaten us with death. For we are Christians, not Arians[4]; would that they too, who have written these things, had not embraced the doctrines of Arius! Yea, brethren, there is need now of such boldness of speech; for we have not received *the spirit of bondage again to fear,* but God hath called us *to liberty* And it were indeed disgraceful to us, most disgraceful, were we, on account of Arius or of those who embrace and advocate his sentiments, to lose the faith which we have received from our Saviour through His Apostles Already very many in these parts, perceiving the craftiness of these writers, are ready even unto blood to oppose their wiles, especially since they have heard of your firmness. And seeing that the refutation of the heresy hath gone forth from you[5], and it has been drawn forth from its concealment, like a serpent from

his hole, the Child that Herod sought to destroy is preserved among you, and the Truth lives in you, and the Faith thrives among you.

§. 21. 18. Wherefore I exhort you, having always in your hands the confession which was framed by the Fathers at Nicæa, and defending it with great zeal and confidence in the Lord, be ensamples to the brethren every where, and shew them that a struggle is now before us in support of the Truth against heresy, and that the wiles of the enemy are various. For a martyr's token lies[1], not only in refusing to burn incense to idols; but to refuse to deny the Faith is also an illustrious testimony[2] of a good conscience. And not only those who turned aside unto idols were condemned as aliens, but those also who betrayed the Truth. Thus Judas was degraded from the Apostolical office, not because he sacrificed to idols, but because he was a traitor; and Hymenæus and Alexander fell away not by betaking themselves to the service of idols, but because they *made shipwreck concerning the faith*. On the other hand, the Patriarch Abraham received the crown, not because he suffered death, but because he was faithful unto God; and the other Saints, of whom Paul speaks, Gedeon, Barak, Samson, Jephtha, David, and Samuel, and the rest, were not made perfect by the shedding of their blood, but by faith they were justified; and to this day they are the objects of our admiration, as being ready even to suffer death for piety towards the Lord.

19. And if one may add an instance from our own times, ye know how the blessed Alexander contended even unto death against this heresy, and what great afflictions and labours, old man as he was, he sustained, until in extreme age he also was gathered to his fathers. And how many beside have undergone great toil, in their teachings against this impiety, and now enjoy in Christ the glorious reward of their confession! Wherefore, let us also, considering that this struggle is for our all, and that the choice is now before us, either to deny or to preserve the faith, let us also make it our earnest care and aim to guard what we have received, taking as our instruction the Confession framed at Nicæa, and let us turn away from novelties, and teach our people not to give heed

to *seducing spirits*[1], but altogether to withdraw from the impiety of the Arian fanatics, and from the coalition which the Meletians have made with them.

20. For you perceive how, though they were formerly at variance with one another, they have now, like Herod and Pontius, agreed together in order to blaspheme our Lord Jesus Christ. And for this they truly deserve the hatred of every man, because they were at enmity with one another on private grounds, but have now become friends and join hands, in their hostility to the Truth and their impiety towards God. Nay, they are content to do or suffer any thing, however contrary to their principles, for the satisfaction of securing their several objects; the Meletians for the sake of preeminence and the mad[2] love of money, and the Arian fanatics for their own impiety. And thus by this coalition they are able to assist one another in their malicious designs, while the Meletians pretend to the impiety of the Arians, and the Arians from their own wickedness concur in their baseness, so that by thus mingling together their respective crimes, like the cup of Babylon, they may carry on their plots against the orthodox worshippers of our Lord Jesus Christ. The wickedness and falsehood of the Meletians were indeed even before this evident unto all men; so too the impiety and godless heresy of the Arians have long been known every where and to all; for the period of their existence has not been a short one. The former became schismatics five and fifty years ago, and it is thirty-six years since the latter were pronounced heretics[a], and they were rejected from the Church by the judgment of the whole Ecumenic Council. But by their present proceedings they have proved at length, even to those who seem openly to favour them, that they have carried on their designs against me and the rest of the orthodox Bishops from the very first solely for the sake of advancing their own impious heresy.

For observe, that which was long ago the great object of

TR.III.
21, 22.
1 Tim.4, 1.
[1] supr. p. 149.
§. 22.

[2] μανίαν

---

[a] This ἀπόδειξις or declaration is ascribed to S Alexander, (as Montfaucon would explain it, supr. p. 125.) supr. p. 43. p. 146, r. 5. p. 148, r. 3. p. 149, r. 5. vid. also p. 150. It should be observed that an additional reason for assigning this Letter to the year 356, is its resemblance in parts to the Orations which were written not long after.

the Eusebians is now brought about. They have caused the Churches to be snatched out of our hands, they have banished, as they pleased, the Bishops and Presbyters who refused to communicate with them; and the laity who withdrew from them they have excluded from the Churches, which they have given up into the hands of the Arians who were condemned so long ago, so that with the assistance of the hypocrisy of the Meletians they can without fear pour forth in them their impious language, and make ready, as they think, the way of deceit for Antichrist[1], who sowed among them the seeds[2] of this heresy.

§ 23. Let them however dream and imagine vain things. We know that when our gracious Emperor shall hear of it, he will put a stop to their wickedness, and they will not continue long, but according to the words of Scripture, *the hearts of the impious shall quickly fail them.* But let us, as it is written, *put on the words of holy Scripture,* and resist them as apostates who would set up fanaticism[3] in the house of the Lord. And let us not fear the death of the body, nor let us emulate their ways; but let the word of Truth be preferred before all things. I also, as you all know, was formerly required[4] by the Eusebians either to make pretence of their impiety, or to expect their hostility; but I would not engage myself with them, but chose rather to be persecuted by them, than to imitate the conduct of Judas. And assuredly they have done what they threatened; for after the manner of Jezebel, they engaged the treacherous Meletians to assist them, knowing how the latter resisted the blessed[5] martyr Peter, and after him the great Achillas, and then Alexander, of blessed memory[6], in order that, as being practised in such matters, the Meletians might pretend against me also whatever might be suggested to them, while the Eusebians gave them an opening for persecuting and for seeking to kill me. For this is what they thirst after; and they continue to this day to desire to shed my blood..

21 But of these things I have no care, for I know and am persuaded that they who endure shall receive a reward from our Saviour; and that ye also, if ye endure as the Fathers did, and shew yourselves examples to the people, and

overthrow these strange and alien devices of impious men, shall be able to glory, and say, " We have *kept the Faith ;*" and ye shall receive the *crown of life,* which God *hath promised to them that love Him.* And God grant that I also together with you may inherit the promises, which were given, not to Paul only, but also to all them that *have loved the appearing* of our Lord, and Saviour, and God, and universal King, Jesus Christ; through whom to the Father be glory and dominion in the Holy Spirit, both now and for ever, world without end. Amen.

Tr.III. 23.

2 Tim.4, 7.

James 1, 12.

IV.

APOLOGY

OF OUR HOLY

FATHER ATHANASIUS,

ARCHBISHOP OF ALEXANDRIA.

ADDRESSED TO THE EMPEROR CONSTANTIUS.

[This Apology, which was written with a view to delivery in the Emperor's presence, (vid. "stretching out my hand," § 3 "I have obtained a hearing," § 6. also § 8 init "I see you smile," §. 16 also § 22 fin § 27 init) is the most finished work of its Author It professes to answer the new charges with which Athanasius was assailed after his return from exile upon the Council of Sardica, i e. between 349, when he was recalled, and 356, which is the date of its composition. These charges were, 1. that he had influenced the Emperor Constans to act against his brother Constantius; 2 that he had been a zealous supporter of Magnentius, who had killed the former; 3. that he had used a new Church for worship without the Emperor's leave, and 4 that he had refused to leave Alexandria, which he had been forced to do since, and to present himself at Court, which he was meditating when he wrote this Apology. Towards the end of it, he hears news of his own proscription, which changes his intention, and also his feelings towards Constantius, though he preserves his respectful tone in speaking of him to the conclusion]

§. 1.   1. KNOWING that you have been a Christian for many years[a], most religious Augustus, and that you are godly by descent, I cheerfully undertake to answer for myself at this time,—for

[a] Constantius, though here called a Christian, was not baptized till his last illness, A.D. 361, and then by the Arian Bishop of Antioch, Euzoius   At this time he was 39 years of age. Theodoret represents him making a speech to his whole army on one occasion, exhorting them to baptism previously to going to war, and recommending all to go thence who could not make up their mind to the Sacrament. Hist. iii. 1   Constantius, his grandfather, had rejected idolatry and acknowledged the One God, according to Eusebius, V. Const. i. 14. though it does not appear that he had embraced Christianity

First of the four charges against Athanasius, 155

I will use the language of the blessed Paul, and make him my advocate before you, considering that he was a preacher of the truth, and that you are an attentive hearer of his words.

2. With respect to those ecclesiastical matters, which have been made the ground of a conspiracy against me, it is sufficient to refer your Piety to the testimony of the many Bishops who have written in my behalf[1]; enough too is the recantation of Ursacius and Valens[2], to prove to all men, that none of the charges which they set up against me had any truth in them. For what evidence can others produce so strong, as what they declared in writing? "We lied, we invented these things; all the accusations against Athanasius are full of falsehood[3]." To this clear proof may be added, if you will vouchsafe to hear it, this circumstance, that the accusers brought no evidence against Macarius the presbyter while we were present; but in our absence[4], when they were by themselves, they managed the matter as they pleased. Now, the Divine Law first of all, and next our own Laws[5], have expressly declared, that such proceedings are of no force whatsoever. From these things the piety of your Majesty, as a lover of God and of the truth, will, I am sure[6], perceive that we are free from all suspicion, and will pronounce our opponents to be false accusers.

3. But as to the slanderous charge which has been preferred against me before your Grace, respecting correspondence with the most pious Augustus, your brother Constans[b], of blessed and everlasting memory, (for my enemies report this of me, and have ventured to assert it in writing,) the result of their former[7] accusation is sufficient to prove this also to be untrue. Had it been alleged by another set of persons, the matter would indeed have been a fit subject of enquiry, but it would have required strong evidence, and open proof in presence of both parties: but when the same persons who

Tr. IV. 1, 2.

[1] supr.
[2] p. 14. pp 14, 86.
[3] not supr. In Counc.
Milan, 349 ? Montf.
[4] pp. 31, 47 &c.
[5] Const. Apol. 11. 51. Montf.
[6] οἶδας qu. οἶδα
§. 2.
[7] vid. Apol. contr. Arian. *pass.*

---

[b] Constans had so zealously taken the part of S. Athanasius, as to threaten his brother Constantius with war, if he did not restore him to his see. vid. Lucifer. Op. p. 91. (ed. Ven. 1778.) This led to the Council of Sardica. Constantius complains of Athan in his conference with Liberius, as "not ceasing to exasperate Constans to quarrel with me, had not I with superior meekness sustained the attack both of the exasperator and the exasperated." Theod. Hist. ii. 13. And he says, infra, Hist. Arian. §. 50 that he only permitted Athan.'s return for the sake of peace.

invented the former charge, are the authors also of this, is it not reasonable to conclude from the issue of the one, the falsehood of the other? For this cause they again conferred together in private, thinking to be able to deceive your Piety before I was aware. But in this they failed: you would not listen to them as they desired, but patiently gave me an opportunity to make my defence. And, in that you were not immediately moved to demand vengeance, you acted only as was righteous in a Prince, whose duty it is to wait for the defence of the injured party. Which if you will vouchsafe to hear, I am confident that in this matter also, you will condemn those reckless men, who have no fear of that God, who has commanded us not to speak falsely before the king[1].

4. But in truth I am ashamed even to have to defend myself against charges such as these, which I do not suppose that even the accuser himself would venture to make mention of in my presence. For he knows full well that he speaks untruly, and that I was never so mad, so reft of my senses, as even to be open to suspicion of having conceived any such thing. So that had I been questioned by any other on this subject, I would not have answered, lest, while I was making my defence, my hearers should for a time have suspended their judgment concerning me. But to your Piety I answer with a loud and clear voice, and stretching forth my hand, as I have learned from the Apostle, *I call God for a record upon my soul*, and as it is written in the book of Kings, (let me be allowed to say the same,) *The Lord is witness, and His Anointed is witness*, I have never spoken evil of your Piety before your brother Constans, the most religious Augustus of blessed memory. I have never exasperated him against you, as these falsely accuse me. But whenever in my interviews with him he has mentioned your Grace, (and he did mention you at the time that Thalassus[2] came to Pitybion, and I was staying at Aquileia,) the Lord is witness, how I spoke of your Piety in terms which I would that God would reveal unto your soul, that you might condemn the falsehood of these my calumniators.

5. Bear with me, most gracious Augustus, and freely grant me your indulgence while I speak of this matter. Your most Christian brother was not a man of so light a temper, nor was

whereas he never had had any private interview with him, 157

I a person of such a character, that we should communicate together on a subject like this, or that I should slander a brother to a brother, or speak evil of a king before a king. I am not so mad, Sire, nor have I forgotten that divine sentence which says, *Curse not the king, no, not in thy thought; and curse not the rich in thy bedchamber: for a bird of the air shall carry the voice, and that which hath wings shall tell the matter.* If then those things, which are spoken in secret against you that are kings, are not hidden, is it not incredible that I should have spoken against you in the presence of a king, and of so many bystanders? For I never saw your brother by myself, nor did he ever converse with me in private, but I was always introduced in company with the Bishop of the city, where I happened to be, and with others that chanced to be there. We entered the presence together, and together we retired. Fortunatian^c, Bishop of Aquileia, can testify this, the father Hosius is able to say the same, as also are Crispinus Bishop of Padua, Lucillus of Verona, Dionysius of Leis, and Vincentius of Campania. And although Maximinus of Treves, and Protasius of Milan, are dead, yet Eugenius who was Master of the Palace^d can bear witness for me; for he stood before the veil^e, and heard what we requested of the Emperor, and what he vouchsafed to reply to us.

Tr IV. 3.

Eccles. 10, 20.

^c All these names of Bishops occur among the subscriptions at Sardica. supr. pp 76—78. Fortunatian was raised to the see of Aquileia about 344, signed the condemnation of Athanasius at the Council of Milan in 355, the year before this Apology was written, and in 357 was the Eusebian tempter in the fall of Liberius. Lucillus, Maximinus, and Protasius, are in the list of Saints Maximinus will be mentioned just below, note g Vincent, who had been the Pope's legate at Nicæa, lapsed at Arles so far as to give up S. Athanasius, but recovered himself by refusing to acknowledge the proceedings at Ariminum Leis is Lauda, or Laus Pompeia, *hodie* Lodi; Ughelli, Ital. Sacr t 4 p. 656

^d Or, master of the offices, one of the seven Ministers of the Court under the Empire, "He inspected the discipline of the civil and military schools, and received appeals from all parts of the Empire ... The correspondence between the Prince and his subjects was managed by the four *scrinia*, or offices of this minister of state....The whole business was despatched by 148 secretaries, chosen for the most part from the profession of the law.... But the department of foreign affairs, which constitutes so essential a part of modern policy, seldom diverted the attention of the master of the offices, his mind was more seriously engaged by the general direction of 'he posts and arsenals of the Empire." Gibbon, ch. 17

^e πρὸ τοῦ βήλου. The Veil, which in the first instance was an appendage to the images of pagan deities, formed at this time a part of the ceremonial of the imperial Court. It hung over the entrance of the Emperor's bedchamber, where he gave his audiences. It also hung before the secretarium of the Judges vid Hofman in voc. Gotnofred in Cod. Theod 1. tit. vii. 1.

158 *and could not have had, as his wanderings would shew,*

APOL. TO CONST.
§. 4.

¹ ἐγκάρδιος
vid.
p. 100, note z.
² p. 49, §. 29.
³ συνάξεσι.

⁴ A.D. 345.

6. This certainly is sufficient for proof, yet suffer me nevertheless to lay before you an account of my travels, which will further lead you to condemn the unfounded calumnies of my opponents. When I left Alexandria, I did not go to your brother's Court¹, or to any other persons, but only to Rome²; and having laid my case before the Church, (for this was my only concern,) I spent my time in the public worship³. I did not write to your brother, except when the Eusebians had written to him to accuse me, and I was compelled while yet at Alexandria to defend myself; and again when I sent to him volumes ᶠ containing the holy Scriptures, which he had ordered me to prepare for him. It behoves me, while I defend my conduct, to tell the truth to your Piety. When however three years had passed away, he wrote to me in the fourth year⁴, commanding me to meet him, (he was then at Milan;) and upon enquiring the cause, (for I was ignorant of it, the Lord is my witness,) I learnt that certain Bishops ᵍ had gone up and requested him to write to your Piety, desiring that a Council might be called. Believe me, Sire, this is the truth of the matter; I lie not. Accordingly I went to Milan, and met with great kindness from him; for he condescended to see me, and to say that he had despatched letters to you, requesting that a Council might be called. And while I remained in that city, he sent for me again into Gaul, (for the father Hosius was going thither,) that we might travel from thence to Sardica. And after the Council, he wrote to me while I continued at Naissus ʰ, and I went up, and abode afterwards

---

ᶠ πυκτία, a bound book, vid. Montf. Coll. Nov. *infr.* S. Jerome speaks of Hilarion's transcribing a Gospel. Vit. Hilar. 35. and himself the Psalter, (interpretationem Psalmorum,) ad Florent Ep. v. 2. and St. Eusebius of Vercellæ made a copy of the Gospels, which was extant, as it appears, in the last century. vid. Lami Erud. Apost. p. 678. Mabillon, Itin. Ital. t. 1. p. 9. Montfauc. Diar. Ital xxviii. p 445. Tillemont, (t. 8. p 86) considers that Athan. alludes in this passage to the Synopsis Scr Sacr. which is among his works, but Montfaucon, Collect. Nov. t. 2 p. xxviii. contends that a copy of the Gospels is spoken of.

ᵍ Tillemont supposes that Constans was present at the Council of Milan, at which Eudoxius, Martyrius, and Macedonius, sent to the West with the Eusebian Creed, (vid. Libr. F. vol. 8. p. 111.) made their appearance to no purpose. The Bishops principally concerned in persuading Constans seem to have been Pope Julius, Hosius, and Maximinus of Treves. Hil. Fragm. 2. p 16.

ʰ Naissus was situated in Upper Dacia, and according to some was the birthplace of Constantine The Bishop of the place, Gaudentius, whose name occurs among the subscriptions at Sardica, had protected S. Paul of Con-at Aquileia; where the letters of your Piety found me. And again, being summoned thence by your departed brother, I returned into Gaul, and so came at length to your Piety. [Tr. IV. 4—6.]

7. Now what place and time does my accuser specify, at [§. 5.] which I made use of these expressions according to his slanderous imputation? In whose presence was I so mad as to give utterance to the words which he has falsely charged me with speaking? Who is there ready to support the charge, and to testify to the fact? What his own eyes have seen that ought he to speak, as holy Scripture enjoins. But no; he will find no witnesses of that which never took place. But I take your Piety to witness, together with the Truth, that I lie not. I request you, for I know you to be a person of excellent memory, to call to mind the conversation I had with you, when you condescended to see me, first at Viminacium[1], a second time at Cæsarea in Cappadocia, and a third time at Antioch. Did I speak evil before you even of the Eusebians who have persecuted me? Did I cast imputations upon any of those that have done me wrong? If then I imputed nothing to any of those against whom I had a right to speak; how could I be so possessed with madness as to slander a King before a King, and to set a brother at variance with a brother? I beseech you, either cause me to appear before you that the thing may be proved, or else condemn these calumnies, and follow the example of David, who says, *Whoso privily slandereth his neighbour, him will I destroy.* As much as in them lies, they have slain me; for *the mouth that belieth, slayeth the soul.* But your long-suffering has prevailed against them, and given me confidence to defend myself, that they may suffer condemnation, as contentious and slanderous persons. Concerning your most religious brother, of blessed memory[2], this may suffice: for you will be able, according to the wisdom which God has given you, to gather much from the little I have said, and to perceive that this accusation is a mere invention. [Prov. 25, 8.] [1 in Mæsia.] [Ps. 101, 5.] [Wisd. 1, 11.] [2 τῆς μακαρίας μνήμης.]

8. With regard to the second calumny, that I have written [§. 6.] letters to the usurper[1], (his name I am unwilling to pro-

---

stantinople and incurred the anathemas of the Eusebians at Philippopolis. Hil. Fragm. iii. 27.

[1] Magnentius, a barbarian by origin, securing the troops who were about the person of Constans, had taken possession

nounce,) I beseech you investigate and try the matter, in whatever way you please, and by whomsoever you may approve of. The extravagance of the charge so confounds me, that I am in utter uncertainty how to act. Believe me, most religious Prince, many times did I weigh the matter in my mind, but was unable to believe that any one could be so mad as to utter such a falsehood. But when this charge was published abroad by the Arians, as well as the former, and they boasted that they had transmitted to you a copy of the letter, I was the more amazed, and I have passed sleepless nights contending against the charge, as if in the presence of my accusers; and suddenly breaking forth into a loud cry, I have immediately fallen to my prayers, desiring with groans and tears that I might obtain a favourable hearing from you. And now that by the grace of the Lord, I have obtained such a hearing, I am again at a loss how I shall begin my defence; for as often as I make an attempt to speak, I am prevented by my horror at the deed.

9. In the case of your departed brother, the slanderers had indeed a plausible pretence for what they alleged; because I had been admitted to see him, and he had condescended to write to your brotherly affection concerning me; and he had often sent for me to come to him, and had honoured me when I came. But for the traitor[1] Magnentius, *the Lord is witness, and His Anointed is witness*, I know him not: I never did know him. What correspondence then could there be between persons so entirely unacquainted with each other? What reason was there to induce me to write to such a man? How could I have commenced my letter, had I written to him? Could I have said, ' You have done well to murder the man who honoured me, whose kindnesses I shall never forget?' Or, ' I approve of your conduct in destroying our Christian friends, and most faithful brethren?' or, ' I approve of your proceedings in butchering those who so kindly entertained me at Rome; for instance, your departed[2] Aunt Eutropia[k], whose disposition answered to her name, that worthy

---

[1] διάβολος
1 Sam. 12, 5.

[2] μακαρίας

---

of Autun in Gaul, where the Emperor was, and, on the flight of the latter, had sent a party of horse after him, by whom he was despatched. Magnentius, after some successes, was defeated in the great battle of Mursa, and ultimately destroyed himself at Lyons.

[k] Nepotian, the son of Eutropia, Constantine's sister, had taken up arms against Magnentius, got possession of

man, Abuterius, the most faithful Spirantius, and many other excellent persons?" Is it not mere madness in my accuser even to suspect me of such a thing? What, I ask again, could induce me to place confidence in this man? What trait did I perceive in his character on which I could rely? He had murdered his own master; he had proved faithless to his friends, he had violated his oath; he had blasphemed God, by consulting poisoners and sorcerers[1] contrary to his Law. And with what conscience could I send greeting to such a man, whose madness and cruelty had afflicted not me only, but all the world around me? To be sure, I was very greatly indebted to him for his conduct, that when your departed brother had filled our churches with sacred offerings, he murdered him. For the wretch was not moved by the sight of these his gifts, nor did he stand in awe of the divine grace which had been given to him in baptism: but like a deadly and devilish spirit, he raged against him, till your blessed[2] brother suffered martyrdom at his hands, while he, henceforth a criminal like Cain, was driven from place to place, *a fugitive and a vagabond*, to the end that he might follow the example of Judas in his death, by becoming his own executioner, and so bring upon himself a double weight of punishment in the judgment to come.

TR. IV
6—8.
§. 7.

[1] Bingh. Antiqu. xvi. 5. §. 5. &c.

[2] μακα-είτη Gen 4, 12. vid. Hist. Ar §. 7.

10 With such a man the slanderer thought that I had been on terms of friendship, or rather he did not think so, but like an enemy invented an incredible fiction: for he knows full well that he has lied. I would that, whoever he is, he were present here, that I might put the question to him on the word of Truth itself, (for whatever we speak as in the presence of God, we Christians consider as an oath[3],) I say, that I might ask him this question, which of us rejoiced most in the well-being of the departed[4] Constans? who prayed for him most earnestly? The facts of the foregoing charge prove this, indeed it is plain how the case stands. But although he himself knows full well, that no one who was so disposed towards the departed[4] Constans, and who truly loved him, could be a friend to his enemy, I fear that being possessed

§. 8.

[3] vid. Chrys. in Eph. tr p.119, note g.
[4] μακα-είτου

Rome, and enjoyed the title of Augustus for about a month. Magnentius put him to death, and his mother, and a number of his adherents, some of whom are here mentioned.

APOL. TO CONST. with other feelings towards him than I was, he has falsely attributed to me those sentiments of hatred which were entertained by himself.

§. 9. 11. For myself, I am so surprised at the enormity of the thing, that I am quite uncertain what I ought to say in my defence. I can only declare, that I condemn myself to die a thousand deaths, if even the least suspicion attaches to me in this matter. And to you, Sire, as a lover of the truth, I confidently make my appeal. I beseech you, as I said before, to investigate this affair, and especially to call for the testimony of those who were once sent by him as ambassadors to you. These are the Bishops Servatius[1] and Maximus and the rest, with Clementius and Valens. Enquire of them, I beseech you, whether they brought letters to me. If they did, this would give me occasion to write to him. But if he did not write to me, if he did not even know me, how could I write to one with whom I had no acquaintance? Ask them whether, when I saw Clementius, and spoke of your brother of blessed memory[1], I did not, in the language of Scripture, wet my garments with tears, when I remembered his kindness of disposition and his Christian spirit? Learn of them how anxious I was, on hearing of the cruelty of that savage beast, and finding that Valens and his company had come by way of Libya, lest he should attempt a passage also, and like a robber murder those who held in love and memory the departed[2] Prince, among whom I account myself second to none.

[1] τῆς μακαρίας μνήμης, supr p 159, r.2.

[2] μακαρίου

§. 10. 12. How with this apprehension of such a design, was there not an additional probability of my praying for your Grace? Should I feel affection for his murderer, and entertain dislike towards you his brother who avenged his death? Should I remember his crime, and forget that kindness of yours which you vouchsafed to assure me by letter should remain the same towards me after your brother's death of happy memory[3], as it had been during his lifetime? How could I have borne to look upon the murderer? Must I not have thought that the

[3] μακαρίτου

---

[1] Sarbatius or Servatius, and Maximus occur in the lists of Gallic subscriptions at Sardica. The former is supposed to be St. Servatius or Servatio of Tungri, concerning whom at Arimi- num, vid Sulp. Hist. ii. 59. vid. also Greg. Turon. Hist. Franc. ii. 5. where however the Bened. Ed. prefers to read Aravatius, a bishop, as he considers, of the fifth century.

He could not be false to one brother in the presence of another 163

blessed Prince beheld me, when I prayed for your safety? For brothers are by nature the mirrors of each other. Wherefore as seeing you in him, I never should have slandered you before him; and as seeing him in you, never should I have written to his enemy, instead of praying for your safety. Of this, my witnesses are, first of all, the Lord who has heard and has given to you entire the kingdom of your forefathers: and next those persons who were present at the time, Felicissimus, who was Duke of Egypt, Rufinus, and Stephanus, the former of whom was Receiver-general[1], the latter, Master there; Count Asterius, and Palladius Master of the palace, Antiochus and Evagrius Official Agents[m]. I had only to say, "Let us pray for the safety of the most religious Emperor, Constantius Augustus," and all the people immediately cried out with one voice, "O Christ, send thy help to Constantius," and they continued praying thus for some time[n].

Tr. IV. 9—11.

[1] supr.

pp 32, 118.

13 Now I have already called upon God, and His Word, the Only-begotten Son our Lord Jesus Christ, to witness for me, that I have never written to that man, nor received letters from him. And as to my accuser, give me leave to ask him a few short questions concerning this charge also How did he come to the knowledge of this matter? Will he say that he has got copies of the letter? for this is what the Arians have declared till they were weary. Now in the first place, even if he can shew writing resembling mine, the thing is by no means certain, for there are forgers, who have often imitated the hand[2] even of you who are Kings.

§. 11.

[2] χεῖρος, supr. p. 107.

---

[m] 1. The Rationales or Receivers, in Greek writers Catholici, (λογοθεταὶ being understood, Vales. ad Euseb. vii. 10) were the same as the Procurators, (Gibbon, Hist. ch. xvii. note 148.) who succeeded the Provincial Quæstors in the early times of the Empire. They were in the department of the Comes Sacrarum Largitionum, or High Treasurer of the Revenue, (Gothofr. Cod. Theod t. 6 p. 327.) Both Gothofr. however and Pancirolus, p. 134. Ed. 1623. place Rationales also under the Comes Rerum Privatarum. Pancirolus, p. 120 mentions the Comes Rationalis Summarum Ægypti as distinct from other functionaries. Gibbon, ch xvii seems to say that there were in all 29, of whom 18 were counts. 2. Stephanus, μάγιστρος ἔχει, Tillemont translates, "Master of the camp of Egypt." vol. 8 p. 137 3. The Master of the offices or of the palace has been noticed above, p. 157, note d. 4 ἀγεντισηριβους, agentes in rebus. These were functionaries under the Master of the offices, whose business it was to announce the names of the consuls and the edicts or victories of the Empire. They at length became spies of the Court, vid Gibbon, ch. xvii. Gothofr. Cod. Th vi. 27.

[n] "Presbyterum Eraclium mihi successorem voc. A populo acclamatum est, Deo gratias, Christo laudes; dictum est vicies terties. Exaudi Christe, Augustino vita; dictum est sexies decies. Te patrem, te episcopum, dictum est octies." August. Ep 213.

And the resemblance will not prove the genuineness of the letter, unless my customary amanuensis shall testify in its favour. I would then again ask my accusers, Who provided you with these copies? and whence were they obtained? I had my writers[o], and he his servants, who received his letters from the bearers, and gave them into his hand. My assistants are forthcoming, vouchsafe to summon the others, (for they are most probably still living,) and enquire concerning these letters. Search into the matter, as though Truth were the partner of your throne. She is the defence of Kings, and especially of Christian Kings, with her you will reign most securely, for holy Scripture says, *Mercy and truth preserve the king, and they will encircle his throne in righteousness.* And the wise Zorobabel gained a victory over the others by setting forth the power of Truth, and all the people cried out, *Great is truth, and mighty above all things.*

14 Had I been accused before any other, I should have appealed to your Piety, as once the Apostle appealed unto Cæsar, and put an end to the designs of his enemies against him. But since they have had the boldness to lay their charge before you, to whom shall I appeal from you? to the Father of Him who says, *I am the Truth,* that He may incline your heart unto clemency:—

O Lord Almighty, and King of eternity, the Father of our Lord Jesus Christ, who by Thy Word hast given this Kingdom to Thy servant Constantius, do Thou shine into his heart, that he, knowing the falsehood that is set against me, may both favourably receive this my defence; and may make known unto all men, that his ears are firmly set to hearken unto the Truth, according as it is written, *Righteous lips alone are acceptable unto the King.* For Thou hast caused it to be said by Solomon, that thus the throne of a kingdom shall be established.

15. Wherefore at least enquire into this matter, and let the accusers understand that your desire is to learn the truth; and see, whether they will not shew their falsehood by their

---

[o] vid. Rom. xvi. 22. Lucian is spoken of as the amanuensis of the Confessors, who wrote to St. Cyprian, Ep. 16. Ed. Ben. Jader perhaps of Ep. 80. St. Jerome was either secretary or amanuensis to Pope Damasus, vid. Ep ad Ageruch. (123. n. 10. Ed. Vallars.) vid. Lami de Erud. Ap. p. 258.

very looks; for the countenance is a test of the conscience, as it is written, *A merry heart maketh a cheerful countenance, but by sorrow of the heart the spirit is broken*. Thus they who had conspired against Joseph were convicted by their own consciences; and the cruelty of Laban towards Jacob were shewn in his countenance[1]. And thus you see the suspicious alarm of these persons, for they fly and hide themselves; but on my part frankness[2] in making my defence. And the question between us is not one regarding worldly wealth, but concerning the honour of the Church. He that has been struck by a stone, applies to a physician; but sharper than a stone are the strokes of calumny; for as Solomon has said, *A false witness is a maul, and a sword, and a sharp arrow*, and its wounds Truth alone is able to cure, and if Truth be set at nought, they grow worse and worse.

16. It is this that has thrown the Churches every where into such confusion; for pretences have been devised, and Bishops of great authority, and of advanced age[3], have been banished for holding communion with me. However, if matters stop here, our prospect is favourable through your gracious interposition. And that the evil may not extend itself, let Truth prevail before you; and leave not the whole Church under suspicion, as though Christian men, nay even Bishops, could be guilty of plotting and writing in this manner. Or if you are unwilling to investigate the matter, it is but right that we who offer our defence, should be believed, rather than our calumniators. They, like enemies, are occupied in wickedness, we, as earnestly contending for our cause, present to you our proofs. And truly I wonder how it comes to pass, that while we address you with fear and reverence, they are possessed of such an impudent spirit, that they dare even to lie before the King[4]. But I pray you, for the Truth's sake, and as it is written, *search diligently* in my presence, on what grounds they affirm these things, and whence these letters were obtained. But neither will any of my servants be proved guilty, nor will any of his people be able to tell whence they came; for they are forgeries. And perhaps one had better not enquire further. They do not wish it, lest the writer of the letters should be certain of

166 *The third charge, of using an undedicated Church,*

APOL. TO CONST.

detection. For the calumniators alone, and none besides, know who he is.

§. 14.

17. But forasmuch as they have informed against me in the matter of the great Church, that a congregation was holden there before it was completed, I will answer to your Piety on this charge also; for the parties who bear so hearty an enmity against me, constrain me to do so. I confess this did so happen; for, as in what I have hitherto said, I have spoken no lie, I will not now deny this. But the facts are far otherwise than they have represented them. Permit me to declare to you, most religious Augustus, that we kept no day of dedication, (it would certainly have been unlawful to do so, before receiving orders from you,) nor were we led to act as we did through premeditation. No Bishop or other Clergyman was invited to join in our proceedings; for much was yet wanting to complete the building. Nay the congregation was not held on a previous notice, which might give them a reason for informing against us. Every one knows how it happened; hear me, however, with your accustomed equity and patience. It was the feast of Easter, and an exceeding great multitude of Christians was assembled together, such as Christian kings would desire to see in all their cities. Now when the Churches were found to be too few to contain them, there was no little stir among the people, who desired that they might be allowed to meet together in the great Church, where they could all offer up their prayers for your safety[1]. And this they did; for although I exhorted them to wait awhile, and to assemble in the other Churches, with whatever inconvenience to themselves, they would not listen to me; but were ready to go out of the city, and meet in desert places in the open air, thinking it better to endure the fatigue of the journey, than to keep the feast in such a state of discomfort.

[1] supr. p. 163. vol. 8, p. 159.

§. 15.

18. Believe me, Sire, and let Truth be my witness in this also, when I declare that in the congregations held during the season of Lent, in consequence of the narrow limits of our buildings, and the vast multitude of people assembled, a great number of children, not a few of the younger and very many of the older women, besides several young men, suffered so much from the pressure of the crowd, that they were obliged

to be carried home; though by the Providence of God, none perished. All however murmured, and demanded the use of the great Church. And if the pressure was so great during the days which preceded the feast, what would have been the case during the feast itself? Of course matters would have been far worse. It did not therefore become me to change the people's joy into grief, their cheerfulness into sorrow, and to make the festival a season of lamentation.

19. And that the more, because I had a precedent in the conduct of our Fathers. For the blessed Alexander, when the other places of worship were too small, and he was engaged in the erection of what was then considered a very large one, the Church of Theonas[p], held his congregations there on account of the number of the people, while at the same time he proceeded with the building. I have seen the same thing done at Treves and at Aquileia, in both which places, while the building was proceeding, they assembled there during the feasts, on account of the number of the people; and they never found any one to accuse them in this manner. Nay, your brother of blessed memory was present, when a congregation was held under these circumstances at Aquileia. I also followed this course. There was no dedication, but only an assembly for the sake of prayer. You, at least, I am sure, as a lover of God, will approve of the people's zeal, and will pardon me for being unwilling to hinder the prayers of so great a multitude.

20. But here again I would ask my accuser, where was it right that the people should pray? in the desert, or in a place which was in course of building for the purpose of prayer? Where was it becoming and pious that the people should

---

[p] S. Epiphanius mentions 9 Churches in Alexandria. Hær. 69 2 Athan mentions in addition that of Quirinus. Hist. Arian. §. 10. The Church mentioned in the text was built at the Emperor's expense, and apparently upon the Emperor's ground, as on the site was or had been a Basilica, which bore first the name of Hadrian, then of Licinius, Epiph ibid. Hadrian, it should be observed, built in many cities temples without idols, which were popularly considered as intended by him for Christian worship, and went after his name. Lamprid. Vit. Alex. Sev. 43. The Church in question was built in the Cæsareum. Hist. Arian. 74. There was a magnificent Temple, dedicated to Augustus, as ἐπιβατήριος, on the harbour of Alexandria, Philon. Legat ad Caium, pp. 1013, 4. ed 1691. and called the Cæsareum It was near the Emperor's palace, vid. Acad des Inscript vol. 9. p 416 As to the Cæsarean Church, it was begun by Gregory, finished by George, burnt under Julian, rebuilt by Athanasius Tillem. vol. 8 pp. 148, 9

168 *Better to meet together, than to pray separately.*

APOL. TO CONST. answer, Amen[q]? in the desert, or in what was already called the Lord's house? Where would you, most religious Prince, have wished your people to stretch forth their hands, and to pray for you? where the Greeks, as they passed by, might stop and listen, or in a place named after yourself, which all men have long called the Lord's house, even since the foundations of it were laid? I am sure that you prefer your own place; for I see you smile, and that tells me so

21. " But," says the accuser, " it ought to have been in the Churches." They were all, as I said before, too small and confined to admit the multitude. Then again, in which way was it most becoming that their prayers should be made? Should they meet together in parts and separate companies, with danger from the crowded state of the congregations? or, when there was now a place that would contain them all, should they assemble in it, and speak as with one and the same voice in perfect harmony? This was the better course, for this shewed the unanimity of the multitude: in this way God will readily hear prayer. For if, according to the promise
Mat. 18, 19 of our Saviour Himself, where two shall agree together as touching any thing that they shall ask, it shall be done for them, how shall it be when so great an assembly of people with one voice utter their Amen to God? Who indeed was there that did not marvel at the sight? Who but pronounced you a happy prince, when they saw so great a multitude met together in one place? How did the people themselves rejoice to see each other, having been accustomed heretofore to assemble in separate places! The circumstance was a source of pleasure to all; of vexation to the calumniator alone.

§ 17. 22. Now then, I would also meet the other and only remaining objection of my accuser. He says, the building was not completed, and prayer ought not to have been made there.
Mat. 6, 6. But the Lord said, *But thou, when thou prayest, enter into thy closet, and shut the doors* What then will the accuser answer? or rather what will all prudent and true Christians say? Let your Majesty ask the opinion of such: for it is
Is 32, 6 Sept written of the other, *The foolish person will speak foolishness;*

---

[q] Bingham, Antiqu. v. 3 § 25 Suicer Thesaur. *in voc* ἀμὴν, Gavanti,
Tertullian, (O T vol 1 p 214, note n.) Thesaur. vol 1. p. 89. ed. 1763.

Better to pray in a building than in the desert.

but of these, *Ask counsel of all that are wise* When the Churches were too small, and the people so numerous as they were, and desirous to go forth into the desert, what ought I to have done? The desert has no doors, and all who choose may pass through it, but the Lord's house is enclosed with walls and doors, and marks the difference between the pious and the profane. Will not every wise person then, as well as your Piety, Sire, give the preference to the latter place? For they know that here prayer is lawfully offered, while a suspicion of irregularity attaches to it there. Unless indeed, no place proper for it existed, and the worshippers dwelt only in the desert, as was the case with Israel, although after the tabernacle was built, they also had thenceforth a place set apart for prayer.

23 O Christ, Lord and true King of kings, Only-begotten Son of God, Word and Wisdom of the Father, I am accused because the people prayed Thy gracious favour, and through Thee besought Thy Father, who is God over all, to save Thy servant, the most religious Constantius. But thanks be to Thy goodness, that it is for this that I am blamed, and for the keeping of Thy laws. Heavier had been the blame, and more true had been the charge, had we passed by the place which the Emperor was building, and gone forth into the desert to pray. How would the accuser then have vented his folly against me! With what apparent reason would he have said, "He despised the place which you are building; he does not approve of your undertaking, he passed it by in derision; he pointed to the desert to supply the want of room in the Churches; he prevented the people when they wished to offer up their prayers." This is what he wished to say, and sought an occasion of saying it; and finding none he is vexed, and so forthwith invents a charge against me. Had he been able to say this, he would have confounded me with shame; as now he injures me, copying the accuser's[1] ways, and watching for an occasion against those that pray. Thus has he perverted to a wicked purpose his knowledge of Daniel's history. But he has been deceived, for he ignorantly imagined, that Babylonian practices were in fashion with you, and knew not that you are a friend of the blessed Daniel, and worship the same

[1] διαβό-λου, supr. p. 160. r. 1.

God, and do not forbid, but wish all men to pray, knowing that the prayer of all is, that you may continue to reign in perpetual peace and safety[1].

24. This is what I have to complain of on the part of my accuser. But may you, most religious Augustus, live through the course of many years to come, and celebrate the dedication of the Church. Surely the prayers which have been offered for your safety by all men, are no hindrance to this celebrity. Let these unlearned persons cease such misrepresentations, but let them learn from the example of the Fathers; and let them read the Scriptures. Or rather let them learn of you, who are so well instructed in such histories, how that Jesus the son of Josedek the priest, and his brethren, and Zorobabel the wise, the son of Salathiel, and Ezra the priest and scribe of the law, when the temple was in course of building after the captivity, the feast of tabernacles being at hand, (which was a great feast and time of assembly and prayer in Israel,) gathered the people together with one accord in the great court within the first gate, which is toward the East, and prepared the altar to God, and there offered their gifts, and kept the feast. And so afterwards they brought hither their sacrifices, on the sabbaths and the new moons, and the people offered up their prayers. And yet the Scripture says expressly, that when these things were done, the temple of God was not yet built; but rather while they thus prayed, the building of the house was set forward. So that neither were their prayers deferred in expectation of the dedication, nor was the dedication prevented by the assemblies held for the sake of prayer. But the people thus continued to pray; and when the house was entirely finished, they celebrated the dedication, and brought their gifts for that purpose, and all kept the feast for the completion of the work.

25. And thus also did the blessed Alexander, and the other Fathers. They continued to assemble their people, and when they had completed the work they gave thanks unto the Lord, and celebrated the dedication. This also it befits you to do, O Prince, most careful in your inquiries. The place is ready, having been already sanctified by the prayers which have been offered in it, and requires only the presence

Fourth charge, of his disobeying an Imperial order.

of your Piety. This only is wanting to its perfect beauty. Do you then supply this deficiency, and there make your prayers unto the Lord, for whom you have built this house. That you may do so is the trust of all men.

TR. IV. 18, 19.

26. And now, if it please you, let us consider the remaining accusation, and permit me to answer it likewise. They have dared to charge me with resisting your commands, and refusing to leave my Church. Truly I wonder they are not weary of uttering their calumnies, I however am not yet weary of answering them, I rather rejoice to do so; for the more abundant my defence is, the more entirely must they be condemned. I did not resist the commands of your Piety, God forbid; I am not a man that would resist even the Quæstor[r] of the city, much less so great a Prince. On this matter, I need not many words, for the whole city will bear witness for me. Nevertheless, permit me again to relate the circumstances from the beginning; for when you hear them, I am sure you will be astonished at the presumption of my enemies.

§. 19.

27. Montanus the officer of the Palace[1], came and brought me a letter, which purported to be an answer to one from me, requesting that I might go into Italy, for the purpose of obtaining a supply of the deficiencies which I thought existed in the condition of our Churches. Now I desire to thank your Piety, which condescended to assent to my request, on the supposition that I had written to you, and made provision[2] for me to undertake the journey, and to accomplish it without trouble. But here again I am astonished at those who have spoken falsehood in your ears, that they were not afraid, seeing that lying belongs to the Devil, and that liars are alien from Him who says, *I am the Truth.* For I never wrote to you, nor will my accuser be able to find any such letter; and though I ought to have written every day, if I might thereby behold your gracious countenance, yet it would neither have been pious to desert the Churches, nor right to be troublesome to your Piety, especially since you are willing to grant our requests in behalf of the Church, although we are not present to make

[1] vid Cod. Theod. vi. 30.
[2] supr. p. 100, note y.
John 14, 6.

---

[r] λογιστῇ, auditor of accounts᾿ vid. Arist. Polit. vi. 8. Demosth. de Coronâ, p. 290. ed. 1823.

APOL. them. Now may it please you to order me to read what
TO Montanus commanded me to do. This is as follows[1]. * * *
CONST.

[1] lost, or never introduced §. 20.

28. Now I ask again, whence have my accusers obtained this letter also? I would learn of them who it was that put it into their hands? Do you cause them to answer. By this you may perceive that they have forged this, as they did also the former letter, which they published against me, with reference to the wretched Magnentius. And being convicted in this instance also, on what pretence next will they bring me to make my defence? Their only concern is, to throw every thing into disorder and confusion; and for this end I perceive they exercise their zeal. Perhaps they think that by frequent repetition of their charges, they will at last exasperate you against me. But you ought to turn away from such persons, and to hate them; for such as themselves are, such also they imagine those to be who listen to them, and they think that their calumnies will prevail even before you.

1 Sam. 22, 9.

The accusation of Doeg prevailed of old against the priests of God: but it was the unrighteous Saul, who hearkened unto him. And Jezebel was able to injure the most religious

1 Kings 21.

Naboth by her false accusations, but then it was the wicked and apostate Ahab who hearkened unto her. But the most holy David, whose example it becomes you to follow, as all pray that you may, favours not such men, but was wont to turn away from them and avoid them, as raging dogs. He

Ps. 101, 5
Ex. 23, 1 Sept

says, *Whoso privily slandereth his neighbour, him have I destroyed.* For he kept the commandment which says, *Thou shalt not receive a false report.* And false are the reports of these men in your sight. You, like Solomon, have required

Prov. 30, 8

of the Lord, (and believe yourself to have obtained your desire,) that it would seem good unto Him to remove far from you vain and lying words.

§. 21.

29 Forasmuch then as the letter was forged by my calumniators, and contained no order that I should come to you, I concluded that it was not the wish of your Piety that I should come. For in that you gave me no absolute command, but merely wrote as in answer to a letter from me, requesting that I might be permitted to set in order the things which seemed to be wanting, it was manifest to me (although no one told me this) that the letter which I had received did not express the

sentiments of your Clemency. All knew, and I also stated in writing, as Montanus is aware, that I did not refuse to come, but only that I thought it unbecoming to take advantage of the supposition that I had written to you to request this favour, fearing also lest my accusers should find in this a pretence for saying that I made myself troublesome to your Piety. Nevertheless, I made preparations, as Montanus also knows, in order that, should you condescend to write to me, I might immediately leave home, and readily answer your commands, for I was not so mad as to resist such an order from you. When then in fact your Piety did not write to me, how could I resist a command which I never received? or how can they say, that I refused to obey, when no orders were given me? Is not this again the mere fabrication of enemies, pretending that which never took place? I fear that even now, while I am engaged in this defence of myself, they may allege against me that I am doing that which I have never obtained your permission to do. So easily is my conduct made matter of accusation by them, and so ready are they to vent their calumnies in despite of that Scripture, which says, *Love not to slander another, lest thou be cut off.*

30 After a period of six and twenty months, when Montanus had gone away, there came Diogenes the Notary[s], but he brought me no letter, nor did we see each other, nor did he charge me with any commands as from you. Moreover when the General Syrianus entered Alexandria, seeing that certain reports were spread abroad by the Arians, who declared that matters would now be as they wished, I enquired whether he had brought any letters on the subject of these statements of theirs. I confess that I asked for letters containing your commands. And when he said that he had brought none, I requested that Syrianus himself, or Maximus the Prefect of Egypt, would write to me concerning this matter. Which request I made, because your Grace had written to me,

---

[s] Notaries were the immediate attendants on magistrates, whose judgments, &c. they recorded and promulgated. Their office was analogous in the Imperial Court. vid Gothofred in Cod. Theod. vi. 10 Ammian. Marcell. tom. 3 p. 464. ed. Erfurdt, 1808. Pancirol Notit. p 143. Hofman *in voc.* Scharf enumerates with references the civil officers, &c. to whom they were attached in Dissert. l. de Notariis Ecclesiæ, p. 49.

APOL. TO CONST.

desiring that I would not suffer myself to be alarmed by any one, nor attend to those who wished to frighten me, but that I would continue to preside over the Churches without fear. It was Palladius, the Master of the Palace, and Asterius Duke of Armenia, who brought me this letter. Permit me to read a copy of it. It is as follows:

§. 23.

31. *A copy*[1] *of the letter as follows*

Constantius Victor Augustus to Athanasius.

[1] vid. another translation of the Latin, Hist. Arian. §. 24

It is not unknown to your Prudence, how constantly I prayed that success might attend my late brother Constans in all his undertakings, and your wisdom will easily judge how greatly I was afflicted, when I learnt that he had been cut off by the treachery of ruffians. Now forasmuch as certain persons are endeavouring at this time to alarm you, by setting before your eyes that lamentable tragedy, I have thought good to address to your Reverence this present letter, to exhort you, that, as becomes a Bishop, you would teach the people to conform to the established[2] religion, and, according to your custom, give yourself up to prayer together with them. For this is agreeable to our wishes; and our desire is, that you should in every season be a Bishop in your own place

[2] κιχειω- στημένη, vid κρα- τοῦσῃ πίστει, infr. §. 31.

And in another hand:—May divine Providence preserve you, beloved Father, many years.

§. 24. 32. On the subject of this letter, my opponents conferred with the magistrates. And was it not reasonable that I, having received it, should demand their letters, and refuse to give heed to mere pretences? And were they not acting in direct contradiction to the tenor of your instructions to me, while they failed to shew me the commands of your Piety? I therefore, seeing they produced no letters from you, considered it improbable that a mere verbal communication should be made to them, especially as the letter of your Grace had charged me not to give ear to such persons. I acted rightly then, most religious Augustus, that, as I had returned to my country under the authority of your letters, so I should only leave it by your command, and might not render myself liable hereafter to a charge of having deserted the Church, but as receiving your order might have a reason for my secession. This was demanded for me by all my people, who went to Syrianus together with the Presbyters, and the greatest part, to say the least, of the city with them. Maximus the Prefect of Egypt was also there: and their request was that either he would send me a declaration of your wishes in writing, or would forbear to disturb the Churches, while the people themselves were sending a deputation to you respecting the matter. When they persisted in their demand, Syrianus at last perceived the reasonableness of it, and consented, protesting by your life (Hilary was present and witnessed this) that he would put an end to the disturbance, and refer the case to your Piety. The guards of the Duke, as well as those of the Prefect of Egypt, know that this is true; the Prytanis[1] of the city also remembers the words, so that you will perceive that neither I, nor any one else, resisted your commands.

Tr.IV. 23—25.

[1] The Mayor, Tillem. vol. 8. p. 152.

33 All demanded that the letters of your Piety should be exhibited. For although the bare word of a King is of equal weight and authority with his written command, especially if he who reports it, boldly affirms in writing that it has been given him; yet when they neither openly declared that they had received any command, nor, as they were requested to do, gave me assurance of it in writing, but acted altogether as by their own authority; I confess, I say it boldly, I was suspicious of them. For there were many Arians about them, who were their companions at table, and their advisers, and while they attempted nothing openly, they were preparing to assail me, by stratagem and treachery. Nor did they act at all as under the authority of a royal command, but, as their conduct betrayed, at the solicitation of my enemies This made me demand more urgently that they should produce letters from you, seeing that all their undertakings and designs were of a suspicious nature, and because it was unseemly that after I had entered the Church, under the authority of so many letters from you, I should retire from it without such a sanction.

§. 25.

34. When however Syrianus gave his promise, all the people assembled together in the Churches with feelings of joyfulness and security. But three and twenty days after, he burst into the Church with his soldiers, while we were

engaged in our usual services, as those who entered in there witnessed; for it was a vigil, preparatory to a communion[1] on the morrow. And such things were done that night as the Arians desired and had beforehand denounced against us. For the General brought them with him; and they were the instigators and advisers of the attack. This is no incredible story of mine, most religious Augustus, for it was not done in secret, but was noised abroad every where. When therefore I saw the assault begun, I first exhorted the people to retire, and then withdrew myself after them, God hiding and guiding me, as those who were with me at the time witnessed. Since then, I have remained by myself, though I have all confidence to answer for my conduct, in the first place before God, and also before your Piety, for that I did not flee and desert my people, but can point to the attack of the General upon us, as a proof of persecution. His proceedings have caused the greatest astonishment among all men, for either he ought not to have made a promise, or not to have broken it after he had made it.

§. 26. 35. Now why did they form this plot against me, and treacherously lay an ambush to take me, when it was in their power to enforce the order by a written declaration? The command of a King is wont to give great boldness to those entrusted with it; but their desire to act secretly, made the suspicion stronger that they had received no command. And did I require any thing so very absurd? Let your Majesty's candour decide[2]. Will not every one say, that such a demand was reasonable for a Bishop to make? You know, for you have read the Scriptures, how great an offence it is for a Bishop to desert his Church, and to neglect the flock of God. For the absence of the Shepherd gives the wolves an opportunity to attack the sheep. And this was what the Arians and all the other heretics desired, that during my absence they might find an opportunity to entrap the people into impiety. If then I had fled, what defence could I have made before true Bishops? or rather before Him who has committed to me His flock? He it is who judges the whole earth, the true King of all, our Lord Jesus Christ, the Son of God.

36. Would not every one have rightly charged me with neglect of my people? Would not your Piety have blamed me, and have justly asked, " After you had returned under the authority of our letters, why did you withdraw without such authority, and desert your people?" Would not the people themselves at the day of judgment have reasonably imputed to me this neglect of them, and have said, " He that had the oversight of us fled, and we were neglected, there being no one to put us in mind of our duty?" When they said this, what could I have answered? Such a complaint was made by Ezekiel against the Pastors of old; and the blessed Apostle Paul, knowing this, has charged every one of us, in the person of his disciple, saying, *Neglect not the gift that is in thee, which was given thee, with the laying on of the hands of the presbytery.* Fearing this, I wished not to flee, but to receive your commands, if indeed such was the will of your Piety. But I never obtained what I so reasonably requested, and now I am falsely accused before you; for I resisted no commands of your Piety; nor will I now attempt to return to Alexandria, until your Grace shall desire it. This I say beforehand, lest the slanderers should again make this a pretence for accusing me.

37. Considering these things, I did not give sentence against myself[1], but hastened to come to your Piety, with this my defence, knowing your goodness, and remembering your faithful promises, and being confident that, as it is written in the Proverbs of Scripture, *Just speeches are acceptable to a gracious king*[2]. But when I had already entered upon my journey, and had past through the desert, a report suddenly reached me[t], which at first I thought to be incredible, but which afterwards proved to be true. It was rumoured every where that Liberius Bishop of Rome, the great Hosius of Spain, Paulinus of Gaul, Dionysius and Eusebius of Italy, Lucifer of Sardinia[3], and certain other Bishops, with their Presbyters and Deacons, had been banished because they refused to subscribe to my condemnation. These had been

---

[t] In this chapter he breaks off his Oratorical form, and ends his Apology much more in the form of a letter. vid. however τῶν λόγων καιρὸν, infr. §. 34, 35 init. προσφωνήσω, §. 35 The events which he here records changed his feelings towards Constantius, whom henceforth he accounted as a persecutor, worse than heathen, because an apostate. vid. Lib F. vol. 5. p. 90, note p.

banished, and Vincentius[1] of Capua, Fortunatian[1] of Aquileia, Heremius of Thessalonica, and all the Bishops of the West, were treated with no ordinary vigour, nay were suffering extreme violence and grievous injuries, until they could be induced to promise that they would not communicate with me.

38. While I was astonished and perplexed at these tidings, behold another report[2] overtook me, respecting them of Egypt and Libya, that nearly ninety Bishops had been under persecution, and that their Churches were given up to the professors of Arianism; that sixteen had been banished, and of the rest, some had fled, and others were constrained to dissemble. For the persecution was said to be so violent in those parts, that at Alexandria, while the brethren were praying during Easter and on the Lord's day in a desert place near the cemetery, the General came upon them with a force of soldiery, more than three thousand in number, with arms, drawn swords, and spears, whereupon outrages, such as might be expected to follow so unprovoked an attack, were committed against women and children, who were doing nothing more than praying to God. It would perhaps be unseasonable to give an account of them now, lest the mere mention of such enormities should move us all to tears. But such was their cruelty, that virgins were stripped, and even the bodies of those who died from the blows they received were not immediately given up for burial, but were cast out to the dogs, until their relatives, with great risk to themselves, came secretly and stole them away, and much effort was necessary, that no one might know it.

§. 28. 39. The rest of their proceedings will perhaps be thought incredible, and will fill all men with astonishment, by reason of their extreme wickedness. It is necessary however to speak of them, in order that your Christian zeal and piety may perceive that their slanders and calumnies against us are framed for no other end, than that they may drive us out of the Churches, and introduce their own impiety in our place. For when the lawful Bishops, men of advanced age, had some of them been banished, and others forced to fly, heathens and catechumens, those who hold the first places in the senate, and men who are notorious for their wealth, were straightway commissioned by the Arians to preach the holy faith instead of Christians[1]. And enquiry was no longer made, as the Apostle enjoined, *if any be blameless;* but according to the practice of the impious Jeroboam, he who could give most money, was named Bishop; and it made no difference to them, even if the man happened to be a heathen, so long as he furnished them with money. Those who had been Bishops from the time of Alexander, monks and ascetics, were banished: and men practised only in calumny corrupted, as far as in them lay, the Apostolic rule, and polluted the Churches. Truly their false accusations against us have gained them much, that they should be able to commit iniquity, and to do such things as these in your time[2]; so that the words of Scripture may be applied to them, *Woe unto those through whom My name is blasphemed among the Gentiles.*

TR. IV. 28, 29.
[1] Hist. Ar.§.73. supr. p. 135, r.1.
1 Tim. 3, 2.
[2] καιροῖς, de Syn. fin. (tr. p. 159.)
vid. 2 Sam.12, 14 &c.

40. These were the rumours that were noised abroad, and although every thing was thus turned upside down, I still did not relinquish my earnest desire of coming to your Piety, but was again setting forward on my journey. And I did so the more eagerly, being confident that these proceedings were contrary to your wishes, and that if your Grace should be informed of what was done, you would prevent it for the time to come. For I could not think that a righteous king could wish Bishops to be banished, and virgins to be stripped, or the Churches to be in any way disturbed. While I thus reasoned and hastened on my journey, behold a third report reached me, to the effect that letters had been written to the Princes of Auxumis, desiring that Frumentius[u], Bishop of Auxumis, should be brought from thence, and that search should be made for me even as far as the country of the Barbarians, that I might be handed over to the Commentaries[x]

§. 29.

---

[u] Athan. had consecrated Frumentius for the Ethiopian mission, who had been already successful in introducing Christianity into the heathen court of Auxumis, where he had held the place first of Minister, then of Regent. The two Princes to whom Constantius writes in the letter which is presently to follow were the King's sons, whom Frumentius had first served

[x] That is, the prison. "The official books;" Montfaucon (apparently) in Onomast. vid. Gothofr. Cod. Theod. ix. 3 l. 5. However, in xi. 30. p. 243. he says, Malim pro ipsâ custodiâ accipere. And so Du Cange *in voc.* and this meaning is here followed. vid. supr. p. 25. where commentarius is translated "jailor." Apol. contr. Arian. § 8.

180   Letter of Constantius against Athanasius

Apol. to Consi.

(as they are called) of the Prefects, and that all the laity and clergy should be compelled to communicate with the Arian heresy, and that such as would not comply with this order should be put to death. To shew that these were not merely idle rumours, but that they were confirmed by facts, since your Grace has given me leave, I produce the letter. My enemies, who threatened every one with death, frequently caused it to be read.

§. 30.   41. *A copy of the letter.*

[1] pp. 79, 96, 119, &c

Victor[1] Constantius Maximus Augustus to the Alexandrians.

Your city, preserving its native spirit and temper, and remembering the virtue of its founders, has habitually shewn itself obedient unto us, as it does at this day; and we on our part should consider ourselves greatly wanting in our duty, did not our good will eclipse even that of Alexander himself. For as it belongs to a temperate mind, to behave itself orderly in all respects, so it is the part of royalty, on account of virtue, permit me to say, such as yours, to embrace you above all others, you, who rose up as the first teachers of wisdom;

[2] τὸν ὄντα. infr. p 182, note y

who were the first to acknowledge the God, who is[2], who moreover have chosen for yourselves the most consummate masters; and have cordially acquiesced in our opinion, justly abominating that impostor and cheat, and dutifully uniting yourselves to those venerable men who are beyond all admiration And yet, who is ignorant, even among those who live in the end of the earth, what violent party spirit was displayed in the late proceedings? with which we know not any thing that has ever happened, worthy to be compared. The majority of the citizens had their eyes blinded, and a man who had come forth from the lowest dens of infamy obtained authority among them, entrapping into falsehood, as under cover of darkness, those who were desirous to know the truth;—one who never provided for them any fruitful and edifying discourse, but corrupted their minds with unprofitable subtleties. His flatterers shouted and applauded him; they were astonished at his powers, and they still probably murmur secretly; while the majority of the more simple sort took their cue from them. And thus all went with the stream, as if a flood had broken in, while every thing was entirely neglected. One of the multitude was in power;—how can I describe him more truly, than by saying, that he was superior in nothing to the meanest of the people, and that the only kindness which he shewed to the city was, that he did not thrust her citizens down into the pit. This noble-minded and illustrious person did not wait for judgment to proceed against him, but sentenced himself to banishment as he deserved. So that now it is for the interest of the Barbarians to remove him out of the way, lest he lead some of them into impiety, for he will make his complaint, like distressed characters in a play, to those who shall first fall in with him.

42. To him however we will now bid a long farewell. For yourselves there are few with whom I can compare you: I am bound rather to honour you separately above all others, for the great virtue and wisdom which your actions, that are celebrated almost through the whole world, proclaim you to possess. Go on in this sober course. I would gladly have repeated to me a description of your conduct in such terms of praise as it deserves, O ye who have eclipsed your predecessors in the race of glory, and will be a noble example both to those who are now alive, and to all who shall come after, and alone have chosen for yourselves the most excellent guide you could have for your conduct, both in word and deed, and hesitated not a moment, but manfully transferred your affections, and gave yourselves up to the other side, leaving those grovelling[1] and earthly teachers, and stretching forth towards heavenly things, under the guidance of the most venerable George[2], than whom no man is more perfectly instructed therein. Under him you will continue to have a good hope respecting the future life, and will pass your time in this present world, in rest and quietness. Would that all the citizens together would lay hold on his words, as a sacred anchor, so that we might need neither knife nor cautery, for those whose souls are diseased!

43. Such persons we most earnestly advise to renounce their zeal in favour of Athanasius, and not even to remember the foolish things which he spoke so plentifully among them. Otherwise they will bring themselves before they are aware

APOL. TO CONST.

into extreme peril, from which we know not any one who will be skilful enough to deliver such factious persons. For while that pestilent[1] fellow Athanasius is driven from place to place, being convicted of the basest crimes, for which he would only suffer the punishment he deserves, if one were to kill him ten times over; it would be inconsistent in us to suffer those flatterers and juggling ministers of his to exult against us; men of such a character as it is a shame even to speak of, respecting whom orders have long ago been given to the magistrates, that they should be put to death. But even now perhaps they shall not die, if they desist from their former offences, and repent at last. For that villain Athanasius led them on, and corrupted the whole state, and laid his impious and polluted hands upon the most holy things.

[1] ἔλιθρον

§. 31

44. The following is the letter which was written to the Princes of Auxumis respecting Frumentius Bishop of that place.

45 Victor Constantius Maximus Augustus, to Æzanes and Sazanes.

It is altogether a matter of the greatest care and concern to us, to extend the knowledge of the supreme God[y]; and I think that the whole race of mankind claims from us equal regard in this respect, in order that they may pass their lives in hope, being brought to a proper knowledge of God, and having no differences with each other in their enquiries concerning justice and truth. Wherefore considering that you are deserving of the same provident care as the Romans, and desiring to shew equal regard for your welfare, we command that the same doctrine be professed in your Churches as in theirs. Send therefore speedily into Egypt the Bishop Frumentius, to the most venerable Bishop George, and the rest who are there, who have especial authority to appoint to these offices, and to decide questions concerning them. For of course you know and remember (unless you alone pretend

---

[y] ἡ τοῦ κρείττονος γνῶσις, vid. τὸν κρείττονα, infr. And so in Arius's Thalia, the Eternal Father, in contrast to the Son, is called ὁ κρείττων, τὸν κρείττονα, de Synod. §. 15 So again, θεὸν τὸν ὄντα συνιέντας, supr. §. 30. and συνετῶν θεοῦ in the Thalia, Orat. 1. 5. Again, σοφίας ἐξηγητὰς, supr. §. 30 and τῶν σοφίας μετεχόντων, κατὰ πάντα σοφῶν, in the Thalia, ibid And τῶν ἐξηγητῶν τοὺς ἄκρους εἴλισθι, supr. §. 30. and τούτων κατ' ἴχνος ἦλθον in the Thalia.

addressed to the Ethiopians.

to be ignorant of that which all men are well aware of) that this Frumentius was advanced to his present rank by Athanasius, a man who is guilty of ten thousand crimes; for he has not been able fairly to clear himself of any of the charges brought against him, but was at once deprived of his see, and now wanders about destitute of any fixed abode, and passes from one country to another, as if by this means he could escape his own wickedness.

Tr. IV. 31, 32.

46. Now if Frumentius shall readily obey our commands, and shall submit to an enquiry into all the circumstances of his appointment, he will shew plainly to all men, that he is in no respect opposed to the laws of the Church and the established[1] faith. And being brought to trial, when he shall have given proof of his general good conduct, and submitted an account of his life to those who are to judge of these things, he shall receive his appointment from them, if it shall indeed appear that he has any right to be a Bishop. But if he shall delay and avoid the trial, it will surely be very evident, that he has been induced by the persuasions of the wicked Athanasius, thus impiously to act against divine authority, choosing to follow the course of him whose wickedness has been made manifest. And our fear is lest he should pass over into Auxumis and corrupt your people, by setting before them accursed and impious doctrines, and not only unsettle and disturb the Churches, and blaspheme the supreme[2] God, but also thereby cause utter overthrow and destruction to the several nations whom he visits. But I am sure that Frumentius will return home, perfectly acquainted with all matters that concern the Church, having derived much instruction, which will be of great and general utility, from the conversation of the most venerable George, and such other of the Bishops, as are excellently qualified to communicate such knowledge. May God continually preserve you, most honoured brethren.

[1] κρατού-ση, supr. p. 174. r. 1.

[2] κρίστοτα

47. Hearing, nay almost seeing, these things, through the mournful representations of the messengers, I confess I turned back again into the desert, justly concluding, as your Piety will perceive, that if I was sought after, that I might be sent as soon as I was discovered to the Prefects[3], I should be prevented from ever coming to your Grace; and that if

§. 32.

[3] p. 179, 180 init.

those who would not subscribe against me, suffered so severely as they did, and the laity who refused to communicate with the Arians were ordered for death, there was no doubt at all but that ten thousand new modes of destruction would be devised by the calumniators against me; and that after my death, they would employ against whomsoever they wished to injure, whatever means they chose, venting their lies against us the more boldly, for that then there would no longer be any one left who could expose them. I fled, not because I feared your Piety, (for I know your long-suffering and goodness,) but because from what had taken place, I perceived the spirit of my enemies, and considered that they would make use of all possible means to accomplish my destruction, from fear that they would be brought to answer for what they had done contrary to the intentions of your Excellency. For observe, your Grace commanded that the Bishops should be expelled only out of the cities and the province But these worthy persons presumed to exceed your commands, and banished aged men and Bishops venerable for their years into desert and unfrequented and frightful places, beyond the boundaries of three provinces[1]. Some of them were sent off from Libya to the great Oasis; others from the Thebais to Ammoniaca in Libya.

48. Neither was it from fear of death that I fled; let none of them condemn me as guilty of cowardice; but because it is the injunction of our Saviour[1] that we should flee when we are persecuted, and hide ourselves when we are sought after, and not expose ourselves to certain dangers, nor by appearing before our persecutors inflame still more their rage against us. For to give one's self up to one's enemies to be murdered, is the same thing as to murder one's self; but to flee, as our Saviour has enjoined, is to know our time, and to manifest a real concern for our persecutors, lest if they proceed to the shedding of blood, they become guilty of the transgression of the law, *Thou shall not kill.* And yet these

[1] Egypt was divided into three Provinces till Hadrian's time, Egypt, Libya, and Pentapolis, Hadrian made them four; Epiphanius speaks of them as seven Hær. 68. 1. By the time of Arcadius they had become eight vid. Orlendini Orbis Sacer et Prof vol 1. p 118 The Province specially spoken of seems to be Egypt, which Augustus kept in his own hands vid. supr p. 5, note d p 116, r 1

men by their calumnies against me, earnestly wish that I should suffer death. ^{Tr. IV. 32, 33.}

49. What they have again lately done proves that this is their desire and murderous intention. You will be astonished, I am sure, most religious Augustus, when you hear it; it is indeed an outrage worthy of amazement. What it is, I pray you briefly to hear. The Son of God, our Lord and Saviour §. 33. Jesus Christ, having become man for our sakes, and having destroyed death, and delivered our race from the bondage of corruption, in addition to all His other benefits bestowed this also upon us, that we should possess upon earth, in the state of virginity, a picture of the holiness of Angels. Accordingly such as have attained this virtue, the Catholic Church has been accustomed to call the brides[1] of Christ. [1] νύμφας And the heathen who see them express their admiration of them as the temples of the Word. For indeed this holy and heavenly profession is no where established, but only among us Christians, and it is a very strong argument that with us is to be found the genuine and true religion. Your most religious father Constantine Augustus, of blessed memory[2], honoured the Virgins above all other orders, and [2] τῆς μακαρίας μνήμης. your Piety in several letters has given them the titles of the honourable and holy women. But now these worthy Arians [supr. pp. 159, 162.] who have slandered me, and by whom conspiracies have been formed against most of the Bishops, having obtained the consent and cooperation of the magistrates, first stripped them, and then caused them to be suspended upon what are called the Hermetaries[3], and scourged them on the ribs so [3] a rack, or horse, Tillemont. v. Athan. p. 169. severely three several times, that not even real malefactors have ever suffered the like. Pilate, to gratify the Jews of old, pierced one of our Saviour's sides with a spear. These men have exceeded the madness of Pilate, for they have scourged not one but both His sides; for the limbs of the Virgins are in an especial manner the Saviour's own.

50 All men shudder at hearing the bare recital of deeds like these. These men alone, not only did not fear to strip and to scourge those undefiled limbs, which the Virgins had dedicated solely to our Saviour Christ, but, what is worse than all, when they were reproached by every one for such extreme cruelty, instead of manifesting any shame, they

pretended that it was commanded by your Piety. So utterly presumptuous are they and full of wicked thoughts and purposes. Such a deed as this was never heard of in past persecutions[1]: or supposing that it ever occurred before, yet surely it was not befitting either that Virginity should suffer such outrage and dishonour, in the time of your Majesty a Christian Prince, or that these men should impute to your Piety their own cruelty. Such wickedness belongs only to heretics, to blaspheme the Son of God, and to do violence to His holy Virgins.

[1] vid. Hist. Ar. §40. §. 64.

§. 34. 51 Now when such enormities as these were again perpetrated by the Arians, I surely was not wrong in complying with the direction of Holy Scripture, which says, *Hide thyself for a little moment, until the indignation be overpast.* This was another reason for my withdrawing myself, most religious Augustus; and I refused not, either to depart into the desert, or, if need were, to be let down from a wall in a basket. I endured every thing, I even dwelt among wild beasts, that your favour might return to me, waiting for an opportunity to offer to you this my defence, confident as I am that they will be condemned, and your goodness manifested unto me.

Is. 26, 29

52. O, Augustus, blessed and beloved of God, what would you have had me to do? to come to you while my calumniators were inflamed with rage against me, and were seeking to kill me, or, as it is written, to hide myself a little, that in the mean time they might be condemned as heretics, and your goodness might be manifested unto me? or would you have had me, Sire, to appear before your magistrates, in order that though you had written merely in the way of threatening, they not understanding your intention, but being exasperated against me by the Arians, might kill me on the authority of your letters, and on that ground ascribed the murder to you? It would neither have been becoming in me to surrender, and give myself up that my blood might be shed, nor in you, as a Christian King, to have the murder of Christians, and those too Bishops, imputed unto you.

§ 35. 53. It was therefore better for me to hide myself, and to wait for this opportunity. Yes, I am sure that from your knowledge of the sacred Scriptures you will assent and approve of my conduct in this respect. For you will perceive that, now those who exasperated you against us have been silenced, your righteous clemency is apparent, and it is proved to all men that you never persecuted the Christians at all, but that it was they who made the Churches desolate, that they might sow the seeds[1] of their own impiety every where; on account of which I also, had I not fled, should long ago have suffered from their treachery. For it is very evident that they who scrupled not to utter such calumnies against me, before the great Augustus, and who so violently assailed Bishops and Virgins, sought also to compass my death. But thanks be to the Lord who has given you this kingdom. All men are confirmed in their opinion of your goodness, and of their wickedness, from which I fled at the first, that I might now make this appeal unto you, and that you might find some one towards whom you may shew kindness. I beseech you therefore, forasmuch as it is written, *A soft answer turneth away wrath*, and, *righteous thoughts are acceptable unto the King;* receive this my defence, and restore all the Bishops and the rest of the Clergy to their countries and their Churches; so that the wickedness of my accusers may be made manifest, and that you, both now and in the day of judgment, may have boldness to say to our Lord and Saviour Jesus Christ, the King of all, "*None of Thine have I lost*, but these are they who designed the ruin of all, while I was grieved for those who perished, and for the Virgins who were scourged, and for all other things that were committed against the Christians; and I brought back them that were banished, and restored them to their own Churches."

Tr. IV. 35.

[1] vol. 8. p. 5. note k.

Prov. 15, 1; 16, 13.

vid. p. 177.

John 18, 9.

V.

APOLOGY

OF OUR

HOLY FATHER ATHANASIUS,

ARCHBISHOP OF ALEXANDRIA,

IN VINDICATION OF HIS FLIGHT,

WHEN HE WAS PERSECUTED BY DUKE SYRIANUS.

[This Apology seems to have been written A.D. 357 or 358. The circumstances which led to it are mentioned in the opening sentences. From what he says to Constantius in the foregoing work, p. 177, it might almost be said that, in addition to the considerations insisted on in the following argument, he considered that the command of the Emperor would in itself have been a sufficient reason for his leaving his Church, and it was because he had not received it, that he had not left it before. Now the violence of Syrianus, acknowledged as it was by Constantius, was of the nature of a command. The real reason however was, that, if he had been cut off, there was no one to take his place. vid. supr. p. 184]

---

§. 1. 1. I HEAR that Leontius[1], now in the see of Antioch, and Narcissus[2] of the city of Nero, and George[3], now of Laodicea, and the Arians who are leagued with them, are spreading abroad many slanderous reports concerning me, charging me with cowardice, because forsooth, when myself was sought by them, I did not surrender myself into their hands. Now as to their imputations and calumnies, although there are many things that I could write, which they are unable to deny, and which all who have heard of their proceedings know to be true, yet I shall not be prevailed upon to make any reply to them, except only to remind them of the words of our Lord, and of the declaration of the Apostle, that *a lie is of the Devil*, and that, *revilers shall not inherit the kingdom of God*. For it is sufficient thereby to prove, that neither their thoughts nor their words are according to the Gospel, but that after their own pleasure, whatsoever themselves desire, that they think to be good.

[1] infr. §. 26.
[2] vol. 8. p. 99, supr. p. 74, &c.
vid. 1 John 2, 21.
1 Cor. 6, 10.

§. 2. 2. But forasmuch as they pretend to charge me with cowardice, it is necessary that I should write somewhat concerning this, whereby it shall be proved that they are men of wicked minds, who have not read the sacred Scriptures· or if they have read them, that they do not believe the divine inspiration of the oracles they contain. For had they believed this, they would never have dared to act contrary to them, nor have imitated the malice of the Jews who slew the Lord. For God having given them a commandment, *Honour thy father and thy mother,* and, *He that curseth father or mother,⁴ let him die the death;* that people established a contrary law, changing the honour into dishonour, and alienating to other uses the money which was due from the children to their parents. And though they had read what David did, they acted in contradiction to his example, and accused the guiltless for plucking the ears of corn, and rubbing them in their hands on the Sabbath day. Not that they cared either for the laws, or for the Sabbath, for they were guilty of greater transgressions of the law on that day: but being wicked-minded, they grudged the disciples the way of salvation, and desired that their own private notions should have the sole pre-eminence. They however have received the reward of their iniquity, having ceased to be an holy nation, and being counted henceforth as the rulers of Sodom, and as the people of Gomorrah.

3. And these men likewise, not less than they, seem to me to have received their punishment already in the ignorance with which their own folly possesses them. For they understand not what they say, but think that they know things of which they are ignorant; while the only knowledge that is in them is to do evil, and to frame devices more and more wicked day by day. Thus they reproach me with my present flight, not for the sake of my character, as wishing me to shew my manliness by coming forward; (how is it possible that such a wish can be entertained by enemies in behalf of those who run not with them in the same career of madness?) but being full of malice, they pretend this, and whisper¹ up and down that such is the case, thinking, foolish as indeed they are, that through fear of their revilings, I shall yet be induced to give myself up to them. For this is what they desire: to accomplish this they have recourse to all kinds of schemes: they pretend themselves to be friends, while they search after

¹ περιβομ-βεῖν, vol. 8. p. 22, note y. Greg. Naz. Orat.27. n. 2.

APOL. me as enemies, to the end that they may glut themselves with
FOR
FLIGHT. my blood, and put me also out of the way, because I have
always opposed and do still oppose their impiety, and confute and brand their heresy.

§. 3.   4. For whom have they ever persecuted and taken, that they
have not insulted and injured as they pleased? Whom have
they ever sought after and found, that they have not handled
in such a manner, that either he has died a miserable
[1] ταντα- death, or has been illtreated in every member[1]? Whatever
χόθεν
the magistrates appear to do, it is their work, and the other
are merely the tools of their will and wickedness. In consequence, where is there a place that has not some memorial
of their wickedness? Who has ever opposed them, without
their conspiring against him, inventing pretexts for his ruin
after the manner of Jezebel? Where is there a Church that
is not at this moment lamenting the success of their plots
against her Bishops? Antioch is mourning for the orthodox
Confessor Eustathius[a]; Balaneæ for the most admirable
[2] Hist. Euphration[2]; Paltus and Antaradus for Cymatius[2] and Carte-
Arian.5.
rius; Adrianople for that lover of Christ, Eutropius, and after
him for Lucius, who was often loaded with chains by their
means, and so perished; Ancyra mourns for Marcellus,
[3] Berœa, Berrhœa[3] for Cyrus[2], Gaza for Asclepas.
Hist.
Ar. 5   5. Of all these, after inflicting many outrages, they by their
intrigues procured the banishment; but for Theodulus and
Olympius, Bishops of Thrace, and for me and my Presbyters,
they caused diligent search to be made, to the intent that if we
were discovered we should suffer capital punishment: and pro-

[a] vid. Hist. Arian. §. 4 also Theodoret Hist. l. 20. Eustathius was one
of the original opponents of Arianism.
S. Alexander wrote to him (then Bishop
of Berrhœa) against Arius, as well as to
Philogonius of Antioch and Alexander
of Constantinople. He was deposed
by the Arians A D. 331, on the pretence of Sabellianism and perhaps of
incontinency. Montfaucon, however,
doubts whether the latter was ever
made a charge, though Theodoret
mentions it. V. Athan. p. 14. Another
reason is given Hist. Arian loc cit. The
orthodox succession was continued,
though dispossessed, and gave occasion
to the schism, after the overthrow of
Arianism, which was not terminated
till the time of S. Chrysostom. The
name of Euphration occurs de Syn. 17.
(tr. vol. 8. p. 99) as the Bishop to whom
Eusebius of Cæsarea wrote an heretical
letter. Balaneæ is on the Syrian coast.
Paltus also and Antaradus are in
Syria, and these persecutions took
place about A.D. 340; that of Eutropius,
and of Lucius his successor, about 332,
shortly after the proceedings against
Eustathius. Cyrus too was banished
under pretence of Sabellianism about
340. Asclepas has been mentioned supr.
p. 69. note e. For Theodulus and Olympius vid. Hist. Arian. §. 19. and supr.
p. 71. note g.

bably we should have so perished, had we not fled at that very time contrary to their intentions. For letters to that effect were delivered to the Proconsul Donatus against Olympius and his friends, and to Philagrius respecting me. And having raised a persecution against Paul, Bishop of Constantinople, as soon as they found him, they caused him to be openly strangled[1] at a place called Cucusus in Cappadocia, employing as their executioner for the purpose Philip, who was Prefect. He was a patron of their heresy, and the tool of their wicked designs

_{TR. V.
3—5.}

_{[1] infr
Hist.
Arian.
§. 4.}

6. Are they then satisfied with all this, and content to be quiet for the future? By no means; they have not given over yet, but like the horseleach[2] in the Proverbs, they revel more and more in their wickedness, and fix themselves upon the larger dioceses. Who can adequately describe the enormities they have already perpetrated? who is able to recount all the deeds that they have done? Even very lately, while the Churches were at peace, and the people worshipping in their congregations, Liberius Bishop of Rome, Paulinus[3] Metropolitan of Gaul, Dionysius[4] Metropolitan of Italy, Lucifer[5] Metropolitan of the Sardinian islands, and Eusebius[6] of Italy, all of them excellent Bishops and preachers of the truth, were seized and banished, on no pretence whatever, except that they would not unite themselves to the Arian heresy, nor subscribe to the accusations and calumnies which they had invented against me.

_{§. 4.}

_{[2] Hist.
Arian.
§. 65.}

_{[3] of Treves.
[4] of Milan.
[5] of Cagliari
[6] of Vercellæ.}

7. Of the great Hosius, who answers to his name, that confessor of an happy old age[7], it is superfluous for me to speak, for I suppose it is known unto all men that they caused him also to be banished; for he is not an obscure person, but of all men the most illustrious, and more than this. When was there a Council held, in which he did not take the lead, and convince every one by his orthodoxy? Where is there a Church that does not possess some glorious monuments of his patronage? Who has ever come to him in sorrow, and has not gone away rejoicing? What needy person ever asked his aid, and did not obtain what he desired? And yet even on this man they made their assault, because knowing the calumnies which they invent in behalf of their iniquity, he would not subscribe to their designs against me. And if

_{§. 5.}

_{[7] εὐγηροτάτου, vid supr.
p. 70.}

APOL. FOR FLIGHT.

afterwards, upon the repeated blows that were inflicted upon him above measure, and the conspiracies that were formed against his kinsfolk, he yielded to them for a time, as being old and infirm in body, yet at least their wickedness was shewn even in this circumstance, so zealously did they endeavour by all means to prove that they were not truly Christians[1].

[1] infr. §. 27 init.

§. 6. 8. After this they again fastened themselves upon Alexandria, seeking anew to put me to death: and their proceedings were now worse than before. For on a sudden the Church was surrounded by soldiers, and deeds of war took the place of prayers. Then George[2] of Cappadocia who was sent by them, having arrived during the season of Lent[3], brought an increase of evils which they had taught him. For after Easter week, Virgins were thrown into prison; Bishops were led away in chains by soldiers; the houses of orphans and widows were plundered, and their bread taken away; attacks were made upon houses, and Christians thrust forth in the night, and their dwellings sealed up: the brothers of clergymen were in danger of their lives on account of their relations.

[2] vol. 8. p. 134, note f. supr. p. 181.
[3] supr. p. 7, note h.

9. These outrages were sufficiently dreadful, but more dreadful than these followed. For on the week that succeeded the Holy Pentecost, when the people after their fast had gone out to the cemetery to pray, because that all refused communion with George, that abandoned person, understanding this to be the case, stirred up against them the commander Sebastian, a Manichee, who straightway with a multitude of soldiers with arms, drawn swords, bows, and spears, proceeded to attack the people, though it was the Lord's day: and finding a few praying, (for the greater part had already retired on account of the lateness of the hour,) he committed such outrages as became a disciple of these men. Having lighted a pile, he placed certain virgins near the fire, and endeavoured to force them to say that they were of the Arian faith: and where he saw that they were getting the mastery, and cared not for the fire, he immediately stripped them naked, and wounded their faces in such a manner, that for some time they could hardly be recognised.

§. 7. 10. And having seized upon forty men, he beat them after a new fashion. Cutting some fresh twigs of the palm tree with the thorns upon them[1], he scourged them on the back so severely, that some of them were for a long time under medical treatment on account of the thorns which had entered their flesh, and others unable to bear up under their sufferings died. All those whom they had taken, both the men and the virgins, they sent away together into banishment to the great Oasis. And the bodies of those who had perished they would not at first suffer to be given up to their friends, but concealed them in any way they pleased, and cast them out without burial[2], in order that they might not appear to have any knowledge of these cruel proceedings. But herein their deluded minds greatly misled them. For the relatives of the dead, both rejoicing at the confession, and grieving for the bodies of their friends, published abroad so much the more this proof of their impiety and cruelty. Moreover they immediately banished out of Egypt and Libya the following Bishops[3], Ammonius, Muius, Gaius, Philo[4], Hermes, Plenius, Psenosiris, Nilammon, Agathus, Anagamphus, Marcus, Ammonius, another Marcus, Dracontius[5], Adelphius[6], Athenodorus, and the Presbyters, Hierax[7], and Dioscorus; whom they drove forth under such cruel treatment, that some of them died on the way, and others in the place of their banishment. They caused also more than thirty Bishops to take to flight; for their desire was, after the example of Ahab, if it were possible, utterly to root out the truth. Such are the enormities of which these impious men have been guilty.

11. But although they have done all this, yet they are not ashamed of the evils they have already contrived against me, but proceed now to accuse me, because I have been able to escape their murderous hands. Nay, they bitterly bewail themselves, that they have not effectually put me out of the way; and so they pretend to reproach me with cowardice, not perceiving that by thus murmuring against me, they rather turn the blame upon themselves. For if it be a bad thing to flee, it is much worse to persecute; for the one party hides himself to escape death, the other persecutes with a desire to kill; and it is written in the Scriptures that we ought to flee, but he that seeks to destroy transgresses the law, nay, and is himself the occasion of the other's flight. If

194   *If it be a sin to flee, it is a greater to cause to flee*

APOL. FOR FLIGHT.
[1] vid. supr. p. 18. §. 4.

then they reproach me with my flight, let them be more ashamed of their own persecution[1]. Let them cease to compass my destruction, and I shall without delay cease to flee.

12. But they, instead of giving over their wickedness, are employing every means to obtain possession of my person, not perceiving that the flight of those who are persecuted is a strong argument against them that persecute. For no man flees from the gentle and the humane, but from the cruel and the evil-minded. *Every one that was in distress, and every one that was in debt,* fled from Saul, and took refuge with David. But this is the reason why these men desire to cut off those who are in concealment, that there may be no evidence forthcoming of their wickedness. But herein their minds seem to be blinded with their usual error. For the more the flight of their enemies becomes known, so much the more notorious will be the destruction or the banishment which their treachery has brought upon them[2]; so that whether they kill them outright, their death will be the more loudly noised abroad against them, or whether they drive them into banishment, they will but be sending forth every where monuments of their own iniquity.

1 Sam. 22, 2.

[2] Hist. Arian. § 34. 35.

§. 9.

13. Now if they had been of sound mind, they would have seen that they were in this strait, and that they were defeated by their own arguments. But since they have lost all judgment, they are still led on to persecute, and seek to destroy, and yet perceive not their own impiety. It may be they even venture to accuse Providence itself, (for nothing is beyond the reach of their presumption,) that it does not deliver up to them those whom they desire, certain as it is, according to the saying of our Saviour, that not even a sparrow can fall into the net[3] without our Father which is in heaven. But when these bad spirits obtain possession of any one, they immediately forget not only all other, but even themselves; and raising their brow in very haughtiness, they neither acknowledge times and seasons, nor respect human nature in those whom they injure. Like the tyrant of Babylon[4], they attack more furiously, they shew pity to none, but mercilessly *upon the ancient,* as it is written, *they very heavily lay the yoke,* and *they add to the grief of them that are wounded.*

[3] p. 199, r. 1.

[4] pp. 9. 195.

Is. 47, 6.

Ps. 69, 26.

14. Had they not acted in this manner; had they not driven into banishment those who spoke in my defence against their calumnies, their representations might have appeared to some persons sufficiently plausible. But since they have conspired against so many other Bishops of high character, and have spared neither the great confessor Hosius, nor the Bishop of Rome, nor so many others from Spain and Gaul, and Egypt, and Libya, and the other countries, but have committed such cruel outrages against all who have in any way opposed them in my behalf, is it not plain that their designs have been directed rather against me than against any other, and that their desire is miserably to destroy me as they have done others? To accomplish this they vigilantly watch for an opportunity, and think themselves injured, when they see those safe, whom they wish not to live. Who then does not perceive their profligacy? Is it not very evident to every one that they do not reproach me with cowardice from regard to my character, but that being athirst for blood, they employ these their base devices as a snare, thinking thereby to catch those whom they seek to destroy? That such is their character is shewn by their actions, which have convicted them of possessing dispositions more savage than wild beasts, and more cruel than the Babylonians¹. But although the proof against them is sufficiently clear from all this, yet since they still dissemble with soft words after the manner of their *father the devil*, and pretend to charge me with cowardice, while they are themselves more cowardly than hares; let us consider what is written in the sacred Scriptures respecting such cases as this. For thus they will be shewn to fight against the Scriptures no less than against me, while they detract from the virtues of the Saints.

15. For if they reproach men for hiding themselves from those who seek to destroy them, and accuse those who flee from their persecutors, what will they do when they see Jacob fleeing from his brother Esau, and Moses withdrawing into Midian for fear of Pharaoh? What excuse will they make for David, after all this idle talk, for fleeing from his house on account of Saul, where he sent to kill him, and for hiding himself in the cave, and for changing his appearance, until he withdrew from Abimelech², and escaped his designs

Tr. V. 9, 10.

§. 10.

¹ p 194.

John 8, 44

² Achish. 1 Sam 21, 13.

APOL. FOR FLIGHT. against him? What will they say, they who are ready to say any thing, when they see the great Elias, after calling upon God and raising the dead, hiding himself for fear of Ahab, and fleeing from the threats of Jezebel? At which time also the sons of the prophets, when they were sought after, hid themselves with the assistance of Abdias, and lay concealed in caves[1].

[1] Hist. Ar.§.53.

§. 11. 16. Perhaps they have not read these histories; as being out of date; yet have they no recollection of what is written in the Gospel? For the disciples also withdrew and hid themselves for fear of the Jews; and Paul, when he was sought after by the governor at Damascus, was let down from the wall in a basket, and so escaped his hands. As the Scripture then relates these things of the Saints, what excuse will they be able to invent for their wickedness? To reproach them with cowardice would be an act of madness, and to accuse them of acting contrary to the will of God, would be to shew themselves entirely ignorant of the Scriptures. For there was a command under the Law that cities of refuge should be appointed, in order that they who were sought after to be put to death, might at least have some means of saving themselves. And when He who spake unto Moses, the Word of the Father, appeared in the end of the world, He also gave this commandment, saying, *But when they persecute you in this city, flee ye into another:* and shortly after He says, *When ye therefore shall see the abomination of desolation, spoken of by Daniel the prophet, stand in the holy place, (whoso readeth, let him understand;) then let them which be in Judea flee into the mountains: let him which is on the housetop not come down to take any thing out of his house: neither let him which is in the field return back to take his clothes.* Knowing these things, the Saints regulated their conduct accordingly. For what our Lord has now commanded, the same also He spoke by His Saints before His coming in the flesh[2]; and this is the rule which is given unto men to lead them to perfection,—what God commands, that to do.

Ex. 21, 13.

Mat. 10, 23. Mat 24, 15.

[2] τῆς ἐνσάρκου παρουσίας, supr. p. 129, r. 3.

§. 12. 17. Wherefore also the Word Himself, being made man for our sakes, condescended to hide Himself when He was sought after, as we do: and also when He was persecuted, to flee and avoid the designs of His enemies. For it became Him, as by hunger and thirst and suffering, so also by hiding Himself and fleeing, to shew that He had taken our flesh, and was made man. Thus at the very first, as soon as He became man, when He was a little child, He Himself by His Angel commanded Joseph, *Arise, and take the young Child and His Mother, and flee into Egypt; for Herod will seek the young Child's life.* And when Herod was dead, we find Him withdrawing to Nazareth for fear of Archelaus his son. And when afterwards He was shewing Himself to be God, and made whole the withered hand, the Pharisees went out, and held a council against Him, how they might destroy Him; but when Jesus knew it, He withdrew Himself from thence. So also when He raised Lazarus from the dead, *from that day forth*, says the Scripture, *they took counsel for to put Him to death. Jesus therefore walked no more openly among the Jews; but went thence into a country near to the wilderness.* Again, when our Saviour said, *Before Abraham was, I am, the Jews took up stones to cast at Him; but Jesus hid Himself, and went out of the temple.* And *going through the midst of them, He went His way, and so passed by.* When they see these things, or rather when they hear of them, for see they do not, will they not desire, as it is written, to become *fuel of fire*, because their counsels and their words are contrary to what the Lord both did and taught? Also when John was martyred, and his disciples buried his body, *when Jesus heard of it, He departed thence by ship into a desert place apart.*

Tr. V. 11—13.

Mat. 2, 13.

Mat. 26, 4

John 11, 53, 54.

John 8, 58, 59.

Luke 4, 30.

§. 13.

Is. 9, 5.

Mat. 14, 3.

18. Thus the Lord acted, and thus He taught. Would that these men were even now ashamed of their conduct, and confined their rashness to man, nor proceeded to such extreme madness as even to charge our Saviour with cowardice! for it is against Him that they now utter their blasphemies. But no one will endure such madness; nay it will be seen that they do not understand the Gospels. The cause must be a reasonable and just one, which the Evangelists represent as weighing with our Saviour to withdraw and to flee; and we ought therefore to assign the same for the conduct of all the Saints. (For whatever is written concerning our Saviour in His human nature, ought to be considered as applying to the whole race of mankind[1]; because He took our body, and ex-

[1] vol. 8. p. 241.

hibited in Himself human infirmity.) Now of this cause John has written thus, *They sought to take Him: but no man laid hands on Him, because His hour was not yet come.* And before it came, He Himself said to His Mother, *Mine hour is not yet come.* and to them who are called His brethren, *My time is not yet come.* And again, when His time was come, He said to the disciples, *Sleep on now, and take your rest: for behold, the hour is at hand, and the Son of man is betrayed into the hands of sinners.*

§. 14. 19. Now in so far as He was God and the Word of the Father, He had no time; for He is Himself the Creator of times[1]. But being made man, He shews by speaking in this manner that there is a time allotted to every man; and that not by chance, as some of the Gentiles imagine in their fables, but a time which He, the Creator, has appointed to every one according to the will of the Father. This is written in the Scriptures, and is manifest to all men. For although it be hidden and unknown to all, what period of time is allotted to each, and how it is allotted; yet every one knows this, that as there is a time for spring and for summer, and for autumn and for winter, so, as it is written, there is a time to die, and a time to live. And so the time of the generation which lived in the days of Noah was cut short, and their years were contracted, because the time of all things was at hand. But to Hezekiah were added fifteen years. And as God promises to them that serve Him truly, *I will fulfil the number of thy days;* Abraham dies *full of days,* and David besought God, saying, *Take me not away in the midst of my days.* And Eliphaz, one of the friends of Job, being assured of this truth, said, *Thou shalt come to thy grave in a full age, like as a shock of corn cometh in in his season.* And Solomon confirming his words, says, *The souls of the unrighteous are taken away untimely.* And therefore he exhorts in the book of Ecclesiastes, saying, *Be not overmuch wicked, neither be thou foolish: why shouldest thou die before thy time?*

§. 15. 20. Now as these things are written in the Scriptures, the case is clear, that the saints[2] knew that a certain time was allotted to every man, but that no one knows the end of that time, is plainly intimated by the words of David, *Declare unto me the shortness of my days.* What he did not know, that he desired to be informed of Accordingly the rich man also, while he thought that he had yet a long time to live, heard the words, *Thou fool, this night thy soul shall be required of thee: then whose shall those things be which thou hast provided?* And the Preacher speaks confidently in the Holy Spirit, and says, *Man also knoweth not his time.* Wherefore the Patriarch Isaac said to his son Esau, *Behold, I am old, and I know not the day of my death.* {Tr. V. 15, 16. Luke 12, 20. Eccles. 9, 12. Gen. 27, 2.}

21. Our Lord therefore, although as God, and the Word of the Father, He both knew the period which He had allotted to all, and was conscious of the time for suffering, which He Himself had appointed also to His own body; yet since He was made man for our sakes, He hid Himself when He was sought after before that time came, as we do; when He was persecuted, He fled, and avoiding the designs of His enemies He passed by, and so *went through the midst of them.* But when He had brought on that time which He Himself had appointed, at which He desired to suffer in the body for all men, He announces it to the Father, saying, *Father, the hour is come; glorify Thy Son.* And then He no longer hid Himself from those who sought Him, but stood willing to be taken by them; for the Scripture says, He said to them that came unto Him, *Whom seek ye?* and when they answered, *Jesus of Nazareth,* He saith unto them, *I am He whom ye seek.* And this He did even more than once; and so they straightway led Him away to Pilate. He neither suffered Himself to be taken before the time came, nor did He hide Himself when it was come; but gave Himself up to them that conspired against Him, that He might shew to all men that the life and death of man depends upon the divine sentence; and that without our Father which is in heaven, neither a hair of man's head can become white or black, nor a sparrow fall into the net[1]. {Luke 4, 30. John 17, 1. John 18, 4, 5. Mat. 5, 36; 10, 29.}

[1] p. 194, r. 3.

22. Our Lord therefore, as I said before, thus offered Himself for all; and the Saints having received this example from their Saviour, (for all of them before His coming, nay always, were under His teaching[2],) in their conflicts with their persecutors acted lawfully in flying, and hiding themselves when they were sought after. And being ignorant, as men, of the end of the time which Providence had appointed unto

§. 16.

[2] vol. 8. p. 236, note c.

them, they were unwilling at once to deliver themselves up into the power of those who conspired against them. But knowing on the other hand what is written, that *the times of man are in God's hand,* and that *the Lord killeth,* and *the Lord maketh alive,* they the rather endured unto the end, *wandering about,* as the Apostle has spoken, *in sheepskins, and goatskins, being destitute, tormented, wandering in deserts,* and hiding themselves *in dens and caves of the earth;* until either the appointed time of death arrived, or God who had appointed their time spake unto them, and stayed the designs of their enemies, or else delivered up the persecuted to their persecutors, according as it seemed to Him to be good. This we may well learn respecting all men from David: for when Joab instigated him to slay Saul, he said, *As the Lord liveth, the Lord shall smite him; or his day shall come to die; or he shall descend into battle, and perish; the Lord forbid that I should stretch forth my hand against the Lord's anointed.*

§. 17. 23. And if ever in their flight they voluntarily came unto those that sought after them, they did not do so without reason: but when the Spirit spoke unto them, then as righteous men they went and met their enemies; by which they also shewed their obedience and zeal towards God. Such was the conduct of Elias, when, being commanded by the Spirit, he shewed himself unto Ahab; and of Micaiah the prophet when he came to the same Ahab; and of the prophet who cried against the altar in Samaria, and rebuked Jeroboam; and of Paul when he appealed unto Cæsar. It was not certainly through cowardice that they fled: God forbid. The flight to which they submitted was rather a conflict and war against death. For with wise caution they guarded against these two things; either that they should offer themselves up without reason, (for this would have been to kill themselves, and to become guilty of death, and to transgress that saying of the Lord, *What God hath joined, let not man put asunder;*) or that they should willingly subject themselves to the reproach of negligence, as if they were unmoved by the tribulations which they met with in their flight, and which brought with them sufferings greater and more terrible than death. For he that dies, ceases to suffer[1];

but he that flies, while he expects daily the assaults of his enemies, esteems death a lighter evil. They therefore whose course was consummated in their flight did not perish dishonourably, but attained as well as others the glory of martyrdom. Therefore it is that Job is accounted a man of mighty fortitude, because he endured to live under so many and such severe sufferings, of which he would have had no perception, had he come to his end.

24. Wherefore the blessed Fathers thus regulated their conduct also; they shewed no cowardice in fleeing from the persecutor, but rather manifested their fortitude of soul in shutting themselves up in close and dark places, and living a hard life. Yet did they not desire to avoid the time of death when it arrived; for their concern was neither to shrink from it when it came, nor to forestall the sentence determined by Providence, nor to resist His dispensation, for which they knew themselves to be preserved; lest by acting hastily, they should become to themselves the cause of terror: for thus it is written, *He that is hasty with his lips, shall bring terror upon himself.*

25. Of a truth no one can possibly doubt that they were well furnished with the virtue of fortitude. For the Patriarch Jacob who had before fled from Esau, feared not death when it came, but at that very time blessed the Patriarchs, each according to his deserts. And the great Moses who previously had hid himself from Pharaoh, and had withdrawn into Midian for fear of him, when he received the commandment, *Go into Egypt,* feared not to do so. And again when he was bidden to go up into the mountain Abarim and die, he delayed not through cowardice, but even joyfully proceeded thither. And David who had before fled from Saul, feared not to risk his life in war in defence of his people; but having the choice of death or of flight set before him, when he might have fled and lived, he wisely preferred death. And the great Elias who had at a former time hid himself from Jezebel, shewed no cowardice when he was commanded by the Spirit to meet Ahab, and to reprove Ochozias. And Peter who had hid himself for fear of the Jews, and the Apostle Paul who was let down in a basket, and fled, when they were told, *Ye must bear witness at Rome,* deferred not

APOL. FOR FLIGHT.
¹ vid. Euseb. Hist ii. 25.
2 Tim. 4, 6.

the journey; yea, rather, they departed rejoicing¹; the one as hastening to meet his friends, received his death with exultation; and the other shrunk not from the time when it came, but gloried in it, saying, *For I am now ready to be offered, and the time of my departure is at hand.*

§. 19.

26. These things both prove that their previous flight was not the effect of cowardice; and testify that their after conduct also was of no ordinary character: and they loudly proclaim that they possessed in a high degree the virtue of fortitude. For neither did they withdraw themselves to gratify a slothful timidity, seeing they were at such times under the practice of a severer discipline² than at others; nor were they condemned for their flight, or charged with cowardice, by such as are now so fond of criminating others. Nay they were blessed through that declaration of our Lord, *Blessed are they which are persecuted for righteousness' sake.* Nor yet were these their sufferings without profit to themselves; for having tried them as *gold in the furnace*, as the Book of Wisdom has said, God found them worthy for Himself. And then they shone the more *like sparks*, being saved from them that persecuted them, and delivered from the designs of their enemies, and preserved to the end that they might teach the people, that their flight and escape from the rage of them that sought after them, was according to the dispensation of the Lord. And so they became dear in the sight of God, and obtained the most glorious testimony to their fortitude.

² τὸν τό- νον τῆς ἀσκήσεως

Mat. 5, 10.

§. 20.

27. Thus, for example, the Patriarch Jacob was favoured in his flight with many, even divine visions, and remaining quiet himself, he had the Lord on his side, rebuking Laban, and hindering the designs of Esau; and afterwards he became the father of Judah, of whom sprang the Lord according to the flesh; and he dispensed the blessings to the Patriarchs. And Moses the beloved of God, when he was in exile, then it was that he saw that great sight, and being preserved from his persecutors, was sent as a prophet into Egypt, and being made the minister of those mighty wonders and of the Law, he led that great people in the wilderness. And David when he was persecuted wrote the Psalm, *My heart is inditing a good matter;* and, *Our God shall come, and shall not keep*

Ps. 45, 1.
Ps. 50, 3.

silence. And again he speaks more confidently, saying, *Mine eye hath seen his desire upon mine enemies;* and again, *In God have I put my trust; I will not be afraid what man can do unto me.* And when he fled and escaped from the face of Saul *to the cave,* he said, *He hath sent from heaven, and hath saved me. He hath given them to reproach that would tread me under their feet. God hath sent His mercy and truth, and hath delivered my soul from the midst of lions.* Thus he too was saved according to the dispensation of God, and afterwards became king, and received the promise, that from his seed our Lord should spring. Tr. V. 20, 21. Ps.54,7. Ps. 56, 11. Ps.57,3.

28. And the great Elias, when he withdrew himself to mount Carmel, called upon God, and destroyed at once more than four hundred prophets of Baal; and when there were sent to take him two captains of fifty with their hundred men, he said, *Let fire come down from heaven,* and thus rebuked them. And he too was preserved, so that he anointed Elisha in his own stead, and became a pattern of virtue for the sons of the prophets. And the blessed Paul, after writing these words, *what persecutions I endured; but out of them all the Lord delivered me, and will deliver;* could speak more confidently and say, *But in all these things we are more than conquerors, for nothing shall separate us from the love of Christ*[1]. For then it was that he was caught up to the third heaven, and admitted into paradise, where he heard *unspeakable words, which it is not lawful for a man to utter.* And for this end was he then preserved, that *from Jerusalem even unto Illyricum* he might *fully preach the Gospel.* 2 Kings 1, 10. 2 Tim.3, 11. Rom. 8, 35. 37. [1] pp.149, 220. 2 Cor. 12, 4 Rom. 15, 19.

29. The flight of the saints therefore was neither blameable nor unprofitable. If they had not avoided their persecutors, how would it have come to pass that the Lord should spring from the seed of David? Or who would have preached the glad tidings of the word of truth? It was for this that the persecutors sought after the saints, that there might be no one to teach, as the Jews charged the Apostles; but for this cause they endured all things, that the Gospel might be preached[2] Behold, therefore, in that they were thus engaged in conflict with their enemies, they passed not the time of their flight unprofitably, nor while they were persecuted, did they forget the welfare of others: but as being ministers of the §. 21. [2] p. 184.

good word, they grudged not to communicate it to all men; so that even while they fled, they preached the Gospel, and gave warning of the wickedness of those who conspired against them, and confirmed the faithful by their exhortations.

30. Thus the blessed Paul, having found it so by experience, declared beforehand, *As many as will live godly in Christ, shall suffer persecution.* And so he straightway prepared them that fled for the trial, saying, *Let us run with patience the race that is set before us;* for although there be continual tribulations, *yet tribulation worketh patience, and patience experience, and experience hope, and hope maketh not ashamed.* And the Prophet Esaias when such-like affliction was expected, exhorted and cried aloud, *Come, my people, enter thou into thy chambers, and shut thy doors· hide thyself as it were for a little moment, until the indignation be overpast*[1]. And the Preacher who knew the designs of the wicked against the righteous, and said, *If thou seest the oppression of the poor, and violent perverting of judgment and justice in a province, marvel not at the matter· for He that is higher than the highest regardeth, and there be higher than they moreover there is the profit of the earth.* He had his own father David for an example, who had himself experienced the sufferings of persecution, and who supports them that suffer by the words, *Be of good courage, and He shall strengthen your heart, all ye that put your trust in the Lord;* for them that so endure, not man, but the Lord Himself, (he says,) *shall help them, and deliver them, because they put their trust in Him* for I also *waited patiently for the Lord, and He inclined unto me, and heard my calling; He brought me up also out of the lowest pit, and out of the mire and clay.* Thus is shewn how profitable to the people and productive of good is the flight of the Saints, howsoever the Arians may think otherwise.

§. 22. 31. Thus the Saints, as I said before, were abundantly preserved in their flight by the Providence of God, as physicians for the sake of them that had need. And to all men generally, even to us, is this law given, that we should flee when we are persecuted, and hide ourselves when we are sought after, and not rashly tempt the Lord, but should wait, as I said above, until the appointed time of death arrive, or the Judge determine something concerning us, according as it shall seem to Him to be good: that we should be ready, that, when the time calls for us, or when we are taken, we may contend for the truth even unto death. This rule the blessed Martyrs observed in their several persecutions. When persecuted they fled, while concealing themselves they shewed fortitude, and when discovered they submitted to martyrdom. And if some of them came and presented themselves to their persecutors^a, they did not do so without reason; for immediately in that case they were martyred, and thus made it evident to all that their zeal, and this offering up of themselves to their enemies, were from the Spirit.

Tr. V. 22—24.

32. Seeing therefore that such are the commands of our Saviour, and that such is the conduct of the Saints, let these persons, to whom one cannot give a name suitable to their character,—let them, I say, tell us, from whom they learnt to persecute? They cannot say, from the Saints[1]. No, but from the Devil; (that is the only answer which is left them;)—from him who says, *I will pursue, I will overtake.* Our Lord commanded to flee, and the saints fled: but persecution is a device of the Devil, and one which he desires to exercise against all. Let them say then, to which we ought to submit ourselves; to the words of the Lord, or to their fabrications? Whose conduct ought we to imitate, that of the Saints, or that of those whose example they have adopted? But since it is likely they cannot determine this question, (for, as Esaias said, their minds and their consciences are blinded, and they think *bitter to be sweet*, and *light darkness*[2],) let some one come forth from among us Christians, and put them to rebuke, and cry with a loud voice, "It is better to trust in the Lord, than to attend to the foolish sayings of these men; for the *words* of the Lord have *eternal life*, but the things which these utter are full of iniquity and blood."

§. 23.

[1] Hist. Arian. §§. 33, 67.
Ex. 15, 9.
Is. 5,20.
[2] p. 220. vol. 8. p. 9.
John 6, 68.

33. This were sufficient to put a stop to the madness of these impious men, and to prove that their desire is for nothing else, but only through a love of contention to utter revilings

§. 24.

---

^a Vid. instances and passages collected in Pearson's Vind. Ignat. part ii. c. 9. also Gibbon, ch xvi. p. 438. Mosheim de Reb. Ante Const. p. 941.

APOL. FOR FLIGHT.

and blasphemies. But forasmuch as having once dared to fight against Christ, they have now become officious, let them enquire and learn into the manner of my withdrawal from their own friends. For the Arians were mixed with the soldiers in order to exasperate them against me, and, as they were unacquainted with my person, to point me out to them. And although they are destitute of all feelings of compassion, yet when they hear the circumstances they will surely be quiet for very shame.

[p. 176.] 34. It was now night[1], and some of the people were keeping a vigil preparatory to a communion on the morrow, when the General Syrianus suddenly came upon us with more than five thousand soldiers, having arms and drawn swords, bows, spears, and clubs, as I have related above. With these he surrounded the Church, stationing his soldiers near at hand, in order that no one might be able to leave the Church and pass by them. Now I considered that it would be unfair in me to desert the people during such a disturbance, and not to endanger myself in their behalf; therefore I sat down upon my throne, and desired the Deacon to read the Psalm, and the people to answer, *For His mercy endureth for ever,* and then all to withdraw and depart home. But the General having now made a forcible entry, and the soldiers having surrounded the Chancel for the purpose of apprehending me, the Clergy and those of the laity, who were still there, cried out, and demanded that I should withdraw. But I refused, declaring that I would not do so, until they had retired one and all. Accordingly I stood up, and having bidden prayer, I then made my request of them, that all should depart before me, saying that it was better that my safety should be endangered, than that any of them should receive hurt. So when the greater part had gone forth, and the rest were following, the monks who were there with me and certain of the Clergy came up and dragged me away. And thus, (Truth is my witness,) while some of the soldiers stood about the Chancel, and others were going round the Church, I passed through, under the Lord's guidance, and with His protection withdrew without observation, greatly glorifying God, that I had not

Ps. 136, 1.

betrayed the people, but had first sent them away, and then had been able to save myself, and to escape the hands of them which sought after me.

35. Now when Providence had delivered me in such an extraordinary manner, who can justly lay any blame upon me, because I did not give myself up into the hands of them that sought after me, nor return and present myself before them? This would have been plainly to shew ingratitude to the Lord, and to act against His commandment, and in contradiction to the practice of the Saints. He who censures me in this matter must presume also to blame the great Apostle Peter, because though he was shut up and guarded by soldiers, he followed the angel that summoned him, and when he had gone forth from the prison and escaped in safety, he did not return and surrender himself, although he heard what Herod had done. Let the Arian in his madness censure the Apostle Paul, because when he was let down from the wall and had escaped in safety, he did not change his mind, and return and give himself up; or Moses, because he returned not out of Midian into Egypt, that he might be taken of them that sought after him; or David, because when he was concealed in the cave, he did not discover himself to Saul. As also the sons of the prophets remained in their caves, and did not surrender themselves to Ahab. This would have been to act contrary to the commandment, since the Scripture says, *Thou shalt not tempt the Lord thy God.* Being careful to avoid such an offence, and instructed by these examples, I so ordered my conduct; and I do not undervalue the favour and the help which have been shewn me of the Lord, howsoever these madmen may gnash their teeth[1] against me. For since the manner of my retreat was such as I have described, I do not think that any blame whatever can attach to it in the minds of those who are possessed of a sound judgment: seeing that according to holy Scripture, this pattern has been left us by the Saints for our instruction. But there is no atrocity, it would seem, which these men neglect to practise, nor will they leave any thing undone, which may shew their own wickedness and cruelty.

36. And indeed their lives are only in accordance with their spirit and the follies of their doctrine; for there are no sins

APOL. FOR FLIGHT.

[margin: ¹ Hist. Arian. §. 28.]

that one could charge them with, how heinous soever, that they do not commit without shame. Leontius[1], for instance, being censured for his intimacy with a certain young woman, named Eustolium, and prohibited from living with her, mutilated himself for her sake, in order that he might be able to associate with her freely. He did not however clear himself from suspicion, but rather on this account he was degraded from his rank as Presbyter, although the heretic Constantius by violence caused him to be named a Bishop. Narcissus[2], besides being charged with many other transgressions, was degraded three times by different Councils; and now he is the most wicked among them. And George[3] who was a Presbyter, was degraded on account of his vices, and although he had nominated himself a Bishop, he was nevertheless a second time degraded in the great Council of Sardica. And besides all this, his dissolute life is notorious, for he is condemned even by his own friends, as making the end of existence and happiness to consist in the commission of the most disgraceful crimes.

[margin: ² p. 60. vol. 8. p. 99.]

[margin: ³ p. 25.]

§. 27. 37. Thus each surpasses the other in his own peculiar vices. But there is a common blot that attaches to them all, in that through their heresy they are enemies of Christ, and are no longer called Christians[b], but Arians. They ought indeed to accuse each other of the sins they are guilty of, for they are contrary to the faith of Christ; but they rather conceal them for their own sakes. And it is no wonder, that being possessed of such a spirit, and implicated in such vices, they persecute and seek after those who follow not the same impious heresy as themselves; that they delight to destroy them, and are grieved if they fail of obtaining their desires, and think themselves injured, as I said before, when they see those alive, whom they wish to perish. May they continue to be injured in such sort, that they may lose the power of inflicting injuries, and that those whom they persecute may give thanks unto the Lord, and say in the words of the twenty-sixth Psalm, *The Lord is my light and my salvation; whom then shall I fear? The Lord is the strength of my life; of whom then shall I be afraid? When the wicked, even mine enemies and my foes,*

[margin: Ps.27,1.]

---

[b] Vid. supr. p. 149, r. 4. infr. Hist. 64 init. vol. 8. p. 27, note h. pp. reff. Arian. §§. 17. 34 fin. 41 init. 59 fin. 85, 1. 179, 4. 182. 188, 4. 194, 2.

come upon me to eat up my flesh, they stumbled and fell: *and again in the thirtieth Psalm, Thou hast known my soul in adversities; Thou hast not shut me up into the hands of my enemies; Thou hast set my feet in a large room;* in Christ Jesus our Lord, through whom to the Father in the Holy Spirit be glory and power for ever and ever. Amen.

Tr. V. 27.
Ps. 31, 7. 8.

VI.

AN EPISTLE

OF OUR

HOLY FATHER ATHANASIUS,

ARCHBISHOP OF ALEXANDRIA,

TO HIS BROTHER SERAPION,

CONCERNING THE DEATH OF ARIUS.

[S. Serapion, Bishop of Thmuis, was a friend of St. Anthony's; to him the Saint on his death, which took place shortly before the following Letter from Athanasius, left one of his sheepskins, leaving the other to S Athanasius himself. His fellowship with Athanasius in persecution, has gained him the title of Confessor, and his accomplishments and talents that of Scholasticus. Jerom. de Vir. Illustr. 99. At his suggestion Athanasius about the same date wrote his work upon the divinity of the Holy Spirit, addressing it to him He seems also to have been a correspondent of Apollinaris. His name is found in the Roman Martyrology under March 21. It appears from the commencement of the following Letter, written A.D. 358—360, that Serapion had asked Athanasius, first for a history of his times, next for a refutation of Arianism, and thirdly for an account of the death of Arius. The death of Arius is the subject of this Letter itself, for the history of his times he refers him to his History of Arianism addressed to the Monks, which he sent him at the same time; and the refutation of Arianism, which was also addressed to the Monks, has sometimes been supposed to be the four celebrated Orations which are his principal dogmatic work. Though in strict order of time the Epistles both to Serapion and to the Monks are later than the History, and the latter Epistle, as containing scarcely an allusion to the History, might easily be detached from it, yet it seems best in a matter of this kind to follow the arrangement adopted in the Benedictine Edition.]

---

1. Athanasius to Serapion a brother and fellow-minister sends health in the Lord.

§. 1.   1. I HAVE read the letters of your Piety, in which you have requested me to make known to you the events of my

Arius deceives Constantine by a false oath.

times relating to myself, and to give an account of that most impious heresy of the Arians, in consequence of which I have endured these sufferings, and also of the manner of the death of Arius. With two out of your three demands I have readily undertaken to comply, and have sent to your Godliness the letter which I wrote to the Monks; from which you will be able to learn my own history as well as that of the heresy. But with respect to the other matter, I mean the Death, I debated with myself for a long time, fearing lest any one should suppose that I was exulting in the death of that man. But yet, since a disputation which has taken place amongst you concerning the heresy, has issued in this question, whether Arius died in communion with the Church; I therefore was necessarily desirous of giving an account of his death, as thinking that the question would thus be set at rest, considering also that by making this known I should at the same time silence those who are fond of contention. For I conceive that when the wonderful[1] circumstances connected with his death become known, even those who before questioned it will no longer venture to doubt that the Arian heresy is hateful in the sight of God[2].

2. I was not at Constantinople when he died, but Macarius the Presbyter was, and I heard the account of it from him. Arius had been summoned by the Emperor Constantine, through the interest of the Eusebians; and when he entered the presence the Emperor enquired of him, whether he held the Faith of the Catholic Church? And he declared upon oath that he held the right[3] Faith, and gave in an account of[3] his Faith in writing, suppressing the points for which he had been cast out of the Church by the Bishop Alexander, and speciously[4] alleging expressions out of the Scriptures. When[4] therefore he swore that he did not profess the opinions for which Alexander had excommunicated him, the Emperor dismissed him, saying, "If thy Faith be right, thou hast done well to swear; but if thy Faith be impious, and thou hast sworn, God judge thee according to thy oath." When he thus came forth from the presence of the Emperor, the Eusebians with their accustomed violence desired to bring him into the Church[5]. But Alexander the Bishop of Con-

stantinople of blessed memory[1] resisted them, saying that the inventor of the heresy ought not to be admitted to communion; whereupon the Eusebians threatened, declaring, "As we have caused him to be summoned[2] by the Emperor, in opposition to your wishes, so to-morrow, though it be contrary to your desire, Arius shall have communion with us in this Church." It was the Sabbath when they said this.

§. 3. 3. When the Bishop Alexander heard this, he was greatly distressed, and entering into the Church, he stretched forth his hands unto God, and bewailed himself; and casting himself upon his face in the Chancel[3], he prayed, lying upon the pavement. Macarius also was present, and prayed with him, and heard his words. And he besought these two things, saying, "If Arius is brought to communion to-morrow, let me Thy servant depart, and destroy not the pious with the impious; but if Thou wilt spare Thy Church, (and I know that Thou wilt spare,) look upon the words of the Eusebians, and give not Thine inheritance to destruction and reproach, and take off Arius[4], lest if he enter into the Church, the heresy also may seem to enter with him, and henceforward impiety[5] be accounted for piety." When the Bishop had thus prayed, he retired in great anxiety; and a wonderful and extraordinary circumstance took place. While the Eusebians threatened, the Bishop prayed, but Arius, who had great confidence in the Eusebians, and talked very wildly, urged by the necessities of nature withdrew[6], and suddenly, in the language of Scripture, *falling headlong he burst asunder in the midst,* and immediately expired as he lay, and was deprived both of communion and of his life together.

§. 4. 4. Such was the end of Arius: and the Eusebians, overwhelmed with shame, buried[7] their accomplice, while the blessed Alexander, amidst the rejoicings of the Church, celebrated the Communion with piety and orthodoxy, praying with all the brethren, and greatly glorifying God, not as exulting in his death, (God forbid!) for *it is appointed unto all men once to die,* but because this thing had been shewn forth in a manner surpassing the expectations of all men. For the Lord Himself judging between the threats of the Eusebians and the prayer of Alexander, condemned the Arian heresy, shewing it to be unworthy of communion with the Church, and making manifest to all, that although it receive the support of the Emperor and of all mankind, yet it has been condemned by the Church herself.

5. Thus this antichristian workshop[1] of the Arian fanatics has been shewn to be unpleasing to God and impious; and many of those who before were deceived by it have changed their opinions. For none other than the Lord Himself who was blasphemed by them has condemned the heresy which rose up against Him, and has again shewn, that howsoever the Emperor Constantius may now use violence to the Bishops in behalf of it, yet it is excluded from the communion of the Church, and alien from the kingdom of heaven[e]. Wherefore also let the question which has arisen[2] among you be henceforth set at rest; (for this is the agreement that was made among you,) and let no one join himself to the heresy, but let even those who have been deceived repent. For who shall receive a heresy which the Lord has condemned? And will not he who takes up the support of that which He has made excommunicate, be guilty of great impiety, and manifestly an enemy of Christ?

6. Now this is sufficient to confound the contentious; read it therefore to those who before raised this question, as well as what I have briefly[3] addressed to the Monks against the heresy, in order that they may be led thereby more strongly to condemn the impiety and wickedness of the Arian fanatics. Do not however consent to give a copy of these letters to any one, neither transcribe them for yourself, (I have signified the same to the Monks also[4],) but as a sincere friend, if any thing is wanting in what I have written, add it, and immediately send them back to me. For you will be able to learn from the letter which I have written to the Brethren, what pains it has cost me to write it[5], and also to perceive that it is not safe for the writings of an individual[6] to be published, (especially if they relate to the highest and chief[7] doctrines,) for this reason,—lest what is imperfectly expressed through infirmity or the obscurity of language, do hurt to the reader. For the majority of men do not consider the faith or the aim of the writer[8], but either through envy or a spirit of contention, receive what is

Tr. VI.
4, 5.

[1] ἐργαστήριον
[2] ἀλλοτρία τῶν οὐρανῶν.
Mat. 18, 18.

§. 5.

[3] p. 216, r. 2.

[4] p. 217, r. 7.

[5] p. 215, r. 2.
[6] ἰδιώτου, p. 218, r. 1.
[7] κορυφαιοτάτων.
[8] p. 130, r. 2. p. 134, r. 4.

EPIST. TO SERAP.

written as themselves choose, according to an opinion which they have previously formed, and misinterpret it to suit their pleasure. But the Lord grant that the Truth and a sound[1] faith in our Lord Jesus Christ may prevail among all, and especially among those to whom you read this. Amen.

[1] ὑγιαί-νουσαν, vid. Alex. Ep. Encycl. §. 5 fin.

VII.

AN EPISTLE

OF OUR

HOLY FATHER ATHANASIUS,

ARCHBISHOP OF ALEXANDRIA,

TO THE MONKS

[The beautiful and striking Letter which follows formed the introduction to a work, which the Author, as he says in the course of it, thought unworthy of being preserved for posterity. Some critics have supposed it to be the Orations against the Arians, which form his greatest work; but this opinion can hardly be maintained, though the discussion of it does not belong to this place. The Epistle to the Monks was written in 358, or later, but before the foregoing Epistle to Serapion.]

---

1. To those in every place who are living a monastic life, who are established in the faith of God, and sanctified in Christ, and who say, *Behold, we have forsaken all, and followed Thee,* brethren dearly beloved and longed for, a full greeting in the Lord. §. 1.

Mat. 19, 27.

1. IN compliance with your affectionate request, which you have frequently urged upon me, I have written a short account of the sufferings which ourselves and the Church have undergone, refuting, according to my ability, the accursed[1] heresy of the Arian fanatics, and proving how entirely it is alien from the Truth. And I thought it needful to represent to your Piety what pains[2] the writing of these things has cost me, in order that you may understand thereby how truly the blessed Apostle has said, *O the depth of the*

[1] μυσαράν
[2] p. 213, r. 4.

Rom. 11, 33.

riches both of the wisdom and knowledge of God; and may kindly bear with a weak man such as I am by nature. For the more I desired to write, and endeavoured to force myself to understand the Divinity of the Word, so much the more did the knowledge thereof withdraw itself from me; and in proportion as I thought that I apprehended it, in so much I perceived myself to fail of doing so. Moreover also I was unable to express in writing even what I seemed to myself to understand; and that which I wrote was unequal to the imperfect shadow of the truth which existed in my conceptions.

§. 2. 2. Considering therefore how it is written in the Book of Ecclesiastes, *I said, I will be wise, but it was far from me; That which is far off, and exceeding deep, who shall find it out?* and what is said in the Psalms, *The knowledge of Thee is too wonderful for me; it is high, I cannot attain unto it;* and that Solomon says, *It is the glory of God to conceal a thing;* I frequently designed to stop and to cease writing; believe me[1], I did. But lest I should be found to disappoint you, or by my silence to lead into impiety those who have made enquiry of you, and are given to disputation, I constrained myself to write briefly[2], what I have now sent to your Piety. For although a perfect apprehension of the truth is at present far removed from us by reason of the infirmity of the flesh; yet it is possible, as the Preacher himself has said, to perceive the madness of the impious, and having found it, to say that it is *more bitter than death.* Wherefore for this reason, as perceiving this and able to find it out, I have written, knowing that to the faithful the detection of impiety is a sufficient information wherein piety consists. For although it be impossible to comprehend what God is, yet it is possible to say, what He is not[a]. And we know that He is

---

[a] This negative character of our knowledge, whether of the Father or of the Son, is insisted on by other writers. "When we speak of the substance of any being, we have to say what it is, not what it is not, however, as relates to God, *it is impossible to say* what He is as to His substance. .... All we can know about the Divine Nature is, that it is *not* to be known, and whatever positive statements we make concerning God, relate not to His Nature, but to the accompaniments of His Nature." Damasc. F. O. 1. 4. S. Basil ad Eunom. 1. 10. speaks similarly of the negative attributes, (so to speak,) of the Divine Nature, adding, however, the positive. And St. Austin says, "Totum ab animo rejicite; quidquid occurrerit, negate....dicite *non est illud.*" August. Enarrat. 2. in Psalm 26. 8. "How," says St. Cyril, "the Fa-

not as man; and that it is not lawful to conceive of any created[1] nature as existing in Him. So also respecting the Son of God, although we are by nature very far from being able to apprehend Him; yet it is possible and easy to condemn the assertions of the heretics concerning Him, and to say, that the Son of God is not such; nor is it lawful even to conceive in our minds such things as they speak, concerning His divinity; much less to utter them with the lips.

3. Accordingly I have written as well as I was able; and you, dearly beloved, receive these communications not as containing a perfect exposition of the doctrine of the divinity of the Word, but as being merely a refutation of the impiety of the enemies of Christ, and as containing and affording to those who desire it, suggestions[2] for arriving at a pious and sound[3] faith in Christ. And if in any thing they are defective, (and I think they are defective in all respects,) pardon it with a pure conscience, and only receive favourably the boldness[4] of my good intentions in support of godliness. For an utter condemnation of the heresy of the Arians, it is sufficient for you to know the judgment which has been given by the Lord in the death of Arius, of which you have already been informed by others. *For the Lord of Hosts hath purposed, and who shall disannul it?* and whom the Lord hath condemned who shall justify[5]? After such a sign[6] has been given, who does not now acknowledge, that the heresy is hated of God[7], however it may have men for its patrons?

4. Now when you have read this account, pray for me, and exhort one another so to do. And immediately send it back to me, and suffer no one whatever to take a copy of it, nor transcribe it for yourselves[8]. But like good money-changers[b] be satisfied with the reading; but read it repeatedly if you desire to do so. For it is not safe that the

§. 3.

Tr VII. 2, 3. ¹τῶν γιν- ητῶν, vol. 8. p. 261, note e.

² ἀφορ- μὴν ³ p. 214, r. 1.

⁴ τὸ τολ- μηρὸν

Is. 14, 27.

⁵ so quoted p. 148. ⁶ σημεῖον, vid. p. 211, r 1. ⁷ θεομίση- τος, vid. p. 211, r. 2. ⁸ p. 213, r. 3.

---

ther begat the Son, we profess not to tell; *only* we insist upon its *not* being in *this* manner or *that*.' Catech xi. 11. " Patrem *non* esse Filium, sed habere Filium qui Pater *non* sit, Filium *non* esse Patrem, sed Filium Dei esse natum, sanctum quoque Paracletum esse, qui *nec* Pater sit ipse, *nec* Filius, sed a Patre Filioque procedat. Anonym. in Append. Aug Oper. t. 5 p. 383

[b] On this celebrated text, as it may be called, which is cited so frequently by the Fathers, vid. Coteler. in Const. Apol. n. 36. in Clement. Hom. n. 51. Potter in Clem. Strom. 1. p. 425. Vales. in Euseb. Hist. vii. 7. vid. also S. Cyril, Catech. tr. p. 78, note o.

writings of us babblers and private persons[1] should fall into the hands of them that shall come after. Salute one another in love, and also all that come unto you in piety and faith. For *if any man*, as the Apostle has said, *love not the Lord, let him be anathema. The grace of our Lord Jesus Christ be with you. Amen.*

Epist. to Monks
[1] ἰδιωτῶν,
p. 213, r. 5.
Apol. contr. Ar. §. 9.
supr. p. 27. §. 12.
p. 30.
1 Cor. 16, 22.

VIII.
THE HISTORY OF THE ARIANS,
[*Down to the Year* 357, *the beginning being lost.*]

[The earlier portion of this History, which seems to have commenced with the Author's elevation to his see, has not been preserved, because, as Montfaucon conjectures, it was considered but a repetition of the second part of the Apology against the Arians, §. 59—84. pp. 88—116. supr. He notices a correspondence even in the words employed in the two works, at the place in the Apology where the line of narrative may be considered to be taken up by the opening but broken sentence of the following History. In the beginning of § 84. of the Apology, supr. p. 116, towards the end of its second part, Athanasius says, "As such is the nature of their machinations, so they *very soon* shewed plainly the reasons of their conduct. For, when they went away, they took the Arians with them to Jerusalem, and there *admitted them to communion;*" and in the beginning, as extant, of the History. "And *not long after*, they proceeded to put in execution the designs for the sake of which they had had recourse to these artifices; for they *no sooner* had formed their plans, but they *immediately admitted the Arians to communion*" vid. also infr. p. 220, r. 2. Papebroke, whom Tillemont in the main follows, considers that the whole Apology formed a sort of third part of the Work addressed to the Monks, (the dogmatic treatise being the first of the three) And in maintenance of this opinion he proposes an ingenious though untenable emendation of some words in the text of Athanasius, or rather in the notes added to the text by his copyists. (in Maii 2 p. 187.) A question has been raised about the genuineness of the work before us, under the idea that it probably was the writing of a companion of Athanasius, not of the Saint himself. It cannot be denied that in parts it is written in a livelier and terser, not to say freer, style than his other works, and he speaks of himself in the third person. And there is a passage, where, if the text be not corrupt, the writer distinguishes himself from Athanasius, §. 52. But on the other hand, there is a passage in which he speaks in the first person where none but Athanasius can be meant vid. §. 21. p. 236. And he speaks of himself in other works in the third person, e. g Orat. i. §. 3 Moreover, it is plain that the very circumstance that he was not writing in his own person would make a considerable alteration in his mode of writing, not to dwell on the difference between an apology and what is a history and invective. Some instances of agreement in words, phrases, texts, &c. are pointed out in the margin and notes]

CHAP. I.
ARIAN PERSECUTION UNDER CONSTANTINE.

1. . . . . . . AND not long after they proceeded to put in §. 1. execution the designs for the sake of which they had had

recourse to these artifices; for they no sooner had formed their plans, but they immediately admitted the Arians to communion. They set aside the repeated condemnations which had been passed upon them, and again pretended the imperial authority[1] in their behalf. And they were not ashamed to say in their letters, "since Athanasius has suffered, all opposition[2] has ceased, and let us henceforward receive the Arians;" adding, in order to frighten their hearers, 'because the Emperor has commanded it.' Moreover they were not ashamed to add, "for these men profess orthodox opinions;" not fearing that which is written, *Woe unto them that call bitter sweet, that put darkness for light*[3]; for they are ready to undertake any thing in support of their heresy. Now is it not hereby plainly proved to all men, that we both suffered heretofore, and that you now persecute us, not under the authority of an Ecclesiastical sentence[4], but on the ground of the Emperor's threats, and on account of our Piety towards Christ? As also they conspired in like manner against the Bishops, fabricating charges against them also; some of whom are fallen asleep in the place of their exile, having attained the glory of Christian confession; and others are at this day banished from their country, and contend still more and more manfully against their heresy, saying, *Nothing shall separate us from the love of Christ*[5].

§. 2. 2. And hence also you may discern its character, and be able to condemn it more confidently. The man who is their friend and their associate in impiety, although he is open to ten thousand charges for other enormities which he has committed; although the evidence and proof against him are most clear; he is approved of by them, and straightway becomes the friend of the Emperor, obtaining favour by his impiety; and making large gains, he acquires confidence before the magistrates to do whatever he desires. But he who exposes their impiety, and honestly advocates the cause of Christ, though he is pure in all things, though he is conscious of no delinquencies, though he meets with no accuser; yet on the false pretences which they have framed against him, is immediately seized and sent into banishment under a sentence of the Emperor, as if he were guilty of the crimes which they wish to charge upon him, or as if, like Naboth, he had blasphemed the king. While he who advocates the cause of their heresy, is sought for and immediately sent to take possession of the other's Church; and henceforth confiscations and insults, and all kinds of cruelty are exercised against those who do not receive him. And what is the strangest thing of all[1], the man whom the people desire, and know to be *blameless*[2], the Emperor takes away and banishes; but him whom they neither desire, nor know, he sends to them from a distant place[3] with soldiers and letters[4] from himself. And henceforward a strong necessity is laid upon them, either to hate him whom they love; who has been their teacher, and their father in godliness; and to love him whom they do not desire, and to trust their children to one of whose life and conversation and character they are ignorant; or else certainly to suffer punishment, if they disobey the Emperor.

3. In this manner the impious are now proceeding, as heretofore, against the orthodox; giving proof of their malice and impiety amongst all men every where. For granting[5] that they have justly accused Athanasius; yet what have the other Bishops done? On what grounds can they charge them? Has there been found in their case too the dead body of an Arsenius? Is there a Presbyter Macarius, or has a chalice been broken amongst them? Is there a Meletian to play the hypocrite? No: but as their proceedings against the other Bishops shew the charges which they have brought against Athanasius, in all probability, to be false; so their attacks upon Athanasius make it plain, that their accusations of the other Bishops are unfounded likewise. This heresy has come forth upon the earth like some wild monster, which not only injures the innocent with its words, as with teeth[6]; but it has also hired external power to assist it in its designs.

4. And strange it is that, as I said before, no accusation is brought against any of them; or if any be accused, he is not brought to trial; or if a shew of enquiry be made, he is acquitted against evidence, while the convicting party is plotted against, rather than the criminal put to shame. Thus the whole party of them is full of vileness[7]; and their spies[8], for

Bishops[1] they are not, are the vilest of them all. And if any one among them desires to become a Bishop, he is not told, *a Bishop must be blameless*[2]; but only, "Take up opinions contrary to Christ, and care not for manners. This will be sufficient to obtain favour for you, and friendship with the Emperor." Such is the character of those who support the tenets of Arius. And they who are zealous for the truth, however holy and pure they shew themselves, are yet, as I said before, made criminals, whenever these men choose, and on whatever pretences it may seem good to them to invent. The truth of this, as I before remarked, you may clearly gather from their proceedings.

§. 4. 5. There was one Eustathius[3], Bishop of Antioch, a Confessor, and sound in the Faith. This man, because he was very zealous for the truth, and hated the Arian heresy, and would not receive those who adopted its tenets, is falsely accused before the Emperor Constantine, and a charge invented against him, that he had insulted his mother[a]. And immediately he is driven into banishment, and a great number of Presbyters and Deacons with him. And immediately after the banishment of the Bishop, those whom he would not admit into the clerical order on account of their impiety were not only received into the Church by them, but were even appointed the greater part of them to be Bishops, in order that they might have accomplices in their impiety. Among these was Leontius the eunuch[4], now of Antioch, and before him Stephanus, George of Laodicea, and Theodosius who was of Tripolis, Eudoxius of Germanicia, and Eustathius[5] now of Sebastia.

§. 5. 6. Did they then stop here? No. For Eutropius[3] who was Bishop of Adrianople, a good man, and excellent in all respects, because he had often convicted Eusebius, and had

---

[a] If the common slander of the day concerning St. Helena was imputed to St. Eustathius, Constantine was likely to feel it keenly. "Stabulariam," says St Ambrose, "hanc primò fuisse asserunt, sic cognitam Constantio" de Ob. Theod 42. Stabularia, i.e. an innkeeper; so Rahab is sometimes considered to be "cauponaria sive tabernaria et meretrix,"Cornel à Lap in Jos ii 1. ἐξ ὁμιλίας γυναικὸς οὐ σεμνῆς, οὐδὲ κατὰ νόμον συνηλθού σης Zosim.Hist.ii.p.78. Constantinus ex concubinâ Helenâ procreatus. Hieron. in Chron. Euseb. p 773 (ed. Vallars) Tillemont however maintains, (Empereurs, t 4. p. 613) and Gibbon fully admits (Hist ch. 14. p. 190.) the legitimacy of Constantine. The latter adds, "Eutropius (x 2) expresses in a few words the real truth, and the occasion of the error, 'ex *obscuriori matrimonio* ejus filius'"

advised them who came that way, not to comply with his impious dictates, suffered the same treatment as Eustathius, and was cast out of his city and his Church. Basilina¹ was the most active in the proceedings against him. And Euphration of Balanea, Cymatius of Paltus, another Cymatius of Taradus, Asclepas of Gaza, Cyrus of Berea² in Syria, Diodorus of Asia, Domnion of Sirmium, and Ellanicus of Tripolis, were merely known to hate³ the heresy; and some of them on one pretence or another, some without any, they removed under the authority of royal letters⁴, drove them out of their cities, and appointed others whom they knew to be impious men, to occupy the Churches in their stead.

TR VIII 4—7. ¹Julian's mother. ²qu. Berrhœa? ³ p. 217, r. 7. ⁴ p. 221, r. 3.

7. Of Marcellus⁵ the Bishop of Galatia it is perhaps superfluous for me to speak; for all men have heard how the Eusebians, who had been first accused by him of impiety, brought a counter-accusation against him, and caused him to be banished in his old age. He went up⁶ to Rome, and there made his defence, and being required by them, he offered a written declaration of his faith, of which the Council of Sardica approved. But the Eusebians made no defence, nor, when they were convicted of impiety out of their writings, were they put to shame, but rather assumed greater boldness against all. For they had interest with the Emperor through the women⁷, and were formidable to all men.

§. 6. ⁵ p. 52, note 1. ⁶ἀνελθὼν, vid Acts 21, 15. infr. pp 239, r. 3. 242, r. 4. ⁷ i. e. Constantia, Const.'s sister.

8. And I suppose no one is ignorant of the case of Paul⁸, Bishop of Constantinople; for the more illustrious any city is, so much the more that which takes place in it is not concealed. A charge was fabricated against him also. For Macedonius his accuser, who has now become Bishop in his stead, (I was present myself at the accusation,) afterwards held communion with him, and was a Presbyter under Paul himself. And yet when Eusebius with an evil eye⁹ wished to seize upon the Bishopric of that city, (he had been translated in the same manner from Berytus to Nicomedia,) the charge was revived against Paul, and they did not give up their plot, but persisted in the calumny. And he was banished first into Pontus by Constantine, and a second time by Constantius he was sent bound with iron chains to Singara in Mesopotamia, and from thence transferred to

§. 7. ⁸ p. 191, r. 1. ⁹ ἐπ' ὀφθαλμίᾳ, supr. p. 23.

Emesa, and a fourth time he was banished to Cucusus in Cappadocia, near the deserts of mount Taurus; where, as those who were with him have declared, he died by strangulation[1] at their hands. And yet these men who never speak the truth, though guilty of this, were not ashamed after his death to invent another story, representing that he had died from disease; although all who live in that place know the circumstances. And even Philagrius[b] who was then Deputy-Governor[c] of those parts, and represented all their proceedings in such manner as they desired, was yet astonished at this; and being grieved perhaps that another, and not himself, had done the evil deed, he informed Serapion the Bishop as well as many other of our friends, that Paul was shut up by them in a very confined and dark place, and left to perish of hunger; and when after six days they went in and found him still alive, they immediately set upon him, and strangled him.

9. This was the end of his life; and they said that Philip who was Prefect was their agent in the perpetration of this murder. Divine Justice however did not overlook this; for not a year had past, when Philip was deprived of his office in great disgrace, so that being reduced to a private station, he became the mockery of those whom he least desired to be the witnesses of his fall. For in extreme distress of mind, *a fugitive and a vagabond*, like Cain[2], and expecting every day that some one would destroy him, far from his country and his friends, he died, like one astounded at his misfortunes, in a manner that he least desired. Moreover these men spare not even after death those against whom they have invented charges whilst living. They are so eager to shew themselves formidable to all, that they banish the living, and shew no mercy on the dead; but alone of all the

---

[b] It is remarkable that this Philagrius, who has been so often mentioned with dishonour in these Tracts of St. Athanasius, as an apostate and a persecutor, vid. supr. pp. 5, 31, &c. is represented by St. Greg. Naz. as very popular in Alexandria, and as on that account appointed to the prefecture there a second time. He compares his entry into the city on this occasion to that of St Athan.'s after banishment. vid. Greg. Orat. 21. 28. St. Athan. however wrote on the spot and at the time, and there is nothing inconsistent in his being a popular magistrate and an enemy of the Church.

[c] Vicarius, i. e. "vicarius Præfecti, agens vicem Præfecti;" Gothofred in Cod. Theod. 1. tit. 6. vid. their office, &c. drawn out at length, ibid. t. 6. p. 334.

world they manifest their hatred to them that are departed, and conspire against their friends, truly inhuman as they are, and haters of that which is good, savage in temper beyond mere enemies, in behalf of their impiety, who eagerly plot the ruin of me and of all the rest, with no regard to truth, but by false charges.

TR VIII 7, 8.

10. Perceiving this to be the case, the three brothers, Constantine, Constantius, and Constans, caused us all after the death of their father to return to our own country and Church; and while they wrote letters concerning the rest to their respective Churches, concerning Athanasius they wrote the following; which likewise shews the violence of the whole proceedings, and proves the murderous disposition, of the Eusebian party.

§. 8.

11. *A copy of the Letter of Constantine Cæsar to the people of the Catholic Church in the city of the Alexandrians.*

I suppose that it has not escaped the knowledge of your pious minds[1], &c.

12. This is his letter; and what more credible witness of their conspiracy could there be than this, who knowing these circumstances has thus written of them?

[1] vid. Apol. contr. Arian. §. 87. supr. p. 121.

CHAP. II

FIRST ARIAN PERSECUTION UNDER CONSTANTIUS.

§. 9.   1. THE Eusebians however, seeing the declension of their heresy, wrote to Rome, as well as to the Emperors Constantine and Constans, to accuse Athanasius: but when the persons who were sent by Athanasius disproved the statements which they had written, they were repulsed with disgrace by the Emperors, and Julius, Bishop of Rome, wrote to say that a Council ought to be held, wherever we should desire, in order that they might exhibit the charges which they had to make, and might also freely defend themselves concerning those things of which they themselves were accused. The Presbyters also who were sent by them, when they saw themselves making an exposure, requested that this might be done Whereupon these men, whose conduct is suspicious in all that they do, when they see that they are not likely to get the better in an Ecclesiastical trial, betake themselves to Constantius alone, and there bewail themselves, as to the patron[1] of their heresy. "Spare," they say, "the heresy, you see that all men have withdrawn from us; and very few of us are now left. Begin to persecute, for we are being deserted even of those few, and are left destitute. Those persons whom we forced over to our side, when these men were banished, they now by their return have persuaded again to take part against us. Write letters therefore against them all, and send out Philagrius a second time[2] as Prefect of Egypt, for he is able to carry on a persecution favourably for us, as he has already shewn upon trial, and the more so, as he is an apostate[3] Send also Gregory as Bishop to Alexandria, for he too is able to strengthen our heresy."

§. 10.   2 Accordingly Constantius at once writes letters, and commences a persecution against all, and sends Philagrius as Prefect with one Arsacius an eunuch, he sends also Gregory with a military force. And the same consequences

[1] προστά-την, de Syn. §. 31. tr p. 127.
[2] p. 224, note b.
[3] παρα-βάτης, p. 5.

followed as before[1]. For gathering together[2] a multitude of herdsmen and shepherds, and other dissolute youths belonging to the town, armed with swords and clubs, they attacked in a body the Church which is called the Church of Cyrinus[3]; and some they slew, some they trampled under foot, others they beat with stripes and cast into prison or banished. They haled away many women also, and dragged them openly into the court, and insulted them, dragging them by the hair. Some they proscribed; from some they took away their bread[4] for no other reason, but that they might be induced to join the Arians, and receive Gregory who had been sent by the Emperor.

3. Athanasius however, before these things happened, at the first report of their proceedings, sailed to Rome, knowing the rage of the heretics, and for the purpose of having the Council held as had been determined. And Julius wrote letters to them, and sent the Presbyters Elpidius and Philoxenus[5], appointing a day[6], and saying, that either they must come, or consider themselves as altogether suspected persons. But as soon as the Eusebians heard that the trial was to be an Ecclesiastical one, at which no Count would be present[7], nor soldiers stationed before the doors, and that the proceedings would not be regulated by royal order, (for they have always depended upon these things to support them against the Bishops, and without them they have no boldness even to speak;) they were so alarmed that they detained the Presbyters till after the appointed time, and pretended this indecent excuse, that they were not able to come now on account of the war which was begun by the Persians[8]. But this was not the true cause of their delay, but the fears of their own consciences. For what have Bishops to do with war? Or if[9] they were unable on account of the Persians to come to Rome, although it is at a distance and beyond sea, why did they like lions[9] traverse[10] the parts of the East and those which are near the Persians, seeking who was opposed to them, that they might falsely accuse and banish them?

4. However when they had dismissed the Presbyters with this improbable excuse, they said to one another, "Since we are unable to get the advantage in an Ecclesiastical trial,

ARIAN HIST.

¹ pp. 51, 53.

let us exhibit our usual audacity." Accordingly they write to Philagrius, and cause him after a while to go out with Gregory into Egypt. Whereupon the Bishops are severely scourged and cast into chains¹; Sarapammon, for instance, Bishop and Confessor, they drive into banishment; Potammon, Bishop and Confessor, who had also lost an eye in the persecution, they beat with stripes on the back so cruelly, that he appeared to be dead before they came to an end. In which condition he was cast aside, and hardly after some hours, being carefully attended and fanned, he revived, God granting him his life; but a short time after he died of the sufferings caused by the stripes, and attained in Christ to the glory of a second martyrdom. And besides these, how many monks were scourged, while Gregory sat by with Balacius the Duke! how many Bishops were wounded! how many virgins were beaten!

§. 13.
² p. 8.

5. After this the wretched Gregory called upon all men to have communion with him²; but if thou didst demand of them communion, they were not worthy of stripes: and if thou did scourge them as if evil persons, why didst thou ask it of them as if holy? But he had no other end in view, except to fulfil the designs of them that sent him, and to establish the heresy. Wherefore he became in his folly a murderer and

³ δήμιος. pp 133 fin. 247, r. 2.
⁴ p. 178, § 27 fin.

an executioner³, injurious, crafty, and profane; in one word, an enemy of Christ. He so cruelly persecuted the Bishop's aunt, that even when she died he would not suffer her to be buried⁴. And this would have been her lot; she would have been cast away without burial, had not they who attended on the corpse carried her out as one of their own kindred. Thus even in such things he shewed his profane temper. And again when the widows and other mendicants ᵃ had received alms, he commanded what had been given them to be seized, and the vessels in which they carried their oil and wine to be broken, that he might not only shew impiety by robbery, but in his deeds dishonour the Lord; from whom

vid. Mat. 25, 45.

very shortly ᵇ he will hear those words, *Inasmuch as thou hast dishonoured these, thou hast dishonoured Me.*

ᵃ ἀνεξόδων, vid. infr. §. 60. Tillemont translates it, prisoners. Montfaucon has been here followed; vid. Collect. Nov. t. 2. p. xliii.

ᵇ ὅσον εἰδίπω, vid. p. 245, r. 4. George was pulled to pieces by the populace, A.D. 362. This was written A.D. 358, or later.

6. And many other things he did, which exceed the power of language to describe, and which whoever should hear would think to be incredible. And the reason why he acted thus was, because he had not received his ordination according to ecclesiastical rule, nor had been called to be a Bishop by apostolical tradition[b], but had been sent out from court with military power and pomp, as one entrusted with a secular government. Wherefore he boasted rather to be the friend of Governors, than of Bishops and Monks. Whenever therefore Father Antony wrote to him from the mountains, as godliness is an abomination to a sinner, so he abhorred the letters of the Saint. But whenever the Emperor, or a General, or other magistrate, sent him a letter, he was as much overjoyed as those in the Proverbs, of whom the Word has said indignantly, *Woe unto them who leave the paths of uprightness; who rejoice to do evil, and delight in the frowardness of the wicked.* And so he honoured with presents the bearers of these letters; but once when Antony wrote to him he caused Duke Balacius to spit upon the letter, and to cast it from him. But Divine Justice did not overlook this; for no long time after, when the Duke was on horseback, and on his way to the first halt[c], the horse turned his head, and biting him on the thigh, threw him off; and after three days he died.

TR. VIII.
13, 14.
§. 14.

Prov. 2, 13. 14.
Sept.

---

[b] He had neither apostolical calling, nor canonical ordination, for he was a layman, nominated to his see by the Emperor, and that, when there was a lawful occupant, and consecrated by heretics. "Tradition" and "Canon" seem used nearly as synonymous. p.249, r. 6.

[c] μονήν. vid. supr. p. 50, note h. This halt or station which lay up the Nile was called Cereu, (Athan. V. Ant. §. 86.) or Chæreus, or the land or property of Chæreus, vid. Naz. Orat. 21, 29. who says it was the place where the people met Athanasius on his return from exile on Constantius's death.

CHAP. III.

RESTORATION OF THE CATHOLICS ON THE COUNCIL OF SARDICA.

§. 15.   1. WHILE they were proceeding in like measures towards all, at Rome about fifty Bishops assembled[1], and denounced the Eusebians, as persons suspected, afraid to come, and also condemned as unworthy of credit the written statement they had sent; but us they received, and gladly embraced[2] our communion. While these things were taking place, a report of the Council held at Rome, and of the proceedings against the Churches at Alexandria, and through all the East, came to the hearing of the Emperor Constans[3]. He writes to his brother Constantius, and immediately they both determine[4] that a Council shall be called, and matters be brought to a settlement, so that those who had been injured may be released from further suffering, and the injurious be no longer able to perpetrate such outrages. Accordingly there assemble at the city of Sardica both from the East and West to the number of one hundred and seventy Bishops[a], more or less; those who came from the West were Bishops only, having Hosius for their father[5], but those from the East brought with them instructors of youth and advocates, Count Musonianus[6], and Hesychius[6] the Castrensian ; on whose account they came with great alacrity, thinking that every thing would be again managed by their authority. For thus by means of these persons they have always shewn themselves formidable to any whom they wished to intimidate, and have prosecuted their designs against whomsoever they chose. But when they arrived and saw that the

[1] p. 14, note b.
[2] and p 232, r.3. *ἠγάπη-σαν.* vid. *ἀγάπην,* p. 39, r. 2.
[5] p. 60, r. 2.
[3] p. 158, note g.
[4] infr. §. 50.
[5] vid. p. 158, and *ἱ πατὴρ τῶν ἐπισ-κόπων,* infr. pp. 255,256.
[6] p. 59, notes a, b.

---

[a] vid. supr. p. 78, note o. Montfaucon argues in the Addenda in his Præf p. xxxiv. from the subscriptions in St. Hilary, p. 1292. that the Bishops whose signatures occur without provinces annexed, (supr. p 76.) were the Bishops present—whereas those who were absent signed with a mention of their provinces. Accordingly he considers the number of orthodox to be 86; to which if we add the 70 or 80 Eusebians, we approximate to the number 170   If the parties were so nearly matched, it is very remarkable that the Eusebians should withdraw. But they had the Pope, Athanasius, and Hosius against them.

cause was to be conducted as simply an ecclesiastical one, without the interference of the Count or of soldiers; when they saw the accusers who came from every church and city, and the evidence which was brought against them, when they saw the venerable Bishops Arius and Asterius[1], who came up in their company, withdrawing from them and siding with us, and giving an account of their profligate conduct; as their whole proceedings had been suspicious, so now they fear the consequences of a trial, lest they should be convicted by us of being false informers, and it should be discovered by those whom they produced in the character of accusers, that they had themselves suggested all they were to say, and were the contrivers of the plot.

2. Perceiving this to be the case, although they had come with great zeal, as thinking that we should be afraid to meet them, yet now when they saw our alacrity, they shut themselves up in the Palace[b], (for they had their abode there,) and proceeded to confer with one another in the following manner, "We came hither for one result; and we see in prospect another, we arrived in company with Counts, and the trial is proceeding without them. We are certainly condemned. You all know the orders that have been given. The Athanasians have the reports of the proceedings in the Mareotis[2], by which he is cleared, and we are covered with disgrace. Why then do we delay? why are we so slow? Let us invent some excuse and be gone, or we shall be condemned if we remain. It is better to suffer the shame of fleeing, than the disgrace of being convicted as false accusers. If we flee, we shall find some means of defending our heresy; and even if they condemn us for our flight, still we have the Emperor as our patron[3], who will not suffer the people to expel us from the Churches."

3. They reasoned with themselves in this manner: and

---

[b] The word Palatium sometimes stands for the space or limits set apart in cities for the Emperor, Cod. Theod. xv. 1. 47. sometimes for the buildings upon it, ibid. vii 10, 2. which were one of the four public works mentioned in the Laws. ibid. xv. 1. 35. and 36. None but great officers of state were admitted into it. xv. 1. 47. Even the judges might not lodge in it, except there was no Prætorium, vii. 10. 2. Gothofr. in vii. 10, 1. enumerates (with references) the Palatia in Antioch, Daphne, Constantinople, Heraclea, Milan, Treves, &c. It was a great mark then of imperial favour that the Eusebians were accommodated in the Palatium at Sardica.

Proceedings of the Council of Sardica.

ARIAN HIST.

Hosius and all the other Bishops repeatedly signified to them the alacrity of the Athanasians, saying, 'They are ready with their defence, and pledge themselves to prove you false accusers.' They said also, 'If you fear the trial, why did you come to meet us? either you ought not to have come, or now that you have come, not to flee.' When they heard this, being still more alarmed, they had recourse to an excuse even more indecent than that they pretended at Antioch[1], viz. that they betook themselves to flight because the Emperor had written to them the news of his victory over the Persians. And this excuse they were not ashamed to send by Eustathius a Presbyter of the Sardican Church. Nevertheless their flight did not succeed according to their wishes; for immediately the holy Council, of which the great Hosius was president, wrote to them plainly, saying, "Either come forward and answer the charges which are brought against you, for the false accusations which you have made against others, or know that the Council will condemn you as guilty, and declare Athanasius and his friends free and clear from all blame." Whereupon they were rather impelled to flight by the alarms of conscience, than to compliance with the proposals of the letter: for when they saw those who had been injured by them, they did not even turn their faces to listen to their words, but fled with greater speed.

[1] p. 227, r. 8.

§. 17. 4. Under these disgraceful and unseemly circumstances their flight took place. And the holy Council, which had been assembled out of more than five and thirty provinces[2], perceiving the malice of the Arians, admitted the Athanasian party to answer to the charges which they had brought against them, and to declare the sufferings which they had undergone. And when they had thus made their defence, as we said before, they approved and so highly admired their conduct, that they gladly embraced[3] our communion, and wrote letters to all quarters, to the diocese of each, and especially to Alexandria, and Egypt, and the Libyas, declaring Athanasius and his friends to be innocent, and free from all blame, and their opponents to be calumniators, evil-doers, and every thing rather than Christians[4]. Accordingly they dismissed them in peace; but deposed[5] Stephanus and Menophantus, Acacius and George of Laodicea, Ursacius and

[2] pp. 14, 60, r. 9.

[3] p. 230, r. 2.

[4] p. 208, note b.
[5] p. 75.

Valens, Theodorus and Narcissus. And against Gregory who had been sent to Alexandria by the Emperor, they put forth a proclamation to the effect that he had never been made a Bishop, and that he ought not to be called a Christian[1]. They therefore declared the ordinations which he professed to have conferred to be void, and commanded that they should not be even named in the Church, on account of their novel and illegal nature. Thus Athanasius and his friends were dismissed in peace (the letters concerning them are inserted at the end on account of their length[2]; and the Council was dissolved.

marginal notes: TR. VIII 16—18. [1] p. 68. [2] not found there, but in Apol. contr. Ar. supr. p 60—76.

5. But the deposed persons, who ought now to have remained quiet, with those who had separated after so disgraceful a flight, were guilty of such conduct, that their former proceedings appear trifling in comparison of these. For when the people of Adrianople would not have communion with them, as men who had fled from the Council, and had been declared guilty, they carried their complaints to the Emperor Constantius, and succeeded in causing ten of the laity to be beheaded, belonging to the Manufactory of arms[3] there, Philagrius, who was there again as Count, assisting their designs in this matter also. The tombs of these persons, which we have seen in passing by, are in front of the city.

marginal notes: §. 18. [3] de Fabricis, vid. Gothofr. in Cod. Theod.

6. Then as if they had been quite successful, because they had fled lest they should be convicted of false accusation, they prevailed with the Emperor to command whatsoever they wished to be done. Thus they caused two Presbyters and three Deacons to be banished from Alexandria into Armenia. As to Arius and Asterius, the former Bishop of Petræ[c] in Palestine, the latter Bishop in Arabia, who had

marginal note: x. 21.

---

[c] This seems to be the famous Petra, the capital of Edom, which has lately been discovered by travellers; Edom being formed into the Province Tertia Palestina, or at least called Palestine, about or soon after the time of St. Athanasius. But a difficulty arises from a passage in the Tomus ad Antioch. §. 10. where Asterius, the fellow-sufferer with Arius, (or Macarius, as he is called supr. p. 74.) is said to be Bishop of Petræ of Arabia, as if the Petræ of Palestine were distinct from it. Reland observes, Palestine, p. 928, (in answer to Cellarius, who considered in consequence that there were two Petræ, Le Quien Orien. Christ. t. 3. pp. 665. 666.) that as there is already one error of text in this passage (as it appears), of Arius for Macarius, so the word Petra may have fallen into the wrong place, instead of "the one of Palestine, the other of Petra of Arabia," or that Petra may be a marginal note, which has been incorporated with the text in the wrong place, as is con-

234 Tyrannical measures against the Alexandrians.

ARIAN HIST.
§. 19.
[1] p. 71, note f.
p. 190.

[2] of Tenedos, vid. pp. 76, 223.
[3] p. 71, note g.

[4] Acacians, &c. p. 241, r. 1. vol. 8. p. 7, note p.

[5] this accounts for Ath.'s caution, pp. 79, 80, and 236, r. 5.

withdrawn from their party, they not only banished into upper Libya, but also caused them to be treated with insult; and as to Lucius[1], Bishop of Adrianople, when they saw that he used great boldness of speech against them, and exposed their impiety, they again, as they had done before, caused him to be bound with iron chains on the neck and hands, and so drove him into banishment, where he died, as they know. And Diodorus the Bishop[2] they transported from his place; but against Olympius of Æni, and Theodulus of Trajanople[3], both Bishops of Thrace, good and orthodox men, when they perceived their hatred of the heresy, they brought false charges.

7. This the party of Eusebius had done first of all, and the Emperor Constantius wrote letters on the subject; and next these men[4] revived the accusation. The purport of the letters was, that they should not only be expelled from their cities and churches, but should suffer capital punishment, wherever they were discovered. However surprising this conduct may be, it is only in accordance with their principles; for as being instructed by the Eusebians in such proceedings, and as heirs of their impiety and evil principles, they wished to shew themselves formidable at Alexandria, as their fathers had done in Thrace. They caused an order to be written, that the ports and gates of the cities should be watched, lest availing themselves of the permission granted by the Council, the banished persons should return to their churches. They also cause orders to be sent to the magistrates at Alexandria, respecting Athanasius and certain Presbyters, named therein, that if either the Bishop[5], or any of the others, should be found coming to the city or its borders, the magistrate should have power to behead those who were

firmed by the run of the passage supr. p. 74. and by passages to which he refers in St Hilary. He observes moreover, on the improbability of the silence of Eusebius, St. Jerome, the acts of Councils, and ancient Notitiæ, supposing there were two Petræ. Dr. Robinson, who in his recent elaborate and useful work on Palestine, referring to Reland, observes, that "the passage [in the text] is usually referred to as contained in the 'Epist. ad solitariam Vitam agentes,' though in the Benedictine Edition at least, it is found, not in that Epistle, but in the Historia Arianor. § 18." Palest vol. 2. p. 655. But these were but two titles of the same work, till Montfaucon more correctly confined the former to the short introduction to a lost dogmatic work which is prefixed to the History, (vid. supr. pp. 210, 215, and note of Amanuensis in Calc. Hist) yet even Montf. calls the History, "Ep. ad Sol." Notes, tom. 1. p 150, 151. correcting himself in Præf xxxiii. And it is called "Epistle to the Solitaries" by Ceillier even since Montfaucon.

so discovered. Thus this new Jewish heresy[1] does not only deny the Lord, but has also learnt to commit murder.

8. Yet even after this they did not rest; but as the father of their heresy goeth about[2] like a lion, seeking whom he may devour, so these obtaining the use of the public posts[3] went about, and whenever they found any that reproached them with their flight, and that hated the Arian heresy, they scourged them, cast them into chains, and caused them to be banished from their country; and they rendered themselves so formidable, as to induce many to dissemble, many to fly into the deserts, rather than willingly even to have any dealings with them. Such were the enormities which their madness prompted them to commit after their flight.

9. Moreover they perpetrate another outrageous act, which is indeed in accordance with the character of their heresy, but is such as was never heard of before, nor is likely soon to take place again, even among the more dissolute of the Gentiles[4], much less among Christians. The holy Council had sent as Legates the Bishops Vincentius[5] of Capua, (this is the Metropolis of Campania,) and Euphrates of Agrippina[6], (this is the Metropolis of Upper Gaul,) that they might obtain the Emperor's consent to the decision of the Council, that the Bishops should return to their Churches, inasmuch as he was the author of their expulsion. The most religious Constans had also written to his brother[7], and supported the cause of the Bishops. But these admirable men, who are equal to any act of audacity, when they saw the two Legates at Antioch, consulted together and formed a plot, which Stephanus[8] undertook by himself to execute, as being a suitable instrument for such purposes. Accordingly they hire a common harlot, even at the season of the most holy Easter, and stripping her introduce her by night into the apartment of the Bishop Euphrates. The harlot who thought that it was a young man who had sent to invite her, at first willingly accompanied them, but when they thrust her in, and she saw the man asleep and unconscious of what was going on, and when presently she distinguished his features, and beheld the face of an old man, and the figure of a Bishop, she immediately cried aloud, and declared that violence was used towards her. They desired her to be

silent, and to lay a false charge against the Bishop; and so when it was day, the matter was noised abroad, and all the city ran together; and those who came from the Palace[1] were in great commotion, wondering at the report which had been spread abroad, and demanding that it should not be passed by in silence. An enquiry therefore was made, and her master[2] gave information concerning those who came to fetch the harlot, and these informed against Stephanus; for they were his Clergy. Stephanus therefore is deposed, and Leontius the eunuch[3] appointed in his place, only that the Arian heresy may not want a supporter.

§. 21. 10. And now the Emperor Constantius, feeling some compunctions, returned to a right[4] mind; and concluding from their conduct towards Euphrates, that their attacks upon the others were of the same kind, he gives orders that the Presbyters and Deacons who had been banished from Alexandria into Armenia should immediately be released. He also writes publicly to Alexandria commanding that the clergy and laity who were friends of Athanasius should suffer no further persecution. And when Gregory died about ten months after, he sends for Athanasius with every mark of honour, writing to him no less than three times a very friendly letter[5], in which he exhorted him to take courage and come. He sends also a Presbyter and a Deacon, that he may be still further encouraged to return; for he thought that, through alarm at what had taken place before, I[6] did not care to return. Moreover he writes to his brother Constans, that he also would exhort me to return. And he affirmed that he had been expecting Athanasius a whole year, and that he would not permit any change to be made, or any ordination to take place, as he was preserving the Churches for Athanasius their Bishop.

§. 22. 11. When therefore he wrote in this strain, and encouraged him by means of many, (for he caused Polemius, Datianus, Bardion, Thalassus[7], Taurus[8], and Florentius, his Counts, in whom Athanasius could best confide, to write also;) Athanasius committing the whole matter to God, who had stirred the conscience of Constantius to do this, came with his friends to him; and he gave him a favourable audience, and sent him away to go to his country and his Churches, writing at the same time to the magistrates in the several places, that whereas he had before commanded the ways to be guarded, they should now grant him a free passage. Then when the Bishop complained of the sufferings he had undergone, and of the letters which the Emperor had written against him, and besought him that the false accusations against him might not be revived by his enemies after his departure, saying, " If you please, summon these persons; for as far as we are concerned they are at liberty to stand forth, and we will expose their conduct;" he would not do this, but commanded that whatever had been before slanderously written against him should all be destroyed and obliterated, affirming that he would never again listen to any such accusations, and that his purpose was fixed and unalterable. This he did not simply say, but sealed his words with an oath, calling upon God to be witness of them. And so encouraging him with many other words, and desiring him to be of good courage, he sends the following letters to the Bishops and Magistrates.

12. Constantius Augustus, the Great, the Conqueror, to the Bishops and Clergy of the Catholic Church.

The most Reverend Athanasius has not been deserted by the grace of God [1], &c.

Another Letter.

From Constantius to the people of Alexandria.

Desiring as we do your welfare in all respects [2], &c.

Another Letter.

Constantius Augustus, the Conqueror, to Nestorius, Prefect of Egypt.

It is well known that an order was heretofore given by us, and that certain documents are to be found prejudicial to the character of the most reverend Bishop Athanasius; and that these exist among the Orders [3] of your worship. Now we desire your Prudence, of which we have good proof, to transmit to our Court, in compliance with this our order, all the letters respecting the fore-mentioned person, which are found in your Order-Book [3].

[1] vid. Apol. contr. Arian. §. 54. supr. p. 82.
[2] vid. Apol. contr. Arian. §. 55. supr. p. 83.
[3] or Acta Publica, vid. supr p. 84.

13. The following is the letter which he wrote after the death of the blessed Constans. It was written in Latin, and is here translated into Greek[1].

Constantius Augustus, the Conqueror, to Athanasius.

It is not unknown to your Prudence, that it was my constant prayer, that prosperity might attend my late brother Constans in all his undertakings; and your wisdom may therefore imagine how greatly I was afflicted when I learnt that he had been taken off by most unhallowed hands. Now whereas there are certain persons who at the present time endeavour to alarm you by that so melancholy event, I have therefore thought it right to address this letter to your Constancy, to exhort you that, as becomes a Bishop, you would teach the people those things which pertain to the service of God, and that, as you are accustomed to do, you would employ your time in prayers together with them, and not give credit to vain rumours, whatever they may be. For our fixed determination is, that you should continue, agreeably to our desire, to perform the office of a Bishop in your own place. May Divine Providence preserve you, most beloved Father[2], many years.

14. Under these circumstances, when they had at length taken their leave, and commenced their journey, those who were friendly to them rejoiced to see their friend; but of the other party, some were confounded at the sight of him; others not having the confidence to appear, hid themselves; and others repented of what they had written against the Bishop. Thus all the Bishops of Palestine, except some two or three, and those men of suspected character, so willingly received Athanasius, and embraced communion with him[3], that they wrote to excuse themselves, on the ground that in what they had formerly written, they had acted, not according to their own wishes[4], but by compulsion. Of the Bishops of Egypt and the Libyan provinces, of the laity both of those countries and of Alexandria, it is superfluous for me to speak. They all ran together, and were possessed with unspeakable delight, that they had not only received their friends alive contrary to their hopes; but that

they were also delivered from the heretics who were as tyrants and as raging dogs towards them. Accordingly great was their joy, the people in the congregations encouraging one another in virtue. How many unmarried women, who were before ready to enter upon marriage, now remained virgins to Christ! How many young men, seeing the examples of others, embraced the monastic life! How many fathers persuaded their children, and how many were urged by their children, to submit themselves to Christian discipline[1]! How many wives persuaded their husbands, and how many were persuaded by their husbands, to give themselves to prayer, as the Apostle has spoken! How many widows and how many orphans, who were before hungry and naked, now through the great zeal of the people, were no longer hungry, and went forth clothed! In a word, so great was their emulation in virtue, that you would have thought every family and every house a Church, by reason of the goodness of its inmates, and the prayers which were offered to God. And in the Churches there was a profound and wonderful peace, while the Bishops wrote from all quarters, and received from Athanasius the customary letters of peace.

15. Moreover Ursacius and Valens, as if suffering the scourge of conscience, came to another mind, and wrote to the Bishop himself a friendly and peaceable letter[2], although they had received no communication from him. And going up[3] to Rome they repented, and confessed that all their proceedings and assertions against him were founded in falsehood and mere calumny. And they not only voluntarily did this, but also anathematized the Arian heresy, and presented a written declaration of their repentance, addressing to the Bishop Julius the following letter in Latin, which has been translated into Greek. The Latin copy was sent to us by Paul[4] Bishop of Tibur.

Translation from the Latin.

Ursacius and Valens to my[5] Lord the most blessed Pope Julius.

Whereas it is well known that we[6], &c.

TR VIII. 25, 26.

§. 26.

[1] ἀσκή-σεως: vid. p. 202, r. 2.

[2] p. 86, note q.

[3] ἀναλ-θόντες, p 26. r. 2. 39. and p. 242, r. 4.

[4] Pauli-nus, supr. p. 86. Paulia-nus? p. 78.

[5] κυρίῳ μου, supr. p. 113.

[6] vid. Apol. contr. Ar § 58. supr. p. 86.

Translation from the Latin.

The Bishops Ursacius and Valens to my[1] Lord and Brother, the Bishop Athanasius.

Having an opportunity of sending[2], &c.

After writing these, they also subscribed the letters of peace which were presented to them by Peter and Irenæus, Presbyters of Athanasius, and by Ammonius a layman, who were passing that way, although Athanasius had sent no communication to them by these persons.

§. 27. 16. Now who was not filled with admiration at witnessing these things, and the great peace that prevailed in the Churches? who did not rejoice to see the concord of so many Bishops? who did not glorify the Lord, beholding the delight of the people in their assemblies? How many enemies repented! How many excused themselves who had formerly accused him falsely! How many who formerly hated him, now shewed affection for him! How many of those who had written against him, recanted[3] their assertions! Many also who had sided with the Arians, not through choice but by necessity, came by night and excused themselves. They anathematized the heresy, and besought him to pardon them, because, although through the plots and calumnies of these men they appeared bodily on their side, yet in their hearts they held communion with Athanasius, and were always with him. Believe me, this is true[4].

[1] κυρίῳ μου, supr. p. 113.
[2] vid. Apol. con. Ar. §. 58. supr. p. 87.
[3] παλινῳ-δίαν ᾖσαν
[4] pp.158, 216.

CHAP. IV.

SECOND ARIAN PERSECUTION UNDER CONSTANTIUS.

1. BUT the inheritors[1] of the opinions and impiety of the Eusebians, the eunuch Leontius[a], who ought not to remain in communion even as a layman[2], because he mutilated himself that he might henceforward be at liberty to sleep with one Eustolium[3], who is a wife as far as he is concerned, but is called a virgin; and George and Acacius, and Theodorus, and Narcissus, who were deposed by the Council; when they heard and saw these things, were greatly ashamed. And when they perceived the unanimity and peace that existed between Athanasius and the Bishops; (they were more than four hundred[4], from great Rome, and all Italy, from Calabria, Apulia, Campania, Bruttia, Sicily, Sardinia,

§. 28.
[1] p. 234, r. 4.
[2] Can. Ap. 17. but vid. Morin. de Pæn. p. 185.
[3] p. 208.
[4] after Sardica, vid. p. 78, note o.

[a] Various writers have treated on the subject of that great scandal of the early centuries, the συνείσακτοι. The most charitable account of it is to be found in the unprotected state of women dedicated to a single life when or where Convents did not exist. "She says that she has no protector, husband, guardian, father, nay, nor brother," &c. Chrysost. ap. Basn. Dissert. vii. 19. ad Arn Eccles. t. 2. And the example of the Holy and Blessed Virgin was adduced, whom our Lord consigned to the care of St. John, Epiph. Hær. 78. 11. which the Nicene Council so far acknowledged that it dispensed with its prohibition in favour of mother, sister, aunt, or other person, to whom no suspicion could attach. Nay, even in the case of the atrocious extravagance, which St. Cyprian reprobates, Ep. 62 (ed. Ben.) and which in a still more perverted and shocking form is spoken of in the text, it must be recollected that it was not unknown to primitive times for husband and wife to vow continency and yet to cohabit. Theodoret gives an instance in which a youth persuades his bride, ἐν αὐτῇ τῇ παστάδι, τῇ πρωτῇ τῶν γάμων ἡμέρᾳ Hist iv. 12. Another is the instance so beautifully related by St. Gregory of Tours, in which the bride persuades her husband; "puella, graviter contristata, aversa ad parietem, amarissime flebat," till "tunc ille, armatus crucis vexillo, ait, Faciam quæ hortaris, et datis inter se dextris, quieverunt." He adds, "Multos postea in uno strato recumbentes annos, vixerunt cum castitate laudabili." Hist. Franc. 1. 42. What was found possible in the married, others had the indecency and wildness to attempt in the single state. On the συνείσακτοι, vid. Mosheim de Rebus Ante Const. p. 599. Routh, Reliqu. Sacr. t 2. p. 506. t 3. p. 445. Basnag. Diss. vii. 19. in Ann Eccles. t. 2 Muratori Anecdot Græc. p. 218. Dodwell, Dissert Cyprian iii. Bevereg. in Can Nic. 3. Suicer. Thesaur. in voc. &c. &c. It is conjectured by Beveridge, Dodwell, Van Espen, &c. that Leontius gave occasion to the first Canon of the Nicene Council, περὶ τῶν τολμώντων ἑαυτοὺς ἐκτέμνειν.

Corsica, and the whole of Africa, and those from Gaul, Britain, and Spain, with the great Confessor Hosius; and also those from Pannonia, Noricum, Siscia, Dalmatia, Dardania, Dacia, Mysia, Macedonia, Thessaly, and all Achaia, and from Crete, Cyprus, and Lycia, with most of those from Palestine, Isauria, Egypt, the Thebais, the whole of Libya, and Pentapolis;) when I say they perceived these things, they were possessed with envy and fear; with envy, on account of the communion of so many together; and with fear, lest those who had been entrapped by them should be brought over by the unanimity of so great a number, and henceforth their heresy should be triumphantly exposed, and every where proscribed.

§. 29. 2. First of all they persuade Ursacius and Valens to change sides again, and like dogs to return to their own vomit, and like swine to wallow again in the former mire of their impiety; and they make this excuse for their retractation, that they did it through fear of the most religious Constans. And yet even had there been cause for fear, yet if they had confidence in what they had done, they ought not to have become traitors to their friends But when there was no cause for fear, and yet they were guilty of a lie, are they not deserving of utter condemnation? For no soldier was present, no Palatine[1] or Notary[2] had been sent, as they now send them, nor yet was the Emperor there, nor had they been summoned[3] by any one, when they wrote their recantation. But they voluntarily went up[4] to Rome, and of their own accord recanted and wrote it down in the Church, where there was no fear from without, where the only fear is the fear of God, and where every one has liberty of conscience[5]. And yet although they have a second time become Arians, and then have devised this indecent excuse for their conduct, they are still without shame.

§. 30. 3 In the next place they went in a body to the Emperor Constantius, and besought him, saying, "When we first made our request to you, we were not believed; for we told you, when you sent for Athanasius, that by inviting him to come forward, you were expelling our heresy. For he has been opposed to it from the very first, and never ceases to anathematize it He has already written letters against us into all parts of the world, and the majority of men have embraced communion with him; and even of those who seemed to be on our side, some have been gained over by him, and others are likely to be. And we are left alone, so that the fear is, lest the character of our heresy become known, and henceforth both we and you gain the name of heretics. And if this come to pass, you must take care that we be not classed with the Manichæans. Therefore begin again to persecute, and support the heresy, for it accounts you its king." Such was the language of their iniquity. And the Emperor, when in his passage through the country on his hasty march against Magnentius[1], he saw the communion of the Bishops with Athanasius, like one set on fire, suddenly changed his mind, and no longer remembered his oaths, but was alike forgetful of what he had written, and regardless of the duty he owed his brother. For in his letters to him, as well as in his interview with Athanasius, he took an oath that he would not act otherwise than as the people should wish, and as should be agreeable to the Bishop But his zeal for impiety caused him at once to forget all these things. And yet one ought not to wonder that after so many letters and so many oaths Constantius had altered his mind, when we remember that Pharaoh[2] of old, the tyrant of Egypt, after frequently promising and by that means obtaining a remission of his punishments, likewise changed, until he at last perished together with his associates in wickedness.

4. He compelled then the people in every city to change their party, and on arriving at Arles and Milan, he proceeded to act entirely in accordance with the designs and suggestions of the heretics; or rather they acted themselves, and receiving authority from him, furiously attacked every one Letters and orders were immediately sent hither to the Prefect, that for the future the corn should be taken from Athanasius and given to those who favoured the Arian doctrines, and that whoever pleased might freely insult them that held communion with him; and a threat was held out to the magistrates, if they did not hold communion with the Arians. These things were but the prelude to what afterwards took place under the direction of the Duke Syrianus.

5. Orders were sent also to the more distant parts, and

Notaries despatched to every city, and Palatines, with threats to the Bishops and Magistrates, directing the Magistrates to urge on the Bishops, and informing the Bishops that either they must subscribe against Athanasius, and hold communion with the Arians, or themselves undergo the punishment of exile, while the people who took part with them were to understand that chains, and insults, and scourgings, and the loss of their possessions, would be their portion. These orders were not neglected, for the commissioners had in their company the Clergy of Ursacius and Valens, to inspire them with zeal, and to inform the Emperor if the Magistrates neglected their duty. The other heresies, as younger sisters of their own[1], they permitted to blaspheme the Lord, and only conspired against the Christians, not enduring to hear orthodox language concerning Christ. How many Bishops in consequence, according to the words of Scripture, were brought before rulers and kings, and received this sentence from magistrates, "Subscribe, or withdraw from your churches, for the Emperor has commanded you to be deposed!" How many in every city were made to waver, lest they should accuse them as friends of the Bishops! Moreover letters were sent to the city authorities, and a threat of a fine was held out to them, if they did not compel the Bishops of their respective cities to subscribe. In short, every place and every city was full of fear and confusion, while the Bishops were dragged along to trial, and the magistrates witnessed the lamentations and groans of the people.

§. 32. 6. Such were the proceedings of the Palatine commissioners; on the other hand, those admirable persons, confident in the patronage which they had obtained, display great zeal, and cause some of the Bishops to be summoned before the Emperor, while they persecute others by letters, inventing charges against them; to the intent that the one might be overawed by the presence of Constantius, and the other, through fear of the commissioners and the threats held out to them in these pretended accusations, might be brought to renounce their orthodox and pious opinions[2]. In this manner it was that the Emperor forced so great a multitude of Bishops, partly by threats, and partly by promises, to declare, "We will no longer hold communion with Athanasius." For those who came for an interview, were not admitted to his presence, nor allowed any relaxation, not so much as to go out of their dwellings, until they had either subscribed, or refused and incurred banishment thereupon. And this he did because he saw that the heresy was hateful[1] to all men. For this reason especially he compelled so many to add their names to the small number[2] of the Arians, his earnest desire being to collect together a crowd of names, both from envy of the Bishop, and for the sake of making a shew in favour of the Arian impiety, of which he is the patron; supposing that he will be able to alter the truth, as easily as he can influence the minds of men. He knows not, nor has ever read, how that the Sadducees and the Herodians, taking unto them the Pharisees, were not able to obscure the truth; rather it shines out thereby more brightly every day, while they crying out, *We have no king but Cæsar*[3], and obtaining the judgment of Pilate in their favour, are nevertheless left destitute, and wait in utter shame, expecting shortly[4] to become bereft, like the partridge, when they shall see their patron near his death.

[TR VIII 32, 33.]

[1 p. 217, r. 7 p. 223, r. 3.]
[2 p. 248, r. 3 p. 259]
[2 p. 132, r. 5.]
[John 19, 25.]
[3 vol. 8. p 190.]
[4 ἴσον οὐ δίπω. p. 228, note b. Const. died in 362, aged 45.]
[vid. Jer. 17, 11. Sept.]

§. 33.

7. Now if it was altogether unbecoming in any of the Bishops to change their opinions merely from fear of these things, yet it was much more so[a], and not the part of men who have confidence in what they believe, to force and compel the unwilling. In this manner it is that the Devil, when he has no truth on his side[b], attacks and breaks down the doors of them that admit him with axes and hammers. But our Saviour is so gentle that He teaches thus, *If any man wills to come after Me*, and, *Whoever wills to be My disciple*, and coming to each He does not force them, but knocks at the door and says, *Open unto Me, My sister, My spouse*; and if they open to Him, He enters in, but if they delay and will not, He departs from them. For the truth is not preached with swords or with darts, nor by means of soldiers; but by persuasion and counsel. But what persuasion is there where fear of the Emperor prevails? or what counsel is there, when he who withstands them receives at

[5 p. 193 fin.]
[vid. Ps. 74, 6.]
[Mat. 16, 24.]
[Cant. 5, 2.]

---

[b] The fault consists in substituting *persecution for* the power of truth. vid. p. 279, note c.

last banishment and death? Even David, although he was a king, and had his enemy in his power, prevented not the soldiers by an exercise of authority when they wished to kill his enemy, but, as the Scripture says, David persuaded his men by arguments, and suffered them not to rise up and put Saul to death. But he, being without arguments of reason, forces all men by his power, that it may be shewn to all, that their wisdom is not according to God, but merely human, and that they who favour the Arian doctrines have indeed no king but Cæsar; for by his means it is that these enemies of Christ accomplish whatsoever they wish to do.

8. But while they thought that they were carrying on their designs against many by his means, they knew not that they were making many to be confessors, of whom are those who have lately made so glorious a confession, religious men, and excellent Bishops, Paulinus[1] Bishop of Treves the Metropolis of Gaul, Lucifer[2] Bishop of the Metropolis of Sardinia, Eusebius of Vercelli in Italy, and Dionysius of Milan, which is the Metropolis of Italy. These the Emperor summoned before him, and commanded them to subscribe against Athanasius, and to hold communion with the heretics; and when they were astonished at this novel procedure, and said that there was no Ecclesiastical Canon[3] to this effect, he immediately said, "Whatever I will, be that esteemed a Canon; the Bishops of Syria let me thus speak. Either then obey, or go into banishment."

§ 34. 9. When the Bishops heard this they were utterly amazed, and stretching forth their hands to God, they used great boldness of speech against him, teaching him that the kingdom was not his, but God's who had given it to him, whom also they bid him fear, lest He should suddenly take it away from him. And they threatened him with the day of judgment, and warned him against infringing Ecclesiastical order, and mingling Roman sovereignty with the constitution[4] of the Church, nor to introduce the Arian heresy into the Church of God. But he would not listen to them, nor permit them to speak further, but threatened them so much the more, and drew his sword against them, and gave orders for some of them to be led to punishment; although afterwards, like Pharaoh[5], he repented. The holy men therefore shaking off the dust, and looking up to God, neither feared the threats of the Emperor, nor betrayed their cause before his drawn sword; but received their banishment, as a service pertaining to their ministry. And as they passed along, they preached the Gospel in every place and city[1], although they were in bonds, proclaiming the orthodox faith, anathematizing the Arian heresy, and stigmatizing the recantation of Ursacius and Valens. But this was contrary to the intention of their enemies; for the greater was the distance of their place of banishment, so much the more was the hatred against them increased, while the wanderings of these men were but the heralding of their impiety. For who that saw them as they passed along, did not greatly admire them as Confessors, and renounce and abominate the others, calling them not only impious men, but executioners[2] and murderers, and every thing rather than Christians[3]?

[1] infr. p. 253, r 2. vid. Acts 8, 4. Phil. 1, 12.
[2] δημίους, vid. p. 133, r. 12.
[3] supr. p. 208, note b.

CHAP. V.

PERSECUTION AND LAPSE OF LIBERIUS.

§. 35.   1. Now it had been better if from the first Constantius had never become connected with this heresy at all; or being connected with it, if he had not yielded so much to those impious men; or having yielded to them, if he had stood by them only thus far, so that judgment might come upon them all for these atrocities alone. But as it would seem, like madmen, having entangled themselves in the bonds of impiety, they are drawing down upon their own heads a more severe judgment. Thus from the first[1] they spared not even Liberius Bishop of Rome, but extended[a] their fury[2] even to those parts, they respected not his bishopric, because it was an Apostolical throne; they felt no reverence for Rome, because she is the Metropolis of Romania[b]; they remembered not that formerly in their letters they had spoken of her Bishops as Apostolical men. But confounding all things together, they at once forgot every thing, and cared only to shew their zeal in behalf of impiety. When they perceived that he was an orthodox man, and hated[3] the Arian heresy, and earnestly endeavoured to persuade all persons to renounce and withdraw from it, these impious men reasoned thus with themselves: "If we can persuade Liberius, we shall soon prevail over all."

[1] in contrast to date of his fall, p. 255, r. 6.
[2] μανίαν
[3] pp 245, r. 1 254, r. 2

[a] τὴν μανίαν ἐξέτειναν; vid. ἐκτεῖναι τὴν μανίαν infr. p 254. r. 1. And so in the letter of the Council of Chalcedon to Pope Leo, which says that Dioscorus, κατ' αὐτοῦ τῆς ἀμπέλου τὴν φυλακὴν παρὰ τοῦ σωτῆρος ἐπιτετραμμένου τὴν μανίαν ἐξέτεινε λέγομεν δὴ τῆς σῆς ὁσιότητος Hard. Conc t 2. p 656   As to the words ὅτι ἀποστολικός ἐστι θρόνος, the phrase "Apostolical throne or see," is given also, though not as an appellative, to the sees of Antioch, Ephesus, &c. vid. Tertull. de Præscript 36. August Ep. 43. 7. Even were it to be here construed "because it is the Apostolical see," yet perhaps Athanasius uses it from his familiarity with Latin ideas during his frequent exiles in the West, just as he also adopts some of their theological terms. The Eusebians had in the first instance resisted the authority of Rome, though with expressions of respect. supr. p. 40, note c.

[b] By Romania is meant the Roman Empire, according to Montfaucon after Nannius. vid. Præfat xxxiv. xxxv And so Epiph. Hær. lxvi. 1 fin. p 618. and lxviii 2 init. p. 728 Nil. Ep. i. 75. vid. Ducange Gloss Græc. in voc.

2. Accordingly they accuse him falsely before the Emperor; and he, expecting easily to draw over all men to his side by means of Liberius, writes to him, and sends a certain eunuch called Eusebius with letters and offerings, to cajole him with the presents, and to threaten him with the letters. The eunuch accordingly went to Rome, and first proposed to Liberius to subscribe against Athanasius, and to hold communion with the Arians, saying, " The Emperor wishes it, and commands you to do so." And then shewing him the offerings, he took him by the hand, and again besought him, saying, " Be persuaded to comply with the Emperor's request, and receive these." But the Bishop endeavoured to convince him, reasoning with him thus: " How is it possible for me to do this against Athanasius? how can we condemn a man, whom not one[1] Council only, but a second[2] assembled from all parts of the world[3], has fairly acquitted, and whom the Church of Rome dismissed in peace? who will approve of our conduct, if we reject in his absence one, whose presence[4] amongst us we gladly welcomed[5], and admitted him to our communion? There is no Ecclesiastical Canon[6] which can authorize such a proceeding; nor have we had transmitted to us any such tradition[7] from the Fathers, which they might have received from the great and blessed Apostle Peter[8].

3. " But if the Emperor is really concerned for the peace of the Church, if he requires our decrees respecting Athanasius to be reversed, let their proceedings both against him and against all the others be reversed also; and then let an Ecclesiastical Council be called at a distance from the Court[9], at which the Emperor shall not be present, nor any Count be admitted, nor magistrate to threaten us, but where only the fear of God, and the Apostolical rule[10] shall prevail; that so in the first place, the faith of the Church may be secured, as the Fathers defined it in the Council of Nicæa, and the supporters of the Arian doctrines may be cast out, and their heresy anathematized. And then after that, an enquiry being made into the charges brought against Athanasius, and any other beside, as well as into those things of which the other party is accused, let the guilty be cast out, and the innocent receive encouragement

ARIAN HIST.

¹ vid. Palla-vicin. Conc. Trid. vi. 7. Sarpi. Hist. ii. 37.

and support. For it is impossible that they who maintain an impious creed can be admitted as members of a Council; nor is it fit that an enquiry into matters of conduct should precede the enquiry concerning the faith[1]; but all diversity of opinion on points of faith ought first to be eradicated, and then the enquiry made into matters of conduct. Our Lord Jesus Christ did not heal them that were afflicted, until they shewed and declared what faith they had in Him. These things we have received from the Fathers; these report to the Emperor; for they are both profitable for him and edifying to the Church. But let not Ursacius and Valens be listened to, for they have retracted their former assertions, and in what they now say they are not to be trusted."

§. 37. 4. These were the words of the Bishop Liberius. And ²εὐνοῦχος the eunuch[2], who was vexed, not so much because he would not subscribe, as because he found him an enemy to the ³ πρὸς ἐ- heresy, forgetting that he was in the presence of a Bishop[3], πίσκοπον ἦν. after threatening him severely, went away with the offerings; and proceeded to perpetrate an offence, which is foreign ⁴ σπαδόν-from a Christian, and too audacious for a eunuch[4]. In των imitation of the transgression of Saul, he went to the Martyry[c] of the Apostle Peter, and then presented the offerings. But Liberius having notice of it, was very angry with the person who kept the place, that he had not prevented him, and cast out the offerings as an unlawful sacrifice, ⁵τὸν θλα-which increased the anger of the mutilated[5] creature against δίαν him. Consequently he exasperates the Emperor against him, saying, "The matter that concerns us is no longer the obtaining the subscription of Liberius, but the fact that he is so resolutely opposed to the heresy, that he anathematizes the Arians by name." He also stirs up the other eunuchs to say the same, for many of those who are about Con-

⁶ vid. Gibbon, Hist ch. 19 init.

stantius, or rather the whole number of them, are eunuchs[6],

[c] "Under this canopy,"[the Baldacchino in the present St. Peter's Church,] is the high altar, which is only used on the most solemn ceremonies, and beneath it repose the bodies of St Peter and St. Paul That of St. Peter lies in the place where it was first buried It is said that Pope Anacletus, while he was only a priest, constructed a chapel here in 106, which was called the Confessional of St. Peter, and inclosed the body of the Apostle in a marble urn Constantine is reported to have covered the urn with metal, so that it can never be seen." Burton's Rome, p 425.

who engross all the influence with him, and it is impossible to do any thing there without them. The Emperor accordingly writes to Rome, and again Palatines, and Notaries, and Counts are sent off with letters to the Prefect, in order that either they may inveigle Liberius by stratagem away from Rome and send him to the Court to him, or else persecute him by violence.

Tr. VIII. 37, 38.

5. Such being the tenor of the letters, there also fear and treachery forthwith prevailed throughout the whole city. How many were the families against which threats were held out! How many received great promises on condition of their acting against Liberius! How many Bishops hid themselves when they saw these things! How many noble women retired to their estates in consequence of the calumnies of the enemies of Christ! How many ascetics were made the objects of their plots! How many who were sojourning there, and had made that place their home, did they cause to be persecuted! How often and how strictly did they guard the harbour[1] and the approaches to the gates, lest any orthodox person should enter and visit Liberius! Rome also had trial of the enemies of Christ, and now experienced what before she would not believe, when she heard how the other Churches in every city were ravaged by them.

§. 38.

[1] Ostia, vid. Gibbon, Hist. ch 31. p 303.

6. It was the eunuchs who instigated these proceedings against all. And the most remarkable circumstance in the matter is this; that the Arian heresy which denies the Son of God, receives its support from eunuchs, who, as both their bodies are fruitless, and their souls barren of the seeds of virtue, cannot bear even to hear the name of son The Eunuch of Ethiopia indeed, though he understood not what he read, believed the words of Philip, when he taught him concerning our Saviour; but the eunuchs of Constantius cannot endure the confession of Peter[2], nay, they turn away when the Father manifests the Son, and madly rage against those who say, that the Son of God is His genuine Son, thus claiming as a heresy of eunuchs, that there is no genuine and true offspring of the Father. On these grounds it is that the law forbids such persons to be admitted into any ecclesiastical Council[3]; notwithstanding which these have now regarded them as competent judges of eccle-

[2] Mat. 16, 16. allusion to Liberius° vid. p. 57, note u. Hard.

[3] Conc. t. 2 p.305, E. Can Nic. 1

siastical causes, and whatever seems good to them, that Constantius decrees, while men with the name of Bishops dissemble with them. Oh! who shall be their historian? who shall transmit the record of these things to future generations? who indeed would believe it, were he to hear it, that eunuchs who are scarcely entrusted with household services (for theirs is a pleasure-loving[1] race, that has no serious concern but that of hindering in others what nature has taken from them); that these, I say, now exercise authority in ecclesiastical matters, and that Constantius in submission to their will treacherously conspired against all, and banished Liberius!

§. 39. 7. For after the Emperor had frequently written to Rome, had threatened, sent commissioners, devised schemes, on the persecution subsequently breaking out at Alexandria, Liberius is dragged before him, who uses great boldness of speech towards him. "Cease," he said, "to persecute the Christians; attempt not by my means to introduce impiety into the Church. We are ready to suffer any thing rather than to be called Arian fanatics. We are Christians; compel us not to become enemies of Christ. We also give you this counsel: fight not against Him who gave you this empire, nor shew impiety towards Him instead of thankfulness[2]; persecute not them that believe in Him, lest you also hear the words, *It is hard for thee to kick against the pricks.* Nay, I would that you might hear them, that you might obey, as the holy Paul did. Behold, here we are; we are come, before they fabricate charges. For this cause we hastened hither, knowing that banishment awaits us at your hands, that we might suffer before a charge encounters us, and that all may clearly see that all the others too have suffered as we shall suffer, and that the charges brought against them were fabrications of their enemies, and all their proceedings are mere calumny and falsehood."

§. 40. 8. These were the words of Liberius at that time, and he was admired by all men for them. But the Emperor instead of answering, only gave orders for their banishment, separating each of them from the rest, as he had done in the former cases. For he had himself devised this plan in the banishments which he inflicted, that so the severity of his

[1] φιλήδο-νον, this the key to his severity towards them.

[2] p. 246. §. 34. Acts 9, 5.

punishments might be greater than that of former tyrants and persecutors[1]. In the former persecution Maximian who was then Emperor commanded a number of Confessors to be banished together, and thus lightened their punishment by the consolation which he gave them in each other's society. But this man was more savage than he; he separated those who had spoken boldly and confessed together, he put asunder them who were united by the bond of faith, that when they came to die they might not see one another; thinking that bodily separation can disunite also the affections of the mind, and that being severed from each other, they would forget the concord and unanimity which existed among them. He knew not that however each one may remain apart from the rest, he has nevertheless with him that Lord, whom they confessed in one body together, who will also provide, (as he did in the case of the prophet Elisha,) that more shall be with each of them, than there are soldiers with Constantius. Of a truth iniquity is blind; for in that they thought to afflict the Confessors, by separating them from one another, they rather brought thereby a great injury upon themselves. For had they continued in each other's company, and abode together, the pollutions of those impious men would have been proclaimed from one place only; but now by putting them asunder, they have made their impious heresy and wickedness to spread abroad and become known in every place[2].

9 Who that shall hear what they did in the course of these proceedings will not think them to be any thing rather than Christians[3]? When Liberius sent Eutropius a Presbyter and Hilarius a Deacon with letters to the Emperor, at the time that Lucifer and his friends made their confession, they banished the Presbyter on the spot, and after stripping Hilarius[d] the Deacon and scourging him on the back, they banished him too, exclaiming, " Why didst thou not resist Liberius instead of being the bearer of letters from him." Ursacius and Valens with the eunuchs who sided with them were the authors of this outrage. The Deacon, while he was

---

[d] This Hilary afterwards followed Lucifer of Cagliari in his schism. He is supposed to be the author of the Comments on St. Paul's Epistles attributed to St. Ambrose, who goes under the name of Ambrosiaster.

being scourged, praised the Lord, remembering his words, *I gave My back to the smiters;* but they while they scourged him laughed and mocked him, feeling no shame that they were insulting a Levite. Indeed they acted but consistently in laughing while he continued to praise God; for it is the part of Christians to endure stripes, but to scourge Christians is the outrage of a Pilate or a Caiaphas[1].

10. Thus they endeavoured at the first to corrupt the Church of the Romans, wishing to introduce impiety into it as well as others. But Liberius after he had been in banishment two years gave way, and from fear of threatened death was induced to subscribe. Yet even this only shews their violent conduct, and the hatred[2] of Liberius against the heresy, and his support of Athanasius, so long as he was suffered to exercise a free choice. For that which men are forced by torture to do contrary to their first judgment, ought not to be considered the willing deed of those who are in fear, but rather of their tormentors[3]. They however attempted every thing in support of their heresy, while the people in every Church, preserving the faith which they had learnt, waited for the return of their teachers, and cast from them, and all avoided, as they would a serpent, the Antichristian heresy.

CHAP. VI.

PERSECUTION AND LAPSE OF HOSIUS

1. BUT although they had done all this, yet these impious men thought they had accomplished nothing, so long as the great Hosius escaped their wicked machinations. And now they undertook to extend their fury[1] to that venerable old man. They felt no shame at the thought that he is the father of the Bishops[2], they regarded not that he had been a Confessor[3], they reverenced not the length of his Episcopate, in which he had continued more than sixty years; but they set aside every thing, and looked only to the interests of their heresy, as being of a truth such as neither fear God, nor regard man. Accordingly they went to Constantius, and again employed such arguments as the following, "We have done every thing; we have banished the Bishop of the Romans, and before him a very great number of other Bishops, and have filled every place with alarm. But these strong measures of yours are as nothing to us, nor is our success at all more secure, so long as Hosius remains. While he is in his own place, the rest also continue in their Churches, for he is able by his arguments and his faith to persuade all men against us. He is the president of Councils[4], and his letters are every where attended to. He it was who put forth the Nicene Confession, and proclaimed every where that the Arians were heretics. If therefore he is suffered to remain, the banishment of the rest is of no avail, for our heresy will be destroyed. Begin then to persecute him also, and spare him not, ancient[5] as he is. Our heresy knows not to honour the hoary hairs of the aged."

§. 42.

[1] ἐκτεῖναι τὴν μανίαν, p 248, note a.
[2] pp.158, 230,256.
[3] under Maximian.
vid. Luke18, 2.

[4] of Nicæa and Sardica.

[5] ἀρχαῖος, vid p 284.

§. 43.

2. Upon hearing this, the Emperor no longer delayed, but knowing the man, and the weight of his years, wrote to summon him. This was when he first[6] began his attempt

[6] supr p 248,1 1. i. e. two years before his fall.

upon Liberius. Upon his arrival he desired him, and urged him with the usual arguments, with which he thought also to deceive the others, that he would subscribe against us, and hold communion with the Arians. But the old man, scarcely bearing to hear the words, and grieved that he had even ventured to utter such a proposal, severely rebuked him, and after endeavouring to convince him of his error, withdrew to his own country and Church. But the heretics still complaining, and instigating him to proceed, (he had the eunuchs also to remind him and to urge him further,) the Emperor again wrote in threatening terms; but still Hosius, while he endured their insults, was unmoved by any fear of their designs against him, and remaining firm to his purpose, as one who had built the house of his faith upon the rock, he spoke boldly against the heresy, regarding the threats held out to him in the letters but as drops of rain and blasts of wind. And although Constantius wrote frequently, sometimes flattering him with the title of Father[1], and sometimes threatening and recounting the names of those who had been banished, and saying, "Will you continue the only person to oppose the heresy? Be persuaded and subscribe against Athanasius; for whoever subscribes against him thereby embraces with us the Arian cause;" still Hosius remained fearless, and while suffering these insults, wrote an answer in such terms as these. We have read the letter, which is placed at the end[2].

[1] p. 255, r. 2.

[2] transferred by copyists hither.

§. 44. 3. Hosius to Constantius the Emperor sends health in the Lord.

I was a Confessor at the first, when a persecution arose in the time of your grandfather Maximian; and if you shall persecute me, I am ready now too to endure any thing rather than to shed innocent blood and to betray the truth. But I cannot approve of your conduct in writing after this threatening manner. Cease to write thus; adopt not the cause of Arius, nor listen to those in the East, nor give credit to Ursacius and Valens. For whatever they assert, it is not on account of Athanasius, but for the sake of their own heresy. Believe my statement, O Constantius, who am of an age to be your grandfather. I was present at the

Council of Sardica, when you and your brother Constans of blessed memory assembled us all together; and on my own account I challenged the enemies of Athanasius, when they came to the Church where I abode[1], that if they had any thing against him they might declare it; desiring them to have confidence, and not to expect otherwise than that a right judgment would be passed in all things. This I did once and again, requesting them, if they were unwilling to appear before the whole Council, yet to appear before me alone; promising them also, that if he should be proved guilty, he should certainly be rejected by us; but if he should be found to be blameless, and should prove them to be calumniators, that if they should then refuse to hold communion with him, I would persuade him to go with me into Spain. Athanasius was willing to comply with these conditions, and made no objection to my proposal; but they, altogether distrusting their cause, would not consent. And on another occasion Athanasius came to your Court[2], when you wrote for him, and his enemies being at the time in Antioch, he requested that they might be summoned either altogether or separately, in order that they might either convict him, or be convicted, and might either in his presence prove him to be what they represented, or cease to accuse him when absent. To this proposal also you would not listen, and they equally rejected it.

4. Why then do you still give ear to them that speak evil of him? How can you endure Ursacius and Valens, although they have retracted, and made a written confession of their calumnies? For it is not true, as they pretend, that they were forced to confess; there were no soldiers at hand to influence them; your brother was not cognizant of the matter[3]. No, such things were not done under his government, as are done now; God forbid. But they voluntarily went up[4] to Rome, and in the presence of the Bishop and Presbyters wrote their recantation, having previously addressed to Athanasius a friendly and peaceable letter. And if they pretend that force was employed towards them, and acknowledge that this is an evil thing, which you also disapprove of; then do you cease to use force[5]; write no letters, send no Counts; but release those that have been

TR VIII
44.

[1] Coruduba.

[2] στρατόπεδον, p. 100, note z.

[3] p. 15, note f. p. 242.

[4] p. 223, r. 6.

[5] pp. 19, 205, 221, n. 3 fin. 242, r. 5. 245, note b. 267, r. 2. 279, note c.

banished, lest while you are complaining of violence, they do but exercise greater violence. When was any such thing done by Constans? What Bishop suffered banishment at his hands? When did he appear in presence at an Ecclesiastical trial? When did any Palatine of his compel men to subscribe against any one, that Valens and his fellows should be able to affirm this?

5. Cease these proceedings, I beseech you, and remember that you are a mortal man Be afraid of the day of judgment, and keep yourself pure thereunto. Intrude not yourself into Ecclesiastical matters, neither give commands unto us concerning them; but learn them from us. God hath put into your hands the kingdom; to us He hath entrusted the affairs of His Church; and as he who should steal the empire from you would resist the ordinance of God, so likewise fear on your part lest by taking upon yourself the government of the Church, you become guilty of a great offence It is written, *Render unto Cæsar the things that are Cæsar's, and unto God the things that are God's.* Neither therefore is it permitted unto us to exercise an earthly rule, nor have you, Sire, any authority to burn incense[a]. These things I write unto you out of a concern for your salvation. With regard to the subject of your letters, this is my determination: I will not unite myself to the Arians; I anathematize their heresy. Neither will I subscribe against Athanasius, whom both we and the Church of the Romans, and the whole Council pronounced to be guiltless. And yourself also, when you understood this, sent for the man, and gave him permission to return with honour to his country and his Church. What reason then can there be for so great a change in your conduct? The same persons who were his enemies before, are so now also; and the things they now whisper to his prejudice, (for they

---

[a] Incense is mentioned in the Apostolical Canon III. but apparently no where else till this date Hippol de Consumm. Mund adduced by Beveridge on the Canon is not genuine. At the same time it must be recollected, that Hosius was at this time 100 years old, and a rite which he singles out (if he does not speak figuratively) to describe the Eucharistic Sacrifice, could not be a recent one. From Tertull. Apol. 42. and Arnobius, contr. Gent. VII 27. it appears to have been unknown to the African Churches in their day. vid. Bon. Rer. Lit. 1. 25. n. 9. Bellarm. de Miss II.15. Bevereg. Cod. Can. Vind. II. 2. r. 5. Dall. de Pseudepig. Apost. III. 14. §. 4. Dodwell, Use of Incense.

do not declare them openly in his presence,) the same they spoke against him, before you sent for him; the same they spread abroad concerning him when they came to the Council. And when I required them to come forward, as I have before said, they were unable to produce their proofs; had they possessed any, they would not have fled so disgracefully. Who then has persuaded you so long after to forget your own letters and declarations? Forbear, and be not influenced by evil men, lest while you act for the mutual advantage of yourself and them, you bring guilt upon yourself. For here you comply with their desires, hereafter in the judgment you will have to answer for doing so alone. These men desire by your means to injure their enemy, and wish to make you the minister of their wickedness, in order that through your help they may sow the seeds[b] of their accursed heresy in the Church. Now it is not a prudent thing to cast one's self into manifest danger for the pleasure of others. Cease then, I beseech you, O Constantius, and be persuaded by me. These things it becomes me to write, and you not to despise.

6. Such were the sentiments, and such the letter, of the Abraham-like old man, Hosius[1], truly so called[c]. But the Emperor desisted not from his designs, nor ceased to seek an occasion against him; but continued to threaten him severely, with a view either to bring him over by force, or to banish him if he refused to comply. And as the Officers and Satraps of Babylon[2] seeking an occasion against Daniel, found none except in the law of his God; so likewise these present Satraps of impiety were unable to invent any charge against the old man, (for this true Hosius, and his blameless life were known to all,) except the charge of hatred[3] to their heresy. They therefore proceeded to accuse him; though not under the same circumstances as those others accused Daniel to Darius, for Darius was grieved to hear the

§. 45.
[1] i. e. sacred, saintly.
[2] p. 195, r. 1.
[3] p. 260, r. 1.

---

[b] vid. vol. 8. p. 5. note k. It is remarkable, this letter having so much its own character, and being so unlike Athanasius's writings in style, that a phrase characteristic of him should here occur in it. Did Athan. translate it from Latin?

[c] ὁ ἀληθῶς "Ὅσιος κατάσκοποι, οὐ γὰρ ἐπίσκοποι, supr. §. 3. infr. §§. 48, 75 fin. and so ἀληθῶς Εὐσέβιος, Theod. Hist. 1. 4. Ὀνήσιμον, τόν ποτέ σοι ἄχρηστον, νυνὶ δὲ εὔχρηστον, Ep ad Phil. 10. vid. vol. 8. p. 114, note b

ARIAN charge, but as Jezebel accused Naboth, and as the Jews
HIST. applied themselves to Herod. And they said, "He not
only will not subscribe against Athanasius, but also on his
[1] p. 245, account condemns us; and his hatred[1] to the heresy is so
r 1 great, that he also writes to others, that they should rather
suffer death, than become traitors to the truth. For, he
says, our beloved Athanasius also is persecuted for the
Truth's sake, and Liberius Bishop of Rome, and all the rest,
are treacherously assailed."

[2] vid. pp. 7. When this patron of impiety, and Emperor of heresy[2],
226, r. 1. Constantius, heard this, and especially that there were
243, 267,
r. 3. others also in Spain of the same mind as Hosius, after he
had tempted them also to subscribe, and was unable to
compel them to do so, he sent for Hosius, and instead of
banishing him, detained him a whole year in Sirmium.
Godless, unholy, without natural affection, he feared not
God, he regarded not his father's love for Hosius, he
reverenced not his great age, for he was now a hundred
years old [d]; but all these things this modern Ahab, this
second Belshazzar of our times, disregarded for the sake of
impiety. He used such violence towards the old man, and
confined him so straitly, that at last, broken by suffering,
he was brought, though hardly, to hold communion with
Valens and Ursacius, though he would not subscribe against
Athanasius. Yet even thus he forgot not his duty, for at
the approach of death, as it were by his last testament, he
bore witness to the force which had been used towards him,
and anathematized the Arian heresy, and gave strict charge
that no one should receive it.

§. 46. 8. Who that witnessed these things, or that has merely
heard of them, will not be greatly amazed, and cry aloud unto
Ez. 11, the Lord, saying, *Wilt Thou make a full end of the remnant*
13. *of Israel?* Who that is acquainted with these proceed-
Jer. 5, ings, will not with good reason cry out and say, *A wonderful*
30, 2, 12. *and horrible thing is committed in the land;* and, *The*
heavens are astonished at this, and the earth is even more
horribly afraid. The fathers of the people and the teachers
of the faith are taken away, and the impious are brought into

---

[d] οὔτε τὸν Θεὸν φοβηθεὶς ὁ ἄθεος οὔτε τοῦ τὸ γῆρας αἰσχυνθεὶς ὁ ἄστοργος.
πατρὸς τὴν διάθεσιν αἰδεσθεὶς ὁ ἀνόσιος, οὔτε

Constantius forerunner of Antichrist.

the Churches? Who that saw when Liberius Bishop of Rome was banished, and when the great Hosius the father[1] of the Bishops suffered these things, or who that saw so many Bishops banished out of Spain and the other parts, could fail to perceive, however little sense he might possess, that the charges[2] against Athanasius also and the rest were false, and altogether mere calumny? For this reason those others also endured all suffering, because they saw plainly that the conspiracies laid against these were founded in falsehood. For what charge was there against Liberius? or what accusation against the aged Hosius? who bore even a false witness against Paulinus, and Lucifer, and Dionysius, and Eusebius? or what sin could be laid to the account of the rest of the banished Bishops, and Presbyters, and Deacons? None whatever; God forbid. There were no charges against them on which a plot for their ruin might be formed; nor was it on the ground of any accusation that they were severally banished. It was a breaking out of impiety against godliness[3]; it was zeal for the Arian heresy, and a prelude to the coming of Antichrist, for whom Constantius is thus preparing the way.

[TR VIII 46. p. 230, r. 5.

2 vid. in Apol. contr. Ar. and ad Const.

3 ἀσεβίας, ib. σιβσίας, vol. 8. p. 1, note a.]

CHAP. VII.

PERSECUTION AT ALEXANDRIA.

§. 47. 1. AFTER he had accomplished all that he desired against the Churches in Italy, and the other parts; after he had banished some, and violently oppressed others, and filled every place with fear, he at last turned his fury, as it had been some pestilential disorder, against Alexandria. This was artfully contrived by the enemies of Christ; for in order that they might have a show of the signatures of many Bishops, and that Athanasius might not have a single Bishop in his persecution to whom he could even complain, they therefore anticipated his proceedings, and filled every place [1] with terror, which they kept up to second[1] them in the prosecution of their designs. But herein they perceived not through their folly that they were not exhibiting the free sentiments[2] of the Bishops, but rather the violence which themselves had employed; and that, although his brethren should desert him, and his friends and acquaintance stand afar off, and no one be found to sympathise with him and console him, yet far above all these, a refuge with his God was sufficient for him. For Elias also was alone in his persecution, and God was all in all to the holy man. And our Saviour has given us an example herein, who also was left alone, and exposed to the designs of His enemies, to teach us, that when we are persecuted and deserted by men, we must not faint, but place our hope in Him, and not betray the Truth. For although at first it may seem to be afflicted, yet even they who persecute shall afterwards acknowledge it.

[1] ἔφεδρον
[2] p 141, note a, p 257, r. 5.

§. 48. 2. Accordingly they urge on the Emperor, who first writes a menacing letter, which he sends to the Duke and the soldiers. The Notaries Diogenius[1] and Hilarius[1], and certain Palatines with them were the bearers of it; upon whose arrival those terrible and cruel outrages were committed against the Church, which I have briefly related a little above[2], and which are known to all men from the protests put forth by the people, which are inserted at the end of this history[3], so that any one may read them. Then after these proceedings on the part of Syrianus, after these enormities had been perpetrated, and violence offered to the Virgins, as approving of such conduct and the infliction of these evils upon us, he writes again to the senate and people of Alexandria, instigating the younger men, and requiring them to assemble together, and either to persecute Athanasius, or consider themselves as his enemies. He however had withdrawn before these instructions reached them, and from the time when Syrianus broke into the Church; for he remembered that which is written, *Hide thyself as it were for a little moment, until the indignation be overpast*[4].

[TR VIII 47—50. vid. pp 173, 175, 294. p 243, &c]

[3 vid. p. 293, note a.]

[Is. 26, 20.]

[4 pp.186, 204.]

3. One Heraclius, by rank a Count, was the bearer of this letter, and the precursor of a certain George that was dispatched by the Emperor as a spy, for one that was sent from him cannot be a Bishop[5]; God forbid. And so indeed his conduct and the circumstances which preceded his entrance sufficiently prove. Heraclius then published the letter, which reflected great disgrace upon the writer. For whereas, when the great Hosius wrote to Constantius, he had been unable to make out any plausible pretext for his change of conduct, he now invented an excuse much more discreditable to himself and to his advisers. He said, " From regard to the affection I entertained towards my brother of divine and pious memory, I endured for a time the coming of Athanasius among you." This proves that he has both broken his promise, and behaved ungratefully to his brother after his death. He then declares him to be, as indeed he is, " deserving of sacred and pious remembrance;" yet as regards a command of his, or to use his own language, the " affection" he bore him, even though he complied merely " for the sake" of the blessed Constans, he ought to deal fairly by his brother, and make himself heir to his

[5 κατα- σκόπου, οὐκ ἐπί- σκοπος, vid. p. 259, note c.]

[§ 50. [there is no § 49 in Montf]]

sentiments as well as to the Empire. But, although, when seeking to obtain his just rights, he deposed Vetranio, with the question, " To whom does the inheritance belong after a brother's death ᵃ ?" yet for the sake of the accursed heresy of the enemies of Christ, he disregards the claims of justice, and behaves undutifully towards his brethren.

4. Nay, for the sake of this heresy, he would not consent to observe his father's wishes without infringement; but, in what he may gratify those impious men, he pretends to adopt his intention, while in order to distress the others, he cares not to shew the reverence which is due unto a father. For in consequence of the calumnies of the Eusebians, his father sent the Bishop for a time into Gaul to avoid the cruelty of his persecutors, (this was shewn by the blessed Constantine, the brother of the former, after their father's death, as appears by his letters¹,) but he would not be persuaded by the Eusebians to send the person whom they desired for a Bishop, but prevented the accomplishment of their wishes, and put a stop to their attempts with severe threats.

§. 51. 5. If therefore, as he declares in his letters, he desired to observe his father's practice, why did he first send out Gregory, and now this George, who eats his own stores ᵇ ? Why does he endeavour so earnestly to introduce into the Church these Arians, whom his father named Porphyrians ᶜ, and banish others while he patronises them ? Although his

---

ᵃ " It was an easy task to deceive the frankness and simplicity of Vetranio, who, fluctuating some time between the opposite views of power and interest, displayed to the world the insincerity of his temper, and was insensibly engaged in the snares of an artful negociation. Constantius acknowledged him as a legitimate and equal colleague in the Empire, on condition that he would renounce his disgraceful alliance with Magnentius, and appoint a place of interview on the frontiers of their respective provinces.... The united armies were commanded to assemble in a large plain near the city [Sardica]. In the centre, according to the rules of ancient discipline, a military tribunal, or rather scaffold, was erected, from whence the Emperors were accustomed, on solemn and important occasions, to harangue the troops ...The first part of his [C.'s] Oration seemed to be pointed only against the tyrant of Gaul [Magnentius], but while he tragically lamented the cruel murder of Constans, he insinuated, that *none, except a brother, could claim a right to the succession of his brother*. He displayed, with some complacency, the glories of his Imperial race, &c..... The contagion of loyalty and repentance was communicated from rank to rank; till the plain of Sardica resounded with the universal acclamation of 'Away with these upstart usurpers!'" &c. Gibbon, Hist. ch. xviii.

ᵇ George had been pork-contractor to the army, and had been detected in peculation. vid. vol. 8. p. 89, r. 1. p 134, note f. and infr. p. 286.

ᶜ Constantine called the Arians by this title after the philosopher Porphyry, the great enemy of Christianity. Socrates has preserved the Edict Hist. 1 9

father admitted Arius to his presence, yet when Arius perjured himself and burst asunder[1], he lost the compassion of his father; who, on learning the truth, condemned him as a heretic.

6. Why moreover, while pretending to respect the Canons of the Church, has he ordered the whole course of his conduct in opposition to them? For where is there a Canon that a Bishop should be appointed from Court? Where is there a Canon[2] that permits soldiers to invade Churches? What tradition[3] is there allowing counts and ignorant eunuchs to exercise authority in Ecclesiastical matters, and to make known by their edicts the decisions of those who bear the name of Bishops? He is guilty of all manner of falsehood for the sake of this unholy heresy. At a former time he sent out Philagrius as Prefect a second time[5], in opposition to the opinion of his father, and we see what has taken place now.

7. Nor " for his brother's sake" does he speak the truth. For after his death he wrote as often as three times to the Bishop, and repeatedly promised him that he would not change his behaviour towards him, but exhorted him to be of good courage, and not suffer any one to alarm him, but to continue to abide in his Church in perfect security[6]. He also sent his commands by Count Asterius, and Palladius the Notary, to Felicissimus who was then Duke, and to the Prefect Nestorius, that if either Philip the Prefect, or any other should venture to form any plot against Athanasius, they should prevent it. Wherefore when Diogenes came, and Syrianus laid in wait for us, both he[7] and we and the people demanded to see the Emperor's letters, supposing that, as it is written, *Let not a falsehood be spoken before the king*[8]; so when a king has made a promise, he will not lie, nor change. If then " for his brother's sake he complied," why did he also write those letters upon his death? And if he wrote them for " his memory's sake," why did he afterwards behave so very unkindly towards him, and persecute the man, and write what he did, alleging a judgment of Bishops, while in truth he acted only to please himself[9]?

8. Nevertheless his craft has not escaped detection, but we have the proof of it ready at hand. For if a judgment

had been passed by Bishops, what concern had the Emperor with it? Or if it was only a threat of the Emperor, what need in that case was there of the so-named Bishops? When was such a thing heard of before from the beginning of the world? When did a judgment of the Church receive its validity[1] from the Emperor? or rather when was his decree ever recognised by the Church? There have been many Councils held heretofore; and many judgments passed by the Church; but the Fathers never sought the consent of the Emperor thereto, nor did the Emperor busy himself with the affairs of the Church. The Apostle Paul had friends among them of Cæsar's household, and in his Epistle to the Philippians he sent salutations from them; but he never took them as his associates in Ecclesiastical judgments[2]. Now however we have witnessed a novel sight, which is a discovery of the Arian heresy. Heretics have assembled together with the Emperor Constantius, in order that he, alleging the authority of the Bishops, may exercise his power against whomsoever he pleases, and while he persecutes may avoid the name of persecutor[3]; and that they, supported by the Emperor's government, may conspire the ruin of whomsoever they will[d]; and these are all such as are not as impious as themselves. One might look upon their proceedings as a comedy which they are performing on the stage, in which the pretended Bishops are actors[4], and Constantius the performer of their behests, who makes promises to them, as Herod did to the daughter of Herodias, and they dancing before him, accomplish, through false accusations[5], the banishment and death of the true believers in the Lord.

§. 53. 9. Who indeed has not been injured by their calumnies? Whom have not these enemies of Christ conspired to de-

---

[1] τὸ κῦρος

[2] p. 249, r. 9.

[3] p. 279, note c.

[4] p. 34, r. 6.

[5] ἄρχουσιν μένους τὰς διαβολὰς ἱπλ, vid. Herod. Hist. vi. 129 fin.

d οἷς ἂν ἐθέλωσι, and just before ὧν ἂν ἐθέλοι. [And more strikingly just below, § 53 fin ἃ θέλουσι πράττει, ἐπεὶ καὶ αὐτὸς ἅπερ ἤθελεν ἥκουσι παρ' αὐτῶν.] This is a very familiar phrase with Athan. 1 e ὡς ἐθέλησιν, ἅπερ ἐθέλησαν, ὅταν θέλωσιν, οὓς ἐθέλησαν, &c. &c. Some instances have been given supr. p. 15, note e. and vol. 8. p. 92, note r Among the many passages that might be noticed, are the following, de Decr. §. 3 A. de Syn. §. 13 A. Apol contr. Arian §§. 2 C. 14 D. 35 D. 36 D. 73 A. B. 74 F.

77 D Ep. Æg. §§. 5 B 19 A. 22 B. Ap. ad Const. §. 1 C. de Fug. §§ 3 C. 7 E. ad Serap. fin. And so in this History, besides the above passage, the phrase is found in §§. 2 D. 3 fin. 7 C. ib. D twice 47 C 54 init. 59 A. 60 fin. In like manner, ὡς ἠβούλοντο, ἃ βούλονται, &c. Ep. Encycl § 7 D Apol. contr. Arian §§. 36 D. 73 A. 74 A. 77 B. twice. ibid. D. 82 init. 83 F. ibid B. Ep. Æg §. 6 B. C. Apol. ad Const. § 32 D. de Fug. §. 1 fin And so in this History, §§. 2 D. 15 D. 18 C.

stroy? Whom has Constantius failed to banish upon charges which they have brought against them? When did he refuse to hear them willingly? And what is most strange¹, when did he permit any one to speak against them, and did not more readily receive their testimony, of whatever kind it might be? Where is there a Church which now enjoys the privilege of worshipping Christ freely²? If a Church be a maintainer of true piety, it is in danger; if it dissemble, it abides in fear. Every place is full of hypocrisy and impiety, so far as he is concerned; and wherever there is a pious person and a lover of Christ, (and there are many such every where, as were the prophets and the great Elias,) they hide themselves, if so be that they can find a faithful friend like Abdias, and either they withdraw into caves and dens of the earth, or pass their lives in wandering about in the deserts. These men in their madness prefer such calumnies against them, as Jezebel invented against Naboth, and the Jews against our Saviour, while the Emperor, who is the patron³ of the heresy, and wishes to pervert the truth, as Ahab wished to change the vineyard into a garden of herbs, does whatever they desire him to do, for the suggestions he receives from them are agreeable to his own wishes⁴.

^{TR VIII 53, 54.}
^{1 p. 221, r. 1. de Decr. §. 3. F.}
^{2 p. 262, r. 2.}
^{3 p. 260, r. 2.}
^{4 p. 265, r. 9}

10. Accordingly he banished, as I said before, the genuine Bishops, because they would not profess impious doctrines, to suit his own pleasure; and now he has sent Count Heraclius to proceed against Athanasius, who has publicly made known his decrees, and announced the commands of the Emperor to be, that unless they complied with the instructions contained in his letters, their bread⁵ should be taken away, their idols overthrown, and the persons of many of the city-magistrates and people delivered over to certain slavery. After threatening them in this manner, he was not ashamed to declare publicly with a loud voice, "The Emperor disclaims Athanasius, and has commanded that the Churches be given up to the Arians." And when all wondered to hear this, and made signs to one another, exclaiming, "What! has Constantius become a heretic?" instead of blushing as he ought, this man the more strictly obliged the senators and heathen magistrates and wardens of the idol temples to subscribe to these conditions, and to

^{§. 54.}
^{5 p. 243, §. 31.}
^{p. 276, note a.}

ARIAN HIST. agree to receive as their Bishop whomsoever the Emperor should send them. Of course Constantius was strictly upholding the Canons[1] of the Church, when he caused this to be done; when, instead of requiring letters[2] from the Church, he demanded them of the market-place[3], and instead of the people he asked them of the wardens of the temples. He was conscious that he was not sending a Bishop to preside over Christians, but a certain pragmatical person for those who subscribed to his terms.

[1] p. 249, r. 6.
[2] p. 221, r. 4.
[3] infr. note f.

§. 55. 11. The Gentiles accordingly, as purchasing by their compliance the safety of their idols, and certain of the trades[e], subscribed, though unwillingly, from fear of the threats which he had held out to them, just as if the matter had been the appointment of a general, or other magistrate. Indeed what, as heathen, were they likely to do, except whatever was pleasing to the Emperor? But the people having assembled in the great Church[4], (for it was the fourth day of the week,) Count Heraclius on the following day takes with him Cataphronius the Prefect of Egypt, and Faustinus the Receiver-General[5], and Bithynus a heretic; and together they stir up the younger men of the common multitude[f] who worshipped idols, to attack the Church, and stone the people, saying that such was the Emperor's command. As the time of separation[6] however had arrived, the greater part had already left the Church, but there being a few women still remaining, they did as these men had charged them, whereupon a piteous spectacle ensued. The few women had just risen from prayer and had sat down, when the youths having stripped themselves suddenly came upon them with stones and clubs. Some of them the godless[7] wretches stoned to death; they lacerated with stripes the holy persons of the Virgins, tore off their veils[8] and exposed their heads, and when they resisted the insult, the cowards kicked them with their feet. This was dreadful, exceedingly dreadful; but what ensued was worse, and

[4] vid. p. 167, note p.
[5] Catholic, p. 163, note m.
[6] ἀπολύσεως, vid. Suicer. in voc
[7] οἱ ἄθλιοι, vid. p. vol. 8. p. 3, note f.
[8] p. 7, r. 3.

[e] τῶν ἐργασιῶν,—trades, or workmen. vid supr. p. 33, r. 2. Montfaucon has a note upon the word in the Collect. Nov. t 2. p. xxvi. where he corrects his Latin *in loc.* of the former passage very nearly in conformity to the rendering given of it above, p 33 "In Onomastico monui-mus, hic ἐργασίας *officinarum operas* commodius exprimere." And he quotes an inscription discovered by Spon, τοῦτο τὸ ἡρῷον στιφανοῖ ἡ ἐργασία τῶν βαφέων

[f] τῶν ἀγοραίων, vid. Acts xvii. 5. ἀγορὰ has been used just above. vid. Suicer. Thesaur *in voc.*

more intolerable than any outrage. Knowing the holy character of the virgins, and that their ears were unaccustomed to pollution, and that they were better able to bear stones and swords than expressions of obscenity, they assailed them with such language. This the Arians suggested to the young men, and laughed at all they said and did; while the holy Virgins and other godly women fled from such words as they would from the bite of asps, but the enemies[1] of Christ assisted them in the work, nay even, it may be, gave utterance to the same; for they were well-pleased with the obscenities which the youths vented upon them.

12. After this, that they might fully execute the orders they had received, (for this was what they earnestly desired, and what the Count and the Receiver-General instructed them to do,) they seized upon the seats, the throne, and the table which was of wood[g], and the curtains[h] of the Church, and whatever else they were able, and carrying them out burnt them before the doors in the great street, and cast frankincense upon the flame. Alas! who will not weep to hear of these things, and, it may be, close his ears[2], that he may not have to endure the recital, esteeming it hurtful merely to listen to the accounts of such enormities? Moreover they sang the praises of their idols, and said, "Constantius hath become a heathen, and the Arians have acknowledged our customs;" for indeed they scruple not even to pretend heathenism, if only their heresy may be established. They even were ready to sacrifice a heifer which drew the water for the gardens at the Cæsareum[1]; and would have sacrificed it, had it not been a female[k]; for they said that it was unlawful for such to be offered among them.

TR VIII. 55, 56

§ 56.

[1] p. 270, note l.

[2] p. 140 fin.vol.8. p. 188 init.

---

[g] vid. Fleury's Church History, xxii. 7. p. 129, note k. [Oxf. tr. 1843.] By specifying the material, Athan. implies that altars were sometimes not of wood.

[h] Curtains were at the entrance, and before the chancel. vid. Bingh. Antiqu. viii. 6. § 8. Hofman. Lex in voc. *velum.* also Chrysost. Hom. iii in Eph. [tr. p. 133, note o.]

[i] The royal quarter in Alexandria, vid. supr p. 167, note p. In other Palatia an aqueduct was necessary,

[e g] vid. Cod. Theod. xv. 2 even at Daphne, though it abounded in springs, ibid l. 2.

[k] vid. Herodot. ii. 41. who says that cows and heifers were sacred to Isis. vid. Jablonski Pantheon Æg 1. 1. § 15 who says that Isis was worshipped in the shape of a cow, and therefore the cows received divine honours. Yet bulls were sacrificed to Apis, ibid. iv. 2. §. 9. vid. also Schweighæuser *in loc.* Herod.

13. Thus acted the impious[1] Arians in conjunction with the heathens, thinking that these things tended to our dishonour. But Divine justice reproved their iniquity, and wrought a great and remarkable miracle[2], thereby plainly shewing to all men, that as in their acts of impiety[1] they had dared to attack none other but the Lord, so in these proceedings also, they were again attempting to do dishonour unto Him. This was more manifestly proved by the marvellous[3] event which now came to pass. One of these licentious youths ran into the Church, and ventured to sit down upon the throne; and as he sat there the wretched man uttered with a nasal sound some lascivious song. Then rising up he attempted to pull away the throne, and to drag it towards him; he knew not that he was drawing down vengeance upon himself. For as of old the inhabitants of Azotus, when they ventured to touch the Ark, which it was not lawful for them even to look upon, were immediately destroyed by it, being first grievously tormented by emerods; so this unhappy person who presumed to drag the throne, drew it upon himself, and, as if Divine justice had sent the wood to punish him, he struck it into his own bowels; and instead of carrying out the throne, he brought out by the blow his own entrails, so that the throne took away his life, instead of his taking it away. For, as it is written of Judas, his bowels gushed out, and he fell down and was carried away, and the day after died. Another also entered the Church with boughs of trees, and, as in the Gentile manner he waved them in his hands and mocked, he was immediately struck with blindness, so as straightway to lose his sight, and to know no longer where he was; but as he was about to fall, he was taken by the hand and supported by his companions out of the place, and when on the following day he was with difficulty brought to his senses, he knew not either what he had done or suffered in consequence of his audacity.

§. 58. 14. The Gentiles, when they beheld these things, were seized with fear, and ventured on no further outrage; but the Arians were not yet touched with shame, but, like the

---

[1] vid. vol. 8. p. 1, note 1 This is a remarkable instance of the special and technical sense of the words, εὐσέβεια, ἀσεβοῦντες, &c. being here contrasted with pagan blasphemy, &c. vid. also p. 269, r. 1.

Jews when they saw the miracles, were faithless and would not believe, nay, like Pharaoh, they were hardened; they too having placed their hopes below, on the Emperor and his eunuchs. They permitted the Gentiles, or rather the more abandoned of the Gentiles, to act in the manner before described; for they found that Faustinus, who is the Receiver-General by style, but is a vulgar[1] person in habits, and profligate in heart, was ready to play his part with them in these proceedings, and to stir up the heathen. Nay, they undertook to do the like themselves, that as they had struck off their heresy from all other heresies together[2], so they might divide their wickedness with the more depraved part of mankind. What they did through the instrumentality of others I have described above, the enormities they committed themselves, surpass the bounds of all wickedness; and they exceed the vileness of any hangman[3]. Where is there a house which they did not ravage? where is there a family they did not plunder on pretence of searching for their opponents? where is there a garden they did not trample under foot? what tomb[4] they did not open, pretending they were seeking for Athanasius, though their sole object was to plunder and spoil all that came in their way? How many men's houses were sealed up! From how many did they accept hospitality to give it to the soldiers who assisted them! Who had not experience of their wickedness? Who that met them in the market-place but was obliged to hide himself? Did not many an one leave his house from fear of them, and pass the night in the desert? Did not many an one, while anxious to preserve his property from them, lose the greater part of it? And who, however inexperienced, did not choose rather to commit himself to the sea, and to risk all its dangers, than to witness their threatenings? Many also changed their residences, and removed from street to street, and from the city to the suburbs. And many submitted to severe fines, and when they were unable to pay, borrowed of others, merely that they might escape their machinations.

15. For they made themselves formidable to all men, and treated all with great arrogance, using the name of the Emperor, and threatening them with his displeasure. They had to

assist them in their wickedness the Duke Sebastianus, a Manichee, and a profligate young man; the Prefect, the Count, and the Receiver-General to play his part. Many Virgins who condemned their impiety, and professed the truth, they threw down from the houses; others they insulted as they walked along the streets, and caused their heads to be uncovered[1] by their young men. They also gave permission to the females of their party to insult whom they chose; and although the holy and faithful women withdrew on one side, and gave them the way, yet they gathered round them like Bacchanals and Furies[m], and esteemed it a misfortune if they found no means to injure them, and spent that day sorrowfully on which they were unable to do them some mischief. In a word, so cruel and bitter were they against all, that all men called them hangmen[2], murderers, lawless, intruders, evil-doers, and by any other name rather than that of Christians[3].

§. 60. 16. Moreover, imitating the savage practices of Scythians[4], they seized upon Eutychius the Sub-deacon, a man who had served the Church honourably, and causing him to be scourged on the back with a heathen whip, till he was at the point of death, they demanded that he should be sent away to the mines; and not simply to any mine, but to that of Phæno[n], where even a condemned murderer is hardly able to live a few days. And what was most unreasonable in their conduct, they would not permit him even a few hours to have his wounds dressed, but caused him to be sent off immediately, saying, " If this is done, all men will be afraid, and henceforward will be on our side." After a short interval however, being unable to accomplish his journey to the mine on account of the pain of his wounds, he died on the way. He perished rejoicing, having obtained the glory of martyrdom.

---

[m] vid vol. 8. p 91, note q. also Greg Naz. Orat. 35. 3. Epiph. Hær. 69 3 Theod. Hist. 1. 3 (p. 730. ed. Schulze)

[n] The mines of Phæno lie almost in a direct line between Petræ and Zoar, which is at the southern extremity of the Dead Sea They formed the place of punishment of Confessors in the Maximinian Persecution, Euseb. de Mart.Pal.7. and in the Arian Persecution at Alexandria after Athan. Theod. Hist. iv. 19. p 996. Phænon was once the seat of a Bishopric, which sent a Bishop to the Councils at Ephesus, the Ecumenical, and the Latrocinium. vid. Reland, Palestine, pp. 951, 952 Montfaucon *in loc.* Athan. Le Quien. Or Christ. t. 3 p. 745

17. But the miscreants[1] were not even yet ashamed, but in TR VIII. §. 60, 61. the words of Scripture, *having bowels without mercy*, they acted accordingly, and now again perpetrated a devilish[2] deed. When the people prayed them to spare Eutychius and besought them for him, they caused four honourable and free citizens to be seized, one of whom was Hermias who washed the beggars' feet[o]; and after scourging them very severely, the Duke cast them into the prison. But the Arians, who are more cruel even than Scythians[3], when they saw that they did not die from the stripes they had received, complained of the Duke and threatened, saying, "We will write and tell the eunuchs, that he does not flog as we wish." Hearing this he was afraid, and was obliged to beat the men a second time; and they being beaten, and knowing for what cause they suffered and by whom they had been accused, said only, "We are beaten for the sake of the Truth, but we will not hold communion with the heretics; beat us now as thou wilt; God will judge thee for this." The impious heretics[4] wished to expose them to danger in the prison, that they might die there; but the people of God observing their time, besought him for them, and after seven days or more they were set at liberty.

[1] ἀσεβεῖς
[2] Prov. 10, 12.
[2 σαταν-ικόν, vol. 8. p. 9, note s.]
[3] pp. 272, r. 4. 275, r. 4.
[4] miscreants.

18. But the Arians, as being grieved at this, again devised §. 61. another yet more cruel and unholy deed; cruel in the eyes of all men, but well suited to their antichristian heresy. Our Lord commanded that we should remember the poor; He said, *Sell that ye have, and give alms;* and again, *I was a hungred, and ye gave Me meat; I was thirsty, and ye gave Me drink; for inasmuch as ye have done it unto one of these little ones, ye have done it unto Me.* But these men, as being in truth opposed to Christ, have presumed to act contrary to His will in this respect also. For when the Duke gave up the Churches to the Arians, and the destitute persons and widows were unable to continue any longer in

Luke 12, 33.
Mat. 25, 35. 40.

---

[o] Ἑρμείαν λούοντα τοὺς ἀνεξόδους, "Inauspicato verterat Hermantius, qui angiportos non pervios lavabat." Montfaucon, Coll. Nov. t. 2. p. xliii. who translates as above, yet not satisfactorily, especially as there is no article before λούοντα. Tillemont says, "qui avait quelle charge dans la police de la ville," understanding by ἀνέξοδοι, "inclusi sive incarcerati homines;" whereas they are "i qui ἀνὰ τὰς ἐξόδους in exitibus viarum, stipem rogunt." Montf. ibid. For the custom of washing the feet, vid. Bingh. Antiqu. xii. 4. §. 10. Justinian in 1 Ep. ad Trin. v. 10.

them, the widows sat down in places which the Clergy entrusted with the care of them appointed. And when the Arians saw that the brethren readily ministered unto them and supported them, they persecuted them also, beating them on the feet[1], and accused those who gave to them before the Duke. This was done by means of a certain soldier named Dynamius. And it was well-pleasing to Sebastian, for there is no mercy in the Manichæans; nay, it is considered a hateful thing among them to shew mercy to a poor man. Here then was a novel subject of complaint; and a new kind of court now first invented by the Arians. Persons were brought to trial for acts of kindness which they had performed; he who shewed mercy was accused, and he who had received a benefit was beaten; and they wished rather that a poor man should suffer hunger, than that he who was willing to shew mercy should give to him. Such sentiments these modern Jews, for such they are, have learned from the Jews of old, who when they saw him who had been blind from his birth recover his sight, and him who had been a long time sick of the palsy made whole, accused our Lord who had bestowed these benefits upon them, and judged them to be transgressors who had experienced His goodness[2].

19. Who was not struck with astonishment at these proceedings? Who did not execrate both the heresy, and its defenders? Who failed to perceive that the Arians are indeed more cruel than wild beasts? For they had no prospect of gain[3] from their iniquity, for the sake of which they might have acted in this manner; but they rather increased the hatred[4] of all men against themselves. They thought by treachery and terror to force certain persons into their heresy, so that they might be brought to communicate with them; but the event turned out quite the contrary. The sufferers endured as martyrdom whatever they inflicted upon them, and neither betrayed nor denied the true faith in Christ. And those that were without and witnessed their conduct, and at last even the heathen when they saw these things, execrated them as antichristian[5], as cruel executioners[6]; for human nature is prone to pity and sympathise with the poor. But these men have lost even the common senti-

ments of humanity; and that kindness which they would have desired to meet with at the hands of others, had themselves been sufferers, they would not permit others to receive, but employed against them the severity and authority of the magistrates, and especially of the Duke.

20. What they did to the Presbyters and Deacons; how they drove them into banishment under sentence passed upon them by the Duke and the Magistrates, causing the soldiers to throw down their kinsfolk from the houses[1], and Gorgonius the commander of the police[2] to beat them with stripes; and how (most cruel act of all) with much insolence they plundered the bread[a] of these and of those who were now dead; these things it is impossible for words to describe, for their cruelty surpasses all the powers of language. What terms could one employ which might seem equal to the subject? What circumstances could one mention first, so that those next recorded would not be found more dreadful, and the next more dreadful still? All their attempts and iniquities[3] were full of murder and impiety; and so unscrupulous and artful are they, that they endeavour to deceive by promises of protection, and by bribing with money[4], that so, since they cannot recommend themselves by fair means, they may thereby appear to the simple to make some show.

---

[a] τοὺς ἄρτους, the word occurs above, pp. 7, 192, 267. in this sense; but Nannius, Hermant, and Tillemont, with some plausibility understand it as a Latin term naturalized, and translate "most cruel of all, with much insolence they tore the *limbs* of the dead," alleging that merely to take away *loaves* was not so "cruel" as to take away *lives*, which the Arians had done.

CHAP. VIII.

PERSECUTION IN EGYPT.

§. 64.   1. Who would call them even by the name of Gentiles;
¹ p. 208, much less by that of Christians¹? Would any one regard their
note b. habits and feelings as human, and not rather those of wild
beasts, seeing their cruel and savage conduct? They are
² p. 274, more malignant than public hangmen²; more audacious than
r. 6. all other heretics. To the Gentiles they are much inferior,
³pp 235, and stand far apart and separate from them³. I have heard
r. 4.
253,r 1. from our fathers, and I believe their report to be a faithful
one, that long ago, when a persecution arose in the time of
Maximian, the grandfather of Constantius, the Gentiles
concealed our brethren the Christians, who were sought
after, and frequently suffered the loss of their own substance, and had trial of imprisonment, solely that they
might not betray the fugitives. They protected those who
fled to them for refuge, as they would have done their own
persons, and were determined to run all risks on their
behalf. But now these admirable persons, the inventors of
⁴ p. 275 a new heresy, act altogether the contrary part⁴, and are dis-
init. tinguished for nothing, but their treachery. They have
appointed themselves as executioners², and seek to betray
all alike, and make those who conceal others the objects of
their plots, esteeming equally as their enemy both him that
conceals and him that is concealed. So murderous are

they; so emulous in their evil-doings of the wickedness of Judas.

2. The crimes these men have committed cannot worthily be described. I would only say, that as I write and wish to enumerate all their deeds of iniquity, the thought enters my mind, whether this heresy be not the fourth daughter of the horse-leach[1] in the Proverbs, since after so many acts of injustice, so many murders, it hath not yet said, ' It is enough.' No; it still rages, and goes about[2] seeking after those whom it has not yet discovered, while those whom it has already injured, it is eager to injure anew. After the midnight attack, after the evils committed in consequence of it, after the persecution brought about by Heraclius, they cease not yet to accuse us falsely before the Emperor, (and they are confident that as impious persons they will obtain a hearing,) desiring that something more than banishment may be inflicted upon us, and that hereafter those who do not consent to their impieties may be destroyed. Accordingly, being now emboldened in an extreme degree, that most abandoned Secundus[3] of Pentapolis, and Stephanus[4] his accomplice, conscious that their heresy was a defence of any injustice they might commit, on discovering a Presbyter at Barea who would not comply with their desires, (he was called Secundus, being of the same name, but not of the same faith with the heretic,) they kicked till he died[b]. While he was thus suffering he imitated the Saint and said, " Let no one avenge my cause before human judges; I have the Lord for my avenger, for whose sake I suffer these things at their hands." They however were not moved with pity at these words, nor did they feel any awe of the sacred season; for it was during the time of Lent[5] that they thus kicked the man to death.

3. O new heresy, that hast put on the whole devil in impiety and wicked deeds! For in truth it is but a lately invented evil; and although certain heretofore appear to have adopted its doctrines, yet they concealed them and were not known to hold them. But Eusebius and Arius,

---

[b] In like manner the party of Dioscorus at the Latrocinium, or Eutychian Council of Ephesus, A.D. 449. kicked to death Flavian, Patriarch of Constantinople,

ARIAN like serpents coming out of their holes, have vomited¹ forth
HIST. the poison² of this impiety; Arius daring to blaspheme
¹ de Syn. openly, and Eusebius defending his blasphemy. He was
tr. p. 96.
Orat. 1. not however able to support the heresy, until, as I said
tr. p 232.
² Orat. 1. before, he found a patron³ for it in the Emperor. Our
tr. pp. fathers called an Ecumenical Council, when three hundred
177, 189, of them, more or less, met together and condemned the
218.
³ p. 260, Arian heresy, and all declared that it was alien and strange
r. 2.
⁴ ἐκκλη- to the faith of the Church⁴. Upon this its supporters,
σιαστι-
κῆς, perceiving that they were dishonoured and had now no
Orat. 1. good ground of argument to insist upon, devised a different
tr p.242,
r. 4. method, and attempted to vindicate it by means of external
Ep. Æg. power⁵.
§.18 init.
Vales. 4. And herein one may especially admire the novelty as
in Eus. well as wickedness of their device, and how they go beyond
Hist. 11.
25. all other heresies. For these support their fond⁶ inventions
⁵ p. 279, by persuasive arguments calculated to deceive the simple;
r. 1
⁶ τὴν μα- the Greeks, as the Apostle has said, make their attack with
νίαν
sublime and enticing words, and with plausible fallacies;
the Jews, leaving the divine Scriptures, now, as the Apostle
1 Tim.1, again has said, contend about *fables and endless genealogies;*
4.
and the Manichees and Valentinians with them, and others,
corrupting the divine Scriptures, put forth fables in terms of
their own invention. But the Arians are bolder than them
all, and have shewn that the other heresies are but their
⁷ p. 244. younger sisters⁷, whom, as I have said, they surpass in
impiety, emulating them all, and especially the Jews, in
their iniquity. For as the Jews, when they were unable to
prove the charges which they pretended to allege against
Paul, straightway led him to the chief captain and the
governor; so likewise these men, who surpass the Jews in
their devices, make use only of the power of the judges; and
if any one so much as speaks against them, he is dragged
§. 67. before the Governor or the General. The other heresies
also, when the very Truth has refuted them on the clearest
evidence, are wont to be silent, being simply confounded by
their conviction. But this modern and accursed heresy,
when it is overthrown by argument, when it is cast down
and covered with shame by the very Truth, forthwith endeavours to reduce by violence and stripes and imprison-

ment those whom it has been unable to persuade by argument, thereby acknowledging itself to be any thing rather than godly. For it is the part of true godliness not to compel^c, but to persuade, as I said before¹. Thus our Lord Himself, not as employing force, but as offering to their free choice, has said to all, *If any man will follow after Me;* and to His disciples, *Will ye also go away?*

<small>TR. VIII. 66, 67.

¹ p. 257, r. 5.

Mat.16, 24.
John 6, 67.</small>

5. This heresy however is altogether alien from godliness; and therefore how otherwise should it act, than contrary to our Saviour, seeing also that it has enlisted that enemy of Christ Constantius, as it were Antichrist himself², to be its leader in impiety? He for its sake has earnestly endeavoured to emulate Saul in savage cruelty. For when the priests gave victuals to David, Saul commanded, and they were all destroyed, in number three hundred and five³; and this man, now that all avoid the heresy, and confess a sound faith in the Lord, overthrows a Council of full three hundred Bishops, banishes the Bishops themselves, and hinders the people from the practice of piety, and from their prayers to God, preventing their public assemblies. And as Saul overthrew Nob, the city of the priests, so this man, advancing even further in wickedness, has given up the Churches to the impious. And as he honoured Doeg the accuser before

<small>² vid. vol. 8. p. 79, note q.

³ 85 priests, rec.text.</small>

<small>^c The early theory about persecution seems to have been this,—that that was a bad cause which *depended* upon it, but that, when a *cause* was good, there was nothing wrong in using force in due *subordination* to argument; that there was as little impropriety in the civil magistrate's inducing *individuals* by force, when they were incapable of higher motives, as by those secular blessings which follow on Christianity. Our Lord's kingdom was not of this world, that is, it did not depend on this world; but, as subduing engrossing, and swaying this world, it at times condescended to make use of this world's weapons against itself. The simple question was *whether a cause depended on force for its existence.* St. Athanasius declared, and the event proved, that Arianism was so dependent. When Emperors ceased to persecute, Arianism ceased to be; it had no life in itself. Again, all cruel persecution, or long continued, or on a large scale, was wrong, as arguing *an absence* of moral and rational grounds in the *cause* so maintained. Again, there was an evident *impropriety* in ecclesiastical functionaries using secular weapons, as there would be in their engaging in a secular pursuit, or forming secular connections; whereas the soldier might as suitably, and should as dutifully, defend religion with the sword, as the scholar with his pen. And further there was an abhorrence of cruelty natural to us, which it was a duty to cherish and maintain. All this being considered, there is no inconsistency in St. Athanasius denouncing persecution, and in Theodosius decreeing that "the heretical teachers, who usurped the sacred titles of Bishops or Presbyters," should be "exposed to the heavy penalties of exile and confiscation." Gibbon, Hist. ch 27. For a list of passages from the Fathers on the subject, vid. Limborch on the Inquisition, vol. 1. Bellarmin. de Laicis, c. 21. 22. and of authors in favour of persecution, vid. Gerhard de Magistr. Polit p. 741, &c</small>

the true priests, and persecuted David, giving ear to the Ziphites; so this man prefers heretics to the godly, and even persecutes them that flee from him, giving ear to his own eunuchs, who falsely accuse the orthodox. He does not perceive that whatever he does or writes in behalf of the heresy of the Arians, amounts to an attack upon his Saviour.

§. 68. 6. Ahab himself did not act so cruelly towards the priests of God, as this man has acted towards the Bishops. For he was at least pricked in his conscience when Naboth had been murdered, and was afraid at the sight of Elias; but this man neither reverenced the great Hosius, nor was wearied or pricked in conscience, after banishing so many Bishops; but like another Pharaoh, the more he is afflicted, the more he is hardened, and imagines greater wickedness day by day. And the most extraordinary instance of his iniquity was the following. It happened that when the Bishops were condemned to banishment, certain other persons also received their sentence on charges of murder or sedition or theft, each according to the quality of his offence. These men after a few months he released, on being requested to do so, as Pilate did Barabbas; but the servants of Christ he not only refused to set at liberty, but even sentenced them to more unmerciful punishment in the place of their exile, proving himself a perpetual torment to them. To the others through congeniality of disposition he became a friend; but to the orthodox he was an enemy on account of their true faith in Christ. Is it not clear to all men from hence, that the Jews of old when they demanded Barabbas, and crucified the Lord, acted but the part which these present enemies of Christ are acting together with Constantius? nay, that he is even more bitter than Pilate. For Pilate when he perceived the injustice of the deed, washed his hands; but this man, while he banishes the saints, gnashes[1] his teeth against them more and more.

§. 69. 7. But what wonder is it if, after he has been led into impious errors, he is so cruel towards the Bishops, since the common feelings of humanity could not induce him to spare even his own kindred? His uncles[d] he slew; his cousins

---

[d] The brothers of Constantine were Julius Constantius, and Dalmatius; of these Julius Constantius was father of Gallus and Julian, and Dalmatius of

he put out of the way, he commiserated not the sufferings of his father-in-law, though he had married his daughter, or of his kinsmen; but he has ever been a transgressor of his oath towards all. So likewise he treated his brother in an unholy manner; and now he pretends to build his sepulchre, although he delivered up to the barbarians his betrothed wife Olympias, whom he had protected till his death, and had brought up as his intended consort. Moreover he attempted to set aside his wishes, although he boasts to be his heir[1]; for so he writes, in terms which any one possessed but of a small measure of sense would be ashamed of. But when I compare his letters, I find that he does not possess common understanding, but that his mind is solely regulated by the suggestions of others, and is by no means in his own power. Now Solomon says, *If a ruler hearken to lies, all his servants are wicked.* This man proves by his actions that he is such an unjust one, and that those about him are wicked.

8. How then, being such an one, and taking pleasure in such associates, can he ever design any thing just or reasonable, entangled as he is in the iniquity of his followers, men given to sorcery, who have trampled his brains

---

Dalmatius and Hannibalianus. (vid. supr. p 94, note s. p. 108, note c.) Constantine had put his two last-mentioned nephews almost on an equality with his three sons, Dalmatius being a Cæsar, and Hannibalianus "King," the only prince with that title in any age of the Empire. On the Emperor's death some of his great officers as well as the soldiers and people came to a resolution that none but his sons should be their masters. Constantius promised his kinsmen his protection under an oath; but Eusebius of Nicomedia produced a last will of Constantine's, in which he declared his suspicions that he had been poisoned by his brothers, and called on his sons to avenge him. Vid. Gibbon, ch. 18. who continues, "The spirit, and even the forms of legal proceedings were repeatedly violated in a promiscuous massacre; which involved the two uncles of Constantius, seven of his cousins, of whom Dalmatius and Hannibalianus were the most illustrious, the Patrician Optatus, who had married a sister of the late Emperor, and the Prefect Ablavius, whose power and riches had inspired him with some hope of obtaining the purple." p. 132 Constantius had married the daughter of his uncle Julius Constantius, and had given his sister in marriage to his cousin Hannibalianus. "Of so numerous a family," continues Gibbon, "Gallus and Julian alone, the two youngest children of Constantius, were saved from the hands of the assassins." Constantius married Gallus to his sister, and made him Cæsar. Gallus abused his power, was recalled from the seat of his government, and beheaded in prison. Olympias was the daughter of Ablavius, who was betrothed to the Emperor Constans; about the time of Ath.'s writing, Constantius married her to Arsaces, king of Armenia. Amm. Marcell. xx. 11 init. We may suppose Athan. in the text expresses the feeling of the day at this alliance, or of Constantius's enemies. Arsaces was a Christian. St. Olympias was niece to this Olympias. Tillem. Empereurs, t. 4. p. 219.

under the soles of their feet? Wherefore he now writes letters, and then repents that he has written them, and after repenting is again stirred up to anger, and then again laments his fate, and being undetermined what to do, he shews a soul destitute of understanding. Being then of such a character, one would rather pity him, because that under the semblance and name of freedom he is the slave of those who drag him on to gratify their own impious pleasure. In a word, while through his folly and inconstancy, as the Scripture saith, he is willing to comply with the desires of others, he has given himself up to condemnation, to be consumed by fire in the future judgment; at once consenting to do whatever they wish, and gratifying them in their designs against the Bishops, and in their exertion of authority over the Churches.

9. For behold, he has now again thrown into disorder all the Churches of Alexandria and of Egypt and Libya, and has publicly given orders, that the Bishops of the Catholic Church and faith be cast out of them, and that they be given up to the professors of the Arian doctrines. The General began to carry this order into execution; and straightway Bishops were sent off in chains, and Presbyters and Monks bound with iron, after being almost beaten to death with stripes. Disorder prevails in every place; all Egypt and Libya are in danger, the people being indignant at this unjust command, and seeing in it the preparation for the coming of Antichrist, and beholding their property plundered by others, and given up into the hands of the heretics.

§. 71. 10. When was ever such iniquity heard of? when was such an evil deed ever perpetrated, even in times of persecution? They were heathens who persecuted formerly; but they did not bring their idols into the Churches. Zenobia was a Jewess, and a supporter of Paul of Samosata; but she did not give up the Churches to the Jews for Synagogues. This is a new piece of iniquity[1]. It is not simply persecution, but more than persecution, it is a prelude and preparation[2] for the coming of Antichrist. Even if it be admitted[3] that they invented false charges against Athanasius and the rest of the Bishops whom they banished, yet what is this to their later practices? What charges have they to allege

[1] μύσος
[2] vol. 8. p. 79, note q.
[3] ἴστω, p. 221, r. 5.

against the whole of Egypt and Libya and Pentapolis[1]? For they have begun no longer to lay their plots against individuals, in which case they might be able to frame a lie against them; but they have set upon all in a body, so that, however they may wish to invent accusations against them, they must be condemned. Thus their wickedness has blinded their understanding; and they have required, without any reason assigned, that the whole body of the Bishops shall be expelled, and thereby they shew that the charges they framed against Athanasius and the rest of the Bishops whom they banished were false, and invented for no other purpose than to support the accursed heresy of the Arian enemies of Christ.

11. This is now no longer concealed, but has become most manifest to all men. He commanded Athanasius to be expelled out of the city, and gave up the Churches to them. And the Presbyters and Deacons that were with him, who had been appointed by Peter and Alexander, were also expelled and driven into banishment; and the real Arians, who not through any suspicions arising from circumstances[2], but on account of the heresy had been expelled at first together with Arius himself by the Bishop Alexander, Secundus in Libya, in Alexandria Euzoius[3] the Chananean, Julius, Ammon, Marcus, Irenæus, Zozimus, and Serapion surnamed Pelycon, and in Libya Sisinnius, and the younger men with him, associates in his impiety; these obtained possession of the Churches. And the General Sebastian wrote to the governors and military authorities in every place; and the true Bishops were persecuted, and those who professed impious doctrines were brought in in their stead. They banished Bishops who had grown old in orders[4], and had been many years in the Episcopate, having been ordained by the Bishop Alexander; Ammonius[5], Hermes, Anagamphus, and Marcus, they sent to the Upper Oasis; Muis, Psenosiris, Nilammon, Plenes, Marcus, and Athenodorus to Ammoniaca, with no other intention than that they should perish in their passage through the deserts. They had no pity on them though they were suffering from disease, and indeed proceeded on their journey with so much difficulty on account of their weakness, that they were

TR. VIII
70—72.
[1] p. 221,
§. 3.

[2] ἔξωθεν

[3] infr.
Dep.
Ar.

§. 72.

[4] κλήρῳ
[5] p. 193.

ARIAN HIST.
¹ pp.228, 193, r.2.
² p. 193.
³ ἀρχαί-ους, p. 255, r.5.
⁴ p. 192.
⁵ p 193. of the 40 men.
⁶ misbe- hevers.
⁷ p. 280, r. 1.
⁸ p 275, r. 4.
⁹ μονα- στήρια
¹⁰ p.274, r. 1.
§. 73.

obliged to be carried in litters, and their sickness was so dangerous that the materials for their burial accompanied them. One of them indeed died, but they would not even permit the body to be given up to his friends for interment¹. With the same purpose they banished also the Bishop Dracontius² to the desert places about Clysma, Philo to Babylon, Adelphius to Psinabla in the Thebais, and the Presbyters Hierax and Dioscorus to Syene. They likewise drove into exile Ammonius, Agathus, Agathodæmon, Apollonius, Eulogius, Apollo, Paphnutius, Gaius, and Flavius, ancient³ Bishops, as also the Bishops Dioscorus, Ammonius, Heraclides, and Psais; some of whom they gave up to work in the stone-quarries, others they persecuted with an intention to destroy, and many others they plundered.

12. They banished also forty of the laity, with certain virgins whom they had before exposed to the fire⁴; beating them so severely with rods taken from the palm-tree, that after lingering five days some of them died, and others had recourse to medical treatment on account of the thorns left in their limbs, from which they suffered torments worse than death⁵. But what is most dreadful to the mind of any man of sound understanding, though characteristic of these miscreants⁶, is this: When the Virgins during the scourging called upon the Name of Christ, they gnashed their teeth against them with increased fury⁷. Nay more, they would not give up the bodies of the dead to their friends for burial, but concealed them that they might appear to be ignorant of the murder. They did not however escape detection; the whole city perceived it, and all men withdrew from them as executioners⁸, as malefactors and robbers. Moreover they overthrew monasteries⁹, and endeavoured to cast the Monks into the fire; they plundered houses, and breaking into the house of certain free citizens where the Bishop had deposited a treasure, they plundered and took it away. They scourged the widows on the soles of their feet¹⁰, and hindered them from receiving their alms.

13. Such were the iniquities practised by the Arians; and as to their further deeds of impiety, who could bear the account of them without shuddering? They had caused these venerable old men and aged Bishops to be sent into

banishment; they now appointed in their stead profligate heathen youths, whom they thought to raise at once to the highest dignity, though they were not even Catechumens[1]. And others who were accused of bigamy[e], and even of worse crimes, they nominated Bishops on account of the wealth and civil power which they possessed, and sent them out as it were from a market, upon their giving them gold[2]. And now more dreadful calamities befel the people. For when they rejected these mercenary dependents of the Arians, so alien from themselves, they were scourged, they were proscribed, they were shut up in prison by the General, (who did all this readily, being a Manichee,) in order that they might no longer seek after their own Bishops, but be forced to accept those whom they abominated, men who were now guilty of the same mockeries as they had before practised among their idols.

14. Will not every just person break forth into lamentations at the sight or hearing of these things, at perceiving the arrogance and extreme injustice of these impious men? *The righteous lament in the place of the impious.* After all these things, and now that the impiety has reached such a pitch of audacity, who will any longer venture to call this Costyllius[f] a Christian, and not rather the image of Antichrist? For what mark of Antichrist is yet wanting to him? How can he in any way fail to be regarded as he? or how can the latter fail to be supposed such a one as he is? Did not the Arians and the Gentiles offer those sacrifices in the great Church in the Cæsareum[3], and utter their blasphemies against Christ as by His command? And does not the vision of Daniel thus describe Antichrist; that he shall make war with the saints, and prevail against them, and exceed all that have been before him in evil deeds, and shall humble three kings, and speak words against the Most High, and shall think to change times and laws? Now what other person besides Constantius has ever attempted to do these things? He is surely such a one as Antichrist would be. He speaks words against the Most High by supporting this

TR VIII
72—74.
[1] vid. Hallier de Ordin. part 2. 1, 1. art. 2.
[2] p 5, r. 1. p 135, r. 1.

§. 74.
Prov. 28, 28. Sept.

[3] p. 269, note 1.

[e] διγυναίοις, not διγάμοις, on the latter, vid. Suicer, Thes. in voc. διγαμία. Tertull. Works, tr. vol. 1. p. 419, note N.
[f] An irregularly formed diminutive, or a quasi diminutive from Constantius, as Agathyllus from Agathocles, Heryllus from Heracles, &c. vid. Matth. Gr. Gramm. §. 102. ed. 1820.

impious heresy: he makes war against the saints by banishing the Bishops; although indeed he exercises this power but for a little while[g] to his own destruction. Moreover he has surpassed those before him in wickedness, having devised a new mode of persecution; and after he had overthrown three kings, namely Vetranio, Magnentius, and Gallus, he straightway undertook the patronage[1] of impiety; and like a giant[h] he has dared in his pride to set himself up against the Most High.

15. He has thought to change laws, by transgressing the ordinance of the Lord given us through His Apostles, by altering the customs of the Church, and inventing a new kind of ordinations. For he sends from strange places distant a fifty days' journey[2], Bishops attended by soldiers to people unwilling to receive them; and instead of an introduction to the acquaintance of their people, they bring with them threatening messages, and letters to the magistrates. Thus he has sent Gregory from Cappadocia to Alexandria; he has transferred Germinius[3] from Cyzicus to Sirmium; he has removed Cecropius[4] from Laodicea to Nicomedia. Again he transferred from Cappadocia to Milan one Auxentius[5], a man pragmatical rather than Christian, whom he commanded to stay there after he had banished for his piety towards Christ, Dionysius the Bishop of the place, a godly man. But this person was as yet even ignorant of the Latin language, and unskilful in every thing except impiety. And now one George a Cappadocian, who was contractor of stores[6] at Constantinople, and having embezzled all monies that he received, was obliged to fly, he commanded to enter Alexandria with military pomp, and supported by the authority of the General. And he, finding there one Epictetus[i] a novice, a bold young

---

[g] Short lives are generally considered the destiny of the Church's persecutors, and length of days the token of her protectors. What of old was said of pain, applies to persecution—si gravis, brevis; Antichrist's oppression seems to be marked out as three years and a half. Constantius died at 45, having openly apostatized for about six years. Julian died at 32, after a reign of a year and a half. vid. supr. p. 245, r 4. vid. also Bellarmin. de Notis Eccl. 17. and 18.

[h] vid. de Decr. §. 32. tr. p. 58, note m. Orat. ii. §. 32. Naz. Orat. 43, 26. Socr. Hist. v. 10. p. 268.

[i] Epictetus is mentioned above, p. 133, where he is called ὑποκρίτης, which after Montfaucon was translated "stage-player." It is a question, however, especially considering the correspondence between that passage and the present, whether more than 'actor' is meant by it, alluding to the mockery of an ordination in which he seems to have taken part. Though an Asiatic apparently

Substitution of Felix at Rome for Liberius. 287

man, made him his friend[k], perceiving that he was ready for any wickedness; and by his means he carries on his designs against those of the Bishops whom he desires to ruin. For he is prepared to do every thing that the Emperor wishes; who accordingly availing himself of his assistance, has committed at Rome a strange act, but one truly resembling the malice of Antichrist. Having made preparations in the Palace instead of the Church, and caused some three of his own eunuchs to attend instead of the people, he then compelled three[l] ill-conditioned spies[l], (for one cannot call them Bishops,) to ordain forsooth as Bishop one Felix[m], a man worthy of them, then in the Palace. For the people perceiving the iniquitous proceedings of the heretics would not allow them to enter the Churches, and withdrew themselves entirely from them.

TR VIII.
74—76.

pp.221,
fin. 263,
f. 5.

16. Now what is yet wanting to make him Antichrist? what more could Antichrist do at his coming than this man has done? Will he not find when he comes that the way has been already prepared for him by this man easily to deceive the people? Again, he claims to himself the right of deciding causes, which he refers to the Court instead of the Church, and presides at them in person. And strange it is to say, when he perceives the accusers at a loss, he takes up the accusation himself, so that the injured party may no longer be able to defend himself on account of the violence which he displays. This he did in the proceedings against Athanasius. For when he saw the boldness of the Bishops Paulinus, Lucifer, Eusebius, and Dionysius, and how out of

§. 76.

---

by birth, he was made Bishop of Civita Vecchia. We hear of him at the conference between Constantius and Liberius. Theod. Hist. ii. 14. Then he assists in the ordination of Felix. Afterwards he made a martyr of S. Ruffinian by making him run before his carriage; and he ends his historical career by taking a chief part among the Arians at Ariminum, vid. Tillem. t. 6. p. 380, &c. Ughell. Ital. t. 10. p. 56

[k] The Greek is 'Επιτηδειότητά τινα... νεώτερον... ἠγάπησεν, ἐρῶν π. τ λ So in the account of the νεανίσκος, 'Ο δὲ Ἰησοῦς ἐμβλέψας αὐτῷ, ἠγάπησεν αὐτόν. Mark x. 21.

[l] i. e. to keep up the form of the canonical number; and so a century earlier, in the case of Novatian, in the same see, while the capital was still heathen, we read in Eusebius that he brought from some obscure part of Italy "three Bishops," "rustic and ignorant," who after a full meal, when they were not themselves, consecrated him. Hist. vi. 43. On the custom itself, vid. Bingh. Antiqu ii. 11. §. 4.

[m] This Felix has been in after times accounted a true Pope and Martyr, and has been supposed to have condemned Constantius. The circumstances will be found in Tillemont, Mem. t. 6. p. 778. Bolland. Catal. Pontif. Gibbon, ch. 21. p. 390.

the recantation of Ursacius and Valens they confuted those who spoke against the Bishop, and advised that Valens and his associate should no longer be believed since they had already retracted what they now asserted, he immediately stood up and said, " I am now the accuser of Athanasius; on my account you must believe what these assert." And then, when they said,—" But how can you be an accuser, when the accused person is not present? and if you are his accuser, yet he is not present, and therefore cannot be tried. And the cause is not one that concerns Rome, so that you should be believed as being the Emperor; but it is a matter that concerns a Bishop; and the trial ought to be conducted on equal terms both to the accuser and the accused. And besides, how can you accuse him? for you could not be present to witness the conduct of one who lived at so great a distance from you; and if you speak but what you have heard from these, you ought also to give credit to what he says; but if you will not believe him, while you do believe them, it is plain that they assert these things for your sake, and accuse Athanasius only to gratify you[1]?"—when he heard this, thinking that what they had so truly spoken was an insult to himself, he sent them into banishment; and being exasperated against Athanasius, he wrote in a more savage strain, requiring that he should suffer what has now befallen him, and that the Churches should be given up to the Arians, and that they should be allowed to do whatever they pleased.

§. 77. 17. Terrible indeed, and worse than terrible are such proceedings; and yet is this conduct suitable to him who represents the character of Antichrist. Who that beheld him bearing sway over his pretended Bishops, and presiding in Ecclesiastical causes, would not justly exclaim that this was *the abomination of desolation* spoken of by Daniel? For having put on the profession of Christianity, and entering into the holy places, and standing therein, he lays waste the Churches, transgressing their Canons, and enforcing the observance of his own decrees. Will any one now venture to say that this is a peaceful time with Christians, and not a time of persecution? A persecution indeed, such as never arose before, and such as no one perhaps will again stir up, except *the son of lawlessness*, do these enemies of Christ exhibit, who already present a picture of him in their own persons   Wherefore it especially behoves us to be sober, lest this heresy which has reached such a height of impudence, and has diffused itself abroad like the *poison of an adder*, as it is written in the Proverbs, and which teaches doctrines contrary to the Saviour; lest, I say, this be that *falling away*, after which He shall be revealed, of whom Constantius is surely the forerunner[1]. Else wherefore is he so mad against the godly? wherefore does he contend for it as his own heresy, and call every one his enemy who will not comply with the madness of Arius, and admit gladly the allegations of the enemies of Christ, and dishonour so many venerable Councils? why did he command that the Churches should be given up to the Arians? was it not that, when that other comes, he may thus find a way to enter into them, and may take to himself him who has prepared those places for him?

TR. VIII 77, 78. 2 Thess. 2, 8. Ps. 58, 4. 2 Thess. 2, 3. [1] πρόδρο- μος, vid. vol. 8. p. 79, note q.

18. For the ancient Bishops who were ordained by Alexander, and by his predecessor Achilles, and by Peter before him, have been cast out; and those introduced whom the companions of soldiers nominated; and they nominated only such as promised to adopt their doctrines. This was an easy proposition for the Meletians to comply with; for the greater part, or rather the whole of them, have never had a religious education, nor are they acquainted with the *sound faith*[2] in Christ, nor do they know at all what Christianity is, or what writings we Christians possess. For having come out, some of them from the worship of idols, and others from the senate, or from the first civil offices, for the sake of the miserable exemption[3] from duty and for the patronage they gained, and having bribed[4] the Meletians who preceded them, they have been advanced to this dignity even before they were Catechumens. And even if they pretended to have been such, yet what kind of instruction[5] is to be obtained among the Meletians? But indeed without even pretending to have been instructed, they came at once, and immediately were called Bishops, just as children receive a name. Being then persons of this description, they thought the thing of no great consequence, nor even sup-

§. 78. [2] p. 149, r. 3. [3] pp. 84, 85. [4] pp 89, 151, 291. [5] catechising.

posed that piety[1] was different from impiety. Accordingly from being Meletians they readily and speedily became Arians, and if the Emperor should command them to adopt any other profession, they are ready to change again to that also. Their ignorance of true godliness[1] quickly brings them to submit to the prevailing folly, and that which happens to be first taught them. For it is nothing to them to be carried about by every wind and tempest, so long as they are only exempt from duty, and obtain the patronage of men; nor would they care probably to change again[2] to what they were before, even to become such as they were when they were heathens.

19. Any how, being men of such an easy temper, and considering the Church as a civil senate[3], and like heathen, being infected with the worship of idols, they have put on the honourable name of our Saviour, under which they have polluted the whole of Egypt, were it only that they have caused the name of the Arian heresy to be known therein. For Egypt has heretofore been the only country, throughout which the profession of the orthodox faith was boldly maintained[4]; and therefore these misbelievers have striven to introduce jealousy there also, or rather not they, but the Devil who has stirred them up, in order that when his herald Antichrist shall come, he may find that the Churches in Egypt also are his own, and that the Meletians have already been instructed in his principles, and may recognise himself as already formed[5] in them.

§. 79. Such is the effect of that iniquitous[6] order which was issued by Constantius. On the part of the people there was displayed a ready alacrity to submit to martyrdom, and an increased hatred of this most impious heresy; and yet lamentations for their Churches, and groans burst from all, while they cried unto the Lord, "*Spare Thy people, O Lord, and give not Thine heritage unto Thine enemies to reproach; but make haste to deliver us out of the hand of the lawless*[7]. *For behold, they have not spared Thy servants, but are preparing the way for Antichrist.*"

20. For the Meletians will never resist him, nor will they care for the truth, nor will they esteem it an evil thing to deny Christ. They are men who have not approached the

Lord with sincerity; like the chameleon[1] they assume every various appearance; they are hirelings[2] of any who will make use of them. They make not the truth their aim, but prefer before it their present pleasures; they say only, *Let us eat and drink, for to-morrow we die.* Such a profession and faithless temper is more worthy of the Epicritian[3] players than of the Meletians. But the faithful servants of our Saviour, and the true Bishops who believe with sincerity, and live not for themselves, but for the Lord; they faithfully believing in our Lord Jesus Christ, and knowing, as I said before, that the charges which were alleged against the truth were false, and plainly fabricated for the sake of the Arian heresy, (for by the recantation[4] of Ursacius and Valens they detected the calumnies which were devised against Athanasius, for the purpose of removing him out of the way, and of introducing into the Churches the impieties of the enemies of Christ;) they, I say, perceiving all this, as defenders and preachers of the truth, chose rather, and endured to be insulted and driven into banishment, than to subscribe against him, and to hold communion with the Arian fanatics. They forgot not the lessons they had taught to others; yea, they know well that great dishonour remains for the traitors, but for them which confess the truth, the kingdom of heaven[5]; and that to the careless and such as fear Constantius will happen no good thing, but for them that endure tribulations here, as sailors reach a quiet haven after a storm, as wrestlers receive a crown after the combat, so these shall obtain great and eternal joy and delight in heaven,—such as Joseph obtained after his tribulations; such as the great Daniel had after his temptations and the manifold conspiracies of the courtiers against him; such as Paul now enjoys having received a crown from his Saviour; such as the people of God every where expect. They, seeing these things, were not infirm of purpose, but strong in faith, and increased in their zeal more and more. Being fully persuaded of the calumnies and impieties of the heretics, they condemn the persecutor, and in heart and mind run together the same course with them that are persecuted, that they also may obtain the crown of Confession.

TR VIII 79, 80
[1] vol. 8. p 2.
note c.
[2] p. 289, r. 4.
1 Cor. 15, 32.
[3] histrionum genus Montf.
[4] p. 86.
[5] supr. p 213, r. 1.

21. One might say much more against this accused and §. 80.

ARIAN HIST. antichristian heresy, and might demonstrate by many arguments that the practices of Constantius are a prelude to the coming of Antichrist. But seeing that, as the Prophet has said, from the feet even to the head there is no soundness in it, but it is full of all filthiness and all impiety, so that the very name[1] of it ought to be avoided as a dog's vomit or the poison of serpents; and seeing that Costyllius openly exhibits the image of the adversary[2]; in order that our words may not be too many, it will be well to content[n] ourselves with the divine Scripture, and that we all obey the precept[3] which it has given us both in regard to other heresies, and especially respecting this. That precept is as follows; *Depart ye, depart ye, go ye out from thence, touch no unclean thing; go ye out of the midst of them, and be ye clean, that bear the vessels of the Lord.* This may suffice[n] to instruct us all, so that if any one has been deceived by them, he may go out from them, as out of Sodom, and not return again unto them, lest he suffer the fate of Lot's wife; and if any one has continued from the beginning pure from this impious heresy, he may glory in Christ and say, *" We have not stretched out our hands to a strange god;* neither have we worshipped the works of our own hands, nor served the creature[4] more than Thee, the God that hast created all things through Thy Word, the Only-begotten Son our Lord Jesus Christ, through whom to Thee the Father together with the same Word in the Holy Spirit be glory and power for ever and ever. Amen."

[1] p. 138.
[2] ἀντι-κειμένου, 2 Thess. 2, 4.
[3] supr. p. 148.
Is. 52, 11.
Ps. 44, 20.
[4] supr. p. 141, r l.

[n] καλὸν ἀρκεσθῆναι, τοῦτο ἀρκεῖ and so ἤρκει μὲν γὰρ, Apol. contr. Ar. 2 init. ἱκανὰ μὲν οὖν ταῦτα de Decr. 15 init. καὶ ἤρκει μὲν ταῦτα, de Sent D. 4 init. ἀρκεῖ γὰρ αὐτοὺς, Apol. de Fug. 1 fin. ἱκανὰ μὲν οὖν ταῦτα, ibid 24 init ἱκανὸν μὲν οὖν καὶ τοῦτο, ad Serap. de M A.

5 init. ἔστι μὲν οὖν τοῦτο ἱκανὸν, Orat. 1. 17. ἱκανὰ μὲν οὖν, Ep. ad Serap. iii. 2 init. ἀρκεῖ ταῦτα, ad Serap. iv. 7 init. ἀρκεῖ ὅτι, ad Epict. Vid. also Orat. 1. 7. B. Orat. ii init. Orat. iii 47. Ep Æg. 9 init. ad Serap. iv. 1 init. ad Max. 5. &c

The Second Protest [a].

1. The people of the Catholic Church in Alexandria, which §. 81. is under the government of the most Reverend Bishop Athanasius, make this public protest by those whose names are under-written.

We have already protested against the nocturnal assault which was committed upon ourselves and the Lord's house[1], [1 κυριακὸν] although in truth there needed no protest in respect to proceedings with which the whole city has been already made acquainted. For the bodies of the slain which were discovered were exposed in public, and the bows and arrows and other arms found in the Lord's house loudly proclaim the iniquity.

2. But whereas after our Protest already made, the most illustrious Duke Syrianus endeavours to force all men to agree with him, as though no tumult had been made, nor any had perished, (wherein is no small proof that these things were not done according to the wishes of the most gracious Emperor Augustus Constantius; for he would not have been so much afraid of the consequences of this transaction, had he acted therein by command;) and whereas also, when we went to him, and requested him not to do violence to any, nor to deny what had taken place, he ordered us, being Christians, to be beaten with clubs, thereby again giving proof of the nocturnal assault which has been directed against the Church.—

We therefore make also this present Protest, certain of us being now about to travel to the most religious Emperor

---

[a] Of the two Protests referred to supr. p. 263, the first was omitted by the copyists, as being already contained, as Montfaucon seems to say, in the Apology against the Arians, yet if it be the one to which allusion is made in the beginning of the Protest which follows, it is not found there, nor does it appear what document of A D 356 could properly have a place in a set of papers which end with A D 350.

Augustus: and we adjure Maximus the Prefect of Egypt, and the Controllers[1], in the name of Almighty God, and for the sake of the salvation of the most religious Augustus Constantius, to relate all these things to the piety of Augustus, and to the authority of the most illustrious Prefects[2]. We adjure also all the masters of vessels, to publish these things every where, and to carry them to the ears of the most religious Augustus, and to the Prefects and the Magistrates in every place, in order that it may be known that a war has been waged against the Church, and that, in the times[3] of Augustus Constantius, Syrianus has caused Virgins and many others to become martyrs.

3. As it dawned upon the fifth before the Ides of February[4], that is to say, the fourteenth of the month Mechir, while we were keeping vigil[5] in the Lord's house, and engaged in our prayers (for there was to be a communion on the Preparation[6]); suddenly about midnight, the most illustrious Duke Syrianus attacked us and the Church with many legions of soldiers[7] armed with naked swords and javelins and other warlike instruments, and wearing helmets on their heads; and even while we were praying, and while the lessons were being read, they broke down the doors. And when the doors were burst open by the violence of the multitude, he gave command, and some of them shot their arrows; others shouted; their arms rattled, and their swords flashed in the light of the lamps; and forthwith the Virgins were slain, many men were trampled down, and fell over one another as the soldiers came upon them, and several were pierced with arrows and perished. Some of the soldiers also betook themselves to plundering, and stripped the Virgins naked, who were more afraid of being even touched by them than they were of death.

4. The Bishop continued sitting upon his throne, and exhorted all to pray. The Duke led on the attack, having with him Hilarius the notary, whose part in the proceedings was shewn in the sequel. The Bishop was seized, and hardly escaped being torn to pieces; and having fallen into a state of insensibility, and appearing as one dead, he disappeared from among them, and has gone we know not whither. They were eager to kill him. And when they saw that many had

perished, they gave orders to the soldiers to remove out of sight the bodies of the dead. But the most holy Virgins who were left there were buried in the tombs, having attained the glory of martyrdom in the times[1] of the most religious Constantius. Deacons also were beaten with stripes even in the Lord's house, and were shut up there.

[1] p. 294, r 2.

5. Nor did matters stop even here: for after all this had happened, whosoever pleased broke open any door that he could, and searched, and plundered what was within. They entered even into those places, which not even all Christians are allowed to enter. Gorgonius the commander of the city force[b] knows this, for he was present. And no unimportant evidence of the nature of this hostile assault is afforded by the circumstance, that the armour and javelins and swords borne by those who entered were left in the Lord's house. They have been hung up in the Church until this time, that they might not be able to deny it: and although they sent several times Dynamius the soldier[2], as well as the Commander of the city police, desiring to take them away, we would not allow it, until the circumstance was known to all.

[2] τὸν τῆς τάξεως, 1 e. supr p. 274. στρατιώτου

6. Now if an order has been given that we should be persecuted, we are all ready to suffer martyrdom. But if it be not by order of Augustus, we desire Maximus the Prefect of Egypt and all the city magistrates to request of him that they may not again be suffered thus to assail us. And we desire also that this our petition may be presented to him, that they may not attempt to bring in hither any other Bishop: for we have resisted unto death[3], desiring to have the most Reverend Athanasius, whom God gave us at the beginning, according to the succession of our fathers; whom also the most religious Augustus Constantius himself sent to us with letters and oaths. And we believe that when his Piety is informed of what has taken place, he will be greatly displeased, and will do nothing contrary to his oath, but will

[3] pp. 63, 81

---

[b] στρατηγοῦ. There were two στρατηγοὶ or duumvirs at the head of the police force at Alexandria; they are mentioned in the plural in Euseb. vii. 11. where S. Dionysius speaks of their seizing him. We read of them at Philippi in Luke 16, 35. vid. Vales *in loc.* Euseb. et in Amm. Marc. xxxi. 6. The word is translated in the Justinian Code, Prætor. vid. Du Cange, Gloss. Græc. *in voc.*

again give orders that our Bishop Athanasius shall remain with us.

To the Consuls to be elected^c after the Consulship of the most illustrious Arbæthion and Collianus[1]; on the seventeenth Mechir, which is the day before the Ides of February[2].

¹ Lolli-anus.
² Febr. 12.

^c Since the Consuls came into office on the first of January, and were proclaimed in each city, vid. p 153, note m, it is strange that the Alexandrians here speak in February as if ignorant of their names. The phrase, however, is found elsewhere. Thus in this very year the Anonymus Maffeianus, (who is spoken of in the Preface of this Volume,) dates Jan. 5. as " post Consulatum Arbitionis et Loliani." And in Socr. Hist. ii. 29. in the instance of the year 351, when there were no Consuls, and in 346, when there was a difference on the subject between the Emperors who were eventually themselves Consuls, the first months are dated in like manner from the Consuls of the foregoing year.

APPENDIX.

S. Alexander's Deposition of Arius and his companions, and Encyclical Letter on the subject.

[As Montfaucon has introduced the two documents which follow into his Edition, it has been thought that, though not Athanasius's, they might occupy a place in a volume, like the present, which already contains so large a collection of the ecclesiastical tracts and papers of the day to which it belongs. Should the internal character of the Encyclical Letter lead to the suspicion that it is probably Athan.'s own composition, in his situation of Deacon to St. Alexander, or at least as being in his intimate confidence, there will be a further reason for introducing it here. The grounds of this conjecture are such as the following. 1. It is written in a style altogether unlike S. Alexander's, which, (as we see in his Epistle to S. Alexander of Constantinople contained in Theod. Hist. i. 3) is elaborate and involved and abounding in compound words, with nothing of the simplicity and vigor of St. Athan.'s; with which, 2 the style of this document is identical, using the very same words and terms of expression for which Athan. is so remarkable. 3. The theological terms, nay the theological view, of St Alex , is proper to himself, and could not suitably be ascribed to S. Athan., who, to say no more, has far fewer technical phrases than his predecessor; and here the Encyclical Epistle answers to S Athan's writings, not to St. Alex's. 4 Certain texts quoted in the course of it, are used as Athan quotes and uses them in his acknowledged works. Some of these points of resemblance and dissimilarity shall be mentioned in the notes. The date of St. Alexander's document is 321.]

Alexander, being assembled[1] with his beloved brethren, the Presbyters and Deacons of Alexandria, and the Mareotis, greets them in the Lord.

Although you have already subscribed to the letter I addressed to the followers of Arius, exhorting them to renounce his impiety, and to submit themselves to the sound Catholic Faith, and have shewn your right-mindedness[2] and agreement in the doctrines of the Catholic Church; yet forasmuch as I have written also to our fellow-ministers in every place concerning the Arians, and especially since some of you, as the Presbyters Chares and Pistus[3], and the Deacons Serapion,

[1] παρὼν
[2] ὀρθὴν
[3] pp 37, 44.

Parammon, Zozimus, and Irenæus, have joined the Arian party, and been content to suffer deposition with them, I thought it needful to assemble together you, the Clergy of the city, and to send for you the Clergy of the Mareotis, in order that you may understand what I have now written, and may testify your agreement thereto, and give your concurrence in the deposition of the followers of Arius and Pistus. For it is desirable that you should be made acquainted with the sentiments I have expressed, and that each of you should heartily embrace them, as though he had written them himself.

A Copy.

To his dearly beloved and most honoured fellow-ministers[1] of the Catholic Church in every place, Alexander sends health in the Lord.

[1] συλλειτουργοῖς, colleagues.

1. As there is one body[a] of the Catholic Church, and a command is given us in the sacred Scriptures to preserve the bond of unity and peace, it is agreeable thereto, that we should write and signify to one another whatever is done by each of us individually; so that whether one member suffer or rejoice, we may either suffer or rejoice with one another. Now there are gone forth in this diocese, at this time, certain lawless[b] men, enemies of Christ, teaching an apostasy, which one may justly suspect and designate as the forerunner[c] of Antichrist. I was desirous[d] to pass such a matter by without notice, in the hope that perhaps the evil would spend itself among its supporters, and not extend to other places to defile[e] the ears[f] of the simple[g]. But seeing that Eusebius now of Nicomedia, who thinks that the government of the Church rests with him, because retribution has not come upon him for his desertion of Berytus, when he had cast an eye[h] of desire on the Church of the Nicomedians, begins to support these apostates, and has taken upon him to write letters every where in their behalf, if by any means he may draw in certain ignorant persons to this most base and antichristian heresy; I am therefore constrained, knowing what is written in the law, no longer to hold my peace, but to make it known to you all; that you may understand who the apostates are, and the unhappy terms[i] which their heresy has adopted, and that, should Eusebius write to you, you may pay no attention to him, for he now desires by means of these men to exhibit anew his old

§. 1.
Eph. 4, 3.

---

[a] St. Alexander in Theod. begins his Epistle to his namesake of Constantinople with some moral reflections, concerning ambition and avarice. Athan. indeed uses a similar introduction to his Ep Æg. but it is not addressed to an individual.

[b] παράνομοι vid. Hist. Ar. §. 71 init. §. 75 fin. 79. A.

[c] πρόδρομον Ἀντιχρίστου, vid. Orat. 1. 7. B. Vit. Ant. 69. A vol. 8. p. 79, note q.

[d] καὶ ἐβουλόμην μὲν σιωπῇ ... ἐπειδὴ δὲ ... ἀνάγκην ἔσχον. vid Apol. contr. Ar §. 1 init. de Decr §. 2. F Orat. 1. 23 init Orat. 11 init. Orat. 111. 1. A ad Serap. 1 1. C. 16. C. 11. 1 init. 111 init. iv. 8 init. Ep. ad Mon. § 2 E ad Epict

3 fin. ad Max. §. 1. contr. Apollin. i 1 init.

[e] ῥυπώσῃ, and infr. ῥύπον. vid. Hist. Ar. §. 3. C. §. 80. B. de Decr. §. 2. C. Ep. Æg. 11 fin. Orat. 1. 10. C.

[f] ἀκοὰς, and infr. ἀκοὰς βύει. vid. Ep. Æg. §. 13. A. Orat. 1 §. 7. A. Hist. Ar. § 56. B.

[g] ἀκεραίων Apol. contr. Ar. § 1. A. Ep. Æg. §. 18. E. ad Epict. §. 1. fin. ad Adelph. §. 2. fin. Orat. 1. 8. E.

[h] ἐποφθαλμίσας also used of Eusebius. Apol. contr. Ar. §. 6. D. Hist. Ar. §. 7. A.

[i] ῥημάτια. vid. de Decr. §. 8. A. 18. E. Orat. 1. 10. D. de Sent. D. § 23. init. B. Dionysius also uses it. ibid. § 18. A.

malevolence[k], which has so long been concealed, pretending to write in their favour, while in truth it clearly appears, that he does it to forward his own interests

§. 2. 2. Now the apostates are these, Arius, Achilles, Anthales, Carpones, another Arius, and Sarmates, sometime Presbyters; Euzoius, Lucius, Julius, Menas, Helladius, and Gaius, sometime Deacons; and with them Secundus and Theonas, sometime called Bishops. And the novelties they have invented and put forth contrary to the Scriptures are these following:—God was not always a Father[l], but there was a time when God was not a Father. The Word of God was not always, but was made of things that were not: for God that is, made Him that was not, of things that were not; wherefore there was a time when He was not; for the Son is a creature and a work. Neither is He like in substance to the Father; neither is He the true and natural Word of the Father; neither is He His true Wisdom; but He is one of the things made and created, and is called the Word and Wisdom by an abuse of terms, since He Himself was made by the proper Word of God, and by the Wisdom that is in God, by which God made not only all other things but Him also. Wherefore He is by nature subject to change and variation, as are all rational creatures. And the Word is foreign from the substance[m] of the Father, and is alien and separate therefrom. And the Father cannot be described by the Son, for the Word does not know the Father perfectly and accurately, neither can He see Him perfectly. Moreover, the Son knows not His own substance as it really is; for He was created for us, that God might create us by Him, as by an instrument; and He would not have existed, had not God wished to create us. Accordingly, when some one asked them, whether the Word of God can possibly change as the devil changed, they were not afraid to say that He can; for being something made and created, His nature is subject to change.

§. 3. 3. Now when the Arians made these assertions, and shamelessly avowed them, we being assembled with the Bishops of Egypt and Libya, nearly a hundred in number, anathematized both them and

---

[k] κακόνοιαν vid. Hist Ar. §. 75 E. de Decr §. 1. D. et al.

[l] οὐκ ἀεὶ πατήρ This enumeration of Arius's tenets, and particularly the mention of the first, corresponds to de Decr. §. 6. Ep. Æg. § 12. as being taken from the Thalia Orat. 1 §. 5. and far less with Alex. ap. Theod p. 731, 2. vid also Sent. D. §. 16. καταχρηστικῶς, which is found here, occurs de Decr. §. 6. B.

[m] οὐσίαν οὐσία τοῦ λόγου or τοῦ υἱοῦ is a familiar expression with Athan. e. g Orat. 1 45 11 7 B.9. B.11.B.12 A 13. B C. 18 init 22. E. 47 init 56 init &c. for which Alex. in Theod. uses the word ὑπόστασις. e. g. τὴν ἰδιότροπον αὐτοῦ ὑπόστασιν τῆς ὑποστάσεως αὐτοῦ ἀτεκμηγάστου νεωτέραν τῆς ὑποστάσεως γένεσιν ἢ τοῦ μονογενοῦς ἀνεκδιήγητος ὑπόστασις τὴν τοῦ λόγου ὑπόστασιν

Appendix.

their followers. But the Eusebians admitted them to communion, being desirous to mingle falsehood with the truth, and impiety with piety But they will not be able to do so, for the truth must prevail; neither is there any *communion of light with darkness*, nor any *concord of Christ with Belial*[n]. For who ever heard such assertions before[o]? or who that hears them now is not astonished and does not stop his ears lest their filthy language should touch them? Who that has heard the words of John, *In the beginning was the Word*, will not denounce the saying of these men, that " there was a time when He was not?" Or who that has heard in the Gospel, *the Only-begotten Son*, and *by Him were all things made*, will not detest their declaration that He is " one of the things that were made " For how can He be one of those things which were made by Himself? or how can He be the Only-begotten, when, according to them, He is counted as one among the rest, since He is Himself a creature and a work? And how can He be "made of things that were not," when the Father saith, *My heart hath brought forth a good Word*, and, *Out of the womb I have begotten Thee before the morning star?* Or again, how is He " unlike in substance to the Father," seeing He is the perfect *image* and *brightness* of the Father, and that He saith, *He that hath seen Me hath seen the Father*[p]? And if the Son is the *Word* and *Wisdom* of God, how was there " a time when He was not?" It is the same as if they should say that God was once without Word and without Wisdom[q]. And how is He " subject to change and variation," who says, by Himself, *I am in the Father, and the Father in Me*, and, *I and the Father are one*[p]; and by the Prophet, *Behold Me, for I am, and I change not*[r]? For although one may refer this expression to the Father, yet it may now be more aptly spoken of the Word, viz. that though He has been made man, He has not changed; but as the Apostle has said, *Jesus Christ is the same yesterday, to-day, and for ever*. And who can have persuaded them to say, that He was made for us, whereas Paul writes, *for whom are all things, and by whom are all things?* As to their blasphemous position that " the

2 Cor 6, 14

John 1, 1.

Ib. 14. and 18. 3.

Ps. 45, 1. Ib 110, 3.

Heb. 1, 3. John 14, 9.

v. 10, Ib. 10, 30. Mal. 3, 6.

Heb 13, 8.

Ib 2, 10.

§. 4.

---

[n] κοινωνία φωτί. This is quoted Alex. ap. Theod. Hist. 1. 3. p. 738; by S. Athan in the Letter published by Maffei, ed. Patav. t. 3. p. 87. It seems to have been a received text in the controversy, as the Sardican Council uses it supr. p. 76. and S Athan. seems to put it into the mouth of St. Anthony, Vit. Ant 69. A

[o] τίς γὰρ ἤκουσι. Ep. Æg § 7 init ad Epict. §. 2 init. Crat. 1. 8. B. C. Apol. contr. Ar. 85 init. Hist. Ar. § 46 init. § 73 init § 74 init. ad Serap iv.

2 init.

[p] On the concurrence of these three texts in Athan (though other writers use them too, and Alex. ap Theod has two of them,) v. d. vol. 8 p. 229, note g

[q] ἄλογον καὶ ἄσοφον τὸν θεόν. de Decr § 15 Orat. 1. ς. 19 vid. vol. 8 p. 25, note c. p. 208, note b.

[r] This text is thus applied by Athan. Orat 1. 36. D n. 10. A. In the first of these passages he uses the same apology, nearly in the same words, which is contained in the text.

Son knows not the Father perfectly," we ought not to wonder at it; for having once set themselves to fight against Christ, they contradict even His express words, since He says, *As the Father knoweth Me, even so know I the Father.* Now if the Father knows the Son but in part, then it is evident that the Son does not know the Father perfectly; but if it is not lawful to say this, but the Father does know the Son perfectly, then it is evident that as the Father knows His own Word, so also the Word knows His own Father whose Word He is.

<small>John 10, 15.</small>

§. 5. 4. By these arguments and appeals to the sacred Scriptures we frequently overthrew them, but they changed like chameleons[s], and again shifted their ground, striving to bring upon themselves that sentence, *when the impious falleth into the depth of evils, he is filled with contempt.* There have been many heresies before them, which, venturing further than they ought, have fallen into folly; but these men by endeavouring in all their positions to overthrow the Divinity of the Word, have justified the other in comparison of themselves, as approaching nearer to Antichrist. Wherefore they have been excommunicated and anathematized by the Church. We grieve for their destruction, and especially because, having once been instructed in the doctrines of the Church, they have now fallen away. Yet we are not greatly surprised; for Hymeneus and Philetus did the same, and before them Judas, who followed our Saviour, but afterwards became a traitor and an apostate. And concerning these same persons, we have not been left without instruction; for our Lord has forewarned us; *Take heed lest any man deceive you: for many shall come in My name, saying, I am Christ, and the time draweth near, and they shall deceive many; go ye not after them.* And Paul, who was taught these things by our Saviour, wrote, that *in the latter times some shall depart from the sound faith, giving heed to seducing spirits and doctrines of devils, which reject the truth*[t].

<small>Prov. 18, 3.</small>

<small>2 Tim. 2, 17.</small>

<small>Luke 21, 8.</small>

<small>1 Tim. 4, 1.</small>

§. 6. 5. Since then our Lord and Saviour Jesus Christ hath instructed us by His own mouth, and also hath signified to us concerning such men by the Apostle, we accordingly being personal witnesses of their impiety, have anathematized, as we said, all such, and declared them to be alien from the Catholic Faith and Church. And we have made this known to your piety, dearly beloved and most honoured fellow-ministers, in order that should any of them have the boldness[u] to come

---

[s] χαμαιλέοντες. vid. de Decr. §. 1. D. Hist. Ar. §. 79.
[t] Into this text which Athan. also applies to the Arians, (vid. vol. 8. p. 191, note e.) Athan. also introduces, like Alexander here, the word ὑγιαινούσης, e.g. Ep. Æg. §. 20 Orat. 1. 8 fin de Decr 3. E. Hist. Arian. §. 78 init. &c. It is quoted without the word by Origen contr. Cels. v. 64. but with ὑγιοῦς in Matth t. xiv. 16. Epiphan. has ὑγιαινούσης διδασκαλίας, Hær. 78. 2. ὑγιοῦς διδ. ibid. 23. p. 1055.
[u] προπιστεύσαντο vid. de Decr. §. 2. B.

Appendix.

unto you, you may not receive them, nor comply with the desires of Eusebius, or any other person writing in their behalf. For it becomes us who are Christians to turn away from all who speak or think any thing against Christ, as being enemies of God, and destroyers[x] of souls; and not even to *bid such God speed*, lest we become partakers of their sins, as the blessed John hath charged us. Salute the brethren that are with you. They that are with me salute you.

2 John 10.

Presbyters of Alexandria.

§. 7. 6. I, Colluthus, Presbyter, agree with what is here written, and give my assent to the deposition of Arius and his associates in impiety.

Alexander[1], Presbyter, likewise	Nemesius, Presbyter	[1] vid. Presbyters p. 105.
Dioscorus[1], Presbyter, likewise	Longus[1], Presbyter	
Dionysius[1], Presbyter, likewise	Silvanus, Presbyter	
Eusebius, Presbyter, likewise	Perous, Presbyter	
Alexander, Presbyter, likewise	Apis, Presbyter	
Nilanus[2], Presbyter, likewise	Proterius, Presbyter	[2] Nilaras? p. 105.
Arpociation, Presbyter, likewise	Paulus, Presbyter	
Agathus, Presbyter	Cyrus, Presbyter, likewise	

Deacons.

Ammonius[3], Deacon, likewise	Ambytianus, Deacon	[3] vid. Presbyters p. 105.
Macarius, Deacon	Gaius[3], Deacon, likewise	
Pistus[3], Deacon, likewise	Alexander, Deacon	
Athanasius[3], Deacon	Dionysius, Deacon	
Eumenes, Deacon	Agathon, Deacon	
Apollonius[3], Deacon	Polybius, Deacon, likewise	
Olympius, Deacon	Theonas, Deacon	
Aphthonius[3], Deacon	Marcus, Deacon	
Athanasius, Deacon	Comodus, Deacon	
Macarius, Deacon, likewise	Serapion[3], Deacon	
Paulus, Deacon	Nilus, Deacon	
Petrus, Deacon	Romanus, Deacon, likewise	

---

[x] φθορέας τῶν ψυχῶν but S. Alex. in Theod uses the compound word φθοροποιός. p. 731. Other compound or recondite words (to say nothing of the construction of sentences) found in S Alexander's Letter in Theod, and unlike the style of the Circular under review, are such as ἡ φίλαρχος καὶ φιλάργυρος πρόθεσις χριστεμπορίαι φρενοβλαβοῦς ἰδιότροπον ἐμφιστοίχοις συλλαβαῖς θεηγόρους ἀποστόλους ἀντιδιαστολὴν τῆς πατρικῆς μαιεύσεως μιλαγχολικὴν φιλόθεος σαφήνεια ἀνοσιουργίας φληνάφων μύθων. Instances of theological language in S. Alex. to which the Letter in the text contains no resemblance are ἀχώριστα πράγματα δύο ὁ υἱὸς τὴν κατὰ πάντα ὁμοιότητα αὐτοῦ ἐκ φύσεως ἀπομαξάμενος δι' ἰσότερον ἀκηλιδώτου καὶ ἐμψύχου θείας εἰκόνος μεσιτεύουσα φύσις μονογενής τὰς τῇ ὑποστάσει δύο φύσεις

Presbyters of the Mareotis.

I, Apollonius, Presbyter, agree with what is here written, and give my assent to the deposition of Arius and his associates in impiety.

[1] p. 107.

[2] Heraclius? p. 107.

Ingenius[1], Presbyter, likewise	Serenus, Presbyter
Ammonius, Presbyter	Didymus, Presbyter
Dioscorus[1], Presbyter	Heracles[2], Presbyter
Sostras, Presbyter	Boccon[1], Presbyter
Theon[1], Presbyter	Agathus, Presbyter
Tyrannus, Presbyter	Achillas, Presbyter
Copres, Presbyter	Paulus, Presbyter
Ammonas[1], Presbyter	Thalelæus, Presbyter
Orion, Presbyter	Dionysius, Presbyter, likewise

Deacons.

[3] p. 107.

[4] p. 107.

Serapion[3], Deacon, likewise	Didymus, Deacon
Justus, Deacon, likewise	Ptollarion[3], Deacon
Didymus, Deacon	Seras, Deacon
Demetrius[3], Deacon	Gaius[3], Deacon
Maurus[4], Deacon	Hierax[3], Deacon
Alexander, Deacon	Marcus, Deacon
Marcus[3], Deacon	Theonas, Deacon
Comon, Deacon	Sarmaton, Deacon
Tryphon[3], Deacon	Carpon, Deacon
Ammonius[4], Deacon	Zoilus, Deacon, likewise

INDEX.

A

Abuterius, 161
Achillas, 29, 88, 152
Æzanes, 182.
Alexander, Bishop of Thessalonica, some account of, 33, a. n. no friend to the Arians, 33
Alexander, S. Bishop of Alexandria, 21. excommunicated Arius, 139. used Church of Theonas before it was dedicated, 167. prays against Arius being admitted to Communion, 212 Deposition of Arius and his companions, &c. 297 reasons for its being placed here, and grounds for its being probably St. Athan.'s, ibid. writes to his brethren exhorting them to renounce Arian impiety, ibid copy of his Letter, 299. exhorts to unity, ibid. and to have nothing to say to Eusebius of Nicomedia, ibid. cites the novelties of the Arians, 300. and refutes them, 301. shews them to be worse than all other heretics, 302. warns them against them as anathematized and enemies of Christ, ibid and 303
Alexandria, vid *Arians S. Athanasius. Council. Churches. Council of Sardica. George. Gregory. Letter. Syrianus.*
Amen, 168, and n. q.
Ammon, Gregory's secretary, 11.
Antichrist, his marks seen in Constantius, 285. (vid. *Constantius*.) herald of the Devil, 290.
Antony Father, writes to Gregory from the mountains, 229.
Apology of S. Athan. to Constantius, 154. its contents, ibid. (vid. *S Athan.*) for Flight, 188. its contents, ibid.
Apostolical Tradition, 50. see *Tradition*.
Appendix, 297.
Arians, their heresy forerunner of Antichrist, 124, 299. say the Word of God is a creature, 129 substitute a Creed for that of Nicæa, 131. always altering their previous statements, 132. hire George of Cappadocia to be Bishop of Alexandria, 133. their true statements only a cloak, 134 they are Antichrists, 135 attempt to deceive as the Pharisees, Sadducees, and Herodians did, ibid they will not condemn Arius, 136, 149 nor boldly speak truth, 137. their statements about the Word of God, 139, 140 in some sense Manichees, 144 the very dregs of other heresies, 146. not to be trusted because they act like Arius, 147 not Christians, 149, 208, 232, 247, 253, 272, 276. make heathens and catechumens Bishops, 178 corrupt Apostolic rule, 179 prove their murderous intention against S. Athan. by persecuting the Virgins, 185. imitate Jewish malice, 189. insincere in charge against S. Athan ibid their outrages against Bishops, 190. and against Alexandrians, 192 their object is to kill S. Athan. 193 are like Babylonians, 194, 195, (conf. p 9) call him a coward under a pretence, 195 accuse our Lord, if him, of cowardice, 197. act from a love of contention, 205. employ soldiers against S. Athan. 206 their profligate character, 207 their heresy hateful to God, 211, 217. our Lord Himself condemned it, 212, 213. it is accursed and alien from the Truth, 215 sacrifice morality and integrity to their party 220. spies not Bishops, 221, 263, 287. it is like a wild monster on earth, and hires external power, 221 persecute Eustathius, 222. and Eutropius, ibid. and Marcellus, 223. banish Paul, ibid. strangle him, and then tell a lie about it, 224. illtreat the dead, ibid their heresy Jewish, 235. receive support from eunuchs, 251. antichristian, 254. urge on the heathens to persecute Alexandrians, 269. act in conjunction with heathen, 270. persecute

Alexandrians, against miraculous judgments, 271. cause death of Eutychius, 272. scourge the citizens, 273. illtreat the poor, 274. modern Jews, ibid. heathen called them 'antichristian executioners,' ibid 276. illtreat Presbyters and Deacons, 275. worse than Gentiles, 276 inventors of a new heresy, inhuman, ibid. murder Secundus, 277. condemned by the Ecumenical Council, 278 worse than all other heretics because they use force, ibid take Constantius as their friend, 279. worse persecutors than the heathen, and prepare the way for Antichrist, 282 the Arian Bishops banished by S. Alexander, get possession of their Churches, 283. banish Bishops, ibid further iniquities against Laity, Virgins, Widows, Monks, 284 appoint profligate heathen youths and catechumens and men accused of bigamy, 285. their persecution such as never was, 288 its name ought not to be mentioned, 292 (conf p 138) called a strange god, ibid. how the faithful should treat them, ibid. an apostacy, 299 some Arian apostates, 300 their novelties about the Word, ibid they contradict Christ's express words, 302 approach nearer Antichrist than all other heresies by denying the Divinity of the Word, ibid Christ had given warning against them, and S Paul, ibid anathematized by S. Alexander, ibid.

Arius, Bishop of Petræ, 233.

Arius, his death, 147 summoned before Emperor Constantine, gives an account of his faith—takes false oath, 211 dies, 212, 265. could support his heresy only by patronage of the Emperor, 278 blasphemed openly, ibid

Arsenius, said to be murdered by S. Athan but still alive, 25, 26. discovered in concealment, 94. writes in submission to S. Athan 98.

Ascetics, meaning of, 22, n b 179

Asclepas, some account of, 69, n e. clear of heresy, 74, 190.

Assemblies in Churches, when edict came from the Prefect of Egypt, 4. in order to prevent the impiety of the Arians from mingling itself with the faith of the Church, 5

Athanasius, St. flies from the Church in which he principally abode, 8. plots of the Eusebians against him, 9, 10. appeals to the Bishops in behalf of the Alexandrian Church,

10. another judgment demanded upon his case although three had been passed on it already, 14. argument for his innocence from recantation of Ursacius and Valens, 15 and his enemies' confession of their calumnies, 16 account of his election to the Episcopate, 21, 22 the people rejoiced at his return from Gaul, 24 some account of his election, 21, n. a. favourable testimony of, 43 stayed in Rome year and six months; came by summons, 49, and n g. appears against the Eusebians at Council of Sardica, 59. makes his defence, 60. not confounded at Sardica, 63 begs Council to write to Alexandria, 64. invited by the Emperor to his court, 79. goes up to Rome, 80 received kindly by Emperor, 82 passing through Syria is received by the Bishops, 85. recounts proceedings against himself, 87. writes to the Emperor (Constantius), 89 appears before him, 90 sends persons to discover Arsenius, 94. proves accusation of murder, 95. and that Arsenius was alive, 96. shews the same by a letter from Constantine, ib. by a letter from Arsenius, 98. by letter to John, 99. commanded by Emperor to go to Tyre, 101 proves Ischyras no Presbyter, 102 objects to the Commission, 103. proves the plot by letters of the Bishops and Clergy of Egypt, 104, 5, 7, 9, 11, 12 by a letter of Alexander Bishop of Thessalonica to Count Dionysius, 113. by a letter of Count Dionysius to Eusebians, 114. repeats their proceedings against him again, 115. goes up to the Emperor, 119. his interview, ibid sent into Gaul, 121. sent back by Constantine the younger, ibid. proves murderous spirit of Eusebians against him, 122. and their plots again from the sufferings of Liberius and Hosius, 123 writes to warn his Bishops against certain Arians, 125. as being deceivers, 131. as not being needed by them, 135 because they will not openly condemn Arius, 136, 149 and boldly speak truth, 137 cites the Arian statements, 138. his reverent way, ibid. (and v 1) brings proofs from Scripture against them, 141 exhorts his Bishops to make a stand for the Faith, 150 refutes charge of exasperating Constans against Constantius, 155—158. his travels, 158. refutes charge of writing to the usurper, 159—165. refutes

INDEX. 307

charge of using an undedicated Church, 166-170. refutes charge of resisting Emperor's commands, 171-176. escapes from persecution of Syrianus, 176, 294. leaves Alexandria to go to Constantius, 177. hears of the general persecution, 178. hears of his proscription, 179 was coming up still, but turns back from the letter the Emperor sent, 179 defends his flight, 184 expostulates with Constantius, 186. reasons for writing Apol. for Flight, 188. defends it by Scripture examples, 195, and 199—204 by that of our Lord, 197. escapes irruption of Syrianus, 206. his account of the death of Arius in letter to Serapion, 210. not at Constantinople when Arius died, 211. cautions him against making his letters public, 213. sails to Rome to get Council held, 227. comes up to Constantius, 236. and is sent home by him, ibid. what followed on his return from exile, 238, 9, 40. though left quite alone, yet like Elias not forsaken, 262. withdraws from Alexandria, 263. driven from his Church by Constantius, 283. given by God to Alexandrians by succession, and sent with letters and oaths from Constantius, 295.

B.

Balacius, Duke, 228. his sad end, 229.
Baptistery, set on fire, 5.
Basilina, (Julian's mother,) active persecutor of Eutropius, 223.
Beggars, ἀνέξοδοι, 273, and n. o.
Bishops, 4. of equal authority, 45. he should not be a stranger, 50. but taken out of the Clergy of the Diocese, 51. against ancient usage to make a layman a Bishop, 113, n. g.
Blessing, form of, (Pope's,) 58.

C.

Cæsareum, 269, and n. 1. (vid. *Palace*,) 285
Candles, of the Church. 7.
Candlesticks, 7.
Canons and Forms, not given to the Churches at the present day, but wisely transmitted to us from our forefathers, 3. referred to, 41, 45, 49, 53, 55, 56, 249. received from Apostles, 51. referred to, 98, and n. u. do not permit a Bishop to be appointed from the Court, nor soldiers to invade Churches, 265. cannot receive validity from Emperor, 266.
Carpones, 44.
Castrensians, meaning of, 59, n. b.
Catechumens, not present at the oblation, 49, 115 made Bishops by Arians, 177, 285.
' *Cathedræ velatæ*,' 35 (marg. 2.)
Catholicus, 118, 163, n. m.
Cell, 48.
Chalice, 28. not really honoured by the Arians, 35.
Chancel rails taken as spoils out of the Church, 7, 206.
Chorepiscopi, 117, and n. e.
Christ, true God, 141. of same substance and eternity with the Father, ibid. not another Word, and another Wisdom, 142. not a creature, ibid. the One Word, 144. not one among many powers, ibid. knoweth the Father fully, 145. the true Offspring of the Father, ibid (knows His own nature, ibid.) said to be 'created' because He became man, ibid an Example of flight from persecution, 197. what He did in His Human Nature applies to all men, ibid. the Creator of times, 198. and yet had His own time, 199.
Christians, must not allow deceivers to speak ever good words, 128.
Churches, places of assembly on fourth day of week, 4, 268. governed by Apostles in person, 56, n. 2 number of in Alexandria 167, n. p used before dedication, ibid Church of Cyrinus, 227. great Church at Alexandria, 268. pillaged, 269 (vid. *Heraclius*.) called ' Lord's House,' 293.
Colluthus, pretended to the Episcopate, 103. his schism, 109, n. d.
Commentaries, 179, and n. x.
Commission to Mareotis of Eusebians, accused left behind, accuser taken, 103 Presbyters and Clergy of the city and Mareotis not admitted, 104.
Communion, to join (συνάγεσθαι), 147. a communion (σύναξις), 176
Companies, 91
Confessors, enter the kingdom of heaven, 291.
Constans, 14. took part of S. Athan. 155, n. b. most religious, 235 not a persecutor,
Constantine, Emperor, called Victor, 79, 96, 113, 114, r. 2. writes to S. Athan. to allow all to enter the Church, 89. condemns Ision, summons S. Athan. 90. writes to the Alexandrians, ibid. institutes judicial enquiry about Arsenius, and then

condemns Eusebius, 94. writes to S Athan. 96 acquits him of false accusations, 97. condemns Meletians, 98 testifies to correctness of Arian faith, 117. orders Eusebius to come to his court, 119 interview with S Athan. ibid. the barbarians had learnt to fear God through him, 120 sends S. Athan. into Gaul, 121.

Constantine, younger, sends back S. Athan. 121 called 'patron' by Eusebians, 231.

Constantius, most religious, 9, 59, 131, 154, 170, 174, 185. Councils meet by his command, 14, 59, 69. violent and tyrannical, 123 some account of, 154, n a called 'heretic,' 208. spoken of as using violence against Bishops, 213 begins to persecute, 226 returns to a right mind, and invites S. Athan to his court, 236 sends him safe to his Churches, ibid reverses what had been written against him, 237 writes in his favour, ibid. relapses, 243. compels Bishops to subscribe to Arian heresy, 245 banishes the Western Bishops, 246. offends against ecclesiastical rule, ibid sends an eunuch to persuade Liberius to subscribe, 249 banishes Liberius and others, 252 worse than former persecutors, 253 summons Hosius, 255. patron of impiety and emperor of heresy, 260, 267. tortures Hosius to lapse, ibid. forerunner of Antichrist, 261. sends the Duke and soldiers to persecute Alexandrians, 262. instigates young men against S. Athan 263. says he preserved him from regard to Constans, ibid deposed Vetranio, 264. does not follow his father, ibid does not respect canons, 265, 268, 288. persecuted S. Athan after Constans died, ibid. gives up Alexandrian Churches to Arians, 267. sends Heraclius against S. Athan. ibid. (vid. Herac.) sends Bishop with letters from himself, 268 as if Antichrist, 279 overthrows a Council, ibid worse than Saul, ibid than Ahab and Pilate, 280 ill-treatment of his own relations, ibid some account of his connections, ibid n. d inconstant, 282. begins persecution in Egypt, ibid drove S Athan from his Church, 283 called 'Costyllius' and image of Antichrist, 285 the marks of Antichrist seen in him, ibid 286, and n g. 287. takes eunuchs in counsel with him, ibid. claims right of hearing causes, ibid. accuses S Athan. himself, 288 lays waste Churches, ibid forerunner of Antichrist (πρόδρομος), 289 his practices a prelude to the coming of Antichrist, 292.

Constitutions of Paul, 57, and n. t.
Controller, 105, and n a. 294.
Costyllius, a name given to Constantius, 285.
Council [of Bishops] called by Constantine, 59. should be called at a distance from the court, 249. no Emperor should be present, no count, no magistrate, only fear of God and Apostolical religion, ibid should make enquiry first about matters of faith, then matters of conduct, 250. maintainers of an impious creed can not be members, ibid. nor eunuchs, 257

Council of Alexandria, Encyclical Letter, 17. reasons for remaining silent, ibid. answers charges of the Eusebians against S Athan. 19 charge of murder repeated, 20. and of uncanonical election, 22 protest against the commission (vid. Eusebians), 33. send document to refute charges, 34. refutes the charge about the corn, 36. exposes the Eusebians as stirring up the Ariau fanatics, 37. and calls upon the Bishops to avenge the injustice, ibid.

Council of Jerusalem, writes to the Alexandrians, 85.

Council of Sardica, called by the Emperors, 59, 230. condemns Eusebius, acquits S. Athan. 60. writes to Alexandria, and condemns the Arians, allows communion with S. Athan. 61, 232. exposes the Eusebians, 62. exhorts to patience, writes to the Emperors, 63. forbids communion with Gregory, 64, 233. acquits some Presbyters, writes to Bishops of Egypt and Libya, 65, 232. Encyclical Letter of Council, (see Encycl. Letter,) 69. proceedings of the Council again given, 232, 233.

Council of Tyre, documents connected with, 101
Count, a, head of Council of Tyre, 102.
Court (στρατόπεδον), 100. explained, n. z. 249, 257. (see Palace)
Cross roads, (Canalis,) 77 and n. n.
Curtains in a Church, 269, and n. h.

D.

Dalmatius, Censor, 94. and some account of, n. s.
Danius, some account of, 39, n. b. 206.
Deacon, Athanasius a, 21, read the Psalm, 206. called a Levite, 254.

INDEX 309

Decurion, (see margin,) 84.
Dedication, celebrated by the Emperor, 170. by S Alexander, ibid.
Dionysius, Count, 48, 103, 112—114.
Discernment of spirits a gift, 130.
Dog, 118, and n. h.
Ducenary, 107, n. b.
Duke, 96. origin of title, n t. 228.
Dynamius, commander of city police, 295.

E.

Easter, 7, 166, 192.
Ecclesiastical Canons, 3. (vid. *Canon*) the Emperor cannot make, but may break them, 246. referred to as authority, 249.
Ecclesiastical judgments, 249, 266 (vid. *Canon*.)
Ecclesiasticus, contains commands of God, 156. spoken of as a 'divine sentence,' 157. (vid. *Holy Scripture*.)
Egypt, for long boldly maintained the orthodox Faith alone, 290. (conf. p 81.)
Emperor, the, in favour of S. Athan. 27. called 'patron' by Eusebians, 231. has no right to command Bishops about Ecclesiastical matters, nor intrude at Ecclesiastical trials, 258. has no concern in Ecclesiastical judgments, 266.
Encyclical Epistle of S. Athan. to Egypt and Libya, 125. to his fellow-ministers, 1. its contents, ibid
Encyclical Letter of Counc. Sard defends S. Athan., Marcellus, and Asclepas, against calumnies of Arians, 69. refutes their charges, 72. clears Marcellus of heresy, 73. acquits Asclepas, 74. declares S. Athan. Marcellus, Asclepas, innocent, and forbids communion with some, 75 Subscriptions, 76.
Envy, its effects, 90, 91.
Epicritian Players, 29.
Eunuch, one sent to Liberius, 249. his conduct upon refusal of Liberius to submit, 250. in great numbers about the Emperor, ibid why they are Arians and not admitted to a Council, 252.
Eusebians, always supporters and associates of the impious heresy of the Arian fanatics, 4. their wicked calumnies against S. Athanasius, 18. their last charges against him, 19. history of their proceedings and against S. Athan 21 in an unlawful Council at Tyre, ibid saying that he was clandestinely elected, 22 through Eusebius, 23. by accusing him of the murder of Arsenius, 25 who was still alive, 26. of stopping exports of corn from Alexandria to Constantinople, 27. of breaking a chalice, 28. violate reserve about Sacraments, ibid their charge refuted, 30. to investigate same charge send commission to Mareotis, 31. their outrages at Alexandria, 32, 33. proved inconsistent, 35. the real cause of their enmity, 36 refuse to come to the Pope's Council, 42. receive excommunicated Arians to communion, 43. act against the Canon, 45. excuse of day, ibid and times not valid 46 their letters contradictory, 47. their proceedings novel, and appointment of Gregory uncanonical, 50 injuries to other Catholic Bishops, 53. conduct against Pope's prerogatives, 56 at Council of Sardica, 59. retreat to Philippopolis, 60. calumniators, 69. will not come to Council of Sardica, 70. persecute Theodalus, 71. fly from Sardica conscience-stricken, 72. accuse Marcellus falsely, 73 their leaders prevent attendance at Council of Sardica, 74 with Meletians lay plot of the linen vestments, 89. condemned, 90. plot of chalice through Ischyras with Meletians, 92. persuade Emperor to call Council of Tyre, 101. send commission to Mareotis, 103 acted as unjustly as the Jews did against S Paul, 114. examine Catechumens and Jews about mysteries, 115. use violence through soldiers, 116 hide their records, ibid. admit Arians to communion at Jerusalem, ibid. their aim to overthrow the authority of the Council, 47 nominate Ischylas as a Bishop as a reward, 118 some go up to the court and invent another accusation, 121. certain of them try to deceive Alexandrians, 130 proved to be really Arians, 133. employ Meletians against S. Athan 152 charge S. Athan with exasperating Constans against Constantius, 155. accuse him to Constans, 158 of writing to the usurper, 159 of using an undedicated Church, 166. yet Arius summoned to Constantinople, 211. seek to bring him into the Church with violence, ibid and 212 persecuted Marcellus, (vid *Marcellus*,) 223. accuse S Athan. to Emperors Constantius and Constans, 226—90. alone to Constantius, ibid persecute, 227 decline the Council at Rome, ibid.

persecute through Gregory, 228. bring a Count to Council of Sardica, 230. shut themselves up in the palace, 231. fly from the Council, 232 persecute at Adrianople, tyrannical to Alexandrians, 234. plot against Catholic legates at Antioch, 235. persuade Ursacius and Valens to relapse, 242. and Constantius 243 call him king of their heresy, ibid. they force subscription to Arian heresy under pain of banishment, 244. persecute Liberius, 248. persecute Hosius, 255 persecute Alexandrians to force them to leave S. Athan defenceless, 262. persuade the Emperor, ibid.

Eusebian letter to Pope Julius, arrogant, 40. and its contents, n. c.

Eusebius, Bishop of Nicomedia, not appointed canonically, 23 n. e leader of Arians, 89. bribes Meletians, threatens S. Athan 89. plots against him through Meletians, ibid often convicted by Eutropius, 222 covets Bishopric of Constantinople, 223. defends Arius in his blasphemies, 278. deserts Berytus and covets Nicomedia, 299. takes part of Arians, ibid

Eustathius, Bishop of Antioch, 190, and n a persecuted by Arians, 222

Eutropius, Bishop of Adrianople, persecuted by Arians, 222

Eutychius, martyred, 272

Eve, 127.

F

Faith had not its beginning at this time, but it came down to us from the Lord, through His Disciples. vid. *Tradition.*

Feet, washing of, 273, and n o

Flacillus, some account of, 39, n. b.

Flight, 201. vid *Christ. S. Athan. Saints Time.*

Frankincense, 269. (vid. *Incense.*)

Friday, called 'the Preparation,' 7, 294.

Frumentius, Bishop of Auxumis, 179. and some account of, n. n.

G

Gatherings, 91.

Gentiles kinder to Christians than the Arians, 276.

Gibbon, his account of S Athan.'s going up to the Emperor, 26 n. g.

God The Father, Arian novelties of, 300.

Godliness, εὐσέβεια, meaning of, 23.

Gorgonius, commander of the city force of Alexandria, 275, 295.

Gregory, comes from Cappadocia, and what follows from his appointment, 4—9. sent by the Eusebians in the place of Pistus, 9 proved to be an Arian by his secretary Ammon, 11. degraded at Sardica, 63. persecutes at Alexandria, 228. his profaneness, 229. not canonically a Bishop, ibid. and n. t. declared a Bishop by Council of Sardica, 233.

H

Handwriting (χεὶρ), 107, 163.

Heathen. vid *Arians. Miraculous Judgments.*

Helena, S. some account of, 222, n. a.

Heraclius, Count, sent against S. Athan 267. breaks into the great Church, 268. causes Virgins to be persecuted, ibid and the Church to be pillaged, 269. (vid. *Church.*) pillaging miraculously hindered, 270.

Heretics, deceivers like Satan, 128. reject the Law, (vid. *Law*,) ibid. quote Scripture like Satan to deceive the simple, 129. agree to lie, 130. with an unupright mind as a cloak, 134 cannot bear to hear the words of holy men, 142 read but do not believe the Bible, 189 hear, but do not see things it contains, 197 do not understand the Gospels, ibid. persecutors from example of Satan, 205. take kings as their patrons, 243. pay no honour to the aged, 255.

Hermetary, a rack on which Virgins were tortured, 185.

Hilarius, a notary in company with Syrianus, 294.

Hilary, a Deacon, 253. some account of, n d

History of Arians, 217. (see *Arian History.*)

Holy Communion only celebrated on Sundays, probably in Egyptian Churches, 29. n k

Holy Mysteries, how treated by Arians, 51. and n. k. and n. n. Presbyters ministers of them, 52 (v. *Presbyter.*)

Holy Table treated irreverently with

INDEX. 311

Hosius persecuted by Constantius, 123, 177 praises of, 191 a Confessor, 255 persecuted by Arius, ibid. firm against Constantius, 256. writes to him, ibid. warns him against siding with the enemies of S. Athan 257 and not to intrude in Ecclesiastical matters, 258. lapses through torture, 260.

I.

Incense, 258. and n. a.
Ischyras, no Presbyter, false accuser of S. Athan. 30. confesses himself suborned to make a false statement, 34. lived in Peace of Secontaruri, ibid. n. o. and p. 118, 48, 62, 93, 100 retracts and confesses, 93. proved no Presbyter, 102 taken to the Mareotis, 103 deposed by Hosius, 105. no Presbyter, and never had a Church, 108, 118. seven persons in his congregation, 110 112 118.

J

Jews take part with the heathen against the Church, 5.
Job, a man of mighty fortitude, 200. his wife, 127.
John, a Meletian, conduct of him and his partizans, 34.
Judaism brought in by Arians, 141.
Julius, S. Bishop of Rome, 16 his letter to the Eusebians at Antioch, 39. blames their letter, 40 invites them to a revision of their decision, 41. blames them for refusing a Council, 42. for dishonouring Councils, 43. for ordaining Arians, 44. his sentiments those of all, 46. gives reasons for admitting S. Athan 47. by refuting their charges, (vid. *Eusebians*, pp. 22—28.) by their uncanonical appointment of Gregory, 50, 51 and proceedings in the Mareotis, 52 acquits Marcellus, ibid but see n. l. exhorts them to peace, 53. for the welfare of the Church, 54. or they must prove their charges, 55 and not act any longer against his prerogative, 56. and excite God's wrath, 57. blesses them, 58. writes to Alexandrians, 81 invites Eusebians to a Council, 227.

K.

Keepers of idol temples 9, 267, 268

L.

Laity, 50. forty of them banished, 284.
Laws, ecclesiastical different to civil, 98
Law, if you reject it, you reject the Gospel, 128. Heretics reject it, ibid.
Legates, sending of, recognised by Council of Sardica, 39, n a. represent the Ecclesiastical Supremacy, 76 (vid. *Supremacy*)
Lent 7, 166, 192
Letter of Alexander to S. Athan. 95. of Alexander Bishop of Thessalonica to Count Dionysius, 113. of Alexandrian Clergy to the Commission, 104. of Arsenius to S. Athan. 98. of Clergy of Mareotis to the Council of Tyre, 105. of the Clergy of Mareotis to the Controller, &c. 107. of Communion, (*literæ formatæ*,) 8, 99. Emperor cannot send them, 221, 268. of Constantine to Alexandrians, 90. of Constantine the younger to Church of Alexandria, 121. of Constantine to Council of Tyre, 119. of Constantine to John, 96. (part of) of Constantine to S Athan. 89. (2) of Constantine to S. Athan. 96 acquits him of charge of murder, and breaking a Chalice, 97 condemns the Meletians, 98. of Constantius to all Catholic Bishops, 82. of Constantius to the Alexandrians, 84, 180 of Constantius to the Princes of Auxumis, 182. of Constantius to S. Athan. 174 of Council of Jerusalem to Alexandrians, 85. of Council of Jerusalem to Alexandrian Church, 116. of Council of Sardica to Alexandria, (vid. *Council of Sardica*,) 60. of Council of Sardica to Bishops of Egypt and Libya refutes the charges against S Athan. 65. of Count Dionysius to Eusebians, 114. of Egyptian Bishops at Tyre to Council of Tyre, 109. the same to Count Flavius Dionysius, 111. second of the same to the same, 112 Encyclical, of Council of Sardica, (vid. *Council of Sardica*,) 69. Encyclical, to Egypt and Libya, 125. of Hosius to Constantius, 256. of Pope Julius to Alexandrians, rejoices with them that their prayers are heard, and S. Athan. returned to them, 81, 82 of Receiver-General, 118. of S Athan. to Serapion, 210. of Ursacius and Valens to Pope Julius, 86 and n. q. and to S. Athan. 87.
Levite, history of, in Book of Judges not so bad as the sufferings of the Church, 2.

Liberius banished by Constantius, 123, 177. his answer to the Eunuch, 249. what followed at Rome, 251. his speech to the Emperor, 252. sends letters to Emperor to no purpose, 253. lapses, 254.
Lord, (κυρίῳ,) title of the Pope, 86. title of a Bishop, 87, 93, 95, 110, 113 r 2 δισπότῃ, 95, 113, 121.
Lord's Day, 192
Lucius, Bishop of Adrianople, banished by Arians, 234.

M.

Macarius falsely accused of breaking a chalice, 28, 90, 93. sent as prisoner to Corea, Tyre, 101. kept under a guard of soldiers, 103. at Constantinople when Arius dies, 211, 221.
Magistrates attend to civil causes only, 64 and n. c.
Magnentius, 160, 172
Manichees shew no mercy, 274
Marcellus Bishop, favourable testimony of, 43. confesses orthodoxy before Pope Julius, 52. (but see n. l.) Bishop of Ancyro-Galatia, 69. his book not heretical, 73. persecuted by Arians, 223.
Mareotis, some account of, 34. n. o.
Martyrdom, to make a stand for the Faith, 150.
Martyry of the Saviour, 116 of Saint Peter, 250. and n. c.
Master (of the camp), 163. n. m 2.
'*Master* of the Palace,' 157. and n. d. 163 and n. m 3
Maximian grandfather of Constantius, 276
Mechir, February in Egyptian calendar, 294, 296.
Mendicants, 228, and n a
Meletians, false accusers of S. Athan. 27. schismatics since days of S. Peter, 29, 38. received into the Church again, 38 plot with Eusebians against S. Athan 89 conspire with Eusebians in Corea, Tyre, against S. Athan. 101. join Arian fanatics against S Athan. 151 employed by Eusebians against him, 152 how easily they became Arians, 289 look upon the Clergy as a civil senate, 290 introduced Arian heresy into Egypt, ibid.
Meletius Bishop, some account of, 29. n 1 deposed, and made a schism, 88 and n. r.
Miraculous judgments, Arians do not regard them, 271 vid *Heraclius*
Monastery (μόνη), 96 μοναστήρια, 284.
Monks, 6, 179, 284

Montanus, brings S. Athan. a letter from the Emperor, 171.

N.

Nestorius, 84.
Nicæa, Council of, S. Athan. present at, 21. Chrestus appointed, 24. number of Canons, 41 n. d. number present, 43. n. e.
Notary, 173. and n. s.

O.

Oblation, not offered in presence of Catechumens, 49.
Official agents, 163. and n. m. 4.
Oil in stores in the Church, 7.
Order-books, 84.

P.

Phæno, mines of, 272.
Palace, 231. explained, n. b. 249.
Palm tree, scourges made of, 284.
Patrician, 108 and n. c.
Paul, Bishop of Constantinople, martyred by Arians, 223.
Peace given to the Church by our Lord, broken by schism, 53.
Pentecost, 192.
Persecution from the devil, 205. Arian under Constantine, 219. first Arian under Constantius, 226 Arian after Sardica, 233. second Arian under Constantius, 241. cannot influence the will. 245, 246, 254. of Liberius, 248. causes truth to spread, 247 and 253. at Alexandria, 262 in Egypt, 276 in time of Maximian, ibid. the early theory of, 279. n. c.
Petræ, 233. and n. c
Philagrius, Prefect of Egypt, 5. the way in which he took part with Gregory, 4, 5. called the Governor, 7, 31, 224. sent out as Prefect of Egypt, 226, 228. assists Arians to persecute, 233.
Philip, Prefect, agent in murder of Paul, 224
Pistus, sent by the Eusebians to be Bishop of Alexandria before Gregory, and excommunicated, 9. and 37. ordained by Secundus, 44.
Pope, 39 (see *Julius*) his prerogative, 56. nn q. and s. receives from S. Peter, 57 and n. u. and h. 249 and 251 ref 2. called ' brother,' and ' fellow-Bishop,' 61. other Bishops so called, 93, 96, 98

INDEX. 313

Porphyrians; Arians so called by Constantius, 264, and n. c.
Post, 50. explained n. L. 133, 235.
Potamo, Egyptian Bishop, at Council of Tyre, 25, n. e.
Prayer in an undedicated Church, 167. better with many than separately, 168. and in a building than a desert, 169.
Prefect of Egypt puts forth a public letter, having form of an Edict, 4. uses violence in Commission to the Mareotis, 106, 7. v. *Philagrius.*
Preparation, the, (and vid. n. 1.) 7, 294
Prerogative, Pope's, 56 and n. q. and s. and p. 57 of Church of Rome, 80, n p.
Presbyter, 4 Presbyters sent into foreign countries to hear appeals, 39, and n. a. ministers of holy Mysteries, 52.
Prophets, false, Christians warned against, 126.
Protest, the second of the Alexandrians, 293.
Provinces, 184, and n z.
Psalter, 7.
Public conveyance, 100, and n. y.

Q

Quæstor of the City, 171, and n. r.

R.

Receiver-general, 32, 118, 163, n m 268, 269.
Reserve, why necessary now, 28, n. k
Retractation of Ursacius and Valens, 36, and n. q 239.
Romania, 248, and n b.
Rome, 14. an Apostolical Throne, 248, and n. a.
Rowers under command, 91.
Rule, apostolical, 57, 179, 246, 249. v. Tradition, and *Canon.*

S.

Sacred Catalogue, 83. (and see margin.)
Saints, an example of flight from persecution, 196. spoke our Lord's commands before He came, ibid. their conduct like our Lords in fleeing, 197. sacred writers so called, 128, and 198 acted like our Lord in waiting their time, 199 before and after His coming under His teaching,

ibid. their flight not cowardice, but fortitude, 200. examples of great fortitude, 202. their flight neither blameable nor unprofitable, 203. preserved in it for need of others, 204.
Saraca, 14, 65, &c. 230, &c.
Satan attempting to appear holy is detected by Christians as by Christ, 127.
Scripture, 128. (v. *Holy Scripture*)
Seats in a Church, 269.
Secundus, Bishop, Arian, 44.
——— Presbyter at Barea martyred by Arians, 277.
Serapion, S. some account of, 210, 226.
Separation, time of, 268, ref. 6.
Sick persons refuse the ministrations of the Arian heretics, 9
Soldiers employed at the Council of Tyre, 102. sent with Gregory, 226. employed at Councils by Eusebians, 227.
Subintroductæ, 241, n a.
Subscriptions to Encycl Lett. Counc. Sard. 76, and n. l. (v. *Encycl. Lett*) doubt about number, 78, n. o. of Presbyters of Alexandria to deportion of S. Alexander, (v. *Alexander, S*) 303. and of Deacons, ibid and of Presbyters and Deacons of Mareotis, 304.
Sums laid up in the Church by individuals, 7.
Supremacy, 57, and n o. civil and ecclesiastical, 76, n. m. 80, n. p.
Syrianus, general, comes to Alexandria, 173. enters the Church with soldiers, 175, 206. accused to the Emperor of his violence by the Alexandrians, 293. account Alexandrians gave of his violence, 294, 295.

T

Table, Holy, 6. made of wood, 269. and n. g.
Theodorus, some account of, 39 n. b.
Theognius, some account of, 23 n. d. and 39 n b.
Throne in a Church, 269
Time, our Lord's creation of it, 198 appointed for all men, ibid. for flight, 199 for staying, 200.
Trades, ἐργασίαι, 33, 268 n. e
Tradition, Apostolical, 50. of the Fathers, 57. synonymous with 'Canon,' 239 n. b. derived from the Fathers and Apostle Peter, 249. none to allow soldiers and eunuchs authority in Church matters, 265 (v. *Canon.*)
Translation, some account of the lawfulness of, 23 n c.

U.

Unity to be preserved in peace, (App. 299)
Ursacius and Valens, 14, 90. penitent to Rome and retract, 86 and 122, and n. l., and 239. write to S. Athan 87. and 239. not forced to retract, 29
Usurper (Magnentius), 159, and n. i.

V.

Valens, 14. v *Ursacius*.
Veils worn by virgins, 7 v. 3. 157. and n. e. 268.
Vestments, linen, 89. and marg.
Vetranio deposed by Constantius, 264. and n. a. (v. *Constantius*.)
Vigil, 176. kept in the Church, 294.
Viminacium, town where S. Athan. saw Constantius, 159.
Virgins in the Church at Alexandria persecuted, 6, and 192, and 268. their veils, 7. consecrated to God, and called 'brides of Christ,' 185 scourged by Arians, 284. those murdered by Syrians attained the glory of martyrdom, 294.
Volumes containing Holy Scripture, 158. and n. f. τύχτια.

W.

Widows beaten and trampled under foot, 6, 228. clergy took care of them, 274. scourged on the soles of their feet, 284.
Wine in the Church in large quantities, 7.
Word of God, Arian novelties concerning, (App. 300.)
Writers (like an amanuesis), 164. and n. o

INDEX OF TEXTS.

GENESIS.

iv. 12.	στένων καὶ τρέμων	161
	Sept.	224
xxv. 8.		198
xxvii. 12.		199
xxxi. 2.		165
xlii. 21.		ib.

EXODUS.

iii. 10.	201
xv. 9.	205
xx. 13.	184
xxi. 13.	196
xxiii. 1. Sept.	172

DEUTERONOMY.

vi. 16.	207

JOSHUA.

vii. 20. &c.	137

JUDGES.

xix. 19.	2

1 SAMUEL.

iii. 6.	200
xii. 5.	156, 159
xv.	137
xvii. 2.	194
xxi. 13	195
xxii. 9	172
xxvi. 9.	246
10, 11	200
21	16

2 SAMUEL.

xii. 14, &c.	179

1 KINGS.

xxi.	172

2 KINGS.

i. 10.	203
xvii. 9. Sept	152

EZRA.

iii.	170

JOB.

v. 26.	198
xviii. 5.	147
xl. 24. Sept.	127
xli. 4 Sept.	128

PSALMS

xxvii. 1.	208
xxxi. 7, 8.	209
15	210
24.	204
xxxiii. 6.	142
xxxvii. 40.	204
xl. 1.	ib.
xliv. 20.	292
xlv. 1.	202, 201
l. 3	202
16	128
liii 1	146
liv. 7	203

INDEX OF TEXTS.

lvi. 11.	203	xiv. 14.		127
lvii. 3.	ib.	27.	148,	217
lxix. 26.	194	xxvi. 20.		263
lxxiv. 6.	245	29.	186,	204
xciv. 11.	135	xxxii. 6.		168
ci. 5.	159, 172	xlvii. 6.		194
cii. 23. Sept.	198	l. 6.		254
24.	ib.	lii. 11.	148,	292
cx. 3.	301			
cxvi. 16, &c.	145			
cxxxvi. 1.	206			
cxxxix. 6.	216	JEREMIAH.		

		ii. 12.	260
PROVERBS.		v. 30.	ib.
		ix. 2.	114
viii. 22.	145	xiv. 10.	132
x. 12.	273	xvii. 11.	245
20. Sept.	152	xxii. 10.	19
27.	198		
xii 5.	135		
6.	ib.	EZEKIEL.	
xiii. 3. Sept.	201		
xiv. 15.	129	xi. 13.	260
xv. 1.	187	xxxiv. 2, &c.	177
13.	165		
28.	135		
xvi. 13.	164, 177, 187	DANIEL.	
xviii. 3.	302		
xix. 5.	17, 105	vii. 5, 7.	221
xx. 13. Sept.	173	ix. 27.	288
28.	164		
xxv. 2.	216		
7.	105	JOEL.	
8.	159		
18.	165	i. 7. Sept.	165
xxviii. 28. Sept.	285	ii. 17.	290
xxix. 12.	281	25.	140
xxx. 8.	172		
15.	277		

		ESDRAS	
ECCLESIASTES.		iv. 41.	164
iii. 2.	198		
v. 8, 9.	204		
vii. 17.	198	TOBIT.	
23, 24.	216		
26.	ib.	iv. 18.	169
ix. 12.	199	xii. 7.	28
x. 20.	157		

		WISDOM OF SOLOMON.	
CANTICLES.		i. 11.	17, 159
v. 2.	245		

		ECCLESIASTICUS.	
ISAIAH.		vii. 5.	156
v. 20.	205, 220	xv. 9.	128
ix. 5.	197	xxx. 4.	95
x. 14.	127		

INDEX OF TEXTS.

S. MATTHEW

ii. 13.	197
iii. 6.	301
iv. 7.	207
10.	128
v. 10	202
15.	145
36.	199
vi. 6.	168
vii. 6.	28
15.	128
viii. 29.	128, 142
x. 22	63, 67
23.	8, 190
39.	199
xi. 7.	144
xiv. 3.	197
xv. 4.	189
xvi. 16.	251
24.	245, 273
xvii. 5.	142, 143
xviii. 18	213
19.	3, 108
20.	23
xix. 6.	200
27.	215
xxii. 21.	258
29.	135
xxiv. 15.	190
24.	129
24, 25	126
xxv. 35, 40.	273
45.	228
xxvi. 4.	198
45.	197

S. MARK

i. 24.	128, 142

S. LUKE.

iv. 3.	142
30	197, 199
xii. 20.	199
33.	273
xvi. 8.	147
xviii. 2.	255
xxi. 8.	126, 302

S JOHN

i. 1.	141, 145, 301
3.	142, 143 twice
14.	135, 145, 301
45.	129
ii. 4.	198
21.	188
iii. 17	126

v. 17	145
39.	129
46	ib.
vi. 46.	144
67.	273
68.	205
vii. 6.	198
30.	ib
viii. 5	129
42.	135
44.	195
58, 59.	197
x. 15.	145, 302
30.	141, 301
xi 53, 54.	197
xiv. 6.	164, 171
9.	141, 301
10.	143, 301
xvi. 28. ἥκω Athan.	135
xvii. 1.	199
xviii. 4, 5	199
19.	187
xix. 25.	245

ACTS

i. 18.	147, 212
v. 6, 10.	212
viii. 4.	247
27.	251
ix. 5	252
xx 29.	75
xxi. 15.	228
xxiii. 11.	201
xxiv. 18, 19	114
xxv. 16.	ib.

ROMANS.

i. 2.	129
25.	129, 141
v. 4.	204
viii. 35.	149, 220
35, 37.	203
xi. 33.	215
xv 19.	203

I CORINTHIANS.

i. 24.	144
ii. 9.	82
v. 13.	37
vi. 10.	138
vii. 27.	23
xiv. 33.	54
xv. 32.	291
xvi. 22.	218

2 CORINTHIANS.

i. 23.	156
ii. 11.	127
vi. 14, 15.	76, 301
x. 15.	23
xii. 4.	203

GALATIANS.

i. 8, 9.	127
9.	75
v. 13.	149

PHILIPPIANS.

i. 12.	247
ii. 9.	128

2 THESSALONIANS.

ii	289, 290, 292

1 TIMOTHY

i. 18	278
19.	150
iii 2.	179, 221, 222
iv. 1.	149, 151, 302
6	202
14	177
vi. 5.	23

2 TIMOTHY

ii. 17.	131, 302
iii. 11.	203
12.	149, 204
iv. 7.	153

TITUS.

i 14	149

HEBREWS.

i 3	141, 301
ii. 10	143, 301
ix. 27.	212
xi. 37, 38.	200
xii. 1.	204
xiii. 8.	301

JAMES.

i 12.	153

1 PETER.

v. 8.	227

2 PETER.

ii. 22.	88, 242

1 JOHN.

iv. 1.	128
v 20	141

2 JOHN.

10	303

INDEX OF GREEK WORDS.

A

ἀγάπη, ἀγαπᾶν, 60, 230
ἀγεντισηριβους, 163
ἅγιοι, 128
ἀγοραῖος, 268, 271.
ἄθεος, 268
ἀκέραιος, 299.
ἀκοή, 1b
ἀκοινώνητος, 148
ἀληθείας λόγος, 59.
ἀλλότρια τῶν οὐρανῶν, 213.
ἀλογία, ἀλήγιστος, 144, 265. vid 301, n q.
ἀνάθεμα, 2
ἀνελθών, 223, 239
ἀνέξοδος, 228, 273
ἀνθρωποπαθής, 144
ἄνομος, 290.
ἀντικείμενος, 292.
ἀντίχριστος, 274.
ἀξιῶ, 57.
ἀπόδειξις, 151.
ἀπόκοπος, 222, 236.
ἀπόλυσις, 268.
ἀπομαφοριζομεναι, 7.
ἀρειομανῖται, 4, 43.
ἄρον ἄροιον, 212.
ἀρτοὶ, 275
ἀρχα ος, 255, 284
ἀρχὴ, 139.
ἀρχιερεσία, 91.
ἀσιβεια, ἀσιβὴς, 261, 270, 273, 275
ἄσκησις, 239.
ἀφορμὴ, 217.

B

βάλλεται, 126
βῆλον, 157.
βίαρχος, 107.

Γ.

γενέσθαι, 140
γεννητός, γεννηθῆναι, 139, 217
γονεῖς, 238.

Δ

διστατὴς, 95, 121
διστατής μου, 1 3.
δήμιες, 228, 247, 271, 274.
δημιουργῆσαι, 139.
διάβολος, 160, 169.
διαταγὴ, 146
διάταξις τῶν ἀποστόλων, 57, 149.
διγναῖος, 285.
δυσσεβὴς 7, 270.

E.

εἶδος, 145.
ἐκκλησιαστικὸς, 278
ἐκτεῖναι τὴν μανίαν, 248, 255.
ἔνθιος, 109
ἔξαθεν, 283.
ἐπακούειν, 122.
ἐπίνοια, 129, 139, 113
ἐργασίαι, 33, 268.
ἐργαστήριον, 213.
ἔστω, 221, 282.
ἐπιεροτρόφος, 236.
εὐηρότατος, 191.
εὐνοῦχος, 250
εὐσέβεια, 3, 23, 35, 261, 290.
εὐχὴ, 82
ἔφεδρος, 262

H.

ἥκω, 135

INDEX OF GREEK WORDS.

Θ

θαῦμα, 211, 270
θεομάχος, 135
θεομίσητος, 217
θεοστυγὴς, 211
θεραπῶν θεοῦ 120
θλαδίας, 250

Ι

ἴδιος, 139
ἰδιώτης 213, 218
ἱερατεῖον, 212
ἱκανὸν, 292 vid also 299, n. d
ἰσχύσαι 44.

Κ

καθολικὸς, 163
καιροὶ, 179, 294.
κακόνοια, 300
κανάλιον, 77 vid Preface, p xxviii
κανονισθῆναι, 55.
καταχρηστικῶς, 300
κατάσκοπος, 221, 259, 263.
κειλεῦσαι, 59.
κίλλιον, 48
κληθεὶς, 49, 62, 70, 212, 242
κλῆρος 37, 283
κρατοῦσα πίστις, 183
κρείττων, 182, 183
κυριακὸν, 293
κύριος, 85, 86, 87, 93, 95
κύριός μου, 113, 239, 240
κυρῶσαι, κύρος, 60, 266

Λ

λατρεία, 120
λογιστὴς, 171
λογοθέτης 163
λόγος ἀληθείας, 59

Μ

μάγιστρος, 163.
μακαρίτης, μακάριος, τῆς μακαρίας
 μνήμης, 148, 152, 159, 160, 161,
 162, 185
μανία 8, 148, 151, 152, 255, 278.
μαρτύριον 150
μικροψυχία, 41, 55, 56, 99.
μοναστήριον, 284
μονὴ, 50, 96, 229.

μορφωθεὶς 290
μύσος, μυσαρὸς, 215, 282

Ν

νυμφαὶ Χριστοῦ, 185

Ο

ὄλεθρος, 182
ὀρθὸς, 211, 297
ὀρχεῖσθαι τὰς διαβολὰς ἐπὶ, 266.
ὅσον οὐδέπω, 228, 245
οὐσία, 140, 300
ὀφθαλμία, 223, 299.
ὁ ὤν, 180

Π

παλατῖνοι, 89
παλινωδία, 240
παραβατὴς, 226
παραδοξότατον, 221
παράδοσις, 249.
παρὰ ὅμος, 290, 299.
παροικία, 60.
παρουσία ἐν σάρκος, 196
παρῶν παροῦσιν, 297.
πατὴρ τῶν ἐπισκόπων, 230.
περιβομβεῖν, 159
περιέχιται 227, 235
ποίημα, 139.
προαίρεσις, 238
πρόδρομος 289, 299.
προιτρεψάμεθα, 41, 54.
προθεσμία 45, 227.
προσίενιν, 30
προστάτης, 226.
πύκτια, 158.

Ρ

ῥημάτιον, 299
ῥύπος, 221, 99

Σ

σατανικὸν, 273
σημεῖον, 217, 270.
σταδὸν, 250
σ-ιχάριον, 89.
στρατηγὸς, 275, 295.
στρατιώτης, 295
στρατόπεδον, 59, 100, 120, 158, 257.
στρόβιλος 6.
συλλειτούργος, 1, 17, 299.
συνάγεσθαι, σύναξις, 39, 147, 158, 176.
συνείσακται, 241.

INDEX OF GREEK WORDS.

Τ.

τιμᾶν, 40.
τὶς γὰρ ἤκουσε, 301.
τολμηρὸς, 217.
τόνος τῆς ἀσκήσιως, 202.
τριπτὸς, 89.

Υ.

ὑγιαινοῦσα πίστις, 214, 302.
ὑποδικτὴς, 236.
ὑποκρινόμενος, 211.
ὑπόστασις, 300.

Φ.

φθόνος, 220.
φιλήδονος, 252.

Χ.

χαμαὶ, 181.
χαμαιλέοντες, 302.
χεὶρ, 107, 163.
χρηστότης, 86.
χριστόμαχος, 89, 124, 132.

Ω.

ὡς ἐθέλησαν, 15, 266.

FINIS.

www.ingramcontent.com/pod-product-compliance
Lightning Source LLC
Chambersburg PA
CBHW071228230426
43668CB00011B/1348